CRIMINAL JUSTICE
98/99

Twenty-Second Edition

Editor

Joseph L. Victor

Mercy College, Dobbs Ferry

Joseph L. Victor is professor and chairman of the Department of Law, Criminal Justice, and Safety Administration at Mercy College. Professor Victor has extensive field experience in criminal justice agencies, counseling, and administering human service programs. He earned his B.A. and M.A. at Seton Hall University, and his Doctorate of Education at Fairleigh Dickinson University.

A Library of Information from the Public Press
Dushkin/McGraw·Hill
Sluice Dock, Guilford, Connecticut 06437

Visit us on the Internet—**http://www.dushkin.com/**

The Annual Editions Series

ANNUAL EDITIONS, including GLOBAL STUDIES, consist of over 70 volumes designed to provide the reader with convenient, low-cost access to a wide range of current, carefully selected articles from some of the most important magazines, newspapers, and journals published today. ANNUAL EDITIONS are updated on an annual basis through a continuous monitoring of over 300 periodical sources. All ANNUAL EDITIONS have a number of features that are designed to make them particularly useful, including topic guides, annotated tables of contents, unit overviews, and indexes. For the teacher using ANNUAL EDITIONS in the classroom, an Instructor's Resource Guide with test questions is available for each volume. GLOBAL STUDIES titles provide comprehensive background information and selected world press articles on the regions and countries of the world.

VOLUMES AVAILABLE

ANNUAL EDITIONS

Abnormal Psychology
Accounting
Adolescent Psychology
Aging
American Foreign Policy
American Government
American History, Pre-Civil War
American History, Post-Civil War
American Public Policy
Anthropology
Archaeology
Astronomy
Biopsychology
Business Ethics
Canadian Politics
Child Growth and Development
Comparative Politics
Computers in Education
Computers in Society
Criminal Justice
Criminology
Developing World
Deviant Behavior
Drugs, Society, and Behavior
Dying, Death, and Bereavement

Early Childhood Education
Economics
Educating Exceptional Children
Education
Educational Psychology
Environment
Geography
Geology
Global Issues
Health
Human Development
Human Resources
Human Sexuality
International Business
Macroeconomics
Management
Marketing
Marriage and Family
Mass Media
Microeconomics
Multicultural Education
Nutrition
Personal Growth and Behavior
Physical Anthropology
Psychology
Public Administration
Race and Ethnic Relations

Social Problems
Social Psychology
Sociology
State and Local Government
Teaching English as a Second
    Language
Urban Society
Violence and Terrorism
Western Civilization, Pre-Reformation
Western Civilization, Post-Reformation
Women's Health
World History, Pre-Modern
World History, Modern
World Politics

GLOBAL STUDIES

Africa
China
India and South Asia
Japan and the Pacific Rim
Latin America
Middle East
Russia, the Eurasian Republics, and
    Central/Eastern Europe
Western Europe

Cataloging in Publication Data
Main entry under title: Annual Editions: Criminal Justice. 1998/99.
        1. Criminal Justice, Administration of—United States—Periodicals. I. Victor, Joseph L., *comp.* II. Title:
Criminal justice.
HV 8138.A67   364.973.05   77–640116
ISBN 0–697–39137–X   ISSN 0272–3816

Twenty-Second Edition

Cover image © 1998 PhotoDisc, Inc.

Printed in the United States of America

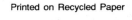

Editors/Advisory Board

Members of the Advisory Board are instrumental in the final selection of articles for each edition of ANNUAL EDITIONS. Their review of articles for content, level, currentness, and appropriateness provides critical direction to the editor and staff. We think that you will find their careful consideration well reflected in this volume.

EDITOR

Joseph L. Victor
Mercy College, Dobbs Ferry

ADVISORY BOARD

Staff

Ian A. Nielsen, Publisher

To the Reader

In publishing ANNUAL EDITIONS we recognize the enormous role played by the magazines, newspapers, and journals of the *public press* in providing current, first-rate educational information in a broad spectrum of interest areas. Many of these articles are appropriate for students, researchers, and professionals seeking accurate, current material to help bridge the gap between principles and theories and the real world. These articles, however, become more useful for study when those of lasting value are carefully *collected, organized, indexed,* and *reproduced* in a *low-cost format,* which provides easy and permanent access when the material is needed. That is the role played by ANNUAL EDITIONS. Under the direction of each volume's *academic editor,* who is an expert in the subject area, and with the guidance of an *Advisory Board,* each year we seek to provide in each ANNUAL EDITION a current, well-balanced, carefully selected collection of the best of the public press for your study and enjoyment. We think that you will find this volume useful, and we hope that you will take a moment to let us know what you think.

During the 1970s, criminal justice emerged as an appealing, vital, and unique academic discipline. It emphasizes the professional development of students who plan careers in the field and attracts those who want to know more about a complex social problem and how this country deals with it. Criminal justice incorporates a vast range of knowledge from a number of specialties, including law, history, and the behavioral and social sciences. Each specialty contributes to our fuller understanding of criminal behavior and of society's attitudes toward deviance.

In view of the fact that the criminal justice system is in a constant state of flux, and because the study of criminal justice covers such a broad spectrum, today's students must be aware of a variety of subjects and topics. Standard textbooks and traditional anthologies cannot keep pace with the changes as quickly as they occur. In fact, many such sources are already out of date the day they are published. *Annual Editions: Criminal Justice 98/99* strives to maintain currency in matters of concern by providing up-to-date commentaries, articles, reports, and statistics from the most recent literature in the criminal justice field.

This volume contains units concerning crime and justice in America, victimology, the police, the judicial system, juvenile justice, and punishment and corrections. The articles in these units were selected because they are informative as well as provocative. The selections are timely and useful in their treatment of ethics, punishment, juveniles, courts, and other related topics.

Included in this volume are a number of features designed to be useful to students, researchers, and professionals in the criminal justice field. These include a *topic guide* for locating articles on specific subjects; the *table of contents abstracts,* which summarize each article and feature key concepts in bold italics; and a comprehensive *bibliography, glossary,* and *index.* In addition, each unit is preceded by an *overview* that provides a background for informed reading of the articles, emphasizes critical issues, and presents challenge questions.

New to this edition are *World Wide Web* sites that can be used to further explore the topics. These sites will be cross-referenced by number in the topic guide.

We would like to know what you think of the selections contained in this edition. Please fill out the postage-paid *article rating form* on the last page and let us know your opinions. We change or retain many of the articles based on the comments we receive from you, the reader. Help us to improve this anthology—annually.

Joseph L. Victor

Editor

Contents

UNIT 1

Crime and Justice in America

Six selections focus on the overall structure of the criminal justice system in the United States. The current scope of crime in America is reviewed, and topics such as criminal behavior, race issues, and policing practices are discussed.

The concepts in bold italics are developed in the article. For further expansion please refer to the Topic Guide, the Glossary, and the Index.

UNIT 2

Victimology

Four articles discuss the impact of crime on the victim. Topics include the rights of crime victims and the consequences of family violence.

UNIT 3

The Police

Five selections examine the role of the police officer. Some of the topics discussed include the stress of police work, multicultural changes, and ethical policing.

UNIT 4

Judicial System

Five selections discuss the process by which the accused are moved through the judicial system. Prosecutors, courts, the jury process, and judicial ethics are reviewed.

The concepts in bold italics are developed in the article. For further expansion please refer to the Topic Guide, the Glossary, and the Index.

vii

UNIT 5

Juvenile Justice

Six selections review the juvenile justice system. The topics include effective ways to respond to violent juvenile crime, juvenile detention, and youths in gangs.

The concepts in bold italics are developed in the article. For further expansion please refer to the Topic Guide, the Glossary, and the Index.

UNIT 6

Punishment and Corrections

Nine selections focus on the current state of America's penal system and the effects of sentencing, probation, overcrowding, and capital punishment on criminals.

The concepts in bold italics are developed in the article. For further expansion please refer to the Topic Guide, the Glossary, and the Index.

ix

The concepts in bold italics are developed in the article. For further expansion please refer to the Topic Guide, the Glossary, and the Index.

x

Charts and Graphs

The concepts in bold italics are developed in the article. For further expansion please refer to the Topic Guide, the Glossary, and the Index.

1

Topic Guide

This topic guide suggests how the selections in this book relate to topics of traditional concern to students and professionals involved with the study of criminal justice. It is useful for locating articles that relate to each other for reading and research. The guide is arranged alphabetically according to topic. Articles may, of course, treat topics that do not appear in the topic guide. In turn, entries in the topic guide do not necessarily constitute a comprehensive listing of all the contents of each selection. **In addition, relevant Web sites, which are annotated on pages 4 and 5, are noted in bold italics under the topic articles.**

TOPIC AREA	TREATED IN	TOPIC AREA	TREATED IN
Attorneys	16. Adversarial Justice 19. 'We're in the Fight of Our Lives' *(1, 3, 16, 19, 20, 21, 22, 23)*	**Crime Victims**	*See* Victimology
		Criminal Justice	1. Overview of the Criminal Justice System 2. Real Problems in American Justice 6. Restorative Justice *(1, 3, 4, 6, 7, 8, 9, 10)*
Battered Families	9. Dynamics of Domestic Abuse *(1, 4, 12)*		
Bias	5. African American Males 18. Jury Nullification 20. Little Learning 32. To Keep Peace 33. Color of Justice *(6, 7, 10, 16, 20, 29)*	**Death Penalty**	33. Color of Justice 35. Death Penalty in 1996 *(30)*
		Defense Counsel	19. 'We're in the Fight of Our Lives' *(22)*
Children	*See* Juveniles	**Delinquency**	*See* Juveniles
Community Policing	3. What to Do about Crime 11. Police and the Quest for Professionalism 13. Better Cops, Fewer Robbers 17. Incorporating Diversity *(16, 18, 19, 20)*	**Drugs**	24. On the Streets of America 31. Prisons Grapple with Rapid Influx of Women *(28)*
Corrections	27. Can We Break the Pattern? 28. Reinventing Parole and Probation 29. Eddie Ellis at Large 30. Ethical Considerations in Probation Practice 31. Prisons Grapple with Rapid Influx of Women 32. To Keep Peace 34. What Works? What Matters? *(29, 30, 31, 32, 33, 34)*	**Ethics**	15. LEN Interview: Prof. Edwin J. Delattre 16. Adversarial Justice 30. Ethical Considerations in Probation Practice *(17, 29)*
		Exclusionary Rule	19. 'We're in the Fight of Our Lives' *(21, 22, 23)*
Courts	16. Adversarial Justice 17. Day of Reckoning 19. 'We're in the Fight of Our Lives' 18. Jury Nullification 20. Little Learning 25. Juvenile Courts in Chaos 26. Teen Court *(21, 22, 23, 24)*	**Expert Witnesses**	20. Little Learning *(21, 22, 23)*
		Family Violence	9. Dynamics of Domestic Violence 10. Victims of Childhood Sexual Abuse *(12, 13, 14, 27)*
Crime	1. Overview of the Criminal Justice System 3. What to Do about Crime 4. Mystery of the Falling Crime Rate 8. True Crime *(1, 4, 6, 7, 8, 9, 10)*	**Fear of Crime**	8. True Crime *(12, 13, 14)*
		Gangs	24. On the Streets of America *(24, 25, 26, 27, 28)*

Selected World Wide Web Sites for
Annual Editions: Criminal Justice

All of these Web sites are hot-linked through the *Annual Editions* home page:
http://www.dushkin.com/annualeditions (just click on this book's title). In addition, these sites are
referenced by number and appear where relevant in the Topic Guide on the previous two pages.

Some Web sites are continually changing their structure
and content, so the information listed may not always
be available.

General Sources

1. American Society of Criminology—*http://www.bsos.umd.edu/asc/four.html*—This is an excellent starting place for study of all aspects of criminology and criminal justice, with links to international criminal justice, juvenile justice, court information, police, governments, and so on.

2. Federal Bureau of Investigation—*http://www.fbi.gov/*—The main page of the FBI Web site leads to lists of the most wanted criminals, uniform crime reports, FBI case reports, major investigations, and more.

3. National Archive of Criminal Justice Data—*http://www.icpsr.umich.edu/NACJD/index.html*—NACJD holds more than 500 data collections relating to criminal justice; this site provides browsing and downloading access to most of these data and documentation. NACJD's central mission is to facilitate and encourage research in the field of criminal justice.

4. Social Science Information Gateway—*http://sosig.esrc.bris.ac.uk*—This is an online catalogue of thousands of Internet resources relevant to social science education and research, including criminal justice. Every resource is selected and described by a librarian or subject specialist.

5. University of Pennsylvania/Library— *http://www.library.upenn.edu/resources/social/sociology/sociology.html*—This site provides a number of indexes of culture and ethnic studies, criminology, population and demographics, and statistical sources.

Crime and Justice in America

6. American Studies Web—*http://www.georgetown.edu/crossroads/asw/*—This eclectic site provides links to a wealth of resources on the Internet related to American studies, including topics in criminal justice, ranging from gender studies to race and ethnicity.

7. Campaign for Equity-Restorative Justice—*http://www.cerj.org/*—This is the home page of CERJ, which sees monumental problems in justice systems and the need for reform. Examine this site and its links for information about the restorative justice movement.

8. Crime-Free America—*http://www.announce.com/cfa/*—Crime-Free America is a grassroots, nonprofit group dedicated to ending the crime epidemic that it feels has gripped the United States over the last four decades. This site has links to the Bureau of Justice Statistics, forums, and crime watch profiles.

9. Crime Times—*http://www.crime-times.org/titles.htm*—This interesting site listing research reviews and other information regarding causes of criminal, violent, and psychopathic behavior consists of many articles, listed by title. It is provided by the Wacker Foundation, publisher of *Crime Times*.

10. Sourcebook of Criminal Justice Statistics Online—*http://www.albany.edu/sourcebook/*—Data about all aspects of criminal justice in the United States are available at this site, which includes more than 600 tables from dozens of sources. The site also has a search mechanism.

11. University of Scranton—*http://academic.uofs.edu/student/jam1/post.html*—Browse through this site for access to some articles and reports that will be of interest to those researching possible relationships between psychiatric disorders and violent crime.

Victimology

12. Connecticut Sexual Assault Crisis Services, Inc.—*http://www.connsacs.org/*—This site has links that provide information about women's responses to sexual assault and related issues. It includes extensive links to sexual violence–related Web pages.

13. National Crime Victim's Research and Treatment Center—*http://www.musc.edu/cvc/*—At this site, find out about the work of NCVC at the Medical University of South Carolina, and click on Related Resources for an excellent listing of additional Web sources.

14. Office for Victims of Crime—*http://www.ojp.usdoj.gov/ovc*—Established by the 1984 Victims of Crime Act, the OVC oversees diverse programs that benefit the victims of crime. This is its Web site, from which you can download a great deal of pertinent information.

15. Ray Jones—*http://blue.temple.edu/~eastern/jones.html*—In this article, subtitled "A Review of Empirical Research in Corporate Crime," Ray Jones explores what happens when business violates the law. An extensive interpretive section and a bibliography are provided.

The Police

16. ACLU Criminal Justice Home Page—*http://aclu.org/issues/criminal/hmcj.html*—This Criminal Justice page of the American Civil Liberties Union Web site highlights recent events in criminal justice, addresses police issues, lists important resources, and contains a search mechanism.

17. Ethics Updates/Lawrence Hinman—*http://ethics.acusd.edu/*—This is Professor Hinman's consummate learning tool. The site provides both simple concept definition and complex analysis of ethics, original treatises, and sophisticated search-engine capability. Subject matter covers the gamut, from ethical theory to applied ethical venues. There are many opportunities for user input.

18. FBI Violent Criminal Apprehension Program—*http://www.fbi.gov/vicap/vicap.htm*—VICAP's mission is to facilitate cooperation, communication, and coordination among law enforcement agencies and provide support in their efforts to investigate, identify, track, apprehend, and prosecute violent serial offenders. This site gives you access to VICAP's data information center resources.

19. Introduction to American Justice—*http://www.uaa.alaska.edu/just/just110/home.html*—Open this site to find an excellent outline of

the causes of crime, including major theories, prepared by Professor Darryl Wood of the Justice Center at the University of Alaska at Anchorage. It provides an introduction to crime, law, and the criminal justice system; police and policing; the court system; corrections; and more.

20. National Institute of Justice—*http://www.ojp.usdoj.gov/nij/lawedocs.htm*—The NIJ sponsors projects and conveys research findings to practitioners in the field of criminal justice. Through this site, you can access the initiatives of the 1994 Violent Crime Control and Law Enforcement Act, apply for grants, monitor international criminal activity, learn the latest about policing techniques and issues, and more.

Judicial System

21. Justice Information Center—*http://www.ncjrs.org/*—Provided by the National Criminal Justice Reference Service, this JIC site connects to information about corrections, courts, crime prevention, criminal justice, statistics, drugs and crime, law enforcement, and victims—among other topics—and presents news and current highlights.

22. National Center for Policy Analysis—*http://www.public-policy.org/~ncpa/pd/law/index3.html*—Through the NCPA's "Idea House," you can click onto links to read discussions of an array of topics that are of major interest in the study of the American judicial system. There are sections on the courts, judges, lawyers, and other aspects of the legal system.

23. U.S. Department of Justice—*http://www.usdoj.gov/*—The DOJ represents the American people in enforcing the law in the public interest. Open its main page to find information about the U.S. judicial system. This site provides links to federal government Web servers, topics of interest related to the justice system, documents and resources, and a topical index.

Juvenile Justice

24. Corrections/Juvenile Delinquency—*http://www.soc.american.edu/justice/corrjuv.htm*—This American University site provides links to many documents, newsletter articles, and fact sheets on a wide variety of juvenile justice issues. Try also *http://www.ncjrs.org/jjhome.htm* for links provided by the Justice Information Center.

25. Gang Land: The Jerry Capeci Page—*http://www.ganglandnews.com/*—Although this site particularly addresses organized-crime gangs, its insights into the gang lifestyle—including gang families and their influence—are useful for those interested in exploring issues related to juvenile justice.

26. Institute for Intergovernmental Research—*http://www.iir.com/*—The IIR is a research organization that specializes in law enforcement, juvenile justice, and criminal justice issues. Explore the projects, links, and search engines from this home page. Topics addressed include youth gangs and white collar crime.

27. National Network for Family Resiliency—*http://www.nnfr.org/nnfr/*—This organization's main Web page will lead you to a number of resource areas of interest in learning about resiliency, including General Family Resiliency, Violence Prevention, and Family Economics.

28. Partnership Against Violence Network—*http://www.pavnet.org/*—The Partnership Against Violence Network is a virtual library of information about violence and youths at risk, representing data from seven different federal agencies—a one-stop searchable information resource.

Punishment and Corrections

29. American Probation and Parole Association—*http://www.csg.org/appa/appa.html*—Open this APPA site to find information and resources related to probation and parole issues, position papers, the APPA code of ethics, and research and training programs and opportunities.

30. Critical Criminology Division of the ASC—*http://sun.soci.niu.edu/~critcrim*—Here you will find basic criminology resources and related government resources, provided by the American Society of Criminology, as well as other useful links. The death penalty is also discussed.

31. David Willshire's Forensic Psychology & Psychiatry Links—*http://www.ozemail.com.au/~dwillsh/*—This site offers an enormous number of links to professional journals and associations. It is a valuable resource for study into possible connections between violence and mental disorders. Topics include serial killers, sex offenders, and trauma.

32. The Keepers' Voice—*http://www.acsp.uic.edu/IACO/*—Visit this site of the International Association of Correctional Officers for links providing insight into the many concerns of inmates and correctional officers. Crime causation from the standpoint of inmates is addressed.

33. Oregon Department of Corrections—*http://www.doc.state.or.us/links/welcome.htm*—Open this site for resources in such areas as crime and law enforcement and for links to U.S. state corrections departments.

34. Stop Prisoner Rape, Inc.—*http://www.spr.org/spr.html*—For a change of pace, open some of the materials available through this site to gain understanding into the social relationships that may develop in incarceration facilities.

We highly recommend that you review our Web site for expanded information and our other product lines. We are continually updating and adding links to our Web site in order to offer you the most usable and useful information that will support and expand the value of your Annual Editions. You can reach us at: *http://www. dushkin.com/annualeditions/.*

Crime and Justice in America

Crime continues to be a major problem in the United States. Court dockets are full, our prisons are overcrowded, probation and parole caseloads are overwhelming, and our police are being urged to do more. The bulging prison population places a heavy strain on the economy of the country. Clearly crime is a complex problem that defies simple explanations or solutions. While the more familiar crimes of murder, rape, and assault are still with us, drugs are an ever-increasing scourge. The debate continues about how best to handle juvenile offenders, sex offenders, as well as those who commit acts of domestic violence. Crime committed using computers and the Internet is already an issue to be dealt with.

Annual Editions: Criminal Justice 98/99 focuses directly upon crime in America and the three traditional components of the criminal justice system: police, courts, and corrections. It also gives special attention to crime victims, in the victimology unit, and to juveniles, in the juvenile justice unit. The articles presented in this section are intended to serve as a foundation for the materials presented in subsequent sections.

The unit begins with "An Overview of the Criminal Justice System," which charts the sequence of events in the administration of justice. The response to crime is a very complex process that involves citizens as well as many agencies, levels, and branches of government. Then, in the *U.S. News & World Report*'s article "The Real Problems in American Justice," it is noted that the criminal justice system is in crisis from "cops to prison." In the

next essay, crime in America and those who commit it are examined. Calls for action to help stem the flow of crime are discussed in "What to Do about Crime." James Q. Wilson offers some controversial suggestions, such as expanding police powers to allow "stop and frisk."

Astute policing, demographic shifts, and tough prison policies are among solutions offered in the next article, "The Mystery of the Falling Crime Rate." Are African American males disproportionately involved in the criminal justice system? Jerome Miller contends that they are in "African American Males in the Criminal Justice System." A different way of doing justice is the theme of "Restorative Justice." This is a fledgling movement in the United States that is based on a theology that could lead us to a different way of providing justice.

Looking Ahead: Challenge Questions

Should the police be given more power to stop and search people on the street? Defend your answer.

How does restorative justice differ from retributive justice?

In your view, what is behind the decline in violent crime?

After reading "The Real Problems in American Justice," do you agree or disagree with article's theme? Why or why not?

An Overview of the Criminal Justice System

The response to crime is a complex process that involves citizens as well as many agencies, levels, and branches of government

The private sector initiates the response to crime

This first response may come from any part of the private sector: individuals, families, neighborhood associations, business, industry, agriculture, educational institutions, the news media, or any other private service to the public.

It involves crime prevention as well as participation in the criminal justice process once a crime has been committed. Private crime prevention is more than providing private security or burglar alarms or participating in neighborhood watch. It also includes a commitment to stop criminal behavior by not engaging in it or condoning it when it is committed by others.

Citizens take part directly in the criminal justice process by reporting crime to the police, by being a reliable participant (for example, witness, juror) in a criminal proceeding, and by accepting the disposition of the system as just or reasonable. As voters and taxpayers, citizens also participate in criminal justice through the policymaking process that affects how the criminal justice process operates, the resources available to it, and its goals and objectives. At every stage of the process, from the original formulation of objectives to the decision

What is the sequence of events in the criminal justice system?

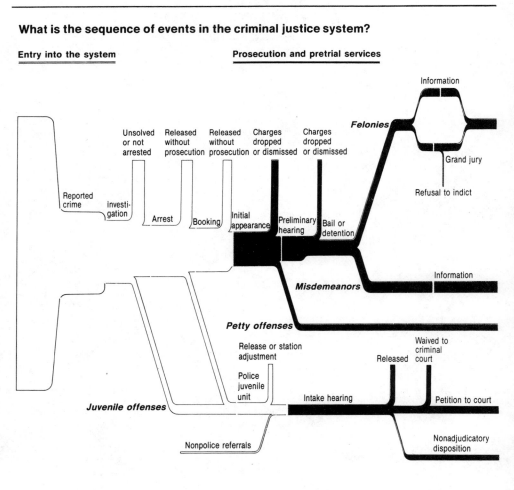

Note: This chart gives a simplified view of caseflow through the criminal justice system. Procedures vary among jurisdictions. The weights of the lines are not intended to show the actual size of caseloads.

From the *Report to the Nation on Crime and Justice,* March 1988, pp. 56–60. Reprinted by permission of the U.S. Department of Justice, Bureau of Justice Statistics.

about where to locate jails and prisons and to the reintegration of inmates into society, the private sector has a role to play. Without such involvement, the criminal justice process cannot serve the citizens it is intended to protect.

The government responds to crime through the criminal justice system

We apprehend, try, and punish offenders by means of a loose confederation of agencies at all levels of government. Our American system of justice has evolved from the English common law into a complex series of procedures and decisions. There is no single criminal justice system in this country. We have many systems that are similar, but individually unique.

Criminal cases may be handled differently in different jurisdictions, but court decisions based on the due process guarantees of the U.S. Constitution require that specific steps be taken in the administration of criminal justice.

The description of the criminal and juvenile justice systems that follows portrays the most common sequence of events in the response to serious criminal behavior.

Entry into the system

The justice system does not respond to most crime because so much crime is not discovered or reported to the police. Law enforcement agencies learn about crime from the reports of citizens, from discovery by a police officer in the field, or from investigative and intelligence work.

Once a law enforcement agency has established that a crime has been committed, a suspect must be identified and apprehended for the case to proceed through the system. Sometimes, a suspect is apprehended at the scene; however, identification of a suspect sometimes requires an extensive investigation. Often, no one is identified or apprehended.

Prosecution and pretrial services

After an arrest, law enforcement agencies present information about the case and about the accused to the prosecutor, who will decide if formal charges will be filed with the court. If no charges are filed, the accused must be released. The prosecutor can also drop charges after making efforts to prosecute (nolle prosequi).

A suspect charged with a crime must be taken before a judge or magistrate without unnecessary delay. At the initial appearance, the judge or magistrate informs the accused of the charges and decides whether there is probably cause to detain the accused person. Often, the defense counsel is also assigned at the initial appearance. If the offense is not very serious, the determination of guilt and assessment of a penalty may also occur at this stage.

In some jurisdictions, a pretrial-release decision is made at the initial appearance, but this decision may occur at other hearings or may be changed at another time during the process. Pretrial release and bail were traditionally intended to ensure appearance at trial. However, many jurisdictions permit pretrial detention of defendants accused of serious offenses and deemed to be dangerous to prevent them from committing crimes in the pretrial period. The court may decide to release the accused on his/her own recognizance, into the custody of a third party, on the promise of satisfying cer-

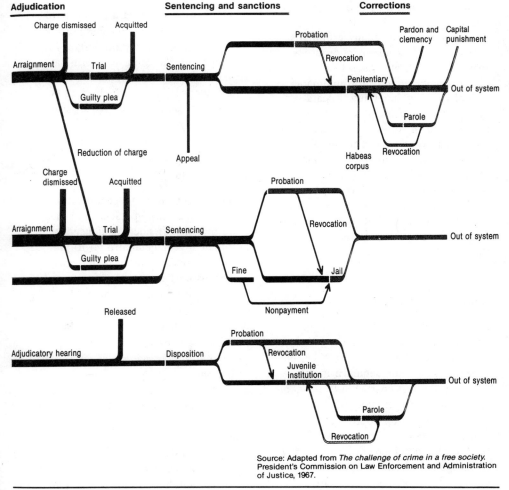

Source: Adapted from *The challenge of crime in a free society*. President's Commission on Law Enforcement and Administration of Justice, 1967.

tain conditions, or after the posting of a financial bond.

In many jurisdictions, the initial appearance may be followed by a preliminary hearing. The main function of this hearing is to discover if there is probable cause to believe that the accused committed a known crime within the jurisdiction of the court. If the judge does not find probable cause, the case is dismissed; however, if the judge or magistrate finds probable cause for such a belief, or the accused waives his or her right to a preliminary hearing, the case may be bound over to a grand jury.

A *grand jury* hears evidence against the accused presented by the prosecutor and decides if there is sufficient evidence to cause the accused to be brought to trial. If the grand jury finds sufficient evidence, it submits to the court an indictment (a written statement of the essential facts of the offense charged against the accused). Where the grand jury system is used, the grand jury may also investigate criminal activity generally and issue indictments called grand jury originals that initiate criminal cases.

Misdemeanor cases and some felony cases proceed by the issuance of an *information* (a formal, written accusation submitted to the court by a prosecutor). *In some jurisdictions,* indictments *may be* required in felony cases. However, the accused may choose to waive a grand jury indictment and, instead, accept service of an information for the crime.

Adjudication

Once an indictment or information has been filed with the trial court, the accused is scheduled for arraignment. At the arraignment, the accused is informed of the charges, advised of the rights of criminal defendants, and asked to enter a plea to the charges. Sometimes, a plea of guilty is the result of negotiations between the prosecutor and the defendant, with the defendant entering a guilty plea in expectation of reduced charges or a lenient sentence.

If the accused pleads guilty or pleads *nolo contendere* (accepts penalty without admitting guilt), the judge may accept or reject the plea. If the plea is accepted, no trial is held and the offender is sentenced at this proceeding or at a later date. The plea may be rejected if, for example, the judge believes that the accused may have been coerced. If this occurs, the case may proceed to trial.

If the accused pleads not guilty or not guilty by reason of insanity, a date is set for the trial. A person accused of a serious crime is guaranteed a trial by jury. However, the accused may ask for a bench trial where the judge, rather than a jury, serves as the finder of fact. In both instances the prosecution and defense present evidence by questioning witnesses while the judge decides on issues of law. The trial results in acquittal or conviction on the original charges or on lesser included offenses.

After the trial a defendant may request appellate review of the conviction or sentence. In many criminal cases, appeals of a conviction are a matter of right; all States with the death penalty provide for automatic appeal of cases involving a death sentence. However, under some circumstances and in some jurisdictions, appeals may be subject to the discretion of the appellate court and may be granted only on acceptance of a defendant's petition for a *writ of certiorari*. Prisoners may also appeal their sentences through civil rights petitions and writs of habeas corpus where they claim unlawful detention.

Sentencing and sanctions

After a guilty verdict or guilty plea, sentence is imposed. In most cases the judge decides on the sentence, but in some States, the sentence is decided by the jury, particularly for capital offenses such as murder.

In arriving at an appropriate sentence, a sentencing hearing may be held at which evidence of aggravating or mitigating circumstances will be considered. In assessing the circum-

stances surrounding a convicted person's criminal behavior, courts often rely on presentence investigations by probation agencies or other designated authorities. Courts may also consider victim impact statements.

The sentencing choices that may be available to judges and juries include one or more of the following:

- the death penalty
- incarceration in a prison, jail, or other confinement facility
- probation—allowing the convicted person to remain at liberty but subject to certain conditions and restrictions
- fines—primarily applied as penalties in minor offenses
- restitution—which requires the offender to provide financial compensation to the victim.

In many States, State law mandates that persons convicted of certain types of offenses serve a prison term.

Most States permit the judge to set the sentence length within certain limits, but some States have determinate sentencing laws that stipulate a specific sentence length, which must be served and cannot be altered by a parole board.

Corrections

Offenders sentenced to incarceration usually serve time in a local jail or a State prison. Offenders sentenced to less than 1 year generally go to jail; those sentenced to more than 1 year go to prison. Persons admitted to a State prison system may be held in prisons with varying levels of custody or in a community correctional facility.

A prisoner may become eligible for parole after serving a specific part of his or her sentence. Parole is the conditional release of a prisoner before the prisoner's full sentence has been served. The decision to grant parole is made by an authority such as a parole board, which has power to grant or revoke parole or to discharge a parolee altogether. The way parole decisions are made varies widely among jurisdictions.

Offenders may also be required to serve out their full sentences prior to release (expiration of term). Those sentenced under determinate sentencing laws can be released only after they have served their full sentence (mandatory release) less any "goodtime" received while in prison. Inmates get such credits against their sentences automatically or by earning it through participation in programs.

If an offender has an outstanding charge or sentence in another State, a detainer is used to ensure that when released from prison he or she will be transferred to the other State.

If released by a parole board decision or by mandatory release, the releasee will be under the supervision of a parole officer in the community for the balance of his or her unexpired sentence. This supervision is governed by specific conditions of release, and the releasee may be returned to prison for violations of such conditions.

The juvenile justice system

The processing of juvenile offenders is not entirely dissimilar to adult criminal processing, but there are crucial differences in the procedures. Many juveniles are referred to juvenile courts by law enforcement officers, but many others are referred by school officials, social services agencies, neighbors, and even parents, for behavior or conditions that are determined to require intervention by the formal system for social control.

When juveniles are referred to the juvenile courts, their *intake* departments, or prosecuting attorneys, determine whether sufficient grounds exist to warrant filing a petition that requests an *adjudicatory hearing* or a request to transfer jurisdiction to criminal court. In some States and at the Federal level prosecutors under certain circumstances may file criminal charges against juveniles directly in criminal courts.

The court with jurisdiction over juvenile matters may reject the petition or the juveniles may be diverted to other agencies or programs in lieu of further court processing. Examples of diversion programs include individual or group counseling or referral to educational and recreational programs.

If a petition for an adjudicatory hearing is accepted, the juvenile may be brought before a court quite unlike the court with jurisdiction over adult offenders. In disposing of cases juvenile courts usually have far more discretion than adult courts. In addition to such options as probation, commitment to correctional institutions, restitution, or fines, State laws grant juvenile courts the power to order removal of children from their homes to foster homes or treatment facilities. Juvenile courts also may order participation in special programs aimed at shoplifting prevention, drug counseling, or driver education. They also may order referral to criminal court for trial as adults.

Despite the considerable discretion associated with juvenile court proceedings, juveniles are afforded many of the due-process safeguards associated with adult criminal trials. Sixteen States permit the use of juries in juvenile courts; however, in light of the U.S. Supreme Court's holding that juries are not essential to juvenile hearings, most States do not make provisions for juries in juvenile courts.

The response to crime is founded in the intergovernmental structure of the United States

Under our form of government, each State and the Federal Government has its own criminal justice system. All systems must respect the rights of individuals set forth in court interpretation of the U.S. Constitution and defined in case law.

State constitutions and laws define the criminal justice system within each State and delegate the authority and responsibility for criminal justice to various jurisdictions, officials, and institutions. State laws also define criminal behavior and groups of children or acts under jurisdiction of the juvenile courts.

Municipalities and counties further define their criminal justice systems through local ordinances that proscribe additional illegal behavior and establish the local agencies responsible for criminal justice processing that were not established by the State.

Congress also has established a criminal justice system at the Federal level to respond to Federal crimes such as bank robbery, kidnapping, and transporting stolen goods across State lines.

The response to crime is mainly a State and local function

Very few crimes are under exclusive Federal jurisdiction. The responsibility to respond to most crime rests with the State and local governments. Police protection is primarily a function of cities and towns. Corrections is primarily a function of State governments. More than three-fifths of all justice personnel are employed at the local level.

	Percent of criminal justice employment by level of government		
	Local	State	Federal
Police	77%	15%	8%
Judicial (courts only)	60	32	8
Prosecution and legal services	58	26	17
Public defense	47	50	3
Corrections	35	61	4
Total	62%	31%	8%

Source: *Justice expenditure and employment, 1985,* BJS Bulletin, March 1987.

(continued)

Discretion is exercised throughout the criminal justice system

Discretion is "an authority conferred by law to act in certain conditions or situations in accordance with an official's or an official agency's own considered judgment and conscience." Discretion is exercised throughout the government. It is a part of decision-making in all government systems from mental health to education, as well as criminal justice.

Concerning crime and justice, legislative bodies have recognized that they cannot anticipate the range of circumstances surrounding each crime, anticipate local mores, and enact laws that clearly encompass all conduct that is criminal and all that is not. Therefore, persons charged with the day-to-day response to crime are expected to exercise their own judgment within *limits* set by law. Basically, they must decide—

- whether to take action
- where the situation fits in the scheme of law, rules, and precedent
- which official response is appropriate.

To ensure that discretion is exercised responsibly, government authority is often delegated to professionals. Professionalism requires a minimum level of training and orientation, which guides officials in making decisions. The professionalism of policing discussed later in this chapter is due largely to the desire to ensure the proper exercise of police discretion.

The limits of discretion vary from State to State and locality to locality. For example, some State judges have wide discretion in the type of sentence they may impose. In recent years other States have sought to limit the judges' discretion in sentencing by passing mandatory sentencing laws that require prison sentences for certain offenses.

Who exercises discretion?

These criminal justice officials...	...must often decide whether or not or how to—
Police	Enforce specific laws
	Investigate specific crimes
	Search people, vicinities, buildings
	Arrest or detain people
Prosecutors	File charges or petitions for adjudication
	Seek indictments
	Drop cases
	Reduce charges
Judges or magistrates	Set bail or conditions for release
	Accept pleas
	Determine delinquency
	Dismiss charges
	Impose sentence
	Revoke probation
Correctional officials	Assign to type of correctional facility
	Award privileges
	Punish for disciplinary infractions
Paroling authority	Determine date and conditions of parole
	Revoke parole

More than one agency has jurisdiction over some criminal events

The response to most criminal actions is usually begun by local police who react to violation of State law. If a suspect is apprehended, he or she is prosecuted locally and may be confined in a local jail or State prison. In such cases, only one agency has jurisdiction at each stage in the process.

However, some criminal events because of their characteristics and location may come under the jurisdiction of more than one agency. For example, such overlapping occurs within States when local police, county sheriffs, and State police are all empowered to enforce State laws on State highways.

Congress has provided for Federal jurisdiction over crimes that—

- materially affect interstate commerce
- occur on Federal land
- involve large and probably interstate criminal organizations or conspiracies
- are offenses of national importance, such as the assassination of the President.

Bank robbery and many drug offenses are examples of crimes for which the States and the Federal Government both have jurisdiction. In cases of dual jurisdiction, an investigation and a prosecution may be undertaken by all authorized agencies, but only one level of government usually pursues a case. For example, a study of FBI bank robbery investigations during 1978 and 1979 found that of those cases cleared—

- 36% were solved by the FBI alone
- 25% were solved by a joint effort of the FBI and State and local police
- 40% were solved by the State and local police acting alone.

In response to dual jurisdiction and to promote more effective coordination, Law Enforcement Coordinating Committees have been established throughout the country and include all relevant Federal and local agencies.

Within States the response to crime also varies from one locality to another

The response differs because of statutory and structural differences and differences in how discretion is exercised. Local criminal justice policies and programs change in response to local attitudes and needs. For example, the prosecutor in one locality may concentrate on particular types of offenses that plague the local community while the prosecutor in an-other locality may concentrate on career criminals.

The response to crime also varies on a case-by-case basis

No two cases are exactly alike. At each stage of the criminal justice process officials must make decisions that take into account the varying factors of each case. Two similar cases may have very different results because of various factors, including differences in witness cooperation and physical evidence, the availability of resources to investigate and prosecute the case, the quality of the lawyers involved, and the age and prior criminal history of the suspects.

Differences in local laws, agencies, resources, standards, and procedures result in varying responses in each jurisdiction

The outcomes of arrests for serious cases vary among the States as shown by Offender-based Transaction Statistics from nine States:

| | % of arrests for serious crimes that result in . . . | | |
	Prose-cution	Convic-tion	Incarcer-ation
Virginia	100%	61%	55%
Nebraska	99	68	39
New York	97	67	31
Utah	97	79	9
Virgin Islands	95	55	35
Minnesota	89	69	48
Pennsylvania	85	56	24
California	78	61	45
Ohio	77	50	21

Source: Disaggregated data used in *Tracking offenders: White-collar crime,* BJS Special Report, November 1986.

Some of this variation can be explained by differences among States. For example, the degree of discretion in deciding whether to prosecute differs from State to State; some States do not allow any police or prosecutor discretion; others allow police discretion but not prosecutor discretion and vice versa.

The real problems in American justice

A system in crisis from cops to courts to prisons

The criminal justice system was low on Americans' list of esteemed institutions long before the O.J. Simpson case became a national obsession. A recent survey by *U.S. News* found only 8 percent with a "great deal" of confidence in the courts, and the public routinely complains of excessive costs and delays, as well as laxity in sentencing.

Clearly, the system is broken in fundamental ways: Each year, 4.3 million violent crimes are committed, but barely more than 200,000 people are convicted of felonies, and a little over half end up going to prison for more than a year. Here's a rundown of the major flaws:

1. Police solve too few crimes. Law enforcers never have had it easy, but their modern success rate is staggeringly low. Only 24 percent of robberies and 13 percent of burglaries are cleared by an arrest. Homicide clearance rates are down from 86 percent in 1970 to 66 percent in 1993. Fewer witnesses are willing to testify against today's armed teens. A larger witness-protection program would help.

But the biggest problem is manpower. Some help is on the way as up to 100,000 community-patrol officers are hired under last year's federal anticrime law. And shootings already are falling in some New York City precincts, where more police are returning to the beat to deal with both serious crimes and low-level offenses. But critics warn that local patrols take away from investigative units.

2. Sleuths lose vital evidence. Harried police officers inadvertently contaminate key items. Crime laboratories, which do everything from alcohol testing to DNA analysis, can compound the problem. Historically, they have been a low priority for public funds. Technicians often receive scant training, and, until recently, few of the nation's 358 labs worked under any quality control. But quality is improving, and new technologies are spreading. An Automated Fingerprint Identification System helps police at more than 80 agencies match fingerprints found at crime scenes to those in a national database. The system registers "hits" in more than 10 percent of cases. One area where quality remains suspect: the system of coroners and medical examiners. One reason is that only a few areas employ doctors trained to investigate unnatural deaths.

3. Dangerous suspects commit crimes while awaiting trials on other charges. Defendants have a legal right to be considered for release before trial, and nearly two thirds of those charged with serious crimes—including one fourth of accused murderers— are allowed out on the street while awaiting trial. While most of them stay out of trouble, a disturbingly high 1 out of 3 either is rearrested, fails to appear in court on time or commits some infraction that results in a bail revocation.

This year, Republicans in the House approved a "jail, not bail" bill that would allow states to spend new federal prison money to build local jails for pretrial inmates. Experts like D. Alan Henry of the Pretrial Services Resource Center complain that such "solutions" will only worsen the system's unfairness: Many of those who can afford to post bail will do so—regardless of how serious their crimes—while poor suspects will remain stuck behind bars.

4. Prosecutors make bargains with too many criminals. In 9 cases out of 10, no trial ever is held. The defendants accept plea bargains that let them plead guilty, usually to just a few of the charges. Critics argue that to move cases along, prosecutors too readily abandon charges that could bring tougher penalties. Although that does happen, just as common is overcharging—filing counts of dubious provability to pressure defendants.

A few places have moved to curb abuses. The most prominent example is Alaska, which banned plea bargaining in 1975. A study by the federal State Justice Institute found that the policy has improved the screening of cases and contributed to longer prison terms. However, researchers found that in some areas, bargaining over pleas has been replaced by bargaining over the charges filed.

5. Criminal cases take too long. The interval between arrest and sentencing averages 274 days nationwide for murders and 172 days for violent crimes generally. The length of the few cases that go to trial is less of a problem. The National Center for State Courts reports that trials average about 11 hours, much shorter than the time it took for single witnesses to testify in the Simpson extravaganza. Murder trials typically last one to two weeks, depending on the circumstances. California trials tend to take longer.

Still, "we can do a lot better" at expediting cases once they reach court, says Barry Mahoney of the Denver-based Justice Management Institute. Mahoney's group and others offer trial-management training to judges, but probably fewer than 10 percent nationwide have taken it. A bigger problem: There aren't enough judges to juggle all witnesses, defendants and lawyers that come to court.

6. The jury system is flawed. It took 11 weeks to choose 12 jurors and 12 alternates in the Simpson trial. Then, the jury was forced to live in a hotel for nine months under guard, which frayed nerves and cost taxpayers more than $2.5 million. The jury process is so cumbersome, says Joseph DiGenova, former federal prosecutor in Washington, D.C., that "procedures instituted a century or two ago . . . are not adequate today."

Ideas abound to simplify jury service. Some reformers urge curtailing the elaborate process of allowing prosecution and defense to eliminate potential jurors, often on the advice of expensive consultants who analyze candidates of expected biases. Once the trial is underway, a few states, including Arizona, are experimenting with permitting jurors to ask questions of witnesses. California prosecutors, noting that 14 percent of Los Angeles County trials end with a hung jury, are pressing the state legislature to allow less-than-unanimous jury verdicts—which Oregon and Louisiana already do.

7. Trials are consumed more with tactics than truth. Many believe that defense lawyers search not for truth but for "preventing evidence of a defendant's guilt from reaching the jury," says James Wootton of the Safe Streets Alliance, an anticrime group based in Washington, D.C. Conservatives in Congress are trying to blunt the "exclusionary rule," which prevents illegally obtained evidence from being used in trials. They would allow such evidence if it was provably gathered in good faith. Others would go further. Law Prof. Joseph Grano of Wayne State University advocates that defense lawyers be required to ask their clients whether they committed the crime and to encourage the guilty to accept responsibility.

But defense lawyers will resist basic changes. "It's been a long time since I went to court looking for the truth," concedes Raymond Brown, a prominent Newark defense attorney. He says a proper role of the defense is forcing prosecutors to prove guilt.

8. Suspects get inadequate legal aid. Simpson is spending millions on a "dream team" defense. The reality for most criminal suspects is that they are fortunate to get much attention at all from overworked public defenders or court-appointed attorneys. Most such advocates are competent: They achieve roughly the same results as high-priced attorneys. The problem is that there are too many cases and too little time. Experts say full-time defense lawyers should handle at most 150 felony cases each year. The actual number in many areas is much higher: Defenders in southwest Florida are assigned some 300 cases and up to 50 appeals a year.

A PORTRAIT OF JUSTICE?

An estimated 4.37 million violent crimes are committed each year (including murder, rape, robbery and aggravated assault), but only a tiny fraction of criminals are put behind bars.

One figure equals 10,000

ANNUAL VIOLENT CRIMES
4.37 million

VIOLENT CRIMES REPORTED TO POLICE
1.85 million

ARRESTS FOR VIOLENT CRIMES
754,110

Note: These data are the latest available. Annual violent crimes and violent crimes reported to police include multiple crimes per defendant.

CONVICTIONS FOR VIOLENT CRIMES
213,100

VIOLENT CONVICTS SENT TO PRISON/JAIL
153,730

VIOLENT CONVICTS PUT ON PROBATION
59,370

USN&WR–Basic data: U.S. Dept. of Justice

Although a system of public defenders is in place, its resources are limited and declining. Congress, for example, is on the verge of eliminating federal funding for a network of centers that help defenders prepare cases of candidates for the death penalty. Critics say the centers help give attorneys ammunition to prolong cases unnecessarily; supporters respond that better sorting of the evidence can actually expedite trials and prevent needless appeals—not to mention helping ensure that innocent persons are not executed or put in prison for life.

9. Some criminals strike over and over. A few criminals commit a disproportionate amount of violence, but identifying and incapacitating them has proved impossible. Limits on prison space and an inability to predict recidivists mean that nearly 6 of every 10 serious offenders are not sentenced to prison. More than 4 in 10 are arrested within three years for another serious crime. Of those who serve time, most are paroled before serving 40 percent of their time.

Several states are moving to abolish parole, and others are clamping down on early releases. Pennsylvania has slowed releases of violent offenders to a trickle. In South Carolina, retired naval officer Jim Grego founded Citizens Against Violent Crime 11 years ago when his daughter was seriously wounded in an assault by a twice-paroled felon. Now that the group has lobbied for tougher standards, the state paroles 25 to 30 percent of applicants compared with 75 percent a decade ago. Meanwhile, many states are beefing up habitual-offender laws, often by requiring life sentences for those who commit two or three violent offenses.

But get-tough measures can backfire. Some states that have eliminated parole have seen costs soar as prison populations explode. And in California, the "three strikes and you're out" law requiring life terms for third-time offenders is causing more defendants to demand trials, thus clogging the courts. "The real crisis in L.A. County is the impact of three strikes," says presiding trial Judge James Bascue.

10. The justice system is insensitive to the public, particularly crime victims. Except for their court testimony, victims traditionally have been shut out when penalties are assessed. This view is changing, albeit slowly. A growing crime-victims movement has succeeded in recognizing victim rights in most states, at least on paper. The challenge is giving those rights real meaning. Victims are campaigning for "restorative justice," a program to involve them more in the sentencing process. In many cases, that means requiring convicts to provide victims restitution for losses or encouraging assailants to face their victims.

Some courts, traditionally remote institutions, are acting to improve public relations. Connecticut indoctrinates its court employees in "total quality management," partly to help citizens seeking information about cases.

Many justice reforms require an infusion of tax money. "The public gets the justice system it pays for," says Donald Rebovich of the National District Attorneys Association. Other changes would necessitate fundamental rewriting of criminal law—something that has proved remarkably resistant to reform. Defense lawyers argue that the system generally works well, even if it results at times in a criminal's going free. So it's reasonable to expect that long after the Simpson case is over, the justice system will lurch along—and so will the public's frustration and outrage.

TED GEST WITH DORIAN FRIEDMAN AND TIMOTHY M. ITO

What To Do About Crime

James Q. Wilson

Few of the major problems facing American society today are entirely new, but in recent years most of them have either taken new forms or reached new levels of urgency. To make matters more difficult, in many cases the solutions formerly relied upon have proved to be ineffective, leaving us so frustrated that we seize desperately on proposals which promise much but deliver little.

In the hope of bringing greater clarity to the understanding of these problems, and of framing workable solutions and policies, we are inaugurating this new series of articles. Like James Q. Wilson's below, each subsequent piece in the series will begin with a reexamination of a particular issue by a writer who has lived with and studied it for a long time and who will then proceed to suggest "What To Do About" it. Among those already scheduled for publication in the coming months are Charles Murray and Richard J. Herrnstein on welfare; Gertrude Himmelfarb on the universities; William J. Bennett on our children; Robert H. Bork on the First Amendment; and Richard Pipes on Russia.

JAMES Q. WILSON, professor of management and public policy at UCLA, is the author of many books and articles on crime, including Thinking about Crime; Varieties of Police Behavior; *and* Crime and Human Nature *(written with Richard J. Herrnstein). He is also the editor of* Crime and Public Policy *and co-editor, with Joan Petersilia, of* Crime *(from ICS Press).*

WHEN the United States experienced the great increase in crime that began in the early 1960's and continued through the 1970's, most Americans were inclined to attribute it to conditions unique to this country. Many conservatives blamed it on judicial restraints on the police, the abandonment of capital punishment, and the mollycoddling of offenders; many liberals blamed it on poverty, racism, and the rise of violent television programs. Europeans, to the extent they noticed at all, referred to it, sadly or patronizingly, as the "American" problem, a product of our disorderly society, weak state, corrupt police, or imperfect welfare system.

Now, 30 years later, any serious discussion of crime must begin with the fact that, except for homicide, most industrialized nations have crime rates that resemble those in the United States. All the world is coming to look like America. In 1981, the burglary rate in Great Britain was much less than that in the United States; within six years the two rates were the same; today, British homes are more likely to be burgled than American ones. In 1980, the rate at which automobiles were stolen was lower in France than in the United States; today, the reverse is true. By 1984, the burglary rate in the Netherlands was nearly twice that in the United States. In Australia and Sweden certain forms of theft are more common than they are here. While property-crime rates were declining during most of the 1980's in the United States, they were rising elsewhere.[1]

America, it is true, continues to lead the industrialized world in murders. There can be

---

[1]These comparisons depend on official police statistics. There are of course errors in such data. But essentially the same pattern emerges from comparing nations on the basis of victimization surveys.

little doubt that part of this lead is to be explained by the greater availability of handguns here. Arguments that once might have been settled with insults or punches are today more likely to be settled by shootings. But guns are not the whole story. Big American cities have had more homicides than comparable European ones for almost as long as anyone can find records. New York and Philadelphia have been more murderous than London since the early part of the 19th century. This country has had a violent history; with respect to murder, that seems likely to remain the case.

But except for homicide, things have been getting better in the United States for over a decade. Since 1980, robbery rates (as reported in victim surveys) have declined by 15 percent. And even with regard to homicide, there is relatively good news: in 1990, the rate at which adults killed one another was no higher than it was in 1980, and in many cities it was considerably lower.

This is as it was supposed to be. Starting around 1980, two things happened that ought to have reduced most forms of crime. The first was the passing into middle age of the postwar baby boom. By 1990, there were 1.5 million fewer boys between the ages of fifteen and nineteen than there had been in 1980, a drop that meant that this youthful fraction of the population fell from 9.3 percent to 7.2 percent of the total.

In addition, the great increase in the size of the prison population, caused in part by the growing willingness of judges to send offenders to jail, meant that the dramatic reductions in the costs of crime to the criminal that occurred in the 1960's and 1970's were slowly (and very partially) being reversed. Until around 1985, this reversal involved almost exclusively real criminals and parole violators; it was not until after 1985 that more than a small part of the growth in prison populations was made up of drug offenders.

Because of the combined effect of fewer young people on the street and more offenders in prison, many scholars, myself included, predicted a continuing drop in crime rates throughout the 1980's and into the early 1990's. We were almost right: crime rates did decline. But suddenly, starting around 1985, even as adult homicide rates were remaining stable or dropping, *youthful* homicide rates shot up.

Alfred Blumstein of Carnegie-Mellon University has estimated that the rate at which young males, ages fourteen to seventeen, kill people has gone up significantly for whites and incredibly for blacks. Between 1985 and 1992, the homicide rate for young white males went up by about 50 percent but for young black males it *tripled*.

The public perception that today's crime problem is different from and more serious than that of earlier decades is thus quite correct. Youngsters are shooting at people at a far higher rate than at any time in recent history. Since young people are more likely than adults to kill strangers (as opposed to lovers or spouses), the risk to innocent bystanders has gone up. There may be some comfort to be had in the fact that youthful homicides are only a small fraction of all killings, but given their randomness, it is not much solace.

T HE United States, then, does not have *a* crime problem, it has at least two. Our high (though now slightly declining) rates of property crime reflect a profound, worldwide cultural change: prosperity, freedom, and mobility have emancipated people almost everywhere from those ancient bonds of custom, family, and village that once held in check both some of our better and many of our worst impulses. The power of the state has been weakened, the status of children elevated, and the opportunity for adventure expanded; as a consequence, we have experienced an explosion of artistic creativity, entrepreneurial zeal, political experimentation—and criminal activity. A global economy has integrated the markets for clothes, music, automobiles—and drugs.

There are only two restraints on behavior—morality, enforced by individual conscience or social rebuke, and law, enforced by the police and the courts. If society is to maintain a behavioral equilibrium, any decline in the former must be matched by a rise in the latter (or vice versa). If familial and traditional restraints on wrongful behavior are eroded, it becomes necessary to increase the legal restraints. But the enlarged spirit of freedom and the heightened suspicion of the state have made it difficult or impossible to use the criminal-justice system to achieve what custom and morality once produced.

This is the modern dilemma, and it may be an insoluble one, at least for the West. The Islamic cultures of the Middle East and the Confucian cultures of the Far East believe that they have a solution. It involves allowing enough liberty for economic progress (albeit under general state direction) while reserving to the state, and its allied religion, nearly unfettered power over personal conduct. It is too soon to tell whether this formula—best exemplified by the prosperous but puritanical city-state of Singapore—will, in the long run, be able to achieve both reproducible affluence and intense social control.

Our other crime problem has to do with the kind of felonies we have: high levels of violence, especially youthful violence, often occurring as part of urban gang life, produced disproportionately by a large, alienated, and self-destructive underclass. This part of the crime problem, though not uniquely American, is more important here than in any other industrialized nation. Britons, Germans, and Swedes are upset about the insecurity of their property and uncertain about what response to make to its theft, but if Americans only had to worry about their homes being burgled and their autos stolen, I doubt that crime would be the national obsession it has now become.

Crime, we should recall, was not a major issue in the 1984 presidential election and had only begun to be one in the 1988 contest; by 1992, it was challenging the economy as a popular concern and today it dominates all other matters. The reason, I think, is that Americans believe something fundamental has changed in our patterns of crime. They are right. Though we were unhappy about having our property put at risk, we adapted with the aid of locks, alarms, and security guards. But we are terrified by the prospect of innocent people being gunned down at random, without warning and almost without motive, by youngsters who afterward show us the blank, unremorseful faces of seemingly feral, presocial beings.

CRIMINOLOGY has learned a great deal about who these people are. In studies both here and abroad it has been established that about 6 percent of the boys of a given age will commit half or more of all the serious crime produced by all boys of that age. Allowing for measurement errors, it is remarkable how consistent this formula is—6 percent causes 50 percent. It is roughly true in places as different as Philadelphia, London, Copenhagen, and Orange County, California.

We also have learned a lot about the characteristics of the 6 percent. They tend to have criminal parents, to live in cold or discordant families (or pseudo-families), to have a low verbal-intelligence quotient and to do poorly in school, to be emotionally cold and temperamentally impulsive, to abuse alcohol and drugs at the earliest opportunity, and to reside in poor disorderly communities. They begin their misconduct at an early age, often by the time they are in the third grade.

These characteristics tend to be found not only among the criminals who get caught (and who might, owing to bad luck, be an unrepresentative sample of all high-rate offenders), but among those who do not get caught but reveal their behavior on questionnaires. And the same traits can be identified in advance among groups of randomly selected youngsters, long before they commit any serious crimes—not with enough precision to predict which individuals will commit crimes, but with enough accuracy to be a fair depiction of the group as a whole.[2]

Here a puzzle arises: if 6 percent of the males causes so large a fraction of our collective misery, and if young males are less numerous than once was the case, why are crime rates high and rising? The answer, I conjecture, is that the traits of the 6 percent put them at high risk for whatever criminogenic forces operate in society. As the costs of crime decline or the benefits increase; as drugs and guns become more available; as the glorification of violence becomes more commonplace; as families and neighborhoods lose some of their restraining power—as all these things happen, almost all of us will change our ways to some degree. For the most law-abiding among us, the change will be quite modest: a few more tools stolen from our employer, a few more traffic lights run when no police officer is watching, a few more experiments with fashionable drugs, and a few more business deals on which we cheat. But for the least law-abiding among us, the change will be dramatic: they will get drunk daily instead of just on Saturday night, try PCP or crack instead of marijuana, join gangs instead of marauding in pairs, and buy automatic weapons instead of making zip guns.

A metaphor: when children play the schoolyard game of crack-the-whip, the child at the head of the line scarcely moves but the child at the far end, racing to keep his footing, often stumbles and falls, hurled to the ground

---

[2]Female high-rate offenders are *much* less common than male ones. But to the extent they exist, they display most of these traits.

by the cumulative force of many smaller movements back along the line. When a changing culture escalates criminality, the at-risk boys are at the end of the line, and the conditions of American urban life—guns, drugs, automobiles, disorganized neighborhoods—make the line very long and the ground underfoot rough and treacherous.

MUCH is said these days about preventing or deterring crime, but it is important to understand exactly what we are up against when we try. Prevention, if it can be made to work at all, must start very early in life, perhaps as early as the first two or three years, and given the odds it faces—childhood impulsivity, low verbal facility, incompetent parenting, disorderly neighborhoods—it must also be massive in scope. Deterrence, if it can be made to work better (for surely it already works to some degree), must be applied close to the moment of the wrongful act or else the present-orientedness of the youthful would-be offender will discount the threat so much that the promise of even a small gain will outweigh its large but deferred costs.

In this country, however, and in most Western nations, we have profound misgivings about doing anything that would give prevention or deterrence a chance to make a large difference. The family is sacrosanct; the family-preservation movement is strong; the state is a clumsy alternative. "Crime-prevention" programs, therefore, usually take the form of creating summer jobs for adolescents, worrying about the unemployment rate, or (as in the proposed 1994 crime bill) funding midnight basketball leagues. There may be something to be said for all these efforts, but crime prevention is not one of them. The typical high-rate offender is well launched on his career before he becomes a teenager or has ever encountered the labor market; he may like basketball, but who pays for the lights and the ball is a matter of supreme indifference to him.

Prompt deterrence has much to recommend it: the folk wisdom that swift and certain punishment is more effective than severe penalties is almost surely correct. But the greater the swiftness and certainty, the less attention paid to the procedural safeguards essential to establishing guilt. As a result, despite their good instincts for the right answers, most Americans, frustrated by the restraints (many wise, some foolish) on swift-ness and certainty, vote for proposals to increase severity: if the penalty is 10 years, let us make it 20 or 30; if the penalty is life imprisonment, let us make it death; if the penalty is jail, let us make it caning.

Yet the more draconian the sentence, the less (on the average) the chance of its being imposed; plea bargains see to that. And the most draconian sentences will, of necessity, tend to fall on adult offenders nearing the end of their criminal careers and not on the young ones who are in their criminally most productive years. (The peak ages of criminality are between sixteen and eighteen; the average age of prison inmates is ten years older.) I say "of necessity" because almost every judge will give first-, second-, or even third-time offenders a break, reserving the heaviest sentences for those men who have finally exhausted judicial patience or optimism.

Laws that say "three strikes and you're out" are an effort to change this, but they suffer from an inherent contradiction. If they are carefully drawn so as to target only the most serious offenders, they will probably have a minimal impact on the crime rate; but if they are broadly drawn so as to make a big impact on the crime rate, they will catch many petty repeat offenders who few of us think really deserve life imprisonment.

Prevention and deterrence, albeit hard to augment, at least are plausible strategies. Not so with many of the other favorite nostrums, like reducing the amount of violence on television. Televised violence may have some impact on criminality, but I know of few scholars who think the effect is very large. And to achieve even a small difference we might have to turn the clock back to the kind of programming we had around 1945, because the few studies that correlate programming with the rise in violent crime find the biggest changes occurred between that year and 1974. Another favorite, boot camp, makes good copy, but so far no one has shown that it reduces the rate at which the former inmates commit crimes.

Then, of course, there is gun control. Guns are almost certainly contributors to the lethality of American violence, but there is no politically or legally feasible way to reduce the stock of guns now in private possession to the point where their availability to criminals would be much affected. And even if there were, law-abiding people would lose a means of protecting themselves long before criminals lost a means of attacking them.

As for rehabilitating juvenile offenders, it has some merit, but there are rather few success stories. Individually, the best (and best-evaluated) programs have minimal, if any, effects; collectively, the best estimate of the crime-reduction value of these programs is quite modest, something on the order of 5 or 10 percent.[3]

WHAT, then, is to be done? Let us begin with policing, since law-enforcement officers are that part of the criminal-justice system which is closest to the situations where criminal activity is likely to occur.

It is now widely accepted that, however important it is for officers to drive around waiting for 911 calls summoning their help, doing that is not enough. As a supplement to such a reactive strategy—comprised of random preventive patrol and the investigation of crimes that have already occurred—many leaders and students of law enforcement now urge the police to be "proactive": to identify, with the aid of citizen groups, problems that can be solved so as to prevent criminality, and not only to respond to it. This is often called community-based policing; it seems to entail something more than feel-good meetings with honest citizens, but something less than allowing neighborhoods to assume control of the police function.

The new strategy might better be called problem-oriented policing. It requires the police to engage in *directed*, not random, patrol. The goal of that direction should be to reduce, in a manner consistent with fundamental liberties, the opportunity for high-risk persons to do those things that increase the likelihood of their victimizing others.

For example, the police might stop and pat down persons whom they reasonably suspect may be carrying illegal guns.[4] The Supreme Court has upheld such frisks when an officer observes "unusual conduct" leading him to conclude that "criminal activity may be afoot"

on the part of a person who may be "armed and dangerous." This is all rather vague, but it can be clarified in two ways.

First, statutes can be enacted that make certain persons, on the basis of their past conduct and present legal status, subject to pat-downs for weapons. The statutes can, as is now the case in several states, make all probationers and parolees subject to nonconsensual searches for weapons as a condition for their remaining on probation or parole. Since three-fourths of all convicted offenders (and a large fraction of all felons) are in the community rather than in prison, there are on any given day over three million criminals on the streets under correctional supervision. Many are likely to become recidivists. Keeping them from carrying weapons will materially reduce the chances that they will rob or kill. The courts might also declare certain dangerous street gangs to be continuing criminal enterprises, membership in which constitutes grounds for police frisks.

Second, since I first proposed such a strategy, I have learned that there are efforts under way in public and private research laboratories to develop technologies that will permit the police to detect from a distance persons who are carrying concealed weapons on the streets. Should these efforts bear fruit, they will provide the police with the grounds for stopping, questioning, and patting down even persons not on probation or parole or obviously in gangs.

Whether or not the technology works, the police can also offer immediate cash rewards to people who provide information about individuals illegally carrying weapons. Spending $100 on each good tip will have a bigger impact on dangerous gun use than will the same amount spent on another popular nostrum—buying back guns from law-abiding people.[5]

Getting illegal firearms off the streets will require that the police be motivated to do all of these things. But if the legal, technological, and motivational issues can be resolved, our streets can be made safer even without sending many more people to prison.

---

[3]Many individual programs involve so few subjects that a good evaluation will reveal no positive effect even if one occurs. By a technique called meta-analysis, scores of individual studies can be pooled into one mega-evaluation; because there are now hundreds or thousands of subjects, even small gains can be identified. The best of these meta-analyses, such as the one by Mark Lipsey, suggest modest positive effects.

[4]I made a fuller argument along these lines in "Just Take Away Their Guns," in the *New York Times Magazine*, March 20, 1994.

---

[5]In Charleston, South Carolina, the police pay a reward to anyone identifying a student carrying a weapon to school or to some school event. Because many boys carry guns to school in order to display or brag about them, the motive to carry disappears once any display alerts a potential informer.

THE same directed-patrol strategy might help keep known offenders drug-free. Most persons jailed in big cities are found to have been using illegal drugs within the day or two preceding their arrest. When convicted, some are given probation on condition that they enter drug-treatment programs; others are sent to prisons where (if they are lucky) drug-treatment programs operate. But in many cities the enforcement of such probation conditions is casual or nonexistent; in many states, parolees are released back into drug-infested communities with little effort to ensure that they participate in whatever treatment programs are to be found there.

Almost everyone agrees that more treatment programs should exist. But what many advocates overlook is that the key to success is steadfast participation and many, probably most, offenders have no incentive to be steadfast. To cope with this, patrol officers could enforce random drug tests on probationers and parolees on their beats; failing to take a test when ordered, or failing the test when taken, should be grounds for immediate revocation of probation or parole, at least for a brief period of confinement.

The goal of this tactic is not simply to keep offenders drug-free (and thereby lessen their incentive to steal the money needed to buy drugs and reduce their likelihood of committing crimes because they are on a drug high); it is also to diminish the demand for drugs generally and thus the size of the drug market.

Lest the reader embrace this idea too quickly, let me add that as yet we have no good reason to think that it will reduce the crime rate by very much. Something akin to this strategy, albeit one using probation instead of police officers, has been tried under the name of "intensive-supervision programs" (ISP), involving a panoply of drug tests, house arrests, frequent surveillance, and careful records. By means of a set of randomized experiments carried out in fourteen cities, Joan Petersilia and Susan Turner, both then at RAND, compared the rearrest rates of offenders assigned to ISP with those of offenders in ordinary probation. There was no difference.

Still, this study does not settle the matter. For one thing, since the ISP participants were under much closer surveillance than the regular probationers, the former were bound to be caught breaking the law more frequently than the latter. It is thus possible that a higher fraction of the crimes committed by the ISP than

of the control group were detected and resulted in a return to prison, which would mean, if true, a net gain in public safety. For another thing, "intensive" supervision was in many cases not all that intensive—in five cities, contacts with the probationers only took place about once a week, and for all cities drug tests occurred, on average, about once a month. Finally, there is some indication that participation in treatment programs was associated with lower recidivism rates.

Both anti-gun and anti-drug police patrols will, if performed systematically, require big changes in police and court procedures and a significant increase in the resources devoted to both, at least in the short run. (ISP is not cheap, and it will become even more expensive if it is done in a truly intensive fashion.) Most officers have at present no incentive to search for guns or enforce drug tests; many jurisdictions, owing to crowded dockets or overcrowded jails, are lax about enforcing the conditions of probation or parole. The result is that the one group of high-risk people over which society already has the legal right to exercise substantial control is often out of control, "supervised," if at all, by means of brief monthly interviews with overworked probation or parole officers.

Another promising tactic is to enforce truancy and curfew laws. This arises from the fact that much crime is opportunistic: idle boys, usually in small groups, sometimes find irresistible the opportunity to steal or the challenge to fight. Deterring present-oriented youngsters who want to appear fearless in the eyes of their comrades while indulging their thrill-seeking natures is a tall order. While it is possible to deter the crimes they commit by a credible threat of prompt sanctions, it is easier to reduce the chances for risky group idleness in the first place.

In Charleston, South Carolina, for example, Chief Reuben Greenberg instructed his officers to return all school-age children to the schools from which they were truant and to return all youngsters violating an evening-curfew agreement to their parents. As a result, groups of school-age children were no longer to be found hanging out in the shopping malls or wandering the streets late at night.

There has been no careful evaluation of these efforts in Charleston (or, so far as I am aware, in any other big city), but the rough figures are impressive—the Charleston crime rate in 1991 was about 25 percent lower than the rate in South Carolina's other principal cities and, for most offenses (including burglaries and larcenies), lower than what that city reported twenty years earlier.

All these tactics have in common putting the police, as the criminologist Lawrence Sherman of the University of Maryland phrases it, where the "hot spots" are. Most people need no police attention except for a response to their calls for help. A small fraction of people (and places) need constant attention. Thus, in Minneapolis, *all* of the robberies during one year occurred at just 2 percent of the city's addresses. To capitalize on this fact, the Minneapolis police began devoting extra patrol attention, in brief but frequent bursts of activity, to those locations known to be trouble spots. Robbery rates evidently fell by as much as 20 percent and public disturbances by even more.

Some of the worst hot spots are outdoor drug markets. Because of either limited resources, a fear of potential corruption, or a desire to catch only the drug kingpins, the police in some cities (including, from time to time, New York) neglect street-corner dealing. By doing so, they get the worst of all worlds.

The public, seeing the police ignore drug dealing that is in plain view, assumes that they are corrupt whether or not they are. The drug kingpins, who are hard to catch and are easily replaced by rival smugglers, find that their essential retail distribution system remains intact. Casual or first-time drug users, who might not use at all if access to supplies were difficult, find access to be effortless and so increase their consumption. People who might remain in treatment programs if drugs were hard to get drop out upon learning that they are easy to get. Interdicting without merely displacing drug markets is difficult but not impossible, though it requires motivation which some departments lack and resources which many do not have.

The sheer number of police on the streets of a city probably has only a weak, if any, relationship with the crime rate; what the police do is more important than how many there are, at least above some minimum level. Nevertheless, patrols directed at hot spots, loitering truants, late-night wanderers, probationers, parolees, and possible gun carriers, all in addition to routine investigative activities, will require more officers in many cities. Between 1977 and 1987, the number of police officers declined in a third of the 50 largest cities and fell relative to population in many more. Just how far behind police resources have lagged

can be gauged from this fact: in 1950 there was one violent crime reported for every police officer; in 1980 there were three violent crimes reported for every officer.

I HAVE said little so far about penal policy, in part because I wish to focus attention on those things that are likely to have the largest and most immediate impact on the quality of urban life. But given the fast gulf between what the public believes and what many experts argue should be our penal policy, a few comments are essential.

The public wants more people sent away for longer sentences; many (probably most) criminologists think we use prison too much and at too great a cost and that this excessive use has had little beneficial effect on the crime rate. My views are much closer to those of the public, though I think the average person exaggerates the faults of the present system and the gains of some alternative (such as "three strikes and you're out").

The expert view, as it is expressed in countless op-ed essays, often goes like this: "We have been arresting more and more people and giving them longer and longer sentences, producing no decrease in crime but huge increases in prison populations. As a result, we have become the most punitive nation on earth."

Scarcely a phrase in those sentences is accurate. The probability of being arrested for a given crime is lower today than it was in 1974. The amount of time served in state prison has been declining more or less steadily since the 1940's. Taking all crimes together, time served fell from 25 months in 1945 to 13 months in 1984. Only for rape are prisoners serving as much time today as they did in the 40's.

The net effect of lower arrest rates and shorter effective sentences is that the cost to the adult perpetrator of the average burglary fell from 50 days in 1960 to 15 days in 1980. That is to say, the chances of being caught and convicted, multiplied by the median time served if imprisoned, was in 1980 less than a third of what it had been in 1960.[6]

Beginning around 1980, the costs of crime to the criminal began to inch up again—the

---

[6]I take these cost calculations from Mark Kleiman, *et al.*, "Imprisonment-to-Offense Ratios," Working Paper 89-06-02 of the Program in Criminal Justice Policy and Management at the Kennedy School of Government, Harvard University (August 5, 1988).

result, chiefly, of an increase in the proportion of convicted persons who were given prison terms. By 1986, the "price" of a given burglary had risen to 21 days. Also beginning around 1980, as I noted at the outset, the crime rate began to decline.

It would be foolhardy to explain this drop in crime by the rise in imprisonment rates; many other factors, such as the aging of the population and the self-protective measures of potential victims, were also at work. Only a controlled experiment (for example, randomly allocating prison terms for a given crime among the states) could hope to untangle the causal patterns, and happily the Constitution makes such experiments unlikely.

Yet it is worth noting that nations with different penal policies have experienced different crime rates. According to David Farrington of Cambridge University, property-crime rates rose in England and Sweden at a time when both the imprisonment rate and time served fell substantially, while property-crime rates declined in the United States at a time when the imprisonment rate (but not time served) was increasing.

Though one cannot measure the effect of prison on crime with any accuracy, it certainly has some effects. By 1986, there were 55,000 more robbers in prison than there had been in 1974. Assume that each imprisoned robber would commit five such offenses per year if free on the street. This means that in 1986 there were 275,000 fewer robberies in America than there would have been had these 55,000 men been left on the street.

Nor, finally, does America use prison to a degree that vastly exceeds what is found in any other civilized nation. Compare the chance of going to prison in England and the United States if one is convicted of a given crime. According to Farrington, your chances were higher in England if you were found guilty of a rape, higher in America if you were convicted of an assault or a burglary, and about the same if you were convicted of a homicide or a robbery. Once in prison, you would serve a longer time in this country than in England for almost all offenses save murder.

James Lynch of American University has reached similar conclusions from his comparative study of criminal-justice policies. His data show that the chances of going to prison and the time served for homicide and robbery are roughly the same in the United States, Canada, and England.

OF LATE, drugs have changed American penal practice. In 1982, only about 8 percent of state-prison inmates were serving time on drug convictions. In 1987, that started to increase sharply; by 1994, over 60 percent of all federal and about 25 percent of all state prisoners were there on drug charges. In some states, such as New York, the percentage was even higher.

This change can be attributed largely to the advent of crack cocaine. Whereas snorted cocaine powder was expensive, crack was cheap; whereas the former was distributed through networks catering to elite tastes, the latter was mass-marketed on street corners. People were rightly fearful of what crack was doing to their children and demanded action; as a result, crack dealers started going to prison in record numbers.

Unfortunately, these penalties do not have the same incapacitative effect as sentences for robbery. A robber taken off the street is not replaced by a new robber who has suddenly found a market niche, but a drug dealer sent away is replaced by a new one because an opportunity has opened up.

We are left, then, with the problem of reducing the demand for drugs, and that in turn requires either prevention programs on a scale heretofore unimagined or treatment programs with a level of effectiveness heretofore unachieved. Any big gains in prevention and treatment will probably have to await further basic research into the biochemistry of addiction and the development of effective and attractive drug antagonists that reduce the appeal of cocaine and similar substances.[7]

In the meantime, it is necessary either to build much more prison space, find some other way of disciplining drug offenders, or both. There is very little to be gained, I think, from shortening the terms of existing nondrug inmates in order to free up more prison space. Except for a few elderly, nonviolent offenders serving very long terms, there are real risks associated with shortening the terms of the typical inmate.

Scholars disagree about the magnitude of those risks, but the best studies, such as the one of Wisconsin inmates done by John DiIulio of Princeton, suggest that the annual

---

[7]I anticipate that at this point some readers will call for legalizing or decriminalizing drugs as the "solution" to the problem. Before telling me this, I hope they will read what I wrote on that subject in the February 1990 issue of COMMENTARY. I have not changed my mind.

costs to society in crime committed by an of-fender on the street are probably twice the costs of putting him in a cell. That ratio will vary from state to state because states differ in what proportion of convicted persons is im-prisoned—some states dip deeper down into the pool of convictees, thereby imprisoning some with minor criminal habits.

But I caution the reader to understand that there are no easy prison solutions to crime, even if we build the additional space. The state-prison population more than doubled between 1980 and 1990, yet the victimization rate for robbery fell by only 23 percent. Even if we assign all of that gain to the increased deterrent and incapacitative effect of prison, which is implausible, the improvement is not vast. Of course, it is possible that the victimi-zation rate would have risen, perhaps by a large amount, instead of falling if we had not increased the number of inmates. But we shall never know.

Recall my discussion of the decline in the costs of crime to the criminal, measured by the number of days in prison that result, on average, from the commission of a given crime. That cost is vastly lower today than in the 1950's. But much of the decline (and since 1974, nearly all of it) is the result of a drop in the probability of being arrested for a crime, not in the probability of being imprisoned once arrested.

Anyone who has followed my writings on crime knows that I have defended the use of prison both to deter crime and incapacitate criminals. I continue to defend it. But we must recognize two facts. First, even modest addi-tional reductions in crime, comparable to the ones achieved in the early 1980's, will require vast increases in correctional costs and en-counter bitter judicial resistance to mandatory sentencing laws. Second, America's most trou-bling crime problem—the increasingly violent behavior of disaffected and impulsive youth—may be especially hard to control by means of marginal and delayed increases in the prob-ability of punishment.

Possibly one can make larger gains by turn-ing our attention to the unexplored area of juvenile justice. Juvenile (or family) courts deal with young people just starting their criminal careers and with chronic offenders when they are often at their peak years of of-fending. We know rather little about how these courts work or with what effect. There are few, if any, careful studies of what hap-pens, a result in part of scholarly neglect and in part of the practice in some states of shrouding juvenile records and proceedings in secrecy. Some studies, such as one by the *Los Angeles Times* of juvenile justice in Califor-nia, suggest that young people found guilty of a serious crime are given sentences tougher than those meted out to adults.[8] This finding is so counter to popular beliefs and the testimony of many big-city juvenile-court judges that some caution is required in interpreting it.

There are two problems. The first lies in de-fining the universe of people to whom sanc-tions are applied. In some states, such as California, it may well be the case that a ju-venile *found guilty of a serious offense* is pun-ished with greater rigor than an adult, but many juveniles whose behavior ought to be taken seriously (because they show signs of being part of the 6 percent) are released by the police or probation officers before ever seeing a judge. And in some states, such as New York, juveniles charged with having committed certain crimes, including serious ones like illegally carrying a loaded gun or committing an assault, may not be finger-printed. Since persons with a prior record are usually given longer sentences than those without one, the failure to fingerprint can mean that the court has no way of knowing whether the John Smith standing before it is the same John Smith who was arrested four times for assault and so ought to be sent away, or a different John Smith whose clean record entitles him to probation.

The second problem arises from the defini-tion of a "severe" penalty. In California, a ju-venile found guilty of murder does indeed serve a longer sentence than an adult con-victed of the same offense—60 months for the former, 41 months for the latter. Many people will be puzzled by a newspaper account that defines five years in prison for murder as a "severe" sentence, and angered to learn that an adult serves less than four years for such a crime.

The key, unanswered question is whether prompt and more effective early intervention would stop high-rate delinquents from be-coming high-rate criminals at a time when their offenses were not yet too serious. Per-haps early and swift, though not necessarily severe, sanctions could deter some budding hoodlums, but we have no evidence of that as yet.

---

[8] "A Nation's Children in Lock-up," *Los Angeles Times*, Au-gust 22, 1993.

For as long as I can remember, the debate over crime has been between those who wished to rely on the criminal-justice system and those who wished to attack the root causes of crime. I have always been in the former group because what its opponents depicted as "root causes"—unemployment, racism, poor housing, too little schooling, a lack of self-esteem—turned out, on close examination, not to be major causes of crime at all.

Of late, however, there has been a shift in the debate. Increasingly those who want to attack root causes have begun to point to real ones—temperament, early family experiences, and neighborhood effects. The sketch I gave earlier of the typical high-rate young offender suggests that these factors are indeed at the root of crime. The problem now is to decide whether any can be changed by plan and at an acceptable price in money and personal freedom.

If we are to do this, we must confront the fact that the critical years of a child's life are ages one to ten, with perhaps the most important being the earliest years. During those years, some children are put gravely at risk by some combination of heritable traits, prenatal insults (maternal drug and alcohol abuse or poor diet), weak parent-child attachment, poor supervision, and disorderly family environment.

If we knew with reasonable confidence which children were most seriously at risk, we might intervene with some precision to supply either medical therapy or parent training or (in extreme cases) to remove the child to a better home. But given our present knowledge, precision is impossible, and so we must proceed carefully, relying, except in the most extreme cases, on persuasion and incentives.

We do, however, know enough about the early causes of conduct disorder and later delinquency to know that the more risk factors exist (such as parental criminality and poor supervision), the greater the peril to the child. It follows that programs aimed at just one or a few factors are not likely to be successful; the children most at risk are those who require the most wide-ranging and fundamental changes in their life circumstances. The goal of these changes is, as Travis Hirschi of the University of Arizona has put it, to teach self-control.

Hirokazu Yoshikawa of New York University has recently summarized what we have learned about programs that attempt to make large and lasting changes in a child's prospects for improved conduct, better school behavior, and lessened delinquency. Four such programs in particular seemed valuable—the Perry Preschool Project in Ypsilanti, Michigan; the Parent-Child Development Center in Houston, Texas; the Family Development Research Project in Syracuse, New York; and the Yale Child Welfare Project in New Haven, Connecticut.

All these programs had certain features in common. They dealt with low-income, often minority, families; they intervened during the first five years of a child's life and continued for between two and five years; they combined parent training with preschool education for the child; and they involved extensive home visits. All were evaluated fairly carefully, with the follow-ups lasting for at least five years, in two cases for at least ten, and in one case for fourteen. The programs produced (depending on the project) less fighting, impulsivity, disobedience, restlessness, cheating, and delinquency. In short, they improved self-control.

They were experimental programs, which means that it is hard to be confident that trying the same thing on a bigger scale in many places will produce the same effects. A large number of well-trained and highly motivated caseworkers dealt with a relatively small number of families, with the workers knowing that their efforts were being evaluated. Moreover, the programs operated in the late 1970's or early 1980's before the advent of crack cocaine or the rise of the more lethal neighborhood gangs. A national program mounted under current conditions might or might not have the same result as the experimental efforts.

Try telling that to lawmakers. What happens when politicians encounter experimental successes is amply revealed by the history of Head Start: they expanded the program quickly without assuring quality, and stripped it down to the part that was the most popular, least expensive, and easiest to run, namely, preschool education. Absent from much of Head Start are the high teacher-to-child case loads, the extensive home visits, and the elaborate parent training—the very things that probably account for much of the success of the four experimental programs.

In this country we tend to separate programs designed to help children from those that benefit their parents. The former are called "child development," the latter "welfare reform." This is a great mistake. Everything we know about long-term welfare recipients indicates that their children are at risk for the very problems that child-helping programs later try to correct.

The evidence from a variety of studies is quite clear: even if we hold income and ethnicity constant, children (and especially boys) raised by a single mother are more likely than those raised by two parents to have difficulty in school, get in trouble with the law, and experience emotional and physical problems.[9] Producing illegitimate children is not an "alternative life-style" or simply an imprudent action; it is a curse. Making mothers work will not end the curse; under current proposals, it will not even save money.

The absurdity of divorcing the welfare problem from the child-development problem becomes evident as soon as we think seriously about what we want to achieve. Smaller welfare expenditures? Well, yes, but not if it hurts children. More young mothers working? Probably not; young mothers ought to raise their young children, and work interferes with that unless *two* parents can solve some difficult and expensive problems.

What we really want is *fewer illegitimate children*, because such children, by being born out of wedlock are, except in unusual cases, being given early admission to the underclass. And failing that, we want the children born to single (and typically young and poor) mothers to have a chance at a decent life.

Letting teenage girls set up their own households at public expense neither discourages illegitimacy nor serves the child's best interests. If they do set up their own homes, then to reach those with the fewest parenting skills and the most difficult children will require the kind of expensive and intensive home visits and family-support programs characteristic of the four successful experiments mentioned earlier.

One alternative is to tell a girl who applies for welfare that she can only receive it on condition that she live either in the home of *two* competent parents (her own if she comes from an intact family) or in a group home where competent supervision and parent training will be provided by adults unrelated to her. Such homes would be privately managed but publicly funded by pooling welfare checks, food stamps, and housing allowances.

A model for such a group home (albeit one run without public funds) is the St. Martin de Porres House of Hope on the south side of Chicago, founded by two nuns for homeless young women, especially those with drug-abuse problems. The goals of the home are clear: accept personal responsibility for your lives and learn to care for your children. And these goals, in turn, require the girls to follow rules, stay in school, obey a curfew, and avoid alcohol and drugs. Those are the rules that ought to govern a group home for young welfare mothers.

Group homes funded by pooled welfare benefits would make the task of parent training much easier and provide the kind of structured, consistent, and nurturant environment that children need. A few cases might be too difficult for these homes, and for such children, boarding schools—once common in American cities for disadvantaged children, but now almost extinct—might be revived.

Group homes also make it easier to supply quality medical care to young mothers and their children. Such care has taken on added importance in recent years with discovery of the lasting damage that can be done to a child's prospects from being born prematurely and with a very low birth weight, having a mother who has abused drugs or alcohol, or being exposed to certain dangerous metals. Lead poisoning is now widely acknowledged to be a source of cognitive and behavioral impairment; of late, elevated levels of manganese have been linked to high levels of violence.[10] These are all treatable conditions; in the case of a manganese imbalance, easily treatable.

MY FOCUS on changing behavior will annoy some readers. For them the problem is poverty and the worst feature of single-parent families is that they are inordinately poor. Even to refer to a behavioral or cultural problem is to "stigmatize" people.

Indeed it is. Wrong behavior—neglectful, immature, or incompetent parenting; the production of out-of-wedlock babies—*ought* to be

---

[9]I summarize this evidence in "The Family-Values Debate," COMMENTARY, April 1993.

[10]It is not clear why manganese has this effect, but we know that it diminishes the availability of a precursor of serotonin, a neurotransmitter, and low levels of serotonin are now strongly linked to violent and impulsive behavior.

stigmatized. There are many poor men of all races who do not abandon the women they have impregnated, and many poor women of all races who avoid drugs and do a good job of raising their children. If we fail to stigmatize those who give way to temptation, we withdraw the rewards from those who resist them. This becomes all the more important when entire communities, and not just isolated households, are dominated by a culture of fatherless boys preying on innocent persons and exploiting immature girls.

We need not merely stigmatize, however. We can try harder to move children out of those communities, either by drawing them into safe group homes or facilitating (through rent supplements and housing vouchers) the relocation of them and their parents to neighborhoods with intact social structures and an ethos of family values.

Much of our uniquely American crime problem (as opposed to the worldwide problem of general thievery) arises, not from the failings of individuals but from the concentration in disorderly neighborhoods of people at risk of failing. That concentration is partly the result of prosperity and freedom (functioning families long ago seized the opportunity to move out to the periphery), partly the result of racism (it is harder for some groups to move than for others), and partly the result of politics (elected officials do not wish to see settled constituencies broken up).

I seriously doubt that this country has the will to address either of its two crime problems, save by acts of individual self-protection. We could in theory make justice swifter and more certain, but we will not accept the restrictions on liberty and the weakening of procedural safeguards that this would entail. We could vastly improve the way in which our streets are policed, but some of us will not pay for it and the rest of us will not tolerate it. We could alter the way in which at-risk children experience the first few years of life, but the opponents of this—welfare-rights activists, family preservationists, budget cutters, and assorted ideologues—are numerous and the bureaucratic problems enormous.

Unable or unwilling to do such things, we take refuge in substitutes: we debate the death penalty, we wring our hands over television, we lobby to keep prisons from being built in our neighborhoods, and we fall briefly in love with trendy nostrums that seem to cost little and promise much.

Much of our ambivalence is on display in the 1994 federal crime bill. To satisfy the tough-minded, the list of federal offenses for which the death penalty can be imposed has been greatly enlarged, but there is little reason to think that executions, as they work in this country (which is to say, after much delay and only on a few offenders), have any effect on the crime rate and no reason to think that executing more federal prisoners (who account, at best, for a tiny fraction of all homicides) will reduce the murder rate. To satisfy the tender-minded, several billion dollars are earmarked for prevention programs, but there is as yet very little hard evidence that any of these will actually prevent crime.

In adding more police officers, the bill may make some difference—but only if the additional personnel are imaginatively deployed. And Washington will pay only part of the cost initially and none of it after six years, which means that any city getting new officers will either have to raise its own taxes to keep them on the force or accept the political heat that will arise from turning down "free" cops. Many states also desperately need additional prison space; the federal funds allocated by the bill for their construction will be welcomed, provided that states are willing to meet the conditions set for access to such funds.

Meanwhile, just beyond the horizon, there lurks a cloud that the winds will soon bring over us. The population will start getting younger again. By the end of this decade there will be a million more people between the ages of fourteen and seventeen than there are now. Half of this extra million will be male. Six percent of them will become high-rate, repeat offenders—30,000 more muggers, killers, and thieves than we have now.

Get ready.

OUNCES OF PREVENTION POUNDS OF FLESH

THE MYSTERY OF THE FALLING CRIME RATE

BY DAVID C. ANDERSON

W hat's behind the declines in violent crime? The question prompts lively discussion among people coming at a huge social issue from different angles: Some point to random demographic changes, others cite lock-'em-up prison policies; still others, most recently, point to more astute policing. This debate is not exactly a replay of the old argument over root causes versus tough law enforcement. The deep social pathologies that breed crime are still there, and that argument unfortunately remains on hold. Instead, the recent drop in crime rates poses a central strategic issue of criminal justice: Should it be reactive, emphasizing the capture, adjudication, and punishment of criminals after they commit crimes? Or proactive, working to prevent crimes from ever occurring? In principle, this should not be an either/or matter, but limited resources force choices.

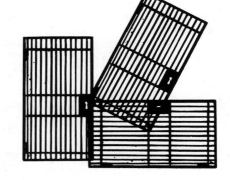

Call it the "back-end/front-end" debate. Back-enders, focusing on events at the conclusion of the criminal justice process, favor punishment for its own sake and for its deterrent effects. They like the death penalty, long prison terms, and limited discretion for judges and parole boards who might be tempted to reduce them. Front-enders look for results from the early stages of justice: policing, gun control, drug treatment, and other kinds of alternative (to prison) programs for young offenders. In general, the back-end approach attracts conservatives who like to sound tough; the front-end approach attracts liberals who focus on broader social dynamics.

Which is the better way to fight crime? While the question ought to be pursued seriously—it is richly complex in practical, economic, and moral issues—it became hopelessly politicized during the decade that began around 1985, when crack and guns produced a surge of urban crime and politicians sought ways to exploit the fear it generated. As it turned out, this politics of crime heavily favored back-enders as it produced fervent support for capital punishment and a nationwide movement toward three-strikes and other mandatory-sentencing laws.

The movement was grounded in valid public anxiety about the level of crime, which no longer could be dismissed as an urban ghetto problem. Millions of middle-class Americans were waking up to the fact that fear had transformed their daily lives. Rising crime imposed surcharges for locks, alarms, and insurance; limited their use of parks, subways, neighborhood streets, and other public places after dark; forced complicated logistics for the supervision and protection of children.

Inevitably, people with narrow agendas sought to exploit fear. Front-enders lamented the new "iron triangle" that lobbied relentlessly, and effectively, for harsher criminal sentences. Its three components: right-wing Republicans seeking to contrast themselves with "soft-on-crime" Democrats; builders, suppliers, and labor unions that benefited from expanding prison construction; and the National Rifle Association, which reflexively sought to fend off serious gun control with proposals for mandatory terms and sentence enhancements for crimes committed with firearms.

Front-enders sputtered in frustration as lawmakers brushed aside evidence that the fear-driven back-end agenda held no promise of greater crime control, and that it created something close to official racism as it forced disproportionate numbers of young black men into prison. What the front-enders failed to grasp was that the discussion had moved away from crime control, where it belongs, and into uglier, more primitive territory. Simply put, the frightened public gave

up on government's ability to prevent crime and turned to other ways of handling its fear.

One of these ways was ad hoc privatization: small armies of security guards for hire; profitable new industries (the Club and Lojack to protect cars; cellular phones with buttons programmed for 911; more sophisticated alarm systems). Another fear-driven remedy was the demand for revenge, or, more precisely, for "expressive punishments" that put more emphasis on venting collective rage than controlling crime. Thus did huge majorities support the death penalty and longer prison sentences; in addition, millions applauded the caning of a young American for vandalism in Singapore and called for legislation to make corporal punishment possible here. They cheered as state lawmakers revived chain gangs and convict stripes and sought to eliminate the "amenities" of prison life. Sensing the public mood, lower-court judges toyed with public "shaming" as an alternative to jail for misdemeanants. Legislators, relieved that they could satisfy voters without having to control crime, were glad to go along with this use of criminal justice for mass therapy.

COST-EFFECTIVE CRIME PREVENTION

While a back-end strategy could guarantee a quick political payoff, no serious policymaker could ignore the longer-term costs. Between 1984 and 1994, according to the Federal Bureau of Justice Statistics, the number of convicts admitted to the nation's state and federal prisons in a year swelled 120 percent, from 246,260 to 541,434, boosting the total incarcerated 116 percent, from 419,346 to 904,647. The taxpayers' overall bill for criminal justice—police, courts, and corrections—also nearly doubled in the period, from $45.6 billion in 1985 to $93.8 billion seven years later, with corrections' share of the total increasing from 28.6 percent to 33.6 percent, or $31.5 billion.

What, in fact, was all this money buying? On this point, the statistics were hardly reassuring. The issue is one of scale. Perhaps half of serious crimes are reported to police. Of these, only about one-fifth result in an arrest. Less than two-thirds of those result in a conviction, and a tiny percentage wind up serving time in a state or federal penitentiary. Thus, the 20 million serious crimes committed each year produce about 500,000 incarcerations—and a third of them are

for nonviolent drug offenses or drunk driving. Even if each convicted felon is responsible for many more than one crime apiece, how can incarceration of so small a fraction of serious criminals have much effect on the crime rate, either directly or as a deterrent? And, if budgets are limited, how is it possible to justify spending 33.6 percent of all the available money to impose serious punishment for a tiny percentage of serious crimes?

People determined to promote the back-end strategy point to studies that document crimes and costs apparently saved by incarceration. William Bennett and his coauthors John DiIulio and John Walters refer in their book *Body Count* to surveys of prison inmates in Wisconsin and New Jersey who claim to have committed numerous crimes in the year before their imprisonment. Both groups of inmates self-reported medians of 12 property or violent crimes, excluding drug crimes. The authors quote other research finding as many as 21 averted crimes for each incarcerated prisoner.

They also quote a study that sought to assess not only direct costs to victims but "monetary value of lost quality of life" caused by crime. "Using various measures," the study put prices on individual murders ($2.4 million each), rapes ($60,000), arson ("almost $50,000"), assault ($22,000), and robbery ($25,000). Multiplying numbers like that by the annual "crimes averted" factors found in the studies of inmates yields amounts that dwarf the average annual cost of keeping an inmate in prison (about $20,000).

However such calculations might provide ammunition for lobbyists of the iron triangle, they remain less than persuasive. Obviously, incarceration incapacitates criminals who are subject to it, and many criminals do commit many crimes per year. But the back-enders leave their audiences with an incomplete picture, for nearly everyone who goes to prison eventually gets released. And given the lack of rehabilitation resoundingly documented by recidivism studies over the years, most of those coming out can be expected to commit new crimes at similar rates. Thus, while 541,434 criminals were sent to prisons in 1994, 456,942 came out, for a net reduction that year of only 84,492 criminals. This does represent an increase over 1984, when 246,260 went in and 221,768 came out, for a net reduction of 24,492. But it's hard to see how incapacitating 60,000 more criminals, a figure that includes nonviolent drug offenders, can have more than a modest impact on serious crime rates even if one believes that each person incapacitated would have committed 10 or 20 crimes in a year. The net incapacitation figure, furthermore, is small enough to be overwhelmed by an increase in the number of young people recruited into lives of drugs, crime, and guns each year, as happened in the late 1980s.

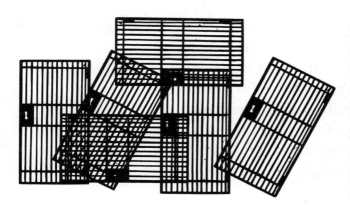

And, of course, as legislatures weary of spending tax dollars for prison expansion, allowing the surge of incarceration to level off, the figures will reverse for a time, with more people coming out than going in, for a net increase of criminals on the street.

As for the claim that the aversion of crimes saves society money, front-end strategies could save as much or more. In any case, estimations of crime control savings don't balance public budgets. And so far, the idea of saving taxpayers so much money in averted costs of crime hasn't led conservative back-enders to support hefty tax increases on them to finance more prison construction.

There simply is no escaping the troubling distortion of spending for corrections at the expense of the rest of the system. Couldn't some of the $31.5 billion that goes to lock up a few hundred thousand serious criminals for a few years each be put to better use preventing some of the 20 million serious crimes?

It's also instructive to think of the issue from the neighborhood's point of view. Suppose that crime may be reduced in equal measure and at equal economic costs either by putting a lot of people in prison or by putting more police on the street and developing other front-end programs to intervene with offenders early. Which strategy leaves the community better off?

Increased police presence risks increased abuse of civil liberties by overzealous officers, a problem that inflicts temporary aggravation on some innocent citizens. But sending people to prison inflicts severe, if not calamitous, emotional and financial stress on their innocent spouses, children, and parents. And their neighborhoods suffer the consequences of having to cope with ex-convicts as they return with their employment prospects permanently stunted and their ability to function in family and community life further impaired by the various brutalities of prison.

Other things being equal, the community clearly is better off with more police and front-end programs than with more people going to prison. In these terms, a strong case could be made for controlling crime with police even if it costs *more* than controlling it by sending people to prison. Any evidence that the police approach produces greater crime control at lower cost should blow the prison strategy out of the water.

OUNCES OF PREVENTION

In a sense, liberals who embrace a front-end law-enforcement strategy are growing up. A crime control agenda based on prevention arguably might include almost any measure that improves education, creates job, supplies day care, improves low-income housing, increases access to health care, and

otherwise supports poor families. But by ignoring the citizenry's immediate anxiety about personal security, liberals who emphasized only "root causes" seemed hopelessly naive, and ceded the whole crime issue to conservatives. A front-end agenda of direct prevention doesn't mean giving up on root causes. But it does allow those with a more social conception of crime to embrace an approach that has two immense advantages over the back-end response: It is less vengeful—and more effective.

Consider New York City: The violent summer of 1990 prompted the city's first black mayor, David Dinkins, and his police commissioner, Lee Brown, to push a proposal for new police hiring—and a tax to pay for it—through the city council and state legislature. The effective expansion of the department from 25,465 to more than 32,000 officers would turn out to be a gift of immeasurable value to Police Commissioner William Bratton, brought in from Boston by Mayor Rudolph Giuliani, who defeated Dinkin's try for a second term in 1993.

Bratton had previously served as chief of New York City's transit police, where he had experimented with new strategies. Now he returned with large ambitions that he would realize all too well, attracting so much attention for genuine achievement that the mayor, feeling upstaged, forced him out after two-and-a-half years.

Bratton's approach was to disperse responsibility for crime fighting downward to precinct commanders while instituting weekly meetings to hold them strictly ac-

> ## Spending on corrections at the expense of the rest of the system doesn't make sense.

countable for results. In order to measure them, he forced precincts to produce a wealth of statistical data. Police computers began to map out crime and enforcement patterns with unprecedented precision and timeliness—they might show, for example, that reports of shootings on a certain street corner occurred mostly on Fridays and Saturdays after 9 p.m.

Precinct commanders were called to account in weekly "COMSTAT" meetings: Why are there so many shootings on that street corner? What do we know about that location and the people who frequent it? What are you doing to get it under control?

At the same time, the new commissioner found excellent use for the new cops coming out of the academy as a result of the Dinkins/Brown hiring plan. He ordered a citywide campaign against "quality of life" offenses—drinking in public, urinating on the street, making noise, and other forms of rowdiness.

Though the endeavor sounded like a public relations stunt, it was deadly serious, with purposes that ran far deeper than simply promoting better manners in public. Bratton was aware of the 1982 *Atlantic Monthly* article "Broken Windows," much discussed in police circles, by James Q. Wilson and George Kelling; it compares a neighborhood where police ignore low-level offenses with a building where the landlord ignores a broken window. As people realize that that they can get away with it, they begin to break more windows until the building is destroyed. Wilson and Kelling used the analogy to argue that determined policing of low-level offenses could inhibit serious criminal activity as well.

In New York, in 1994, "quality of life" became the excuse for an aggressive form of patrolling targeted on youthful lowlifes. It generated complaints of harassment even as it drew praise from older residents of troubled neighborhoods. The routine, based on police lawyers' careful study of Supreme Court "stop and frisk" decisions, called for officers to stop and request identification of anyone they suspected of committing an infraction, accepting only government-issued picture ID.

Those not carrying proper ID or found to be the subject of outstanding warrants were taken into custody, driven to the precinct station, and turned over to detectives who interrogated them for whatever they might tell about drug and gun trafficking and recent crimes in the neighborhood. The process added mightily to the flow of fresh information on which to base new operations.

The effects were immediate and dramatic. The number of homicides in the city had begun a gradual decline in the last years of the Dinkins administration. With the arrival of Bratton, COMSTAT, and aggressive patrolling, the homicide rate began a steep decline that appears to be continuing. Only 985 homicides occurred in the city in 1996, a decline of 57 percent from the peak number of 2,262 in 1990.

Bratton declared that he had proved the broken windows theory. His new measures, he said, had inhibited street criminals, causing them to leave their guns and drugs at home. These claims met with skepticism at first. Weren't crime rates going down all over the country? What was so special about New York? And weren't a lot of things beginning to happen that could be reducing crime independently of the police?

So far, the New York story survives those questions. The nation's big-city homicide rate turned down after 1991 and has continued to fall through 1996. But New York's

> ## "Quality of life" became the rationale for an aggressive form of patrolling targeted on youthful lowlifes.

decline exceeds the national figure. The homicide rate for cities of more than 1 million fell from 33 per 100,000 in 1991 to 21 per 100,000 in 1995. In New York, the rate fell from 29 per 100,000 to 16 per 100,000 in the same period.

Other explanations for declining crime include the natural maturing and waning of the crack epidemic, shifts in drug market patterns, and demographic changes that leave fewer crime-prone teenagers on city streets. But these more gradual events don't explain the close congruence of sharp declines in New York City's crime and the introduction of Bratton's new management and strategies.

Meanwhile, the only independent analysis so far, conducted by Andrew Karmen at John Jay College of Criminal Justice, offers some striking findings. Karmen found that homicides committed with guns and those committed out of doors fell more sharply than those committed indoors or with other weapons. He also found that homicides declined with the rise of patrol strength and with increases in misdemeanor arrests for quality-of-life offenses. Such findings bolster police claims that their greater numbers and aggressive patrols are inhibiting gun use and street crime.

The calculation of costs and benefits extends well beyond the criminal justice system and crime victims. A city experiencing dramatic declines in crime from policing, as opposed to slight or negligible ones from increased incarceration, becomes more hospitable to tourists and to businesses. And the good news, palpable on every street corner, calms the middle-class homeowners whose periodic bouts of panic about the city's future weaken their stabilizing commitments to neighborhoods and schools.

STREET-SMART INTERVENTION

While the New York experience is especially striking given the size of the city and its police department, it isn't unique. Bostonians have recently seen a drastic decline in crime, particularly in gun violence among juveniles. Observers credit a comprehensive police strategy characterized by unprecedented involvement with communities and cooperation among law enforcement agencies. Houston, Dallas, and San Diego have also seen big declines in crime, apparently the result of increased police presence and more aggressive patrolling.

The successes of police-based approaches to crime control encourage thinking about other front-end measures. At least three spring to mind immediately:

Invest more in lower courts, probation departments, and early alternatives. Offenders sentenced to state penitentiaries for serious crime typically wind up there only after committing a number of lower-level crimes (only some of which come to the attention of the authorities) for which they receive insignificant sentences to lightly supervised probation or "time served"—days already spent in jail awaiting court action. Especially if they are relatively young, offenders get off with such sentences because judges are reluctant to expose them to the routine terrors of penitentiary life for a first or second offense.

There is broad agreement that much crime might be averted if courts were able to intervene with offenders more meaningfully after the first or second minor offense, rather than waiting for them to commit more serious crimes. Yet the nation's overcrowded, underfunded urban arraignment courts are a classic horror show of criminal justice. The heavy workload, burnout, and cynicism among criminal justice workers usually preclude any careful consideration of the offender and the underlying problems—substance abuse, lack of education, family crises—that lead people into low-level criminality.

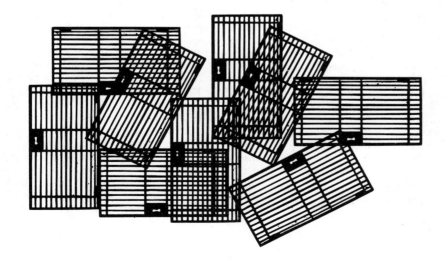

During the 1990s, a few jurisdictions found the will and the resources to improve lower courts. Some set up "drug courts" where judges sentence drug-abusing offenders to treatment programs, then monitor their progress, retaining the power to incarcerate them for failure. New York City set up a somewhat different model in midtown Manhattan. This "community court" arraigned low-level offenders of all sorts, sentencing them to community service projects in the neighborhood, and referring them to a well-staffed social service office located on the premises.

Innovative efforts of lower courts are enhanced when probation departments are able to help. Agencies that deal with offenders released under court supervision are likely to be as underresourced as lower courts. Exceptions are found in Phoenix, Arizona, and in the state of Georgia. Both places offer judges probation-managed "ladders" of sanctions—sentencing options that increase in severity from standard probation supervision through "intensive supervision" (lower caseloads), electronic monitoring, and house arrest, up to work release and boot camp programs based in secure residences. Judges greatly appreciate the chance to move offenders up and down the ladder as they demonstrate more or less willingness to behave.

The possibilities are enhanced further as probation departments get creative with alternative sanctions, finding politically acceptable modes. In South Carolina, for example, judges sentence offenders to pay victims restitution rather than serving time in prison. Offenders who don't have a way to pay are sent to secure residences on the grounds of state prisons, then bused out to work each day in private-sector jobs until they earn enough to pay off their sentence amount. Job developers at the centers come up with the placements, typically hard-to-fill minimum-wage slots where employers frustrated by high turnover welcome the restitution center's steady supply of workers, who are dependably sober, drug free, and motivated by the desire for release.

The restitution centers suggest the potential for public acceptance of front-end programs. Reliable payments of victim compensation defuse much criticism of the non-prison sanction, while the restitution workers' value to local employers builds support for the idea in the business community.

Expand drug treatment. The link between substance abuse and criminal behavior remains obvious and research suggests that as drug abusers recover from addiction, they recover from criminality as well. In large measure, the success of a front-end strategy that calls upon judges and probation agencies to do more with offenders in the early stages of their criminal careers depends upon abundant availability of drug treatment.

The goal should be to develop enough treatment slots so that all addicts who voluntarily seek help may obtain it immediately, and so that judges who wish to make treatment part of a sentence package can order an offender to begin at once. This could be accomplished without any need for big new federal or state bureaucracies simply by amending the Medicaid law so that it will reimburse drug addiction therapy provided through free-standing programs rather than in hospitals.

Skeptics point out that the treatment programs have low rates of success. How can one be sure money spent on them doesn't go down the drain? Yet programs that move even, say, 25 percent of clients into long-term recovery may wind up costing less than sending the same offenders to prison for short terms, then returning them to lives of addiction and crime. Furthermore, treatment managers say that an addict may need several attempts at treatment before it "takes." As courts require offenders to try again and again, the success rate increases.

Get serious about gun control. Researchers confirm the police belief that guns in the hands of kids played a central role in the burst of crime that began in 1985. Even so, lobbying of the National Rifle Association minimized new gun-control legislation during the 1980s and early 1990s. The Brady Bill and the ban on assault weapons, hailed as big symbolic victories, are relatively modest measures. In 1994 and 1995, however, the NRA overreached politically and, by some accounts, financially as well, and its influence began to recede. That makes real gun control look feasible.

A serious gun policy would, at a minimum, require as much of a person who wishes to own and use a gun as of one who wants to own and use a car. Guns should be numbered and registered, with data on guns and owners stored in a computer database instantly accessible by law enforcement agencies.

In addition, gun owners should be licensed, and the burden should be on applicants to demonstrate that they are mentally healthy, have no criminal or spousal abuse records, and have no problems with drugs or alcohol. They should be required to pass written tests on gun law and gun safety as well as practical tests on gun handling on a firing range. And they should have to carry substantial liability insurance. Beyond that, Washington could require manufacturers to build in safety devices like trigger locks that permit use of the gun only by the registered owner, and magnetic strips or computer chips that make guns easier to detect and trace.

Finally, federal law could require that anyone who wants to purchase more than one gun per month make the case for such a need to the local police. Such a law poses no inconvenience to virtually all legitimate gun purchasers, but it could severely inhibit profiteering by gun runners who make legal purchases from retail stores and resell the weapons illegally on the street.

How much would a front-end strategy cost? Obviously the expansion of police departments, lower courts, probation agencies, alternative sanctions, drug treatment, and the bureaucracies necessary to enforce new gun laws would require significant spending. The back-end strategy, however, has already committed the nation to billions in new spending as prisons expand and courts fill them with tens of thousands of new inmates. The issue may not be one of coming up with new money so much as engineering a partial shift of funds already in place.

For now it's enough that police-led victories over crime in New York and other cities revive the front-end/back-end debate and demonstrate an urgent need for research: How are more police used most efficiently? How can lower courts adapt themselves for early intervention and crime control? What are the optimum staffing levels for probation departments? What kinds of alternative sanctions yield the best results? How do different modes of drug treatment work for different kinds of addicts? What would national gun registration and licensing entail and what would be their likely effects?

Such questions, considered marginal where back-end assumptions dominate talk of criminal justice, now belong at the head of the agenda.

AFRICAN AMERICAN MALES

IN THE CRIMINAL JUSTICE SYSTEM

BY JEROME G. MILLER

N THE MIDST of two decades of social neglect, the white majority in America presented its inner cities with an expensive gift—a new and improved criminal justice system. It would, the government promised, bring domestic tranquillity—particularly with regard to African Americans. No expense was spared in crafting it and delivering it inside the city gates. It was, in fact, a Trojan Horse.

While neoconservative commentators such as Charles Murray argued that payments through the Aid to Families with Dependent Children (AFDC) program had undermined family stability and sabotaged work

JEROME G. MILLER is the author of Search and Destroy: African-American Males in the Criminal Justice System *(Cambridge University Press, 1996). He is co-founder of the National Center on Institutions and Alternatives, a nonprofit center dedicated to issues in juvenile justice and located in Washington, D.C. He is now general receiver in charge of the child welfare system for the District of Columbia.*

incentives, the real value of AFDC and food stamp payments to the poor had been steadily declining.[1] Meanwhile, urban schools had deteriorated and fallen into disrepair. Not so with criminal justice. In a society obsessed with single mothers on welfare, more money ($31 billion) was being spent annually at the local, state, and federal levels on a failed drug war alone than on that symbol of vaunted liberal largesse, AFDC ($22 billion).[2]

As government investment in social and employment programs in the inner cities was held stable or cut back during the 1980s, the criminal justice system was ratcheted up to fill the void. Federal, state, and local expenditures for police grew 416%; for courts, 585%; for prosecution and legal services, 1,019%; for public defense, 1,255%; and for corrections, 989.5%. Federal spending for justice grew 668%; county spending increased 710.9%; state spending surged 848%. By 1990 the country was spending $75 billion annually to catch and lock up offenders.[3] For the white majority, it was a popular way to go—particularly as it became clear that these draconian measures would fall heaviest on mi-

norities in general and African American males in particular. The rationale for all this criminal justice activity lay in the putatively exploding crime rates—particularly the rate of violent crime. As it turned out, even this premise was questionable.[4]

In the late 1980s and early 1990s, crime as a social problem and political issue took on the character of a na-

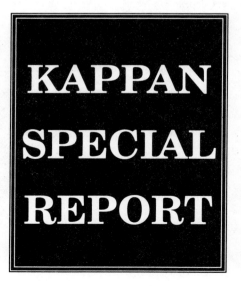

KAPPAN SPECIAL REPORT

From *Phi Delta Kappan*, June 1997, pp. K1-K5, K9-K12. © 1997 by Jerome G. Miller. Reprinted by permission.

tional game of "bait and switch" that meshed with the interests of an aggressive law enforcement establishment. The bait was "violent crime," usually seen as involving inner-city African American youths. The "switch" occurred when law enforcement armamentaria were brought to bear. Since relatively few violent offenders could be found among the millions of citizens of color in the so-called underclass who were being dragged into the justice system, the labels and definitions as to who was dangerous were broadened to include as many as possible as often as possible.

The FBI *Uniform Crime Reports*, on which the media routinely base official estimates of crime, inflated both the numbers and the seriousness of the types of incidents reported. Whereas most European nations report their crime statistics on the basis of convictions, *UCR* statistics are based on complaints or arrests. However, about 43 of every 100 individuals arrested for a felony either were not prosecuted or had their cases dismissed outright at the first court appearance. These dismissals had nothing to do with plea bargains; usually there was not sufficient reason to proceed with the case.[5]

For example, of the 399,277 arrests for "aggravated assault" reported by the FBI in 1990 (a grossly disproportionate percentage of them involving African Americans), only 53,861 (13.4%) resulted in felony convictions.[6] Though figures like this are usually taken by conservative commentators as demonstrating the permissiveness of the justice system, in fact there is quite another phenomenon at work. Police were charging arrestees with violent crimes that they didn't, in fact, commit.

A survey of the "adjudication outcome" for felony defendants in the 75 largest counties in the country revealed that half of the cases of defendants charged with an assault were dismissed outright; half of the remaining charges were reduced to misdemeanors.[7] All of this "overcharging" of defendants comes with a distinctly racial message.

A 1993 California study revealed that, while 64% of the drug arrests of whites were not sustainable, 92% of the black men arrested by police on drug charges were subsequently released for lack of evidence or for inadmissible evidence.[8] These figures are entirely consistent with the thesis that individuals were being routinely overcharged in racially biased ways. Very little of this police activity had to do with serious or violent crime.

By the early 1990s, an absolute majority of young minority males were being arrested—most for minor crimes and misdemeanors. In addition to the approximately three million arrests for "index" (violent or serious) crimes, there were 11 million arrests for lesser

> **By the early 1990s, an absolute majority of young minority males were being arrested—most for minor things.**

crimes and misdemeanors (excluding traffic offenses). Grossly disproportionate percentages of the arrestees were young African American men. The negative effects of this situation on the black community have been largely ignored.

DIFFERENT WORLDS

It is perhaps not so ironic that the incident that plunged South Central Los Angeles into civil disorder involved the acquittal of police officers in the beating of a convicted felon. Dubbed a "gorilla in the mist" on a police radio, a drunken Rodney King had led the police on a high-speed chase. Though a white suburban jury might buy the crisp difference between the "criminal" and the law-abiding citizen, such neat distinctions had limited force in communities where almost everyone has seen a father, son, brother, or close friend given the same "criminal" label.

When Los Angeles city prosecutors ran background checks on the first 1,000 rioters who were arrested and charged with misdemeanors (most having to do with curfew violations), they found that 40% had criminal records and that nearly one-third were on probation or parole. From this important bit of information, the deputy city attorney drew the kind of flawed conclusion that has shaped justice pol-

icy in the inner city for most of the past two decades: "This was not an instantaneous 'good guy rage' kind of thing," he said. "This was a 'bad guy' taking advantage of a situation out of control."[9]

The city attorney's statement was disingenuous at best. He seemed not to realize that, had the police stopped any 1,000 young African American men in the inner city, at least 400 would be found to have criminal records. Moreover, the matter of what kinds of criminal records these LA offenders had was not pursued. The deputy public defender for Los Angeles County cited the case of one of his clients, a 50-year-old man whose criminal record consisted of a single drunk driving arrest 20 years before.[10]

In the year preceding the riots, one-third of all the young black men (between the ages of 20 and 29) living in Los Angeles County had been jailed at least once.[11] At this point, "good guy" versus "bad guy" analyses begin to break down.

The markers for the social disaster that was overtaking African American males had been present for a long time. In a 1967 article, Alfred Blumstein had estimated that, if current patterns continued, the chances of a black male city resident's being arrested at some time in his life for a nontraffic offense were as high as 90%.[12] Later, Blumstein and Elizabeth Graddy looked at arrest statistics gathered from the country's 56 largest cities. They concluded that, whereas one of every four males living in a large city would be arrested for a felony in his lifetime, the majority of non-white males could anticipate being arrested for a felony at some time during their lifetime.[13]

Misdemeanors weren't included in these calculations. Had they been, the percentage of nonwhite males who could anticipate being arrested—and at least briefly jailed—would have reached Blumstein's original 90% prediction. As appalling as these numbers seemed at the time, they were confirmed by others over the ensuing two decades.

In 1987 a California criminologist found a similar pattern in his study of arrests (including misdemeanors) not over a lifetime but in the short 12-year span between ages 18 and 30. Drawing on a statewide sample of males of all races who had been 18 years old in 1974, Robert Tillman traced their arrest records between 1974 and 1986, when they turned 30. Two-thirds of the nonwhite adult males had been arrested and jailed before completing their 29th year (41% for a felony).[14] Tillman included neither juvenile arrests nor arrests after age 30 in his study. Had he done so, the lifetime risk of arrest would easily have reached 90%.

A 1990 RAND Corporation study of the District of Columbia found that one-third of all 18- to 21-year-old African American males who lived there had been arrested and charged with a criminal offense during those three years of their lives. Similarly, the National Center on Institutions and Alternatives found that, on any given day in 1992, 42% of all the 18- to 35-year-old African American males who lived in the District of Columbia were in jail, in prison, on probation/parole, out on bond, or being sought on arrest warrants.[15]

A survey in Baltimore proved to be even more disturbing. Of 60,715 African American males aged 18 to 35 living in Baltimore, 34,025 (56%) were under justice supervision of some sort. The rationale given for the high arrest rates among young black men was fear of violence. However, fewer than one in 10 arrests in Baltimore were for violent crimes. Most young black men who were arrested and jailed were accused of lesser felonies and misdemeanors. The racial disparities were most alarming when drug arrests were singled out. African Americans were being arrested at *six times* the rate of whites, and more than 90% of these arrests were for simple possession.

A 1994 study by the California Commission on the Status of African American Males revealed that one-sixth of California's 625,000 black men 16 years of age and older were being arrested each year, "thereby creating police records which hinder later job prospects." Black men, who make up only 3% of California's population, accounted for 40% of the state's prison inmates.

All these findings challenged what Tillman referred to as the two assumptions that underlie most popular discussion of crime:

• that the world is made up of two types of people—those who commit crimes and those who don't—and

• that criminals form a very small portion of the total population.

As Tillman put it, "The problem appears to be rooted in 'social-structural' conditions, i.e., political, economic, and social institutions that adversely affect large numbers of young adult males, particularly those within certain strata of society. Unless these conditions are recognized and steps taken to alter them, little change can be expected in the frequency with which young men

> **One-fourth of young African American males (aged 18 to 34) in Duval County were being jailed each year.**

become the subjects of the criminal justice system."[16]

The practice of assaulting social problems through our various wars on crime has succeeded in identifying an unusually large number of enemies. By 1994 the number of criminal records in the U.S. approached 50 million—with nearly 60% of the increase occurring in the last decade. With more than 90% of these cases being males and with only about 130 million males residing in the country (including children and the aged), one can only conclude that a larger number of one's young and middle-aged male friends and relatives have a "criminal history" than most would care to acknowledge.[17] Among minority families, the numbers of young men with criminal records would prove to be devastating.

A COUNTY JAIL EXPERIENCE

From 1989 to 1994, I was appointed by the federal court to monitor jail overcrowding in Jacksonville, Florida (Duval County). African American males were being jailed in grossly disproportionate numbers. While African Americans made up about 12% of the county's population, half of the men being brought into the jail each day were African American. Because they were less likely to be able to make even the most modest bail, they tended to stay in jail longer—accounting for 65% to 70% of the population on any given day.

One-fourth of young African American males (aged 18 to 34) in Duval County were being jailed each year.[18] Three-fourths of 18-year-old black youths living in the county would be jailed at least once before reaching age 35. A quarter of all African Americans between the ages of 15 and 17 were arrested during the last four months of 1991 alone.

Very little of this pandemic jailing had to do with serious or violent crime. It was mostly directed at those accused of offenses against "public order" and other lesser offenses. The 10 charges for which individuals were being arrested and jailed most frequently are shown in Table 1.

These figures for Duval County were consistent with national trends. For example, there were an estimated 14,211,900 arrests in the U.S. in 1991. Of these, 2,971,400 were listed as being for index crimes. The remaining 11,240,500 arrests were for nonindex offenses, including everything from forgery (103,700) to public drunkenness (881,100) to curfew and loitering offenses (93,400) to "runaways." The largest single category was the all-inclusive "other." Arrests classified as "other" made up 21% of all reported arrests nationally in 1991. By definition, these arrests were for minor offenses that could not be classified under the "index" categories set forth by the nomenclature of the FBI *Uniform Crime Reports.*[19]

Fewer than 5% of the thousands of young men run through the Duval County Jail ultimately received a state prison sentence. Why? The routine response to this question has been the "commonsense" conclusion that someone is letting the criminals off easy and that slick attorneys are part of the problem. But that conclusion doesn't seem to work in Duval County, which has a statewide reputation as being among the harshest jurisdictions in dealing with offenders.

Most inmates pled guilty to minor charges in order to be released from jail with "time served." Their actual guilt or innocence was beside the point. Because they were poor and could not come up with bail, maintaining their innocence and requesting a trial simply guaranteed that they would sit in jail for weeks or months awaiting a hearing date—a longer wait than many sentences that might later be imposed should they be found guilty of the charges for which they were being held. As for slick lawyers, most inmates were lucky to meet their court-appointed attorneys on the way into the courtroom.

RABBLE MANAGEMENT

At its worst, the experience of the poor and minorities who have over-populated this one large local corrections system lends validity to California sociologist John Irwin's unhappy characterization of jails as institutions for "rabble management." Here are just a few examples.

• A young African American man suffering from asthma and pneumonia had been held in the jail for 22 days on $1,500 bond. He had been jailed on a warrant for not paying $35 in court costs on a four-month-old shoplifting charge. While in jail he lost his job as a truck driver.

• An unemployed 25-year-old African American male had been jailed for "petty theft" and was being held for want of $353 bond. The police arrest report stated, "Investigation revealed that suspect walked into Woolworths, then suspect went to the candy isle [sic] and picked up two Snickers valued at $1.58. Suspect was observed by store security placing the items in bag without paying for the merchandise. Suspect had to be physical [sic] restrained by store security since suspect was uncooperative."

• A frail 81-year-old African American man was arrested for "gambling" (i.e., playing cards for money with friends).

• A 30-year-old man was being held after having been released two weeks earlier from a Florida state prison where he had served six years. He was out three days and, as per the conditions of his release, had reported to the local police station. He was arrested on the spot on an outstanding traffic fine that was four years old. He was in the

state prison when the warrant had been issued and was unaware of it.

Among the "guilty," similar patterns emerged.

• An 18-year-old African American was sentenced to 45 days for taking one cigarette out of a pack on a store shelf, smoking it, and returning the pack to the shelf.

• A 31-year-old African American was given four months in jail for taking a pair of sunglasses from a store.

• A 37-year-old unemployed African American man was sentenced to 150 days in jail for nonpayment of child support.

• A 32-year-old African American man was given 60 days for shoplifting a package of lunch meat.

• A 29-year-old African American man was sentenced to 60 days for petty theft from a gas station convenience store, having put food items into his pants pocket.

• An 18-year-old African American was sentenced to 60 days for selling fake "crack" to vice police for $20.

• A clearly psychotic 54-year-old African American male was sentenced to 60 days for "trespassing" and "resisting arrest without violence." He had been harassing customers at a convenience store and had refused to leave.

• A 34-year-old African American was serving 60 days for shoplifting a package of meat from a supermarket. Pending sentencing, he had been at home, having paid the $150 cash bond. He returned to court for his sentencing and jailing.

Absent some unusual condition, in very few of these cases would a white

person of moderate means, with adequate legal representation, expect to be jailed.

In those rare cases where black men were allowed an "alternative" to incarceration, similar patterns emerged. In the "home detention" program, for example, an electronic "bracelet" is attached to the person's ankle. He or she is unable to leave home without a signal being sent to a central computer system, thereby incurring an "escape" charge. Here are some of those who were sentenced to this alternative.

• A 72-year-old man was sentenced to one year for "driving under the influence" on his moped. He was allowed into the home detention program because of his age and arthritis. Unable to work, he was placed on 24-hour curfew. He lived alone with his dog.

• A 43-year-old man was given four months for "resisting arrest without violence." He was a first offender and a practicing attorney.

• A 22-year-old had been charged with sale and possession of crack cocaine and placed on home detention. He was placed in the program because of his handicapping condition: he had been shot and was totally blind. He was undergoing eye surgery while in home detention.

• A 25-year-old was sentenced to 30 days for petty theft and "resisting and opposing" a police officer. He was in the advanced stages of Hodgkin's disease and, while on home detention, had to be rushed to a hospital emergency room on two occasions to be resuscitated. He died one week prior to the expiration of his 30-day sentence.

One could draw the obvious conclusion from these examples that, at best, the justice system was engaged in some kind of "overkill." Studies in jurisdictions as disparate as Rochester, New York, and Los Angeles showed similar patterns.[20]

Despite legitimate concern over violence among inner-city youths, the bulk of young African American men being dragged into the justice system are charged with misdemeanors and lesser nonviolent felonies. All of this suggests that the currently popular "broken window theory" of arresting individuals for petty violations of public order comes with an ingrained racial twist.

Indeed, according to Shirley Ann Vining Brown, many blacks migrated north in the early 1900s because of their resentment of the law-enforcement tactics in southern counties where officials were paid a bounty for every man arrested. "Large numbers of Black men were rounded up for petty

TABLE 1.

Top 10 Offenses, Duval County, Florida, 1989–94

Offense	Percentage of All Arrests
Other*	18.4
Traffic (excluding drunk driving)	16.3
Shoplifting	9.1
Driving Under Influence	7.0
Assault (simple)	6.6
Drug Sale/Purchase	6.0
Assault (aggravated)	5.0
Disorderly Intoxication	3.0
Worthless Checks	3.0
Burglary	3.0

*"Other" refers to mostly misdemeanor offenses that did not fit the Uniform Crime Report categories (which include all major felony charges). Among offenses classified as "other" in this case were such charges as feeding alligator or crocodile, resisting without violence, loitering, trespassing, nonsupport, technical violations of probation/parole, feeding unsterilized garbage to animals, impersonating a massage license holder, contempt, and 2,990 other transgressions.

infractions of the law such as littering and disorderly conduct. Others were arrested on various charges of suspicion. Heavy fines were often levied for such small violations, and frequently those who could not pay were imprisoned." Black men were arrested "when the labor market was in low supply and workers were needed for road work, ensuring that poor or working-class black males would have to spend time in prison."[21]

As these men came north, arrests there increased dramatically. A U.S. Department of Labor study revealed that, in Cleveland, blacks were routinely being arrested by police and sent to prison on the charge of "suspicion."[22] "It was," as Brown commented, "this type of action by police that accounted for much of the 'Negro Crime' reported during this period (in the 1920s) in the United States."[23]

Continuing into the 1980s and 1990s, this process, so massive in implementation and so racially skewed in outcome, has produced a climate of alienation, hostility, social unrest, and violence in the nation's inner cities.

UNANTICIPATED CONSEQUENCES

On 6 March 1990 an 18-year-old African American man was acquitted of a felony by a black jury in the District of Columbia. That would not have been unusual, but something else was afoot in this courtroom. As the *Washington Post* described the scene: "One young juror was crying when the verdict came. The prosecutor gaped as it was read. The crashing sound in the courtroom was the defendant, whose elation propelled him backward over his chair."[24]

Three weeks later, a letter arrived at D.C. Superior Court. It was from one of the jurors, who wrote that, though most of the jury believed the defendant to be guilty, they had bowed to those who "didn't want to send any more young black men to jail."

The incident was an unsettling example of one of the unanticipated consequences of the national war against crime. It has been repeated in a number of jurisdictions across the nation. In communities in which so many families have seen their sons, brothers, fathers, and friends dragged into the justice system, the idea of galvanizing and organizing the residents against the "criminals"—as though they were outsiders and enemies—is naive. The expectation that the average citizen in an inner-city neighborhood will "in-

form" on young men in trouble so that they might be arrested and jailed is equally naive. The reality is that the

> **Arresting individuals for petty violations of public order comes with an ingrained racial twist.**

massive intrusion of the criminal justice system into the community is perceived as being as destructive and threatening as the harm done by most offenders.

The great University of Chicago social psychologist George Herbert Mead first posed the central dilemma presented to those who would use the justice system to negotiate what he referred to as the "social settlement"— a dilemma that plagues governments run increasingly by lawyers who sometimes seem constitutionally unable to recognize the limitations of their models. Mead wrote:

> We assume that we can detect, pursue, indict, prosecute, and punish the criminal and still retain toward him the attitude of reinstating him in the community as soon as he indicates a change in social attitude himself, that we can at the same time watch for the definite transgression of the statute to catch and overwhelm the offender, and comprehend the situation out of which the offense grows.
> *But the two attitudes, that of control of crime by the hostile procedure of the law and that of control through comprehension of social and psychological conditions, cannot be combined.*[25] (Emphasis added.)

Mead hoped that the newly invented juvenile courts would for the first time be able to consider theretofore "irrelevant" factors associated with delinquency and crime—the familiar root causes, such as unemployment, health problems, emotional disturbance, disorganized communities, and so on. Indeed, Mead's vision led Harvard law professor Roscoe Pound to suggest some 30 years later that the

founding of the juvenile courts was as significant an event in the history of jurisprudence as the signing of the Magna Carta. But Mead's hopes were never realized, and Pound's assessment has not been borne out.

THE VERY LONG ARM OF THE LAW

Since so many young black men are being brought under the auspices of the justice system, it seems sensible to "train" them for the experience. Thus in Washington, D.C., the county police, local educators, the local chapter of the National Association for the Advancement of Colored People, and the black lawyers association sponsor courses that attempt to teach people how they should handle themselves if stopped by the police.

Here is how a reporter described one of those classes in a majority black high school just outside Washington, D.C.

> With his fingers laced behind his head and the Prince George's County police officer grabbing hard at the pager clipped to his waistband, the smile disappeared from 17-year-old Carl Colston's face.
> Later, Colston described his thoughts as the officer frisked him. "You feel uncertain. You don't know what they are going to do."[26]

"I have been pulled over by the police numerous times," said Hardi Jones, president of the county NAACP. To many white people, this seems an odd admission though it is an entirely common experience for a black man.

HOW WIDE A NET?

In 1992 there were more than 12 million bookings into local jails. At least four to five million of those booked were African American males, most accused of minor offenses. Because many of these arrestees were jailed more than once in the same year, it is difficult to know how many individuals were involved. However, there are only about 5.5 million African American men between the ages of 18 and 39 living in the U.S. The percentages mount cumulatively each year as the pool of still unarrested but "arrestable" black men shrinks. Moreover, the process is much more complicated than the simple arrest statistics might suggest, and the implications are more far-reaching than even the most startling statistics indicate.

The scope of the problem was brought home to me in another way in Duval County. I was astonished to find that this one county of approximately 720,000 people maintained more than

> **Contemporary white society confers a perverse identity on the young African American male postulant.**

330,000 active criminal records. The bulk of them had been gathered over the last 15 years. In addition, there were more than 75,000 outstanding misdemeanor arrest warrants and another 10,000 outstanding felony warrants.

RITE OF PASSAGE?

Adolescent bravado notwithstanding, going to jail is not just another rite of passage for a young male—at least not the first or second time. To suggest otherwise is to engage in the kind of nonsensical thinking we would never tolerate if the subjects were middle-class white teenagers from the suburbs. For many African American youths, the experience soon turns into a psychological struggle over whether to meekly assume or to aggressively reject the identity the ritual demands. From "assuming the position," being handcuffed, and being placed in a police van; being moved from place to place, being shackled to a line of peers and older African American males, and posing for a mug shot; being tagged at the wrist or ankle with an ID bracelet; being confined in crowded "tanks" or holding cells with a common toilet or open hole in the middle; to appearing before a robed judge, having a price set on one's head, being detained for want of bail, and, finally, joining one's peers inside or being reunited with anxious relatives outside—the entire experience is a distorted ceremonial expression of manhood for the black male in contemporary American society.

The American anthropologist Robert Linton notes the crucial fact that the identity given a novice is conferred on him by the larger society. "The child becomes a man not when he is physically mature but when he is formally recognized as a man by society. This recognition is almost always given ceremonial expression in what are technically known as puberty rites."[27] In contemporary America, the official representatives of the majority white society confer a perverse identity on the young African American male postulant. He is labeled a renegade, fit to be treated as trash. As one West Coast urban affairs writer put it:

> The L.A.P.D.'s "Operation Hammer" and other antigang dragnets that arrested kids at random . . . have tended to criminalize black youth without class distinction. Between 1987 and 1990, the combined sweeps of the L.A.P.D. and the County Sheriff's Office ensnared 50,000 "suspects." Even the children of doctors and lawyers from View Park and Windsor Hills have had to "kiss the pavement" and occasionally endure some of the humiliations that the homeboys in the flats face every day.[28]

SNITCHING

The most vicious and bloody prison riot of this century, which occurred at the New Mexico State Prison in 1980, provides perhaps the best example of the negative outcomes of snitching, a practice that has fed violence in the inner city. In his study of the riot, Roger Morris discussed the practice of using snitches. "When two or more inmates gathered anywhere, Rodriguez would boast during his tenure as warden and afterward, half of them belonged to him. Snitching and informing in exchange for power, for revenge, for survival, for fear, occasionally even for justice . . . was a way of life at the New Mexico pen."[29]

When the lid blows in such societies, it looses violence that is as much directed at peers as at the authorities. The act of killing a "snitch" is elevated to the level of symbol—a public demonstration to others of the hardness of feeling and the ability to inflict pain or death. In prison society, such displays of violence are related to "fronting," described below. Exposed to this distorted world, the youngest inmates emerge aggressively proud of having taken as their own an identity that, when acted out on the street, ensures their alienation from the larger society.

Probably no single tactic of law enforcement has contributed more to inner-city violence than the practice of seeding the streets with informers and offering deals to snitches. The rise of wanton violence in the early 1990s coincides with the development of a national antidrug strategy based in the widespread use of informers in the cities—particularly in black communities. It has become routine for prosecutors to overcharge defendants and threaten them with stiff sentences unless they give information on a wide array of friends, associates, acquaintances, childhood chums, and relatives.

Law enforcement agencies see informers as crucial in breaking criminal organizations. However, arrests have become so pervasive in the inner city that they have affected most families. The practice of relying on informers threatens and eventually cripples much more than the criminal enterprise; it eats away at whatever social organization there is—including families—that might otherwise keep violence within bounds.

FRONTING

I first became aware of "fronting" when, as Commissioner of Children and Youth for the state of Pennsylvania, I headed an effort to remove 400 teenagers from an adult prison in Pennsylvania. In our debriefing of the young inmates we had placed in alternative settings, the term "fronting" came up repeatedly. Here's how one 16-year-old described his experience.

> When I first got there this guy threatened me and told me he was going to make me his "girl." I yelled that I would beat his butt if he tried. I didn't know it then, but I'd just "fronted" on him. I had challenged him in front of the others. The other inmates told me that I had only a few days to "set up" a confrontation with the guy or I was fair game to be gang raped or taken as someone's "punk."

The young man waited for the appropriate moment when, in front of others, he could accuse the other inmate (falsely) of trying to steal his toothpaste. He then hit the inmate full in the face, breaking his nose. An all-out fight ensued. Both suffered injuries and were sent to the "hole" for a month. But the "new boy" had publicly demonstrated his willingness to be violent and had thereby established his reputation before his peers. When he emerged from the isolation unit, he would have renewed respect. Though the violence was relatively minor, the point was made. Such confrontations are just as likely to involve stabbings, serious injury, or death.

Fronting is a by-product of jailing. It allows a young man to pretend he is in control of a crazy and violent world. You see it in the pathetic posturing, menacing swagger, and cold stares that have come to define the persona of so many young males on the streets of the nation's inner cities; they tell us to watch out. The dynamic is there for all to see in the gratuitous violence of those who beat a white truck driver in LA. It is the stuff of public arguments that turn into shoot-outs and drive-by killings. It betrays the person who has learned never to make an idle threat in front of peers. If you run off at the mouth, you'd best deliver proudly within a relatively short time. It is the royal road to "respect."

It might be well to reexamine here the words of the great American sociologist Gresham Sykes, whose "participant observation" research study, *The Society of Captives,* remains a classic of American criminological literature. Written 30 years ago, it describes the identities conferred by immersion in the criminal justice system.

> Imprisonment [is] directed against the very foundations of the prisoner's being. The individual's picture of himself—as a morally acceptable adult male who can present some claim to merit in his material achievements and his inner strength—begins to waver and grow dim. . . . As one of many, [he] finds two paths open . . . to bind himself to his fellow captives with ties of mutual aid, loyalty, affection, and respect, firmly standing in opposition to the officials. [Or] he can enter into a war of all against all.[30]

Indeed, it is now a sad reality that most of the young black men can anticipate being at least briefly ushered through a series of hothouses for sociopathy: prisons, jails, detention centers, and reform schools—all of which nurture those very characteristics that can subsequently be labeled as pathological.

INTERGENERATIONAL CRIME

In an attempt to measure other unanticipated consequences of the sys-

tem, John Hagan of the University of Toronto and Alberto Palloni of the University of Wisconsin reanalyzed data from the 1960s on working-class boys in London. The original study of 410 boys involved surveys, interviews, and a search of official records. The boys were interviewed at ages 8, 10, 14, 16, 18, 21, and 24. Retrospective data were also collected on the parents. The British researchers had concluded that "a constellation of adverse features of family background (including poverty, too many children, marital disharmony, and inappropriate child-rearing methods), among which parental criminality is likely to be one element, leads to a constellation of antisocial features when sons reach the age of 18, among which criminality is again likely to be one element."[31] These kinds of statements weren't particularly new. They had been made by many over the last century. Hagan and Palloni commented, "This conception of a dangerous, criminal class that is concentrated and reproduced across generations is highly durable."

When Hagan and Palloni reanalyzed the London data, however, they found more important matters at work than "defects in character or behavior." Delinquent careers among inner-city youths—indeed, patterns of intergenerational delinquency in families—were as likely to be due to intervention by the justice system in families' lives as they were to result from variables of culture and character. The better predictor of future delinquency was whether a boy or his father had been effectively labeled as a criminal by the larger society.

In a recent reanalysis of the classic American study of delinquents in Massachusetts by Sheldon Glueck and Eleanor Glueck, sociologists John Laub

and Robert Sampson found essentially the same negative effects from criminal and juvenile justice interventions.[32]

There is little reason to believe that the routing of so many African American youths through the justice system would be any less debilitating than it was for white youths in London or Boston. Indeed, when applied to those with little going for them in the larger society, strategies that rely primarily on deterrence are more likely to exacerbate their situations.

PROBATION

Invented by John Augustus, a Boston shoemaker, over 100 years ago as a way of offering an alternative to jail, probation has deteriorated to the point where the average probation officer is indistinguishable from a policeman. The effects have been only too obvious.

In 1993 almost one-third of the 130,000 inmates in California's state prisons had been put there by their probation officers. These inmates were imprisoned for "technically violating" the conditions of their probation or parole—such things as missing appointments, not attending Alcoholics Anonymous meetings, being unemployed, or moving or marrying without permission. They had not engaged in behavior sufficient to warrant an arrest or criminal charge.

In the world of criminal justice, professional diagnosticians and therapists are expected to deliver one basic commodity, what the late British social anthropologist Sir Edmund Leach called "treatment" when applied to delinquents: "the imposition of discipline by force—the maintenance of the existing order against threats which might arise from its own internal contradictions."[33]

SENTIMENTALIST VERSUS IGNORAMUS

At its best, the criminal justice system affords a democratic society mostly short-term control of and protection from those whose lives are out of control and who represent a threat to others. Such control is obviously necessary in some cases. However, when the justice system becomes the definer of social problems and the foundation of social policy, matters turn dangerous for all concerned. Relying on "experience" emanating from the justice system is dicey even in the best of circumstances. Its rituals and proce-

> ## Most young black men can anticipate being ushered through a series of hothouses for sociopathy.

> **Anticrime policy in the U.S. is highly unlikely to be derived from humane impulse or careful analysis.**

dures distort social realities and feed stereotypes at virtually every step.

It all harks back to George Herbert Mead's comment regarding those who would attempt to solve social problems through the criminal trial process: "The social worker in the court is the sentimentalist, [but] the legalist in the social settlement, in spite of his learned doctrine, is the ignoramus."[34]

The rigid categories that the justice system stands ready to create in abundance seem particularly precious in a society grown vicious over crime—offering refuge in an artificial world of black-and-white issues that carry the system ever further from the complexity of human narrative. Acknowledging the specific conditions out of which a particular violent offender might have arisen is apparently more threatening to our society now than the violent act itself. Such uncomfortable realities undermine the sense of certainty that feeds the moral indignation and drives the punitive response on which the justice system rests. It is much easier to gear the citizenry up to fight the devil than it is to ask it to consider the devilish details that brought the demon to the door. We would rather immerse ourselves in a massive exercise in selective inattention.

THE LIKELY FUTURE

If we have learned anything over the past two decades, it is that anticrime policy in the U.S. is highly unlikely to be derived from either humane impulse or careful analysis. Rather, it is judged for its potential to be distilled into succinct sound bites and applause-garnering throwaway lines. There is less interest in what is correct or even in what "works" than in what sounds good.

Given the racial patterns now firmly fixed in American criminal justice policy and practice, the idea that the costs saved by undoing welfare and family support programs might be used to institutionalize a substantial percentage of the black male population seems increasingly attractive to the majority. One can anticipate ever more florid justifications of the national embarrassment of a nation that will shortly see that it has incarcerated most of its young black men.

DEALING WITH THE DISPOSABLE

Neoconservative dogma currently shapes our national crime policy. It is all there: the objectification of offenders as different from everyone else, the ever larger proportions of minority citizens filling prisons, the destruction of hope through dismissing the possibility of rehabilitation, the shunting of greater numbers of juveniles into adult prisons, and, most recently, the triage management of the disposable through calls to begin removing nondelinquent inner-city youngsters from largely African American single-parent homes to state institutions, camps, or what Charles Murray calls "lavishly funded orphanages" and James Q. Wilson calls "boarding schools."[35] Joining the call for removing children from single-parent homes to "orphanages" is William Bennett.[36]

The Pandora's box that Wilson and Richard Herrnstein opened in their 1985 book, *Crime & Human Nature,* is likely to lead to that more alluring search that has entranced racially obsessed commentators for the last century: the quest for "criminal man." It will set the country on a new adventure that will avoid the murkiness of "root causes" while providing the white majority with a more comforting analysis. We can then move on from deterrence to more sophisticated preventive strategies. The researchers appropriate to this task are standing in line ready to guide us down the slippery slope toward eugenics.

It was Graham Greene, speaking to a conference in France three years after the fall of Nazism, who observed, "The totalitarian state contrives, by educating its citizens, to suppress all sense of guilt, all indecision of mind."[37] One can hope that, when it comes to the African American male, some "indecision of mind" will linger in America for a while longer. And for readers of the *Kappan,* we can also hope that American educators will become in-

creasingly aware of the unstated assumptions that underlie the policies and practices of the criminal justice system in America. Meanwhile, any "solutions" proposed in our current state are likely to smack of finality.

1. E. J. Dionne, *Why Americans Hate Politics* (New York: Simon & Schuster, 1992), p. 6.
2. Patrick Murphy, *Keeping Score: The Frailties of the Federal Drug Budget* (Santa Monica, Calif.: RAND Drug Policy Research Center, Issue Paper, January 1994), p. 5.
3. *Justice Expenditure and Employment, 1990* (Washington, D.C.: Bureau of Justice Statistics, U.S. Department of Justice, Bulletin NCLJ-135777, August 1992), p. 1.
4. Scott Boggess and John Bound, *Comparison Study of Uniform Crime Report, National Crime Survey and Imprisonment Rates* (Ann Arbor: National Bureau of Economic Research, University of Michigan, 1993). In reanalyzing the major sources of crime statistics, the authors concluded that the rate of serious crime as measured by Uniform Crime Report data actually fell by 2% between 1979 and 1991, while the National Crime Survey registered a 27% drop in crimes against persons and a 31% drop in property crimes during the same period.
5. *The Prosecution of Felony Arrests* (Washington, D.C.: Office of Justice Programs, U.S. Department of Justice, 1987).
6. Patrick Langan and John M. Dawson, *Felony Sentences in State Courts, 1990* (Washington, D.C.: Bureau of Justice Statistics, U.S. Department of Justice, NCJ-140186, March 1993), p. 5.
7. Pheny Z. Smith, *Felony Defendants in Large Urban Counties, 1990* (Washington, D.C.: Bureau of Justice Statistics, U.S. Department of Justice, NCJ-1441872, May 1993), p. 13.
8. Sonia Nazario, "Odds Grim for Black Men in California," *Washington Post,* 12 December 1993, p. A-9.
9. Paul Lieberman, "40% of Riot Suspects Found to Have Criminal Records," *Los Angeles Times,* 19 May 1992, p. B-4. A later *Times* survey of 700 people convicted of riot-related felonies (more than 90% convicted of "looting") found that 60% had previously been arrested. See *Los Angeles Times,* 2 May 1993, p. A-34.
10. Lieberman, p. B-4.
11. James Austin and Donald Irie, *Los Angeles County Sheriff's Department Jail Population Analysis and Policy Simulations: Briefing Report* (San Francisco: National Council on Crime and Delinquency, 21 August 1992).
12. Alfred Blumstein, "Systems Analysis and the Criminal Justice System," *Annals of the American Academy of Political and Social Science,* November 1967, p. 99.
13. Alfred Blumstein and Elizabeth Graddy, "Prevalence and Recidivism in Index Arrests: A Feedback Model," *Law and Society Review,* vol. 16, 1981–82, pp. 279–80.
14. Robert Tillman, "The Size of the 'Criminal Population': The Prevalence and Incidence of Adult Arrests," *Criminology,* Fall 1987, pp. 335–47.
15. Jerome Miller and Barry Holman, *Hobbling a Generation: African American Males in the*

District of Columbia's Criminal Justice System (Washington, D.C.: National Center on Institutions and Alternatives, March 1992).

16. Tillman, p. 6.
17. *Proceedings of BJS/SEARCH Conference* (Washington, D.C.: U.S. Department of Justice, January 1992, NCJ-133532).
18. Jerome Miller, *Duval County Jail Report,* submitted to the Honorable Howell W. Melton, U.S. District Judge, Middle District of Florida, Jacksonville, 1 June 1993, pp. 82–83.
19. Federal Bureau of Investigation, *Crime in the United States, 1991* (Washington, D.C.: U.S. Department of Justice, 1992), p. 213.
20. *Justice in Jeopardy,* Report to Monroe County Bar Association Board of Trustees, May 1992; and James Austin, *Los Angeles County Sheriff's Department Jail Population Analysis and Policy Simulations* (San Francisco: National Council on Crime and Delinquency, 21 August 1992).
21. Shirley Ann Vining Brown, "Race as a Factor in the Intra-Prison Outcomes of Youthful First Offenders" (Doctoral dissertation, University of Michigan, 1975).
22. F. D. Tyson, *Negro Migration in 1916–17* (Washington, D.C.: U.S. Department of Labor, 1918), p. 141.
23. Brown, op. cit.
24. Bart Gellman and Sari Horwitz, "Letter Stirs Debate After Acquittal: Writer Says Jurors Bowed to Racial Issue in D.C. Murder Case," *Washington Post,* 29 March 1990, p. A-1.
25. George Herbert Mead, "The Psychology of Punitive Justice," *American Journal of Sociology,* vol. 23, 1917, pp. 577–602.
26. "The Dreaded 'Encounter' with Police," *Washington Post,* 18 January 1994, Metro Section, p. 1.
27. Robert Linton, *The Study of Man* (New York: Appleton-Crofts, 1936).
28. Mike Davis, "In LA, Burning All Illusions," *The Nation,* 1 June 1992, p. 744.
29. Roger Morris, *The Devil's Butcher Shop: The New Mexico Prison Uprising* (New York: Franklin Watts, 1983), p. 87.
30. Gresham Sykes, *The Society of Captives* (Princeton, N.J.: Princeton University Press, 1958), pp. 78–79.
31. John Hagan and Alberto Palloni, "The Social Reproduction of a Criminal Class in Working-Class London Circa 1950–1980," *American Journal of Sociology,* September 1990.
32. John H. Laub and Robert J. Sampson, "The Long-Term Effect of Punitive Discipline," revised version of paper presented at the Life History Research Society Meeting, 6 May 1992, Boston.
33. Edmund Leach, *A Runaway World: The BBC Reith Lectures* (London: British Broadcasting Corporation, 1967).
34. Mead, p. 585.

35. James Q. Wilson, "Redefining Equality: The Liberalism of Mickey Kaus," *Public Interest,* Fall 1992, p. 102.
36. *Washington Times,* 25 January 1994, p. C-3.
37. Graham Greene, *Reflections,* edited by Judith Adamson (London: Reinhardt Books, 1991).

RESTORATIVE JUSTICE

A STORY NEEDING TO BE TOLD

*An exploration of the foundational theology that may lead us
to a different way of doing justice.*

Virginia Mackey

There is a brave, fledgling movement in this country called restorative justice.

This movement is in stark contrast to our present retributive policies in criminal justice. Our country's allegiance to punishment results in our having one of the world's highest incarceration rates and being the only Western democracy to retain the death penalty. Despite this, our fear and preoccupation with crime is overwhelming.

The current concept of restorative justice grew out of the vision and experience of religiously based criminal justice change advocates. It needs to be valued, nurtured, and supported by people of faith.

Ironically, it is gaining more acceptance in the secular—even corrections—world than it appears to have in the religious world. Why do we have so little to say? Our very silence seems to give credence to harsh cries for retribution.

Why does a recent Gallup poll find that support of the death penalty is higher—75 percent—among those who consider religion to be very important in their lives than the 69 percent support among those who say that religion is not very important in their lives?[1]

We have been "so carefully taught" to think punishment.

The reasons for the dichotomy among people of faith are multiple and complex. Criminal matters are sensationalized by the media but are outside the experience of most people.

Even within the portions of our Judeo-Christian tradition that have most influenced our criminal law, there are differing views on the nature of human beings. Some are convinced that our negative instincts must be controlled; others are convinced that our nature is inherently good and can be shaped by nurture and support.

Virginia Mackey is a minister of the United Church of Christ who has chaired and staffed ecumenically sponsored criminal justice projects at the local, state, and national level, including the National Interreligious Task Force on Criminal Justice. For the Presbyterian Church (U.S.A.) she has written Restorative Justice: Toward Nonviolence *and the* Beyond Fear *workshop and packet; her other writings include* Punishment: In the Tradition and Scripture of Judaism, Christianity, and Islam. *She lives in Golden, Colorado. This article is adapted from her address to the Presbytery of the Cascades in June 1996.*

From *Church & Society* magazine, March/April 1997, pp. 23-31. © 1997 by the Presbyterian Church (U.S.A.). Reprinted by permission.

There are differing theologies, among them, one believing that God "says" lawbreakers must be punished, another espousing a theology of restoration.

We have been "so carefully taught" to think punishment. There is a haunting quote from George Bernard Shaw in the Epilog of his play *St. Joan:*

Must then a Christ perish in torment in every age to save those that have no imagination?

Challenges to Our Religious Community

Kay Pranis, now Restorative Justice Planner for the Minnesota Department of Corrections, contends that the biggest gap between what we profess about redemption in most faith gatherings and what we actually do in our daily lives is in the area of criminal justice.

At a 1983 conference on "Breaking the Cycle of Violence and Vengeance," Kay Harris, a professor of criminal justice at Temple University, challenged the religious community:

We need you to help change the terms of the debate, from the repressive and pessimistic context in which we now are forced to operate. We need your help so that the moral turf is not left to the protagonists for law and order and severe penal sanctions.

The way we are treating people is wrong, and must be stopped. Please help in recapturing the moral turf to assert the values and the means you believe should underlie and permeate our responses to conflict, to what we call crime, and to crimes we don't call crimes. Please find a way to be heard and to help change the context of the debate.

Howard Zehr, Mennonite Criminal Justice Coordinator, recommends that we "change lenses."[2] We need to bring the imagination of the faith community to bear on the fear and the realities of crime and injustice.

As William E. Gibson recently wrote in this magazine, "There is a bold word to be spoken for eco-justice against all the forces of eco-injustice, all the oppression of earth and people."[3] I am convinced that is no less true for restorative justice standing against all the forces of criminal injustice, all the oppression of human beings. The concept of restorative justice is truly a story needing to be told.

Renewing Our Vision

Many who advocate punishment claim that it has scriptural justification. We can counter that claim by bringing to speech what we know in our hearts: that our God is a loving God, of enduring patience and will to save.

Revisiting our Judeo-Christian Scripture and tradition can prepare us to make a valid claim that a theology of restorative justice best captures what God "says" about how we are to relate to each other and resolve disputes.

How did Hebrew authors and rabbinic justice-makers fashion a story of restorative justice?

Our Hebrew and Christian ancestors told stories in forming their identity, their sense of values and integrity. These are exceptional stories, rich in metaphors and fraught with hidden meanings. They point not only to maxims for individual morality but to ultimate realities for a people dedicated to being faithful to God, to justice, to nonviolence.

These are *our* stories. But our Western minds, literally and scientifically bent, surely are ethically challenged when the meaning is hidden in story. We're resistant to probing the larger contexts and meanings.

Not so the Hebrews. It was a rabbinic way of reaching a people trying to shift from tribal beliefs in multiple gods to a commitment to monotheism. They first conceptualized the *living* God, the God who is always a reconciling presence.

For the Jew, law is not dictated by God but is revealed in a dynamic and ongoing process. After they had established an identity in creation stories and endless genealogies, they turned to norms, *halakah,* the "way to go."

Since religious leaders were responsible for the resolution of civil, criminal, and family disputes as well as for matters of faith, there was need for guidance on justice. Here it is important to note that the term justice, per se, does not appear in the Old Testament.

Herman Bianchi, professor of law retired from Free University in Amsterdam, reminds us that the closest equivalent is *tsedeqah*—righteousness, making right. He has asserted that

The application of biblical ideas of power and retribution, detached from *tsedeqah,* is one of the most regrettable factors in the history not only of Christianity, but of our entire cultural system.... [Tsedeqah] is a creative and energetic concept. It is valued, as is a fruit tree, by its results.[4]

The very ordering of the books of Scripture has significance. In Genesis, God is depicted as intervening in a case of ultimate violence—murder. God did not rule that Cain "deserved to die" for having slain his brother, Abel. God confronted Cain, obtained a confession, indicated that Cain would never be able to forget his act of violence—"The blood of your brother will haunt you"—and recommended that Cain move to a different place where he could start a life free of violence. And God put a mark of protection on him. In other words, God would be there for him.

Here the redemptive potential was actualized. It applied to later cases such as those of Moses, King David, and Paul.

Early in the Torah, the books of law, the infamous *lex talionis* appears. Granted, "an eye for an eye" is a catchy phrase. It's a tremendous relief to realize that the Hebrew justice-makers coined it to establish limitations on previous tribal practices of "blood revenge," or to indicate that no herder could demand restitution of more than the number of animals that had been killed or stolen.

Were the storytellers advocates of vigilante justice, such as stoning? Did stoning occur? Perhaps. But the accounts in Exodus, Leviticus, and Numbers may be synoptic—repetitive and overstated approaches to deter wickedness.

The rabbis used ingenious argumentation to explain away other legalisms. The phrase *ke-illu* was a legal fiction employed. It was "as if" a penalty had been carried out. The victim was satisfied because the offender had been confronted.

Strict proceduralism was common. The death penalty could not be carried out if there had not been two witnesses to the murder and proof that forewarning had been given.

Substitute penalties were frequent. Religious rituals provided atonement. Social penalties could include expulsion from the synagog, public confession, self-vilification, or the humiliation of a "donkey's burial" near the cemetery fence.

The authors of Proverbs urged persons who had experienced harm not to "emulate the man of violence. Never model your conduct on his."

If your enemies are hungry, give them bread to eat; and if they are thirsty, give them water to drink. (Prov. 25:21)

Or surprise them by grace—a key tenet of Jesus and of nonviolence.

Walter Brueggemann's *The Message of the Psalms*[5] underscores the healing effects of lamentations when we have been the victim of harm or injustice. Psalm 109 spells out the stages:

- In lament, utter your pain and yield it to God.
- Express rage and need for justice. But ask God to be your "prosecutor" and a judge who acts in love.
- Await God's healing and restoration.

How did the Hebrew storytellers convey their concern about the roots of violence?

What are we to make of the stories that depict God's wrath and acts of vengeance? Their context is crucially important. Remember, they were told to peoples who were tempted to return to belief in capricious gods when they needed to explain why evils occurred. When stories depicted God as exacting retribution, they were emphasizing that the sins against God were the most egregious. What were the consequences—not the punishment—of failing God?

Word study is revealing. *Ruah* is key. It can mean "wind," "spirit," or Holy Spirit. What does God breathe life into? Creation. What does God's spirit abide in? That which is good, peaceful, just.

On the other hand, when was God portrayed as being wrathful? The Hebrew terms *aph* or *naqam*, which we translate as "wrath" or "vengeance," imply "heavy breathing." If you wanted to convey what God became angry about, you could depict God as breathing so forcibly that human beings became aware of it. Then, if they paid attention and changed their behavior, they were "avenged" by *naqam*, or God's breathing out with a sigh of relief.

What if God found that the offensive behavior did not cease? Our translations indicate that God punished. But the root words reveal quite different intents such as "to restrain, chasten, instruct, teach." These understandings begin to unravel the seeming contradictions with our notion of God's being "slow to anger and abounding in steadfast love [lovingkindness]" (Ex. 34:6).

There is no doubt that God became "wrathful" about the roots of violence. What upsets God most? Injustice! Anthropomorphically, we can picture God as breathing very heavily.

The prophets understood. God's measure of well-being, says Amos (7:7), is a plumbline. God's plumbline is tied to *shalom* (health, safety, peace) in the community. When injustice and violence interrupt well-being, the plumbline swings to indicate our loss of orientation to God.

The worship of false idols causes God to breathe heavily. In *Restoring Justice: Toward Nonviolence*, the study guide accompanying a 1988 Presbyterian General Assembly policy statement on the violence of prisons, we quoted the book of Habbakuk:

> *What profit is an idol when its maker has shaped it, a metal image, a teacher of lies? . . . Behold, it is overlaid with gold and silver, and there is no breath at all in it.* (2:18,19,RSV)

We meant to draw a parallel to our modern allegiances and devotion of resources to the false idols of punishment and prisons. Surely there is little "breath" in them, and they lack God's spirit.

The nonviolence of Jesus

Scripture calls on us repeatedly to confess our individual and collective complicity in causing the distress of God and of our brothers and sisters. Confession, we hope, will lead to "the greatest story ever told": the nonviolence of Jesus.

Redemption should always be seen as a potential.

God became human, the story goes, to demonstrate unfailing love and compassion and to renew the prophetic call to justice.

Parables were major vehicles for New Testament ethics. In the Parable of the Good Samaritan (Luke 10), Jesus demonstrated that no victim can be neglected and it is our responsibility to provide what is needed: a listening ear, attention to physical needs, financial assistance, a sense of worth, and a path to healing and closure from a bad experience.

Jesus demonstrated repeatedly that he did not assume the hurts we call crimes to be an unalterable state of affairs. He intervened in the lives of "lawbreakers" with radical acceptance and unconditional love. In Luke 19 he afforded dignity to Zacchaeus and caused him to see his own alienation and make amends to those he had cheated.

In John 8 Jesus intervened in the life of the woman doomed to die according to laws about adultery. He turned the question about the death penalty back on those who challenged him to condemn her, saying "Let those who are without sin cast the first stone." No one stepped forward.

Redemption should always be seen as a potential. God loves and wants reconciliation as portrayed in the Parable of the Prodigal Son (Luke 15). The original language conveys that the "father" was so eager to be reunited with his "son" that it was as if his "bowels were yearning."

In Matthew 5, Jesus supplanted the proportional ethic of "an eye for an eye" with one of love. Jesus' sense of nonviolence was so strong that he prayed for his own executioners to be forgiven. Not only are you to love your neighbor but, especially, are you to love those who are unjust. This ethic of nonviolence is a foundation for shalom, for well-being, for a healthy community.

Restorative Justice Is an Ethic of Shalom

An ethic of shalom understands our need for safety and freedom from fear. But it also expects accountability on our part. We must invest and participate in mediating processes and restorative policies. In our responses we must strive for the healing of victim and offender and preventive measures for transformation of communities and social policies.

An ethic of shalom makes our unique responsibility that of being at the forefront of the restorative justice movement. Convinced of the restorative nature of our God, we are to make a bold commitment: covenanting to be restorative justice people, families, congregations, and religious bodies, and telling a restorative justice story that is compelling and can capture the hearts of our people.

Notes

1. *Christian Century*, May 8, 1996.
2. Howard Zehr, *Changing Lenses: A New Focus for Crime and Justice* (Scottdale, Pa.: Herald Press, 1990).
3. William E. Gibson, "Eco-Justice and the Reality of God," in *Church & Society* Magazine, July/August 1996, p. 13.
4. Herman Bianchi, *"Tsedeka* Justice," *Review for Philosophy and Theology*, September 1973.
5. Walter Brueggemann, *The Message of the Psalms: A Theological Commentary* (Minneapolis: Augsburg Publishing, 1984). In *Toward a Justice that Heals: The Church's Response to Crime* (United Church [of Canada] Publishing House, 1988), Morton [MacCallum] Paterson also finds strength in turning to God in lament.

For Reflection, Discussion, and Action

- Virginia Mackey suggests [page 000] that we can counter the claim of scriptural justification for punishment "by bringing to speech what we know in our hearts: that our God is a loving God, of enduring patience and will to save." In what ways do you believe, or know, this? What are your beliefs about, and experiences with, punishment?

- Reflect on the place that lamentation, wrath, and vengeance have in your life. What are your reactions to the author's descriptions of God's wrath? and to her references to Jesus' nonviolence?

- Where in your community and beyond do you see examples of policies of retribution? of restoration? If the concept of restorative justice is a new one, what are your initial reactions to it? If you're familiar with it, where are you seeing it used?

- What are you doing, or what might you do, to advocate for change in the criminal justice system?

Victimology

For many years, crime victims were not considered an important topic for criminological study. Now, however, criminologists consider focusing on victims and victimization essential to understanding the phenomenon of crime. The popularity of this area of study can be attributed to the early work of Hans von Hentig and the later work of Stephen Schafer. These writers were the first to assert that crime victims play an integral role in the criminal event, that their actions may actually precipitate crime, and that unless the victim's role is considered, the study of crime is not complete.

In recent years a growing number of criminologists have devoted increasing attention to the victim's role in the criminal justice process. Generally, areas of particular interest include calculating costs of crime to victims, taking surveys of victims to measure the nature and extent of criminal behavior, establishing probabilities of victimization risks, studying victim precipitation of crime and culpability, and designing services expressly for victims of crime. As more criminologists focus their attention on the victim's role in the criminal process, victimology will take on even greater importance.

This unit provides sharp focus on key issues. In the lead article, "Victimization and the Victim Industry," Joel Best discusses how a widespread ideology of victimization created a victim industry, which now supports the identification of large numbers of victims.

Cheryl Russell, in the next reading, "True Crime," asserts that careful examination of data reveals that much fear among citizens is misplaced. It is true, however, that the worst crimes are increasing and that it is particularly dangerous to live in certain regions of the country.

According to Douglas Marvin, in "The Dynamics of Domestic Abuse," police officers need an in-depth understanding of domestic abuse in order to effectively deal with it. Familiarity with the complex social, economic, and psychological issues that underlie these acts are very important. It is generally believed that children who are abused or neglected will grow up to be violent criminals. Cathy Spatz Widom's study, "Victims of Childhood Sexual Abuse—Later Criminal Consequences," finds that this may not be true.

Looking Ahead: Challenge Questions

What lifestyle changes might you consider to avoid becoming victimized?

How successful are crime victims when they fight their assailants?

Does marital status influence victimization risk? Defend your answer.

Is street crime more harmful that white-collar crime? If you were the victim of a mugging, how would this influence your answer?

Victimization and the Victim Industry

Joel Best

Victimization has become fashionable, the focus of talk shows, political speeches, and concerned commentaries as diverse as Alan Dershowitz's *The Abuse Excuse* (1994), Robert Hughes's *Culture of Complaint* (1993), Wendy Kaminer's *I'm Dysfunctional, You're Dysfunctional* (1992), and Charles Sykes's *A Nation of Victims* (1992). Though these critics approach the topic from different directions, they agree that claims of victimization are spreading, and they worry that this threatens basic assumptions about personal responsibility that are fundamental to the social order. Yet focusing on the moral consequences of claims about victims causes most critics to overlook the social arrangements that foster these claims.

The announcement of new forms of victimization has become commonplace during the last twenty-five years. Journalists, activists, academics, and talk show hosts have called attention to the neglected or unnoticed victims of marital rape, acquaintance rape, date rape, elder abuse, sibling abuse, peer abuse, emotional abuse, telephone abuse, clergy abuse, Satanic ritual abuse, sexual abuse, sexual harassment, sexual addiction, love addiction, food addiction, eating disorders, post-traumatic stress disorder, multiple-personality disorder, chronic fatigue syndrome, false memory syndrome, credit-card dependency, codependency, dysfunctional families, hate crimes, battering, stalking, drunk driving, and UFO abductions. Some of these claims gained wide acceptance, whereas others met with considerable skepticism. But debating the merits of particular claims ignores underlying patterns in the way contemporary Americans interpret victimization. During the 1960s, Americans became sensitized to victims and victimization; by the 1970s, there was a widespread ideology of victimization. As this ideology gained acceptance in key institutions, it created a victim industry—a set of social arrangements that now supports the identification of large numbers of victims.

Discovering Victims in the 1960s

Whether human actions and experiences are best understood as products of individuals' choices or as shaped by social arrangements is a central issue in social theory. Focusing on victims discounts individuals' ability to control their own lives and emphasizes the power of social forces because victims cannot control what happens to them. Contemporary discussions of victimization have their roots in the 1960s and early 1970s, when several developments drew attention to—and reshaped attitudes toward—the social arrangements that produced victims and victimization. During this period, a broad array of activists, conservatives, liberals, therapists, lawyers, and victimologists spoke out about victims and their problems.

The civil rights movement's successes during the early 1960s inspired other social movements demanding equal rights for women, homosexuals, the disabled, the elderly, children, and others. Later movements borrowed tactics, rhetoric, and sometimes personnel from their predecessors. Typically, movement activists identified large segments of the population as victims of prejudice and discrimination (or, in more politicized language, by oppression and exploitation), described the processes of their victimization, and advocated reforms to correct the inequities.

The rhetoric of equal rights also inspired slogans about victims' rights. Many political conservatives deplored the Supreme Court decisions under Chief Justice Earl Warren extending the rights of criminal suspects and restricting police powers; the courts, they argued, protected the rights of criminals but ignored the rights of the criminals' victims. Republican political candidates began advocating victims' rights, and this rhetoric eventually spawned a victims' rights movement that demanded such reforms as victims compensation, victim impact statements, and victim allocution at sentencing and parole hearings.

The Left also adopted victim imagery. In 1971, William Ryan, a psychologist and civil rights activist, published a well-received book *Blaming the Victim*, which focused on the problems of what would later be called the black underclass. Ryan argued that the underclass were victims of racial and class oppression and that criticizing street crime or welfare dependency amounted to blaming powerless people for their own victimization. The expression "blaming the victim" quickly took on a life of its own; Ryan's original focus on the underclass was lost, and the phrase became a rhetorical trump card, playable in almost any political contest. The notion was not new—earlier generations of psychiatrists and social workers had argued that delinquents were "victims of society"—but Ryan's rephrasing caught on. Part of its appeal may have been its ambiguity; it let one identify victims without necessarily specifying who was doing the victimizing.

Furthermore, since 1960 the ranks of mental health professionals has grown more rapidly than has the general population. Public and private medical insurance plans spread and their coverage for mental health services (for example, substance-abuse programs and personal counseling) expanded. These benefits fostered a growing number of therapeutic professionals—clinical psychologists, licensed clinical social workers, family counselors, and so on—whose eligibility to receive compensation from insurers was established in new state and federal legislation. These professionals medicalized family dynamics and other aspects of their patients' lives, often helping them interpret their experiences as forms of victimization. These therapists could apply a growing number of diagnoses; the American Psychiatric Association's *Diagnostic and Statistical Manual* (the official catalog of diagnostic categories) has grown with each revision.

Parallel developments occurred within the law, as reforms made it easier to litigate cases of alleged harms and risks. Following the U.S. Surgeon General's 1964 report on tobacco use, warnings proliferated about risks associated with a wide range of products, foods, and activities. Emerging health and consumer movements focused on those victimized by dangerous technologies, unsafe products, and inadequate regulation. Increasingly, government agencies sought to regulate risks, while hazard victims turned to the civil courts, demanding compensation for their suffering. These regulations and court cases attracted news coverage, contributing to the awareness of risk and victimization.

Increasingly, critical social scientists defined their task as exposing powerful institutions and defending society's most vulnerable members. Within criminology, a growing interest in victimization led to the emergence of victimology as a subspecialty, with its own professional societies, textbooks, and journals. Academics melded activists' calls for equal rights and victims' rights, warnings against blaming victims, therapeutic interpretations of family dynamics, and legal theories of liability into a general study of victims.

The net effect of these developments was to sensitize Americans to the plight of victims and the processes of victimization. Victim advocates argued that victims had long been neglected, even ignored. But by the mid-1970s, victims had become familiar figures on the social landscape.

The Ideology of Victimization

This familiarity coalesced in an ideology of victimization, a set of widely accepted propositions about the nature of victimization. These propositions tend to be invoked piecemeal, that is, in individual campaigns by advocates drawing attention to particular kinds of victims rather than in a general theory of victimization. However, this ideology's seven central tenets underpin most contemporary claims about victims. Each

proposition seems unexceptional by itself, but in combination they form a powerful ideology that makes it easy to identify large numbers of victims.

1. Victimization is widespread. Attempts to draw attention to social problems often emphasize the large numbers of people affected, and claims about victims routinely argue that victimization is widespread, sometimes almost ubiquitous. Thus, for example, we are told that 96 percent of families are dysfunctional or that 96 percent of the population is codependent. Even forms of victimization that might seem rare are alleged to be surprisingly common: A national survey suggested that 1 in 50 adults shows signs of having been abducted by UFOs.

Claims that victimization is common often depend upon broad definitions. Horror stories—especially severe and clear-cut examples—serve to focus attention on a category of victims, but the problem is defined in much broader terms. The problem's domain often expands once the initial claims gain widespread acceptance. Thus, for example, the contemporary campaign against child abuse first addressed the "battered-child syndrome" (typified by severe beatings of very young children); the acceptance of child abuse as a social problem then laid a foundation for expanding its domain to include neglect, sexual abuse, emotional abuse, and so on. Similarly, post-traumatic stress disorder (PTSD) originated as a diagnosis for combat-related psychiatric problems of Vietnam veterans; but the notion of "traumatic stress" proved remarkably flexible, and the PTSD label is now applied to victims whose experiences range from battering and incest to receiving contaminated fast food. Broad definitions, of course, help justify large estimates for the extent of victimization. If the domain of sexual violence includes flashing and "touching assaults by relatively young boys," then the proportion of females who have been victims of sexual violence will be far greater than if some narrower definition is applied.

2. Victimization is consequential. Even a single, brief incident can have consequences that extend throughout the victim's life. One analysis of sexual abuse, for instance, warns that one childhood experience of being flashed or fondled "can have profound and long-term consequences." Victimization's consequences are fundamentally psychological: The victim experiences anxiety, doubt, fear, or other psychological reactions. While victims may have impaired social relationships, the root cause of these problems is not social forces but lasting psychological damage. This characterization invites the medicalization of victimization, since therapists presumably have the appropriate knowledge and skills for treating psychological problems. The theme of lasting consequences is central to the claims of intergenerational victimization—cycles of abuse in which abused children become abusive parents—that have inspired movements of adult children (and grandchildren) of alcoholics, abusive parents, and divorced couples. These reverberating effects further support claims that victimization is widespread. If apparently minor incidents can be consequential, then victimization should be defined broadly.

3. Relationships between victims and their victimizers are relatively straightforward and unambiguous. Most claims about victims describe victimization as exploitative encounters between a victimizer who takes advantage and a victim who suffers. Usually, the perpetrator is portrayed as more powerful than the victim, more aware of the exploitative nature of their relationship, and more responsible for the victimization. In this view, victimization is morally unambiguous: The victimizer is exploitative, the victim innocent.

In practice, people identified as victimizers may dispute that characterization, and even people labeled victims may be unsure whether an offense "really" occurred (as suggested by the title of an influential book on date rape, *I Never Called It Rape*). Victim advocates define these denials and uncertainty as part of the pattern of victimization. Where those involved may see ambiguity, advocates perceive clear-cut, unambiguous exploitation. They make few distinctions among forms of victimization, emphasizing the similarities between, say, forcible rape and date rape rather than exploring any differences.

4. Victimization often goes unrecognized. If victimization is common, consequential, and clear-cut, it should be a visible, prominent part of social life. But victim advocates argue that victimization often goes unrecognized and unacknowledged, not only by the larger society but even by the victims themselves.

Society may simply be unaware of victimization. New ways of thinking about some form of victimization or new evidence or a new willingness of victims to speak up can make a neglected social problem visible. In this view, identifying new types of victims reflects social progress, as a more enlightened society gives victimization the attention it deserves. According to more critical advocates, language, culture, and institutional arrangements obscure victims' suffering. For example, feminists argue that the patriarchy discounts the significance of women's victimization and activists denounce police failures to treat hate crimes seriously.

Victimization also may be deliberately concealed. Some claims describe victimization concealed by numerous or powerful actors, such as a million-member Satanic blood-cult conducting undetected human sacrifices or highly advanced aliens in UFOs experimenting on abducted victims. But secrecy does not require great conspiracies. Offenders may convince individual victims, for example, sexually abused children, to keep the experience secret; if such secrets are widespread, then their sum may be collective invisibility.

Beyond society's failure to acknowledge victims, victims themselves may not recognize victimization for what it is. They may define victimization too narrowly, or they may be ashamed, afraid, or otherwise unwilling to reveal their victimization to others. Some therapists argue that many victims cannot remember their experiences, that a common response to the trauma of victimization is to repress memories of the experience (see Richard Ofshe and Ethan Watters, "Making Monsters," *Society*, March 1993). These victims cannot recall or acknowledge being victimized; they are "in denial." Here again, victimization is portrayed as a psychological problem requiring medical treatment.

5. Individuals must be taught to recognize others' and their own victimization. Because victimization often goes unrecognized by both victims and the larger society, people must be educated. Potential victims may need preventive education,

such as "stranger, danger" and "good touch, bad touch" programs designed to warn preschoolers about abduction and sexual abuse or campus campaigns to make college students aware of—and help them avoid—date rape. Other educational efforts seek to inform the larger society about particular forms of victimization. Newsmagazine feature stories, talk shows, made-for-TV movies, and other press and entertainment genres regularly present information about victims; these treatments routinely adopt the views promoted by victim advocates.

In addition to educational programs aimed at potential victims or the general public, advocates seek to teach victims to recognize, acknowledge, and address their victimization. Therapy and support groups offer ways to deal with one's victimization—once the individual acknowledges that victimization has occurred. But what of those victims said to be in denial, unaware that some prior, now-forgotten victimization continues to trouble them? Though these individuals cannot recall their victimization, they are often aware that something is amiss.

Those unaware of their own victimization must be helped to recognize and identify the root of their problems. Victim advocates offer checklists of symptoms to help diagnose prior victimization. Thus, for example, adult children of alcoholics may "have difficulty following a project through from beginning to end," "feel they are different from other people," and "are either super responsible or super irresponsible"; codependents may "feel angry, victimized, unappreciated, and used," "blame themselves for everything," "come from troubled, repressed, or dysfunctional families," or "deny their family was troubled, repressed, or dysfunctional"; while child victims of ritual abuse may be preoccupied with urine, feces, and flatulation, be clingy, resist authority, destroy toys, or have nightmares. These inventories of symptoms may be lengthy; Melody Beattie's best-selling book *Codependent No More* lists more than 230 characteristics of codependents. Sometimes advocates' lists specify contradictory symptoms. For instance, a review of various guidelines for identifying sexually abused children notes: "Some believe . . . that a reluctance to disclose is characteristic of a true allegation, while others look for spontaneity in the child's disclosure as an index of veracity."

Of course, many—probably more—people display several symptoms on these lists yet deny having been victimized. To victim advocates, a denial of prior victimization may be just another symptom. Regarding her recently recovered memories of childhood sexual abuse, comedienne Roseanne declared: "When someone asks you, 'Were you sexually abused as a child,' there's only two answers. One of them is, 'Yes,' and one of them is, 'I don't know.' You can't say no." Similarly, a failure to display symptoms need not be significant; the review of guidelines for identifying sexual abuse warns: "The absence of positive indicators does not mean the child hasn't been sexually abused." Within such diagnostic frameworks, claims of victimization are easily made but difficult to dismiss. Coupled with the claim that victimization is widespread, these frameworks justify a suspicion that virtually anyone might be victim.

Such checklists of symptoms merely raise the possibility that someone is a victim; confirming this possibility requires additional investigation. Sometimes, the therapist's task is defined as helping the victim "recover the memories" of victimization. Critics note that transcripts of therapists' conversations with patients sometimes reveal leading questions and other tactics that encourage patients to acknowledge their victimization. Or therapists may adopt special techniques to elicit memories of victimization, including hypnosis, play with dolls or puppets, massage, and fantasizing. These methods are often successful. As *The Courage to Heal,* a popular guidebook for survivors of child sexual abuse, notes: "Assume your feelings are valid. So far, no one we've talked to thought she might have been abused, and then later discovered that she hadn't been. The progression always goes the other way, from suspicion to confirmation. If you think you were abused and your life shows the symptoms, then you were." The belief that victimization is widespread but largely hidden justifies extraordinary measures to identify individuals who have been victimized and to encourage them to acknowledge and address their victimization.

6. *Claims of victimization must be respected.* Once individuals learn, via education or therapeutic intervention, to recognize their victimization, their claims to be victims must not be challenged. Victim advocates insist that it takes great courage to step forward and acknowledge one's victimization, that such individuals take a precarious stand against the institutional forces that promote and conceal widespread victimization. Injunctions against challenging claims of victimization often warn against "blaming the victim"; victims have already suffered, and calling their claims into question can only constitute further victimization.

Advocates often argue that skepticism is unwarranted, asserting that some victims' claims should be seen as true by definition (for example, early activists sometimes insisted that children never lie about being sexually abused) or at least that there is no reason for individuals to make false claims about being victimized. Or advocates may suggest that similarities in the stories of many victims (for example, accounts of Satanic ritual abuse or UFO abduction) constitute strong evidence for the stories' truth. Memories of victimization that have been recovered through hypnosis or other therapeutic techniques receive validation from therapists who insist that these techniques elicit reliable information, that challenges are unwarranted and unfair, and that society should support the claims of vulnerable, innocent victims.

7. *The term "victim" has undesirable connotations.* Some advocates reject the very term "victim" on the grounds that it carries negative connotations of being damaged, passive, and powerless. They prefer more positive, "empowering" terms, such as "survivor," "adult child," "recovering," or even "persons" (for example, "persons with AIDS"). This renaming affirms that victimization occurred, while possibly serving to reduce individuals' reluctance to define themselves or others as victims. In addition, to the degree that these category names derive from therapeutic discourse, they offer further medical or scientific legitimacy to claims of victim status.

These seven ideological propositions appear routinely in contemporary discussions of victimization. Combined, they form an extremely powerful ideology, one that encourages

identifying and labeling victims: It defines victimization as common, serious, morally unambiguous, yet largely unrecognized; it justifies methods to identify individuals (and help those individuals recognize themselves) as victims; it delegitimizes doubts about victims' claims; and it provides new, nonstigmatizing labels for those who have suffered.

Again, there is no overarching "victims movement"; rather, advocates address particular forms of victimization. Typically, these campaigns begin modestly, with the initial claims addressing clear-cut, outrageous instances of exploitation. Then, after these initial claims gain acceptance, the problem's domain expands to incorporate other cases. Thus, for example, early claims about sexual harassment focused on instances in which female workers' jobs were overtly threatened unless they complied with their male supervisors' sexual demands. Once sexual harassment gained recognition as a social problem, advocates began expanding its domain to include a broader range of behaviors and conditions, including "conduct that creates an intimidating, hostile, or offensive environment." Such domain expansion is self-reinforcing: Expanded definitions support claims of larger problems; larger problems justify increased attention; and increased attention in turn encourages further expanding the problem's domain.

Institutional Responses to Victimization

Ideologies exist within institutional contexts, receiving more or less ratification and support from different institutions. Campaigns drawing attention to new forms of victimization seek recognition in several institutional arenas. Typically, advocates' initial appeals are sensitizing: They seek to draw an institution's attention to victims whose plights have been neglected. Once an institution acknowledges these victims, advocates call for accommodations to integrate victims' needs within the existing institutional structure. When such accommodation is deemed insufficient, advocates may call for institutional changes—significant alterations to meet the victims' needs.

Typically, the responses to sensitization—accomodation and change—have seemed modest; advocates sought particular reforms to protect particular victims from particular abuses. Thus, a state might pass a law to extend the period within which victims of sexual abuse can file charges or sue for damages, so that adults who recover memories of abuse can bring cases against their abusers, or a university might require all faculty to attend workshops on sexual harassment. Though each reform is limited, taken together they represent considerable institutional support for the ideology of victimization. This support extends across several major institutions, including law, the medical and therapeutic professions, academia, the mass media, and the recovery movement.

Law. Because much of the law concerns protecting individuals against exploitation, it becomes an important institutional arena for claims about victimization. The contemporary ideology of victimization has influenced the law's various facets, including legislation, the criminal justice and court systems, and legal scholarship.

Advocates often call for new laws prohibiting the exploitation of victims or requiring reporting of victimization. For example, following actress Rebecca Schaeffer's well-publicized murder by a fan, claims that stalking was widespread led to California's passing of an antistalking law in 1990. Within two years, forty-seven other states and the District of Columbia had similar laws, and Congress had ordered the National Institute of Justice to devise a model antistalking code and was considering proposals to make stalking a federal crime. Similarly, several states have added a "victims' bill of rights" to their constitutions; state and federal law enforcement agencies have been ordered to collect data on hate crimes; and state laws requiring reporting of various forms of child abuse continue to expand.

In addition to calling for new laws, victim advocates criticize the legal system's failure to protect individuals from victimization, as well as its further failure to treat victims appropriately once they complain to legal authorities. Thus, the criminal justice system's insensitive treatment of victims of rape and child sexual abuse (for example, not responding to all complaints, investigating some allegations with skepticism, and subjecting complainants to humiliating courtroom interrogations) represent a "second rape" or a "second form of child abuse." In this view, the law discourages victims, blames them for their suffering, forces them to humiliate themselves, and then fails to deliver justice. Such claims have inspired reforms to make the legal system more accessible to and protective of victims, ranging from relatively minor accommodations (such as letting child victims testify while seated in child-size chairs) to more substantial institutional changes (such as prohibiting or limiting the cross-examination of child victims giving testimony). The criminal justice system's relatively elaborate arrangements for preserving the rights of defendants (viewed as victimizers by victim advocates) have inspired growing interest in victims using the less restrictive civil courts to bring suits.

Many of these legislative and procedural reforms find support in law schools and law reviews. New claims about victimization often receive sympathetic treatment, as legal scholars recommend ways to modify the law to redress victims' grievances. Though scholars do not agree on all issues (there has, for example, been considerable debate over how to balance the rights of complainants and defendants in sexual abuse trials), many members of law school faculties—and legislatures and courts—accept elements of the ideology of victimization.

The Medical and Therapeutic Professions. Many advocates medicalize victmization, defining treatment as the appropriate response and assigning therapeutic professionals ownership of these social problems. Medicalization carries scientific authority; claims couched in medical language seem almost beyond questioning or criticism. A diverse set of professionals receive this scientific imprimatur, as the medical model—usually associated with physicians, psychiatrists, and perhaps clinical psychologists—has spread throughout the "helping professions." Those who treat victims may have been trained in various disciplines, including social work, family counseling, education, and health science, and their treatment practices may be guided by various other ideologies, ranging from fundamentalist Christianity to feminism. Some therapists are "professional ex's," individuals with little formal training who,

having recovered from victimization, have now begun careers helping others into recovery. Some specialize in identifying and helping particular types of victims (such as helping victims of Satanic ritual abuse to recover those memories), while others address a broad range of problems.

Many of the medical experts who work with victims argue that their principal responsibility is to their patients rather than to abstract principles of inquiry. This rationale justifies therapeutic practices which some critics argue are inconsistent with scientific objectivity or criminal investigations. For example, therapists interviewing children thought to have been sexually abused may use leading questions to elicit acknowledgment of abuse and justify this practice as a necessary therapeutic step, or therapists may urge patients to ignore doubts and ambiguity when acknowledging their victimization. Such practices, justified as therapeutically necessary, distinguish much treatment of victims from traditional medical or scientific inquiry.

Medicalized discussions often focus on the harms experienced by the victims while largely ignoring the victimizers. Whereas earlier psychiatric claims medicalized deviants (such as sexual psychopaths), contemporary claims medicalize victims (such as survivors of sexual abuse). When deviance is deemed extraordinary, we search for explanations in the peculiarities of offenders, but when victimization is seen as commonplace, victimizers seem less remarkable, simply part of an oppressive social system.

Academia. The ideology of victimization also has made significant inroads into education. The need to educate victims, potential victims, and society at large is central to the ideology. Because victimization often occurs during childhood, teachers are encouraged to attend workshops to learn how to teach students to recognize victimization. Within higher education, enthusiasm for the ideology of victimization seems greatest in the helping professions, such as social work, health education, educational counseling, family relations, criminal justice, and child development programs. Students trained in these fields learn to identify and respond to a range of human problems, and claims about victimization are presented as up-to-date knowledge with useful applications. Victims become the subjects of lectures, classes, term papers, theses, and dissertations. Researchers may find foundations and government agencies eager to fund research on victimization, conferences and professional associations emerge as forums for inquiry, and the proliferation of scholarly publishing has produced specialized journals devoted to studying victims (for example, *Dissociation* publishes studies of multiple-personality disorder). Of course, the audience for these conferences and journals largely endorses victimization claims. Concern with victims also appears in more scholarly disciplines, especially in feminist writings, and women's studies programs often provide leadership for on-campus advocacy. Many campuses develop programs to educate or protect students from victimization. Like medicalization, academics' support gives authority to claims about victims.

Mass Media. Most advocates depend upon the mass media to disseminate their claims to the public. In general, claims about victims receive sympathetic coverage in the press, in popular culture, and, most especially, in the talk shows, made-for-TV movies, and other genres that combine news and entertainment. Claims about victims tend to fit the media's template for social problems coverage: They can be typified in dramatic terms (an innocent victim beset by an exploitative villain); they seem relevant (if victimization is widespread, then many people are, might become, or at least have ties to victims); they offer hope (via the intervention of authority figures from law, medicine, or academia); and they lack unacceptable political overtones (so long as the claims focus on the individual victimizer rather than on the social system—for example, patriarchy or the class system—as producing the victimization). Moreover, because most advocates depict victimization as straightforward exploitation and because most claims arouse little organized opposition, the media typically feel no obligation to "balance" their coverage by presenting "both sides" of the issue. Changing media structures also have worked to the advocates' advantage. Cable and satellite delivery have caused television channels to proliferate; broadcasters need relatively inexpensive, relatively popular offerings to fill these channels, and talk shows and "reality shows" (like *America's Most Wanted*) meet these requirements. These genres frequently cover claims about victimization.

The Recovery Movement. U.S. culture has a long fascination with self-help. In recent years, the self-help movement—and Alcoholics Anonymous in particular—has inspired numerous campaigns to help victims recover. This recovery movement has many facets: twelve-step groups, weekend workshops and conferences, lecture tours, and publishers who generate books, pamphlets, magazines, and audio- and videotapes filled with inspirational advice. During the 1980s, most bookstores opened substantial sections devoted to "Recovery." By 1990, nearly three hundred bookstores sold nothing but recovery movement literature, featuring separate sections devoted to alcoholism, adult children of alcoholics, codependency, and so on. The popularity of recovery movement literature seems to transcend otherwise important ideological divisions: Recovery sections can be found in both women's bookstores and Christian book shops. The recovery movement often provides a grassroots embodiment of claims about victims; it offers continual socialization for both neophytes and experienced members, links victims to experts, and often inspires media coverage.

Other institutional supports for victims' claims include policies promoted by government agencies, religious bodies, and private industry. Again, these involve many parallel movements, each promoting recognition of a particular type of victim, each seeking particular reforms within particular institutions. Some campaigns have been more successful than others; issues such as sexual abuse, stalking, and sexual harassment have received widespread institutional validation, whereas, aside from the well-publicized claims of Harvard professor John Mack, victims of UFO abductions have found relatively few visible supporters in law, medicine, and academia. But the overall pattern is clear: Several major institutions respond sympathetically to the ideology of victimization.

The Victim Industry

The ideology of victimization, when coupled with institutional support for that ideology, makes it possible to label large numbers of victims. Studies of witchhunts and political purges speak of social control as an "industry," engaged in the "manufacturing" or the "mass production" of deviants. Analogously, we may speak of a contemporary victim industry mass producing victims. According to Elliott Currie, the great European witchhunt had three key organizational characteristics that fostered the discovery of many thousands of witches: (1) The witchhunters faced few restraints from other social institutions; (2) They had few internal restraints on their powers; and (3) They had a vested interest in identifying witches. Analogous arrangements support the victim industry's campaign to identify large numbers of victims.

Absence of External Restraints. Because the contemporary ideology of victimization has been accepted and incorporated by key institutions, victims advocates face little external opposition. For instance, individuals being treated for some form of victimization may find that their claims—and the claims of their therapists—are protected by sympathetic laws, ratified by academics, depicted favorably in the mass media, and endorsed by the recovery movement. The ideological prohibition against challenging victims' claims further discourages skepticism. Moreover, because identifying victims is defined as beneficial, both to the individual being identified and to the society at large, there is no obvious source of resistance.

It is significant that advocates often demand support for victims while largely ignoring victimizers. Some victimizers cannot be identified: the stranger-rapist who was never apprehended; the unfamiliar adult Satanists who abused the victim as a child; or even extraterrestrial aliens. But for many forms of victimization rooted in family dynamics, the victimizers' identities are presumably known. Yet so long as advocates do not identify and denounce particular people as victimizers, few people have cause to oppose claims about victimization. Thus, for example, claims about recovered memories of Satanic ritual abuse faced little opposition until victims began bringing suits against their relatives for childhood abuse. At that point, a countermovement, the False Memory Syndrome Foundation, emerged. But this is an exception: Relatively few victims' movements generate well-organized opposition because relatively few specify their opponents. Most movements face few external restraints.

Absence of Internal Restraints. The contemporary ideology of victimization offers many alternative ways of identifying victims: long lists of symptoms indicative of victimization, rationales for doubting individuals' denials of victimization, and so on. Moreover, this ideology is endorsed by people with impressive credentials: therapists, lawyers, academics, and professional ex's. Defined as experts, they can influence discussions of putative victimization. Because victimization is often hidden and because these experts have the means to discover and reveal it, their assessments become authoritative. Moreover, under their ideology, these individuals have a right—even an obligation—to label individuals as victims and guide them into accepting that label. Since advocates see themselves as helping both the victim and the larger society understand the truth, they have little reason to question their own actions. The knowledge and techniques needed to detect otherwise hidden victimization give these advocates extraordinary powers to label others as victims, even when those individuals deny that the labels fit. At the same time, the ideology of victimization offers few internal restraints on such labeling.

Vested Interests. Participants in the victim industry often have a stake in the identification of victims. Advocates' vested interests include enhanced prestige and influence for themselves and their professions, supportive validation from important social institutions, and, at least among those therapists who label on a fee-for-service basis, increased income. In addition, some people benefit from being identified as victims: They become professional ex's, write books, travel on the lecture circuit, appear on talk shows, receive praise and favorable attention, and even get treated as experts in their own right. They may become victim-celebrities (known for their experiences as victims)—some, of course, are also celebrity victims (that is, established celebrities who reveal their victimization, such as Roseanne). In short, both those doing the labeling and those being labeled often benefit from the process.

Obviously, the contemporary concern for victims is not a witchhunt. Yet the organizational features that supported large-scale witchhunting also make the victim industry productive. Problems that psychiatrists considered relatively rare twenty or thirty years ago (such as incest or multiple-personality disorder) have been redefined as relatively common conditions, and those labels are often applied. The net effect of the victim industry has been the identification of many thousands of victims.

Why Victims?

No doubt many of the similarities among contemporary victim movements reflect advocates' awareness of one another; rhetoric and methods proven effective in one campaign are borrowed and used to draw attention to other forms of victimization. But this begs a larger question: Why do claims about victims strike a responsive chord in contemporary society? Why are so many kinds of victims being identified at this time and in this society?

The contemporary concern for victims began during the 1960s, when established status hierarchies weakened. Challenges from below—from blacks, women, students, homosexuals, and so on—questioned the legitimacy of existing status arrangements. Talking about victims was often an effective way of pressing these claims. Victimization dramatized the illegitimacy of social arrangements that allowed the exploitation of the vulnerable. Advocates used the ideology of victimization not only to draw attention to specific social problems but also to challenge existing hierarchies. What sort of society fostered and then ignored widespread victimization? Calls to protect victims were also bids to raise the status of those vulnerable to victimization, and victim advocacy was often tied to broader social movements, such as the women's movement.

In addition, victim movements offer a contemporary answer to fundamental, primal issues that every culture must address—issues of justice and evil. Social order is society's most basic accomplishment. But in every society, order sometimes breaks down. Some people do the right thing, but they do not get their just rewards. Other people break the rules. Social control attempts to right these wrongs and restore order to the social system.

In most societies during most of recorded history, punishment has been central to social control. Society roots out the rule breakers, the deviants, and the evildoers and dispenses justice by punishing them. But during the twentieth century, we have become increasingly suspicious of these traditional practices. We favor a rational, scientific point of view, and we suspect that evil is a superstitious notion and that punishment is a barbaric method of achieving justice.

The social sciences bear a good deal of responsibility here. They are in the business of explaining social patterns, of identifying causes and their effects, and they have diligently tried to understand the causes of deviance. But the social scientific perspective on deviance doesn't translate terribly well into social policy. The sticking point, of course, is the notion—fundamental to law—of responsibility. If we can point to the causes of deviant behavior, how can we hold the deviant responsible? Is it just to blame deviants for rule breaking when we believe that their deviance is caused by social conditions? Note the term "blame"—it is central to much social control but largely foreign to social science.

This reveals the attractions of talking about victims. Talking about victims can avoid many of the conflicts between the social scientific and social policy perspectives raised in debates over deviants. To social scientists, victims can be understood as the effects of causal processes. But, as advocates continually warn, social policy must sympathize with—support—victims, not blame them. This helps explain why victims movements tend to gloss over the victimizers. Once advocates start identifying victimizers, they're back in the messy, divisive business of trying to both understand and blame deviants. So long as they stay focused on the victims, advocates can hope to win consensus.

This explanation suggests that victim movements may have more than organizational features in common with witchhunting. The victim plays a symbolic role in our society, not unlike the role played by witches during the witch craze. Both allow society to identify evil and injustice. In societies that interpret events in religious terms, witches consorting with the demonic can explain all sorts of problems. Similarly, our contemporary society, which seeks to understand the world in rational, scientific terms, finds processes of victimization useful explanations for all sorts of contemporary ills. In this way, new victims answer old questions.

Joel Best is professor and chair of the Department of Sociology at Southern Illinois University at Carbondale. He is the editor of the journal Social Problems. *His books include* Threatened Children *and the collection* Images of Issues.

TRUE CRIME

SUMMARY The media and safety-conscious baby boomers fuel an overwhelming public fear of crime. A close look at the data shows that much of the fear is misplaced. Yet the worst crimes are increasing, and life can be especially dangerous in southern and smaller metros. In the next decade, more criminals and a less tolerant public will transform Americans' lives.

by Cheryl Russell

Cheryl Russell is author of The Official Guide to the American Marketplace *(New Strategist, 1995) and editor-in-chief of New Strategist Publications in Ithaca, New York.*

The hour is late. The city street lies dark and empty. Solitary footsteps echo on the pavement. Ahead, an ominous shape lurks in a storefront. Suddenly you're face to face with a gun-wielding, homicidal maniac. You panic. Is it time to run, or time to turn off the TV?

Crime in America has come home. Ask anyone; they can tick off the names, dates, and grisly details from the Oklahoma bombing, the O. J. Simpson double-murder trial, the kidnapping and murder of Polly Klaas, the drowning of Susan Smith's children, the roadside slaying of Michael Jordan's father, the Long Island Railroad massacre, the never-ending string of post office shootings, and on and on. Crime was the number-one issue of concern to the public in 1994, according to the Conference Board. Ninety percent of Americans say that crime is a "serious" problem.

No one escapes the repercussions of Americans' obsession with crime. Some segments of the economy even profit from it. Forty-three percent of Americans have had special locks installed on

their doors, and 18 percent have burglar alarms, according to a 1993 Gallup Poll. Half of American households own guns, and sales of personal-security devices such as mace and pepper spray have been brisk in recent years.

More businesses are hurt than helped by the fear of crime. Downtown areas lose shoppers to suburban shopping malls, while tourists and homebuyers shy away from areas where the media have publicized particularly heinous offenses.

Not only do Americans think crime is a terrible problem; they believe it's getting worse. Nearly nine in ten say there was more crime in 1993 in the U.S. than there was a year before, according to a Gallup poll. This perspective accounts for the popularity of a get-tough attitude toward criminals, from stiffer penalties for juvenile offenders to three-strikes-you're-out life terms for repeat felony criminals. Support for the death penalty has grown from just under 50 percent in the early 1960s to 80 percent in 1994.

But is crime really overwhelming America? The public says yes, but crime statistics are contradictory—and so are the experts. Separating the myths from the facts is the best way to understand the current mood of the public. And when you take a close look, one thing

becomes clear. Every organization should position itself for a future in which fear of crime is likely to play a major role.

FUEL FOR FEAR

Crime has become a hot issue for a number of reasons, beginning with the media. The public's concern with crime rises and falls in lockstep with media reporting about the issue. High-profile crimes create sensational news coverage. And the greater the news coverage, the larger the proportion of Americans who cite crime as the most important problem facing the country, according to a 1994 analysis in *The Public Perspective* by Jeffrey D. Alderman, director of polling for ABC News. Public concern with crime follows news coverage of crimes with an exactness that proves the importance of the media in shaping public opinion.

In 1994, a *Los Angeles Times* poll asked Americans whether their feelings about crime were based on what they read or saw in the media, or on what they had personally experienced. While 65 percent named the media, only 21 percent named personal experience, and 13 percent said both.

Another reason for the public's heightened concern about crime is the

The Books on Crime

*The two sets of government crime statistics are contradictory,
but both agree that violent crime is increasing.*

WHAT POLICE REPORTS SAY

(crimes reported to police per 100,000 population in 1992, 1984, and 1974,
by type of crime, and percent change in crime rate, 1984-92 and 1974-92)

	1992	1984	1974	percent change 1984-92	percent change 1974-92
violent crime, total	757.5	539.2	461.1	40.5%	64.3%
rape	42.8	35.7	26.2	19.9	63.4
robbery	263.6	205.4	209.3	28.3	25.9
aggravated assault	441.8	290.2	215.8	52.2	104.7
property crime, total	4,902.7	4,492.1	4,389.3	9.1	11.7
burglary	1,168.2	1,263.7	1,437.7	–7.6	–18.7
larceny	3,103.0	2,791.3	2,489.5	11.2	24.6
motor-vehicle theft	631.5	437.1	462.2	44.5	36.6

WHAT CRIME VICTIMS SAY

(victimizations per 100,000 people aged 12 or older or per 100,000 households, in 1992,
1984, and 1974, and percent change in victimization rate, 1984-92 and 1974-92)

	1992	1984	1974	percent change 1984-92	percent change 1974-92
violent crime, total	3,210	3,140	3,300	2.2%	–2.7%
rape	70	90	100	–27.3	–30.0
robbery	590	570	720	4.0	–17.3
aggravated assault	900	900	1,040	–0.5	–13.8
property crime, total	15,220	17,870	23,570	–14.8	–35.4
burglary	4,890	6,410	9,310	–23.7	–47.5
larceny	8,320	9,940	12,380	–16.3	–32.8
motor-vehicle theft	2,010	1,520	1,880	32.2	6.9

*Source: Federal Bureau of Investigation, Uniform Crime Reports 1993; and Bureau of Justice Statistics Bulletin,
Criminal Victimization 1992, October 1993*

expansion of the middle-aged population. People in the huge baby-boom generation, now aged 31 to 49, are more concerned than young adults about crime. Baby boomers are also more active in protecting themselves from crime. People aged 30 to 49 are more likely than those younger or older to have installed special locks to have a dog for protection, to have bought a gun, to carry a weapon, or to have a burglar alarm.

In 1995, 38 percent of all American adults are in the 35-to-54 age group, a larger proportion than at any time since the 1950s. The share in this age group will rise to 40 percent by 2000. The middle-aged population is struggling to protect its homes, careers, financial assets, and especially its children. No wonder crime is one of its top concerns.

There is some evidence that the public's fear of crime is driven by a burgeoning population of parents and the crime-crazy media, but not by the facts. Overall crime rates are lower today than they were in the early 1980s. At that time, baby boomers were crime-prone young adults who drove the rates up. And while most Americans believe the crime problem is severe, they think it is much worse elsewhere than it is in their community. Seventy-nine percent of Americans think crime is one of the nation's biggest problems, but only 14 percent name crime as one of the biggest problems in their neighborhood. Sixty-one percent of Americans say they feel "very safe" at home. And most Americans say they are not afraid to walk alone at night near their home.

The average American's fear of crime may be a fear for the future. Forty-three

> Sixty-one percent of Americans say they feel "very safe" at home.

percent say that crime in their local area is increasing. While most Americans feel safe in their home and neighborhood, many do not feel secure in their community or when traveling elsewhere. These feelings will intensify in the years ahead, because those most afraid of crime are a growing segment of the population. Moreover, the worst crime does appear to be on the rise.

A LOOK AT THE DATA

How bad is the crime scene? The answer isn't easy to find, because the United States keeps two sets of books on crime. One, the FBI's Uniform Crime Reports (UCR), is an annual collection of reported crime in over 16,000 communities across the country. The figures are voluntarily submitted to the FBI by police agencies in those communities. Overall, 95 percent of the population is covered by the police agencies that submit their crime data to the FBI, including 97 percent of the metropolitan population and 86 percent of nonmetro residents.

> The public's willingness to report crime varies by type of crime.

The Most Violent Metros

Many smaller metropolitan areas have higher rates of violent crime than the bigger metros Americans fear the most.

(50 metropolitan areas with the largest number of violent crimes* per 100,000 population,1993)

rank	metropolitan area	violent crime rate	rank	metropolitan area	violent crime rate
1	Miami, FL	2,136.2	26	Orlando, FL	1,118.2
2	New York, NY	1,865.5	27	Memphis,TN-AR-MS	1,109.3
3	Alexandria, LA	1,833.0	28	Nashville, TN	1,098.7
4	Los Angeles-Long Beach, CA	1,682.4	29	Stockton-Lodi, CA	1,091.6
5	Tallahassee, FL	1,546.0	30	Riverside-San Bernardino, CA	1,089.8
6	Baton Rouge, LA	1,510.7	31	San Francisco, CA	1,088.1
7	Little Rock-North Little Rock, AR	1,453.1	32	Fresno, CA	1,084.6
8	Jacksonville, FL	1,419.9	33	Greenville-Spartanburg-Anderson, SC	1,080.0
9	Pueblo, CO	1,403.9	34	Fayetteville, NC	1,076.5
10	Baltimore, MD	1,356.1	35	Pine Bluff, AR	1,058.8
11	Gainesville, FL	1,328.6	36	Waco, TX	1,052.6
12	New Orleans, LA	1,312.6	37	Florence, SC	1,045.8
13	Jackson, TN	1,294.7	38	El Paso, TX	1,031.0
14	Albuquerque, NM	1,273.6	39	Newark, NJ	1,030.9
15	Tampa-St. Petersburg-Clearwater, FL	1,223.4	40	Tuscaloosa, AL	1,009.3
16	Charlotte-Gastonia-Rock Hill, NC-SC	1,204.4	41	Fort Lauderdale, FL	1,005.4
17	Anniston, AL	1,183.6	42	Modesto, CA	992.1
18	Sumter, SC	1,179.1	43	Albany, GA	990.0
19	Gadsden, AL	1,177.5	44	Shreveport-Bossier City, LA	987.9
20	Birmingham, AL	1,146.8	45	Lakeland-Winter Haven, FL	984.3
21	Jersey City, NJ	1,144.1	46	Lake Charles, LA	977.7
22	Ocala, FL	1,141.7	47	Greenville, NC	975.5
23	Oakland, CA	1,137.5	48	Monroe, LA	973.5
24	Sioux City, IA-NE	1,133.8	49	Las Vegas, NV-AZ	959.5
25	Columbia, SC	1,129.1	50	Vineland-Millville-Bridgeton, NJ	953.2

* Murder, rape, robbery, aggravated assault

Source: Crime in the United States, 1993, Federal Bureau of Investigation, 1994

The second data set on crime is the Justice Department's national survey of households, called the National Crime Victimization Survey. In this survey, interviewers ask respondents whether anyone in the household has been a crime victim in the past year. Because many crimes are never reported to police, the National Crime Victimization Survey uncovers much more crime than the police report to the FBI.* By comparing these two data sets, analysts can estimate the amount of crime reported to police.

In 1992, only 39 percent of what the Justice Department refers to as "victimizations" were reported to police. Yet the public's willingness to report crime varies by type of crime. In 1992, the public reported 53 percent of rapes, 51 percent of robberies, 49 percent of assaults, 41 percent of household theft, and 30 percent of personal theft. Motor-vehicle theft is most likely to be reported to the police—75 percent in 1992—because

such thefts must be reported to make claims on auto insurance.

Over time, the gap between actual and reported crime has narrowed as Americans have become increasingly willing to complain of misdeeds. The 39 percent reporting level of 1992 was up from 32 percent in 1973. The proportion of aggravated assaults reported to the police increased from 52 percent to 62 percent during those years. The proportion of personal theft reported to police rose from 22 to 30 percent. Today's older, better-educated public is more comfortable interacting with authorities than was the public of two decades ago. This increases the likelihood of reporting crime. In addition, the introduction

---

* The FBI collects statistics on murder and nonnegligent manslaughter, forcible rape, robbery, aggravated assault, burglary, larceny, motor-vehicle theft, and arson. The National Crime Victimization Survey covers all but murder/nonnegligent manslaughter and arson.

of 911 emergency phone services makes it easier for people to report crime.

The two databases on crime seem to contradict each other in many cases. The Uniform Crime Reports show crime rising over the past 20 years, while the National Crime Victimization Survey shows crime falling. The total crime rate rose from 4,850 offenses per 100,000 population in 1974 to 5,660 per 100,000 in 1992, a 17 percent increase, then dropping slightly to 5,483 per 100,000 in 1993, according to the UCR. In contrast, the household survey shows the percentage of households "touched" by crime falling from 32 to 23 percent from 1975 to 1992. The exclusion of murder and arson from the household survey cannot explain this contradiction, because the two datasets show crime rates moving in opposite directions even for specific types of crime. For example, the UCR statistics show the rate of aggravated assault rising from 2.16 to 4.42 assaults per 1,000 people between 1974

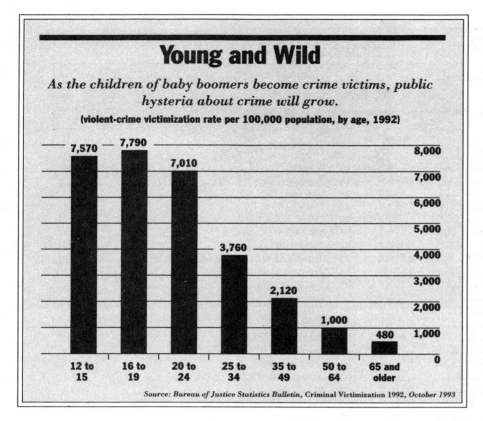

Young and Wild

As the children of baby boomers become crime victims, public hysteria about crime will grow.

(violent-crime victimization rate per 100,000 population, by age, 1992)

12 to 15	7,570
16 to 19	7,790
20 to 24	7,010
25 to 34	3,760
35 to 49	2,120
50 to 64	1,000
65 and older	480

Source: Bureau of Justice Statistics Bulletin, Criminal Victimization 1992, *October 1993*

and 1992, a 105 percent increase. In contrast, the victimization survey shows the aggravated assault rate falling from 10.4 to 9.0 assaults per 1,000 people aged 12 or older during those years.

The trends revealed by the two datasets agree in only two areas. Both show burglary declining and motor-vehicle theft rising. But while the FBI finds that the burglary rate fell 19 percent between 1974 and 1992, the household survey says it fell 48 percent. And while the FBI reports that motor-vehicle theft is up 37 percent, the household survey says just 7 percent.

> The introduction of 911 emergency phone services makes it easier for people to report crime.

Which dataset is right? The public finds the FBI's rising crime rates most believable, because it is closer to the carnage they see on TV. But most experts believe that the trends revealed in the victimization survey are more accurate because of changes in Americans' propensity to report crime. As people report a larger proportion of crime to police, then the UCR statistics will show an increase even if crime rates remain the same. For example, the fact that a larger proportion of aggravated assaults was reported to police in 1993 than in 1974 could account for much of the increase in aggravated assault reported in the UCR.

The trends in the UCR statistics are questionable because of reporting problems. Yet the trends revealed by the victimization survey may not be completely accurate because they are affected by changes in household size, household location, and the age structure of the population. Single-person households are less likely to be victimized by crime than are larger households. Households in central cities are more likely to be victimized than those in suburban areas. If household size declines and an increasing share of households are located in the suburbs, as in

the past 20 years, the proportion of households victimized by crime will decline while crime rates remain unchanged.

The Justice Department reports that if households in 1992 were the same size as those in 1975, the proportion "touched" by crime would have been 23.7 percent in 1992 rather than 22.6 percent. But it would still fall far below the 32 percent of 1975. Adjusting for changes in household location would raise it even further, because it turns out that most of the decline in the proportion of households touched by crime is due to the drop in property crime rather than violent crime. The victimization survey shows the burglary rate dropping by 47 percent between 1973 and 1992, household larceny falling by 22 percent, and personal theft down 35 percent. Violent crime rates, on the other hand, have barely budged.

The changing age structure of the population also affects the crime trends revealed by the victimization survey. Adults are much more likely to be victimized by crime than are older people. Even if crime rates remain unchanged, the overall crime rate should have dropped over the past two decades due to the aging of the population. The fact that the victimization survey shows no significant decline despite the aging of the population suggests that the age-adjusted rate of violent crime is actually on the rise.

Both datasets show violent crime increasing as a proportion of all crime. In the UCR, violent crime grew from 10 to 14 percent of all reported crime from 1974 to 1993. The victimization survey shows the same trend, with violent crime growing from 15 to 20 percent of all crime during those years. This trend alone is enough to alarm the public, since a larger share of the crime around them is of the most-feared type—the random act of violence committed by a stranger.

The UCR shows the rate of violent crime rising fairly steadily since the mid-1970s, peaking in 1992, and standing just below that peak in 1993. The household survey shows the rate of violent crime rising through the early 1980s, falling slightly, then rising again in the early 1990s. The latest statistics from both surveys show violent crime rates today to be close to their all-time high. No wonder people are alarmed.

The trend in violent crime is especially ominous, because the young-adult

SAFETY ZONES

City-dwellers on both coasts tend to think that nothing happens in the Midwest. Although Wisconsinites and Minnesotans may resent having their homes portrayed as boring, they can also have the last laugh. One of the things that isn't happening in the Midwest is crime.

Of the ten metropolitan areas with the lowest assault rates, eight are in Wisconsin and Minnesota, according to the 1993 Federal Bureau of Investigation's Uniform Crime Reports. Bangor, Maine, and Provo-Orem, Utah, are the other two. Four Wisconsin metros rank at the bottom of the list for violent crimes in general.

Wausau, Wisconsin, may be the safest metropolitan area in the country. It has the lowest assault and rape rates, second-lowest burglary rate, third-lowest car-theft rate, fourth-lowest murder rate, and ninth-lowest property-crime rate. Its combined violent crime rate in 1993 was 67 per 100,000 people, versus 2,136 in top-ranked Miami. Other Wisconsin metros also rank tops for lack of crime. Appleton-Oshkosh-Neenah, Sheboygan, and La Crosse each appear on three bottom-ten lists, and Eau Claire appears on two.

Wausau's Deputy Police Chief Paul Luoma modestly declines the credit for his town's low crime rates. "We try to be pro-active, and you have to be visible, but I don't think law enforcement can take credit," Luoma says. "We have a high employment rate—people don't have a lot of time on their hands. The general values of the community and strong education system keep the crime rate low, too."

But even Wausau has an increasing problem with small-gang activity. "It depends on what you call a gang," says Luoma. "Gangs in a small community could be five to ten individuals causing vandalism." The minority population in Wausau has increased tenfold within the last decade, and it consists largely of Hmong and Laotian immigrants who some-times don't get along. He says the kids band together to create self-assurance. "They put tattoos on their arms, wear their hats a different way, and it's all because they want to be recognized. They're saying 'Hey, I'm a person.'" Luoma acknowledges that there's no short-term solution to these problems.

Sergeant John Roach of Bangor says it's difficult to say why the Maine metro places second-lowest in assault rates, but he attributes some of it to an aggressive pursuit of abusers in domestic assault cases. "We count domestic assaults the same as assaults," Roach says. "If there is any sort of evidence of abuse, the abuser is automatically arrested." He says this is true for the entire state of Maine, not just Bangor.

Outside of the Midwest, metros with older residents and low mobility rates have lower-than-average crime rates. Johnstown, Pennsylvania, has the country's largest share of householders who have not moved since 1959—24 percent—and it also has the nation's lowest property-crime and larceny rates, third-lowest burglary rate, and ninth-lowest car-theft rate. One in five householders in Steubenville-Weirton, Ohio-West Virginia, has stayed put for more than 30 years. The metro has the nation's second-lowest property-crime and larceny rates, fifth-lowest rape and burglary rates, and sixth-lowest car-theft rate.

One expects smaller and more out-of-the-way metros such as Lewiston-Auburn, Maine, and Florence, Alabama, to see less crime than New York and Los Angeles. But one of the country's biggest cities also has relatively low crime rates. Pittsburgh ranks no higher than 81st place out of 245 (see "The Most Violent Metros") metro areas for any of the seven types of crimes studied, and it ranks seventh from the bottom for larceny.

SAFE HAVENS

Cooler climates seem to put violence on ice.

(metros with the lowest violent crime rate per 100,000 people, 1993)

rank	metropolitan area	violent crime rate
1	Wausau, WI	66.5
2	Eau Claire, WI	91.4
3	Appleton-Oshkosh-Neenah, WI	106.4
4	Sheboygan, WI	116.1
5	Bangor, ME	125.7
6	Provo-Orem, UT	141.9
7	Bismarck, ND	175.2
8	Williamsport, PA	176.9
9	Lewiston-Auburn, ME	183.5
10	Fayetteville-Springdale-Rogers, AR	196.0

Source: Crime in the United States, 1993, Federal Bureau of Investigation, 1994

—*Jennifer Fulkerson*

population—the segment most likely to commit acts of violence—is currently at a low point, due to the small baby-bust generation. As the young-adult population expands with the children of the baby boom in the next decade or so, we can expect a significant increase in violent crime simply because of demographic change.

SMALL, SOUTHERN, AND DANGEROUS

Crime may be pervasive, but each crime is local. This adds another layer of confusion to the crime story. The media's obsessive reporting of every gory detail has increased the public's fear of crime

> We can expect a significant increase in violent crime simply because of demographic change.

in areas where well-publicized crimes occur. Because the largest number of crimes occur in the most populous metropolitan areas, many people have an exaggerated sense of danger in these places. At the same time, they feel safe in smaller metropolitan areas that may be more dangerous than some big cities. This public confusion is documented in a 1993 Gallup poll that asked Americans to rank cities according to their danger of crime. Out of a list of 15 cities, Americans correctly ranked Miami and New York as first and second in crime danger. UCR statistics show that the metropolitan area with the highest violent crime rate is Miami, with 2,136 per

100,000 people.* Second is New York, with 1,866. The public ranked Washington, D.C., as the 4th most dangerous city, with two-thirds saying Washington, D.C. is a dangerous place to live or visit. But its violent crime rate (771 per 100,000 people) places it 88th among the 245 metro areas reporting violent crimes to the FBI in 1993. This rate is far below that of San Francisco or Dallas. Yet only 42 percent of the public think San Francisco is dangerous, and just 24 percent think Dallas is dangerous.

> The rate of violent crime peaks in July and August, when hot weather shortens tempers.

The metropolitan area with the third-highest rate of violent crime is one most Americans have never heard of: Alexandria, Louisiana. The fourth is no surprise—Los Angeles-Long Beach. Fifth is Tallahassee, Florida. Other lesser-known cities on the top-ten list are Baton Rouge, Louisiana; Little Rock, Arkansas; Jacksonville, Florida; and Pueblo, Colorado.

The UCR statistics show that the South is a region plagued by crime. Of the ten metros with the highest rates of violent crime, seven are in the South. Of the top 20, 16 are in the South. Of the top 50, 35 are in the South. Several factors account for the South's high rate of crime. One is the warm climate, which allows people to get out and into trouble year-round. The rate of violent crime peaks in July and August, when hot weather shortens tempers, according to the FBI.

Another reason for the South's high rate of violent crime may be the rapid growth of many of the region's metropolitan areas. The list of the nation's fastest-growing metros looks very similar to the list of the most dangerous. Florida alone is home to 9 of the 50

Demogram

Peter Tyler

Age: 26
Occupation: Police officer in a small city
Why he's a police officer: "It's just go, go, go. I like the variety of calls. You see rich and poor, young and old. You'll go from breaking up a fight to untangling an automobile accident to rescuing an animal. It's never boring."
How to avoid being mugged: "Use common sense. Don't go in dark unlit areas. Don't walk through bad areas alone. Don't display your money, like counting it at an ATM. Assume that people are always watching you. If it happens, do what you're told and don't try to be a hero. Try to get a good description. When it's over, get to the phone."
How to avoid a burglary: "If the bad guys really want to get in, they will. So if there's something you really value, take it with you or put it in storage. And this is so obvious, but do lock your windows and doors. When I do saturation detail in areas where a lot of young people live, I can't believe how many places we can get into."
The root of all evil: In his experience, drugs and alcohol are directly involved in the vast majority of robberies and assaults by strangers. "I see zombies walking around strung out at 4 a.m., needing a rock of crack, and I know they'll do anything to get the money."
Crime and the young black officer: "When I'm in plain clothes, I do get the feeling, often, that people are wary of me. Race is sort of the baseline. But a lot depends on how you act and what you wear, so I'm careful not to provoke people. It used to bother me, but at this point it's more amusing than anything else. I'll walk into a store and the clerk will run over to me-'can I help you?'-and then keep an eye on me until I leave. All the time I'm thinking, 'You don't know who I am, and you'd sure be embarrassed if you did.' "

---

metropolitan areas with the highest rates of violent crime: Miami (1), Tallahassee (5), Jacksonville (8), Gainesville (11), Tampa (15), Ocala (22), Orlando (26), Fort Lauderdale (41), and Lakeland (45). Other fast-growing metros are also on the list, such as Charlotte-Gastonia, North Carolina (16) and Las Vegas (49). These popular metropolitan areas—many touted as wonderful retirement and recreation areas—have much higher crime rates than the cities Americans fear, such as Atlanta (54th in its rate of violent crime), Boston (85), Washington, D.C. (88), and Philadelphia (114).

The FBI's local crime rates are often criticized by civic leaders in crime-prone cities. And in fact, many variables can skew these data. If fewer robberies are reported in New York City than in Tallahassee, for example, New York's rate will look too low, while Tallahassee's will look too high. When Tallahassee launched an aggressive campaign against sex crimes in the mid-1980s, the number of reported rapes increased three times faster than the overall crime rate. Wherever police are aggressive against criminals but approachable to the public, a high proportion of total crimes will be reported.

Still, the FBI data are the only source of information on local crime rates. And the same regional patterns show up in the crime most difficult to hide: murder. New York ranks 5th and Washington, D.C. ranks 28th among the 255 metropolitan areas that supplied their 1993 murder statistics to the FBI. But the nation's highest murder rate is in New Orleans, followed by Shreveport-Bossier City, Louisiana; Jackson, Mississippi; and Jackson, Tennessee. Of the ten met-

> Of the ten metropolitan areas with the highest murder rates, seven are in the South.

---

* The National Crime Victimization Survey is not large enough to supply data for metropolitan areas, so the Uniform Crime Reports are the only source of local data on crime.

Crime Central

The violent crime rate is dropping in the most violent metros' central cities

(violent crime rate per 100,000 in central cities of the 10 most violent metropolitan areas, 1993, 1994, and percent change 1993-94)

central city	1993	1994	percent change 1993-94
Miami, FL	3,900	3,400	–12.3%
New York, NY	2,100	1,900	–11.0
Alexandria, LA	**	**	**
Los Angeles, CA	2,400	2,100	–13.3
Tallahassee, FL	2,000	1,700	–14.8
Baton Rouge, LA	3,000	2,400	–19.0
Little Rock, AR	3,300	3,000	–10.2
Jacksonville, FL	1,700	1,500	–10.5
Pueblo, CO	1,700	1,400	–17.3
Baltimore, MD	3,000	2,800	–5.3

*See table, p. 25
**Data not available.

Source: Federal Bureau of Investigation

ropolitan areas with the highest murder rates, seven are in the South. Among the top 20, 17 are in the South. Among the top 50, 38 are in the South.

Murder is not included in the Justice Department's victimization survey. But the UCR statistics show that 24,530 Americans were murdered in 1993, or 9.5 murders per 100,000 people. This rate is up 20 percent from a low of 7.9 in 1984 and 1985. This is cause for concern, because the increase occurred despite the shrinking size of the crime-prone young-adult population.

THE NEXT DECADE OF CRIME

The experts agree that violent crime will increase in the years ahead, for demographic reasons alone. The number of Americans aged 15 to 24 is projected to rise 14 percent between 1995 and 2005. Those most likely to commit crime or to be victimized by crime are teenagers and young adults. What's more, crime-prone age groups are getting wilder in the 1990s. The violent crime victimization rate for 16-to-19-year-olds rose from 73.8 to 77.9 per 1,000 between 1989 and 1992, according to the Justice Department's survey. The rate for 12-to-15-year-olds rose from 62.9 to 75.7, and the rate among 20-to-24-year-olds rose from 57.8 to 70.1. Young black men are now so vulnerable to crime that homicide is the leading cause of death for black men aged 15 to 24.

Violent crime may also increase as people's sense of community dwindles. The emergence of highly individualistic generations in the U.S. and other countries has weakened community standards and eroded public trust. The percentage of Americans who think most people can be trusted fell from 55 percent in 1960 to 36 percent in 1993. The emergence of a highly individualis-

> When the baby-boom generation retires, it may retreat behind the walls of a gated community.

TAKING IT FURTHER

ONLINE

Many of the data analyses used to create this article are available online and free to *American Demographics* subscribers. These data are posted as spreadsheets in DBF and WKS formats and are available through our site on the World Wide Web; point your Web browser to http://www.marketingtools.com. If you don't have internet access, dial our electronic bulletin board, modem access number (607) 273-5579.

Our Web site and electronic bulletin board allow you to download rankings of crime rates per 100,000 population based on the FBI's Uniform Crime Reports for 1993. We offer nine tables that cover all metropolitan areas that reported crimes to the FBI. The tables describe the following crimes: overall violent crimes, murder, aggravated assault, rape, robbery, overall property crimes, car theft, burglary, and larceny.

In addition, 1993 and 1994 data are available for these crimes as reported in 194 cities with more than 100,000 population. Please note that 46 metros did not report crime data to the FBI, and an additional 23 are missing some information. These data will be updated on our online services when the 1994 metro data are published in October 1995.

HARDCOPY

To obtain a printed copy of the FBI's Uniform Crime Reports, *Crime in the United States 1993,* call the Superintendent of Documents, U.S. Government Printing Office; telephone (202) 783-3238. A variety of reports analyzing data from the National Crime Victimization Survey are available from the Bureau of Justice Statistics. These include *Crime and the Nation's Households, 1992; Criminal Victimization 1993*; and *Highlights from 20 years of Surveying Crime Victims: The National Crime Victimization Survey, 1973–92.* In addition, the *Sourcebook of Criminal Justice Statistics,* published annually, includes data from both the UCR and the victimization survey. To order these reports, call the Justice Department at (800) 732-3277. Single copies of reports are free.

For more information about international crime statistics, see *Understanding Crime: Experiences of Crime and Crime Control,* edited by Anna Alvazzi del Frate, Ugljesa Zvekic, and Jan. J.M. van Dijk, United Nations Interregional Crime and Justice Research Institute, United Nations Publication No. 49, Rome, August 1993, available for $45 from United Nations Publications, telephone (800) 253-9646.

Most Murderous Metros

Most of the metropolitan areas with the highest murder rates are located in the South.

(50 metropolitan areas with the largest number of murders per 100,000 population, 1993)

rank	metropolitan area	murder rate	rank	metropolitan area	murder rate
1	New Orleans, LA	37.7	26	Monroe, LA	15.8
2	Shreveport-Bossier City, LA	25.8	27	Rocky Mount, NC	15.8
3	Jackson, MS	25.2	28	Washington, DC-MD-VA-WV	15.8
4	Jackson, TN	23.3	29	Galveston-Texas City, TX	15.5
5	New York, NY	23.2	30	Danville, VA	15.3
6	Memphis,TN-AR-MS	21.9	31	Jacksonville, FL	15.1
7	Fayetteville, NC	21.7	32	Vineland-Millville-Bridgeton, NJ	15.0
8	Los Angeles-Long Beach, CA	21.3	33	Montgomery, AL	14.9
9	Gary-Hammond, IN	20.2	34	Dallas,TX	14.6
10	Little Rock-North Little Rock, AR	20.1	35	Riverside-San Bernardino, CA	14.6
11	Alexandria, LA	19.8	36	Savannah, GA	14.6
12	Pine Bluff, AR	19.7	37	Anniston, AL	14.4
13	Birmingham, AL	19.3	38	Oakland, CA	14.4
14	Baton Rouge, LA	19.1	39	Florence, SC	14.2
15	Albany, GA	18.7	40	Laredo, TX	13.9
16	San Antonio, TX	18.6	41	Columbus, GA-AL	13.7
17	Miami, FL	18.1	42	Las Vegas, NV-AZ	13.1
18	Richmond-Petersburg, VA	17.4	43	Mobile, AL	13.0
19	Baltimore, MD	17.2	44	Gadsden, AL	12.9
20	Texarkana, TX-AR	17.1	45	Augusta-Aiken, GA-SC	12.8
21	Fresno, CA	16.9	46	Stockton-Lodi, CA	12.8
22	Charlotte-Gastonia-Rock Hill, NC-SC	16.6	47	Bakersfield, CA	12.5
23	Waco, TX	16.4	48	Flint, MI	12.4
24	Houston, TX	15.9	49	Atlanta, GA	12.2
25	Detroit, MI	15.8	50	Norfolk-Virginia Beach-Newport News, VA-NC	12.1

Source: Crime in the United States, 1993, *Federal Bureau of Investigation, 1994*

tic population that is indifferent toward public judgment has disturbing consequences that ripple through society. One of the consequences is an increase in violence at society's margins.

As violent crime increases in the next decade, the powerful baby-boom generation will have children entering the age group most likely to be victimized by crime. These converging trends will probably increase public hysteria over crime in years to come. Specifically:

• Expect middle-aged Americans to demand more protection for their children, whether they are toddlers in day care or young adults in college. Institutions of higher education are likely to discover that the old-fashioned policy of *in loco parentis* has powerful advantages as a marketing tool. Strict on-campus

discipline will appeal to fearful parents who are unwilling to grant their children independence at the vulnerable age of 18.

• The public's fear of crime will ensure an ongoing fascination with true crime stories. In this respect, the O. J. Simpson trial is just a harbinger of things to come. Expect at least one major crime story to be at the top of the news at all times from now on.

• The public will shy away from gratuitous fictional violence, because they are so afraid of the real thing. Audiences will demand happy endings from their fiction because there are so many tragedies in real life.

• The personal-security industry will offer increasingly creative high-tech ways to protect oneself, from alarms and security cards to hidden cameras. A

growing number of crimes will be captured on videotape and fed to the suppliers of 24-hour news.

• The gun lobby will lose power as an older, educated public demands reasonable compromise in the gun control debate. A growing number of politicians will advocate gun control as their constituents tire of random violence.

• Retailers, restaurateurs, shopping malls, office buildings, train stations, and other public places will offer more visible security. Expect growing demand for guards, metal detectors, and escorts. Even neighborhoods will become more security-conscious. When the baby-boom generation retires, it may retreat behind the walls of a gated community.

The Dynamics of Domestic Abuse

By DOUGLAS R. MARVIN

While on their honeymoon, 23-year-old Mike becomes verbally abusive to his wife, Mary, after she suggests that he has had enough to drink. Mary is surprised by Mike's behavior and his hostile reaction to her. Soon after, however, he apologizes, and because he has always been so kind and gentle, Mary believes him when he tells her that this will never happen again.

Several months later, a similar episode occurs. This time, Mary takes the blame, telling herself that these types of incidents are normal in a new marital relationship. She resolves to do things that will make Mike happy and avert confrontations.

Three weeks later, Mike hits Mary during an argument. After several violent episodes during a 2-month period, Mary finally calls the police because she fears for her safety. Responding officers arrest Mike and charge him with assault under the state's domestic violence laws.

Recognizing the trouble that awaits him, and in an effort to get her back on his side, Mike sends Mary flowers while he is in jail. With the flowers, he includes a long note, in which he expresses his deep sorrow for the pain he has caused her and promises that the behavior will never be repeated. Because his note is so compelling, Mary believes that he has learned his lesson and that their relationship will improve. The following day, she informs the city attorney's office that she does not wish to cooperate with the prosecution. When the prosecutor concludes that the state's case is too weak without Mary as a witness, the state drops its charges against Mike, and he is released from jail.

Scenarios such as this have long constituted a staple of American policing. In many communities, reports related to domestic abuse make up the largest category of calls to which police officers respond. Yet, until fairly recently, police officers rarely ventured into the private domain of the marital relationship. At most, officers responding to calls for help attempted to calm things down and arrange for one party to leave the home for the evening. While such an approach provided a short-term solution, it rarely helped bring about an end to the violence.

During the 1980s, this response began to change as communities implemented more aggressive strategies to address domestic abuse. Many law enforcement agencies began to explore new ways for officers to respond to domestic violence calls. Gradually, the focus shifted from merely "maintaining the peace" to arresting offenders, protecting victims, and referring battered women to shelters and other community resources available to help victims of domestic violence.

This move toward fostering a better understanding of domestic violence represents a clear departure from the approach law enforcement agencies once took toward the issue. However, despite the progressive changes that have taken place during the past two decades, law enforcement still does not address domestic violence in the same way it addresses other violent crimes. While investigators attempt to understand the motivations and characteristics of such offenders as rapists or serial murderers, little attention has been given to profiling batterers. Law enforcement officers who must confront batterers on an almost-daily basis would be well served to develop a better understanding of the dynamics of domestic abuse.

A CLOSER LOOK AT DOMESTIC ABUSE

Officers called upon to respond to and investigate domestic abuse calls need to have a full understanding of the complex social, economic, and psychological issues that surround acts of domestic violence. To assist in the investigation of these cases and to educate police officers about this type of abuse, New Jersey's domestic violence laws require that all police officers receive biannual training in this area. This training brings several pieces of the puzzle together to provide officers with a greater understanding of the dynamics of domestic violence.

From *FBI Law Enforcement Bulletin*, July 1997, pp. 13-18. Reprinted by permission of the U.S. Department of Justice, Federal Bureau of Investigation.

> **Domestic abuse is about one person dominating and controlling another by force, threats, or physical violence.**

Not a Fair Fight

During training, officers learn that domestic violence is not mutual combat. Domestic abuse is about one person dominating and controlling another by force, threats, or physical violence. The long-term affects of domestic violence on victims and children can be profound. A son who witnesses his father abuse his mother is more likely to become a delinquent or batterer himself.[1] A daughter sees abuse as an integral part of a close relationship.[2] Thus, an abusive relationship between father and mother can perpetuate future abusive relationships.

Battering in a relationship will not improve on its own. Interven-

tion is essential to stop the reign of terror. When intervention is lacking, the results can be dire: An average of 1,500 American women are killed each year by husbands, ex-husbands, or boyfriends.[3]

Types of Abuse

Officers investigating domestic violence should have an understanding of the types of abuse they may encounter. Because domestic violence is a pattern of coercive control founded on and supported by violence or the threat of violence, this abuse may take the forms of physical violence, sexual violence, emotional abuse, and/or psychological abuse.

Physical violence includes punching, choking, biting, hitting, hair-pulling, stabbing, shooting, or threats of this type of violence. Sexual violence is characterized by physical attacks of the breast and/or genital area, unwanted touching, rape with objects, and forced sexual relations, including marital rape.

Emotional abuse takes the form of a systematic degrading of the victim's self-worth. This may be accomplished by calling the victim names, making derogatory or demeaning comments, forcing the victim to perform degrading or humiliating acts, threatening to kill the victim or the

victim's family, controlling access to money, and acting in other ways that imply that the victim is crazy.

Psychological battering involves all of these features of emotional abuse, but also consists of at least one violent episode or attack on the victim to maintain the impending threat of additional assaults. Destruction of property is violence directed at the victim even though no physical contact is made between the batterer and the victim. This includes destroying personal belongings, family heirlooms, or even the family pet. This destruction is purposeful and the psychological impact on the victim may be as devastating as a physical attack.

Characteristics of Batterers

Most batterers are masters of deception. Few exhibit violent behavior to anyone other than their victims. Often, batterers possess winning personalities and are well liked in the community. However, they frequently exhibit vastly different public and personal behavior.

In the wake of a violent domestic abuse incident, batterers often attempt to convince responding police officers that their victims are mentally off balance. Many times they fool officers into leaving without conducting a proper, thorough investigation.[4]

Developing a deeper understanding of the characteristics of batterers will help police officers realize when batterers are attempting to manipulate them. To help identify potential batterers, officers should be aware of other common traits they generally possess. These include:

- *Low self-esteem.* This often results from physical or sexual abuse and/or disapproval or neglect by a parent or authoritarian figure from the batterer's childhood.
- *Extreme insecurity and an inability to trust others.* Batterers have difficulty establishing close friendships. They tend to be critical or jealous of their partners.

"Law enforcement officers . . . should make clear to victims that the criminal justice system can help protect them and will work for their benefit."

Lieutenant Marvin serves with the New Providence, New Jersey, Police Department.

- *Denial of responsibility for their behavior.* Batterers often deny that abuse has occurred. They also minimize the impact of their assaultive behavior or blame their partners for causing an incident.
- *Need to control.* Batterers *choose* to abuse their partners. Their purpose is to control them. Batterers use violence or attempted or suggested violence to make their partners comply with their wishes.

THE CYCLE OF VIOLENCE

Police generally become involved in a domestic abuse situation once it has reached a flash point. However, in most domestic abuse cases, physical abuse occurs during one of the three phases that make up the cycle of violence. By becoming familiar with the features of each phase in this cycle, responding officers can help victims understand that the cycle of abuse is likely to continue if nothing is done to address the underlying causes.

In a battering relationship, the cycle of violence includes three distinct phases.[5] Investigating officers who understand these phases can offer objective insight to victims of the violence. For example, if an officer can advise a victim that the batterer's next step likely will be to apologize and possibly send flowers in order to keep her in the relationship, she may be more inclined to understand that the cycle will repeat itself if no intervention occurs.

Tension-Building Phase

During the first—and usually the longest—phase of the overall cycle, tension escalates between the couple. Excessive drinking, illness, jealousy, and other factors may lead to name-calling, hostility, and friction. Unless some type of professional intervention occurs at this point, the second phase of the cycle—acute battering—becomes all but inevitable.

During the tension-building phase, a woman may sense that her partner is reacting to her more negatively, that he is on edge and reacts heatedly to any trivial frustration. Many women recognize these signs of impending violence and become more nurturing or compliant or just stay out of the way.

A woman often will accept her partner's building anger as legitimately directed at her. She internalizes what she perceives as her responsibility to keep the situation from exploding. In her mind, if she does her job well, he remains calm. If she fails, the resulting violence is her fault.

> **"**
> ***... an experienced batterer generally will not leave marks on the victim that would be readily noticeable to others.***
> **"**

Acute-Battering Phase

The second phase of the cycle is the explosion of violence. The batterer loses control both physically and emotionally. Many batterers do not want to hurt their partners, only to teach them a lesson and control them. However, this is the stage where the victim, the batterer, or responding officers may be assaulted or killed.

Unless the battering is interrupted, the violence during this phase will take at least as severe a form as is necessary for the abuser to accomplish his goal. Once he has the victim under his control, he may stop. In other cases, where the batterer completely loses emotional and physical control, the consequences can be deadly.

The violence may be over in a moment or last for several minutes or hours. Although there may be visible injuries, an experienced batterer generally will not leave marks on the victim that would be readily noticeable to others.

After a battering episode, most victims consider themselves lucky that the abuse was not worse, no matter how severe their injuries. They often deny the seriousness of their injuries and refuse to seek medical attention.[6]

Law enforcement officers who respond immediately after a violent episode may find an abusive perpetrator who appears extremely calm and rational. His calm demeanor is deceptive; he has just released his anger and vented his tensions at his victim. The batterer may point to the victim, who may be highly agitated or hysterical because of the abuse, and attempt to blame her for the violence. The victim may, in fact, respond aggressively against officers who attempt to intervene.

Officers should be aware that this reaction may be due to the victim's fear that more severe retaliation awaits her if officers arrest the batterer. The victim also may feel desperate about the impending loss of financial support or even emotional support she receives from the abuser.

Although officers should not make any false promises, they should reassure the victim that the mechanisms are in place for the criminal justice system to help. Officers have a responsibility to provide a complete, professional investigation so that the system will work. A haphazard investigation, or a lack of concern by responding officers, could result in a violent abuser's being released from jail to retaliate against a vulnerable victim.

Honeymoon Phase

The third phase of the cycle is a period of calm, loving, contrite behavior on the part of the batterer. The batterer may be genuinely sorry for the pain he has caused his partner. He acts out of his greatest fear—that his partner will leave him. He attempts to make up for his brutal behavior and believes that he can

New Jersey's Domestic Violence Laws

Domestic violence laws in New Jersey—as in other states—clearly express that the *primary duty* of a law enforcement officer when responding to a domestic violence call is to enforce the laws allegedly violated and to protect the victim. At the same time, the New Jersey statutes provide protection from liability for law enforcement officers who act to enforce domestic violence laws by:
- Making an arrest based on probable cause
- Enforcing a court order in good faith, or
- Acting (or refraining from any action) in good faith under the domestic violence laws.

The statutes clearly define what is expected of law enforcement officers and reflect the legislature's intent to ensure that officers take the necessary steps to protect the victims of domestic violence.

Source: New Jersey Criminal Justice Code 2C:25-18 et. seq.

---

control himself and never again hurt the woman he loves.

The victim wants to believe that her partner really can change. She feels responsible, at least in part, for causing the incident, and she feels responsible for her partner's well-being.

It is at this stage that many victims request that complaints against batterers be dropped. If police conducted a thorough investigation, the prosecutor's office can reacquaint a reluctant victim with photographs of her injuries. When the victim sees the cuts and bruises that she received at the hands of her now-apologetic partner, she may reconsider the wisdom of dropping the charges.

Likewise, if officers had the victim provide a statement of events at the time of the incident, this could prove an invaluable tool for prosecutors. Not only does such a statement establish probable cause, but prosecutors can have the reluctant victim review the details of her abuse or refresh her memory. Officers and prosecutors also can explain that the contrite behavior being exhibited by the batterer may, in all likelihood, give way to a new cycle of violence.

For police officers, the possibility that a victim will forgive her abuser during the honeymoon phase underscores the importance of conducting a thorough investigation. The goal of officers responding to a domestic

abuse call should be able to develop a case that can be prosecuted even if the victim becomes reluctant.[7]

Understanding the Cycle of Violence

While most domestic relationships involving violence include some type of cycle, not all violent relationships go through each phase as described above. Some batterers never express any type of remorse for their actions and, in fact, will continue to use threats and intimidation to discourage a victim from filing a complaint or testifying in court. For such abusers, the thought of resorting to flowers or apologies would never cross their minds. However, most domestic abuse cases follow a pattern corresponding, in some way or another, to the cycle of violence.

CONCLUSION

In recent years, law enforcement has enhanced its ability to resolve various types of cases by studying the motivations and profiling the characteristics of offenders who perpetrate certain types of crimes. The police can apply this same strategy to help address the issues surrounding domestic violence.

Investigations of domestic violence cases should evolve with a full understanding of the characteristics of batterers and the cycle of violence. Law enforcement officers also should

make clear to victims that the criminal justice system can help protect them and will work for their benefit. But the police must back up such guarantees with thorough, professional investigations.

The abusive relationships of the past were allowed to persist, in part, because restrictive statutes and misplaced social mores concerning violence within the domestic setting tied the hands of police and prosecutors. Thanks to new laws and an evolving understanding of the dynamics of domestic abuse, these ties have been cut. Law enforcement should make the most of this new freedom to address an old problem.

Endnotes

1. John Zorza, "The Criminal Law of Misdemeanor Domestic Violence, 1970–1990," *The Journal of Criminal Law and Criminology,* (Chicago, Ill: Northwestern University School of Law—Office of Legal Publications, 1992), 83.
2. Elena Salzman, *The Quincy District Court Domestic Violence Prevention Program: A Model Framework for Domestic Violence Intervention,* 74 B.C.L. REV. 329, (1994).
3. National Woman Abuse Prevention Project, "Understanding Domestic Violence: Fact Sheets," 1989, 21.
4. Ibid.
5. Leonore E. Walker, *The Battered Woman* (New York: Harper-Row, 1979), 43.
6. Domestic Violence Prosecution Protocol, Office of the Attorney General, San Diego, Calif., April 1990.
7. *See* George Wattendorf, "Prosecuting Cases Without Victim Cooperation," *FBI Law Enforcement Bulletin,* April 1996, 18–20.

Victims of Childhood Sexual Abuse—Later Criminal Consequences

Cathy Spatz Widom

Cathy Spatz Widom, Ph.D., is professor of criminal justice and psychology at State University of New York at Albany.

Over the past 25 years, much has been written about the "cycle of violence" or the "intergenerational transmission of violence." These terms refer to the possible negative consequences later in life for children who are sexually or physically abused or neglected. These consequences include an increased potential for violent behavior. In earlier work the researcher examined criminal records on more than 1,500 individuals to determine whether the experience of abuse or neglect during childhood increased the likelihood of arrest as a juvenile or young adult. The research clearly revealed that a childhood history of physical abuse predisposes the survivor to violence in later years, and that victims of neglect are more likely to engage in later violent criminal behavior as well.

Of all types of children maltreatment, physical abuse was the most likely to be associated with arrest for a violent crime later in life. The group next most likely to be arrested for a violent offense were those who had experienced neglect in childhood, a finding of particular interest. Though a more "passive" form of maltreatment, neglect has been associated with an array of developmental problems, and the finding extended that array to include greater risk of later criminal violence.[1]

Focus on sexual abuse

This Research in Brief reports the findings from an analysis of a specific type of maltreatment—childhood sexual abuse—and its possible association with criminal behavior later in life.[2] Using the same cases of individuals studied previously, the researcher sought to find out whether those who had been sexually abused were more likely to engage in later delinquent and criminal behavior than those who had experienced the other types of abuse. Is there an "inevita-ble" or likely progression from being sexually victimized in childhood to being charged with an offense in adulthood, particularly sex offenses?

This examination is part of a two-phase study of the long-term consequences of childhood abuse and neglect. The findings reported here are from the first phase, which used the arrest records of juveniles and adults to measure the criminal consequences of being maltreated. In the second phase, now under way, interviews are being conducted in an attempt to draw a more complete picture of such consequences. The researcher is looking at criminal behavior that may not have been included in official records and at other negative outcomes, including mental health, educational, substance abuse, and other problems. (See "Preview of Work in Progress.")

Evidence from other studies

The link between childhood sexual abuse and negative consequences for

From *National Institute of Justice: Research in Brief*, March 1995, pp. 1–8. Reprinted by permission of the U.S. Department of Justice, Office of Justice Programs.

the victims later in life has been examined in clinical reports and research studies in the past two decades. Frequently reported consequences include acting-out behaviors, such as running away, truancy, conduct disorder, delinquency, promiscuity, and inappropriate sexual behavior. Studies of prostitutes have also revealed an association between sexual abuse during childhood and deviant and criminal behavior.

These and other findings have been the basis for theories linking childhood sexual abuse to the development of deviant and criminal behavior later in life. Among researchers as well as clinicians, acceptance of this link is fairly widespread. However, as a review of research into the impact of childhood sexual abuse has indicated, the empirical evidence may not be sufficient to justify this acceptance.[3] And, a recent review of the long-term effects of childhood sexual abuse—which cited sexual disturbance, depression, suicide, revictimization, and postsexual abuse syndrome—noted criminal consequences only in passing.[4]

The need for a new approach

The methods used to conduct these studies make interpretation difficult. For one thing, most used retrospective self-reports of adults who had been sexually abused as children; that is, they relied on the subjects' own recall. Retrospective accounts of sexual abuse may be subject to bias or error. For example, unconscious denial (or repression of traumatic events in childhood) may prevent recollection of severe cases of childhood sexual abuse. It is also possible that people forget or redefine their behaviors in accordance with later life circumstances and their current situation.

Another difficulty with these methods lies with their reliance on correlation. They involve data collection at only one point in time. In examining the relationship between sexual abuse and later delinquent behavior or adult criminality, it is important to ensure

Preview of Work in Progress

If someone commits a crime but is not apprehended, the crime will not appear in official arrest records. For this reason, in studying the link between childhood victimization and negative consequences in adulthood, including criminal behavior, it is important to examine evidence from other sources. In addition, victims of childhood abuse and neglect may manifest problems other than criminal behavior later in life, and these too cannot be traced through arrest records.

The first phase of this study relied exclusively on official records to document incidents of delinquency and criminality. Because of the limitations of this type of record, the second phase, begun in 1989, used interviews. An attempt is being made to locate as many as possible of the 1,575 people who were studied during the first phase, for the in-person interviews. Since the abuse and/or neglect incidents took place some 20 years ago, most of these people had become young adults in their early 20's and 30's by the time of the interviews.

Information from the interviews is being used to document a number of long-term consequences of childhood victimization, including social, emotional, cognitive and intellectual, occupational, psychiatric, and general health outcomes. Substance abuse is also being studied. Parental alcohol use has been identified in previous research as a risk factor for child abuse, and recent research considers alcohol use to be a possible consequence of early childhood victimization. In view of these intergenerational links, the study will focus on the connections between child abuse, alcohol abuse, and violence.

In addition, because many victimized children appeared not to exhibit adverse effects of abuse and neglect, the research will examine the influence of "protective" factors that might have buffered them from developing negative outcomes, particularly violent criminal behavior.

Data collection and analysis are projected for completion in 1995, and the findings will be prepared for publication. Support received from the National Institute of Justice has been supplemented by a grant from the National Institute of Mental Health.

the correct temporal sequence of events; that is, to make certain that the incident of childhood sexual abuse clearly *preceded* (not followed) delinquency. Thus, multiple data collection points are needed. The few studies that do not rely on retrospection have investigated consequences only over relatively short periods of time.

Perhaps the most serious methodological shortcoming is the frequent lack of appropriate control or comparison groups. Childhood sexual abuse often occurs in the context of multiproblem homes, and sexual victimization of children may be only one of these problems. Without control groups, the effects of other family characteristics, such as poverty, unemployment, parental alcoholism or drug problems, or other inadequate social and family functioning, cannot be easily disentangled from the specific effects of sexual abuse.

The present study

The study posed three questions designed to shed light on the possible long-term criminal consequences of childhood sexual abuse:

• **Is there a higher risk of criminal behavior later in life?** Compared to early childhood experiences of physical abuse and neglect (and also compared to children who did not experience maltreatment, at least as documented by official records), does sexual abuse in early childhood increase the risk of delinquent and criminal behavior?

• **Is there a higher risk of committing sex crimes?** Are childhood sexual abuse victims more likely to commit such crimes as prostitution, rape, and sodomy?

• **Is there a link between sexual abuse, running away, and prostitution?** Is there a significant and direct relationship between early childhood sexual abuse, being arrested as a run-

Table 1: Types of Child Victimization Cases

Type	Number of Cases
Physical Abuse and Neglect	70
Physical Abuse Only	76
Neglect Only	609
Sexual Abuse Only	125
Sexual Abuse Plus (Sexual abuse with physical abuse and/or neglect)	28
Total	908

away as an adolescent, and, in turn, being arrested for prostitution as an adult?

How the study was conducted[5]

The study examined the official criminal histories of a large number of people whose sexual victimization during childhood had been validated. These victims of sexual abuse were compared to cases of physical abuse and neglect and to a control group of individuals who were closely matched in age, race, sex, and approximate family socioeconomic status.

The groups selected for study. The subjects were 908 individuals who had been subjected as children to abuse (physical or sexual) or neglect, and whose cases were processed through the courts between 1967 and 1971. All were 11 years of age or younger at the time of the incident(s).

The research used a "matched cohorts" design. Such studies involve selecting groups of subjects who are similar (matched) to each other but who differ in the characteristic being studied. The "cohort" of children who had been abused or neglected was matched with the control group, which consisted of children who had not been abused or neglected.

Both groups were followed into adolescence and young adulthood to determine if they had engaged in delinquent behavior or had committed crimes as adults. At the time they were chosen for the study, none of them had as yet engaged in delinquent or criminal behavior. The major aim of this analysis was to determine whether sexual abuse during childhood puts victims at greater risk for criminal behavior later in life than do the other types of maltreatment.

Sources of information about maltreatment. Because it was important to use substantiated cases of physical and sexual abuse and neglect, the study relied on the official records of agencies that handled these cases. Detailed information about the abuse and/or neglect incident and family composition and characteristics of study subjects was obtained from the files of the juvenile court and probation department. The records of the sexual abuse cases were obtained from the juvenile courts and from the adult criminal court of a metropolitan area in the Midwest.[6]

Like all sources of information, official records have certain limitations. Some incidents are not reported to law enforcement or social service agencies.

Moreover, the cases studied were processed before the child abuse reporting laws were passed, when many cases of sexual abuse were not brought to the attention of the authorities. For these reasons, the findings cannot be interpreted as applying to all incidents. It is more likely that they represented only the serious and extreme cases—those brought to the attention of the social service and criminal justice systems.

Types of maltreatment. The *sexual abuse* cases represented a variety of charges, from relatively nonspecific ones of "assault and battery with intent to gratify sexual desires" to more specific ones of "fondling or touching in an obscene manner," sodomy, incest, and the like. The *physical abuse* cases included those involving injuries such as bruises, welts, burns, abrasions, lacerations, wounds, cuts, bone and skull fractures. The *neglect cases* reflected the judgment of the court that the parents' deficiencies in child

care was beyond those found acceptable by community and professional standards at the time. They represented extreme failure to provide adequate food, clothing, shelter, and medical attention.

Subgroups created for the study. A case was identified as involving sexual abuse if there was evidence in the records that the charge had been substantiated. Of these cases, most involved sexual abuse only, but some involved physical abuse and/or neglect in addition. Because exposure to these different types of abuse may have different consequences, distinctions were made. Cases involving only sexual abuse are referenced as *Sexual Abuse Only*. The others are referred to as *Sexual Abuse Plus* (sexual abuse plus physical abuse or neglect). (Table 1.)

The sources of information for delinquency and crime. Finding out whether the subjects had become delinquent and/or committed crime as adults required identifying accurate sources of information about these types of behavior. The researcher decided to use official arrest records as the source, for a number of reasons. They are relatively easy to locate and contain reasonably complete information. The source of information about delinquent juveniles was the files of the juvenile probation department.

Criminal consequences

In general, people who experience *any* type of maltreatment during childhood—whether sexual abuse, physical abuse, or neglect—are more likely than people who were not maltreated to be arrested later in life. This is true for juvenile as well as adult arrests. As the figures in Table 2 indicate, 26 percent of the people who were abused and/or neglected were later arrested as juveniles, compared with only 16.8 percent of the people who were not. The figures for adults also indicate a greater likelihood of arrest among people who were maltreated during childhood.

For certain specific offenses, the likelihood of arrest is also greater

Table 2: Likelihood of Arrest Depending on Type of Abuse Experienced

Type of Abuse Subjects	Number of Arrests	Any Juvenile Arrest %	Any Adult Arrest %
All Cases of Abuse and Neglect	908	26.0***	28.6***
Any Sexual Abuse	153	22.2	20.3
Any Physical Abuse	146	19.9	27.4
Any Neglect	609	28.4	30.7
Control Group	667	16.8	21.0

Note: the asterisks indicate instances in which the differences between all cases of abuse/neglect and the control groups were statistically significant.

***p<.001 (The probability is less than 1 in 1,000 that the occurrence could have happened by chance.)

among people who were abused and/or neglected. (These figures are not presented in tabular format.) For example, 14.3 percent of the people who were abused or neglected as children were later charged with property crimes as juveniles, while this was true for only 8.5 percent of the controls. A similar difference in the rate of property crime arrests was found among adults. Childhood abuse and neglect were also associated with later arrest for drug-related offenses. More than 8 percent of the individuals abused or neglected as children were arrested for these offenses as adults, compared to only 5.2 percent of the control group.

Sexual abuse. All types of abuse and neglect in childhood put people at greater risk for arrest later in life. But an important finding of this study is that, in cases of sexual abuse, the risk is no greater than for other types of maltreatment. (See Table 2.) In other words, the victims of sexual abuse are no more likely than other victims to become involved with crime.

A breakdown of the types of offenses reveals one exception. People who were victimized during childhood by either physical abuse or neglect *in addition* to sexual abuse (the Sexual Abuse Plus group) were more likely than those subjected to other types of maltreatment (and also more likely than the controls) to be arrested

as runaways during their juvenile years.

Likelihood of arrest for sex crimes

Could it be that additional breakdowns of types of offenses would reveal greater risk for individuals who were sexually abused in childhood? Previous research indicating that these people are more likely to be arrested for sex crimes suggests this might be the case.

Sex crimes in general. Arrest records revealed that, compared to children who had not been victimized, those who had been were more likely to be arrested for sex crimes. Thus, experiencing any type of abuse/neglect in childhood increases the risk for sex crimes. Children who were sexually abused were about as likely as neglect victims to be arrested for any sex crime and less likely than victims of physical abuse. (See Table 3.)

Calculating the *odds* that abused and neglected children will subsequently be arrested for sex crimes as adults confirmed the statistics on likelihood of arrest. For abused and neglected children in general, the odds of being arrested as adults for a sex crime were higher than for nonvictims. Among sexually abused children, the odds were 4.7 times higher. Among physically abused children, the odds of arrest as adults for a sex crime were only a bit less—more than four times higher than for the controls. Neglected children were also at increased risk of subsequent arrest for a sex crime (2.2 times the rate for the controls). (See Table 3.)

Specific sex crimes. The study also looked at various types of sex crimes, and the breakdown revealed more complexity. The differences among the groups in arrest for one particular sex crime, prostitution, were significant. Arrests for this crime were rare, but child sex abuse victims were more likely to be

Table 3: Likelihood and Odds of Being Arrested for Any Sex Crime[a]

Type of Childhood Victimization	Number of Subjects	Likelihood[b] %	Odds[c]
Any Sexual Abuse	153	3.9	4.7
Any Physical Abuse	146	6.2	4.1
Any Neglect	609	3.6	2.2
Control Group	667	1.6	—

[a]Sex crimes include prostitution, incest, child molestation, rape, sodomy, assault and battery with intent to gratify, peeping, public indecency, criminal deviant conduct, and contributing to the delinquency of a minor.

[b]p<.02

[c]The numbers are odds ratios. They depict the odds that a person who has experienced a certain type of childhood abuse or neglect will commit a sex crime. Thus, for example, the odds that a childhood sexual abuse victim will be arrested as an adult for any sex crime is 4.7 times higher than for people in the control group, who experienced no victimization as children. (In calculating these odds, sex, age, and race were taken into account.)

Table 4: Likelihood and Odds of Being Arrested for a Specific Sex Crime

Type of Childhood Victimization	Number of Subjects	Prostitution		Rape or Sodomy	
		Likelihood[a] %	Odds[b]	Likelihood[a] %	Odds[b]
Any Sexual Abuse	153	3.3	27.7	0.7	[c]
Any Physical Abuse	146	0.7	[c]	2.1	7.6
Any Neglect	609	1.5	10.2	1.1	[c]
Control Group	667	0.1	—	0.4	—

[a]$p < .003$

[b]See Note C on table 3.

[c]Not statistically significant. All other findings on odds were significant at the $p < .05$ level.

This similarity among all three groups of maltreatment victims suggests that for sexual abuse victims, the criminal effect later in life may result not from the specifically sexual nature of the incident but rather from the trauma and stress of these early childhood experiences or society's response to them.

According to this study, child victims arrested as runaways are not arrested for prostitution as adults.

charged with it than were victims of physical abuse and neglect. (Table 4.) The same is true for the odds. Among children who were sexually abused, the odds are 27.7 times higher than for the control group of being arrested for prostitution as an adult.[7] For rape or sodomy, childhood victims of physical abuse were found to be at higher risk of arrest than either other victims or the controls, and the odds of arrest for these crimes were 7.6 times higher than for the controls.

From sexual abuse to running away to prostitution—Is the path inevitable? It may seem logical to assume that children who are sexually abused follow a direct path from being victimized to becoming a runaway as an adolescent, and then becoming a prostitute as an adult. The findings of the current research support the first part of this relationship; 5.8 percent of abused and neglected children became runaways, compared with only 2.4 percent of the controls.

As noted earlier, the researcher found that sexually abused children were more likely than other victims to be arrested for prostitution as adults, and the odds were higher that a sexually abused child would be charged with prostitution as an adult (Table 4). But are juvenile runaways subsequently charged with prostitution? The researcher looked at all runaways in the sample studied, both the victimized groups and the control group. When some of these runaways became adults, they were charged with sex crimes. None of the runaways were arrested for prostitution, however.

Thus, the findings do not support the notion of a direct causal link between childhood victimization, becoming a runaway, and in turn being arrested for prostitution. Some adults were found to be arrested for prostitution, but they were not the runaways in this sample.

Understanding the aftermath of childhood sexual abuse

All types of childhood abuse and neglect put the victims at higher risk for criminal behavior. However, the particular type of victimization suffered by children who are sexually abused does not set them apart. It does not put them at an even higher risk of arrest, for they are no more likely than children who are physically abused or neglected to be charged with a crime later in life.

The same is true for sex crimes. People victimized by sexual abuse as children are also significantly more likely than nonvictims to be arrested for a sex crime, although no more so than victims of physical abuse and neglect.

For prostitution, the likelihood is greater. For prostitution, findings were consistent with those of previous studies: childhood sexual abuse victims run a greater risk than other maltreatment victims of being arrested for prostitution. The percentage of sexual abuse victims arrested for this offense was low, however (3.3 percent).

From runaway to prostitute? As noted earlier, while the findings support the existence of a link between sexual abuse in childhood and becoming a runaway as a juvenile, they do not support a subsequent link to adult prostitution. That is, being arrested as an adolescent runaway does not predispose people who were sexually abused as children to be arrested for prostitution as adults.

The current research is limited because of its exclusive reliance on official criminal histories. Certainly, such records underestimate the number of runaways, since many of them may be brought to the attention of social service agencies without being arrested. For this reason, other types of data should be examined. However, the fact that none of the runaways identified in this study were arrested for prostitution (while other individuals were) suggests that the connection is at least not as strong as would have been previously thought.

Other sex crimes. Childhood sexual abuse victims were not at greater risk later in life of arrest for rape or sodomy. Rather, the findings reveal an association between these crimes and childhood physical abuse, not sexual abuse. Males who were physically abused in childhood showed a greater tendency than other abused and neglected children and the controls to be arrested for these types of sex crimes. This is consistent with earlier findings regarding the "cycle of violence," which indicated that physical abuse in childhood is associated with the highest rates of arrest for violence later in life.[8] Thus, the violent aspect of rape rather than its sexual component or sexual motivation may explain the association. Indeed, practitioners and clinicians who work with these victims commonly refer to rape as a crime of violence, not simply a sex crime.

Patterns of offending

Tentative evidence is offered here to support the notion that when sexual abuse is differentiated by type, the subsequent patterns of juvenile and adult offending are also different. The *Sexual Abuse Plus* group tended to be at greater risk for running away, particularly compared to the other abuse and neglect groups and the controls. Other analysis showed this group more often victimized by family members or relatives in their own homes than the *Sexual Abuse Only* groups. If one's home is abusive in multiple ways, it is not surprising that the victims would resort to running away as an escape.

These tentative differences suggest that studies of the long-term consequences of childhood sexual abuse might find it worthwhile to disaggregate sexual abuse experiences into groups consisting exclusively of sexual abuse in conjunction with other childhood victimization. Future research might examine the question of whether the effect of multiple forms of abuse is additive.

Criminal behavior is not the inevitable outcome

The link between early childhood sexual abuse and later delinquent and adult criminal behavior is not inevitable. Although it is clear that individuals who were sexually abused in childhood are at increased risk of arrest as juveniles and adults, many do not become delinquents or adult criminals. In fact **the majority of the sexually abused children in this study do not have an official criminal history as adults.** Long-term consequences of childhood sexual abuse may be manifest across a number of domains of psychological distress and dysfunction, but not necessarily in criminal behavior. Delinquency and criminality represent only one possible type of outcome of childhood sexual abuse. A number of researchers have described depression, anxiety, self-destructive behavior, and low self-esteem among adults who were sexually abused in childhood. Further research with these samples is under way to document the long-term effects of childhood victimization in a broad array of outcomes. (See "Preview of Work in Progress.")

Implications for policy

In planning and implementing treatment and prevention programs for children who are sexually abused, practitioners need to keep in mind that these children are in no sense destined for later involvement in criminal behavior. Like other victims of abuse and neglect, the majority will manifest no such negative outcome, at least as evidenced by official records or arrest. However, interventions need to be grounded in the knowledge that childhood victims of sexual abuse, as well as other types of abuse and neglect, are at increased risk for criminal involvement compared to nonvictims.

The need to avoid projecting criminal outcomes for sexually abused children has to be balanced by awareness of the particular risks they face. For

example, interventions for sexually abused children should be informed by knowing that the likelihood of becoming a juvenile runaway is not only greater than among nonvictims, but also greater than for other types of childhood maltreatment victims. In developing interventions, it is also important to consider the higher risk for later prostitution that sexual abuse victims face. The health threat posed, not only with respect to the more conventional sexually transmitted diseases, but particularly to HIV infection, makes the need for prevention interventions directed at childhood sexual abuse even more urgent.

As the example of prostitution makes clear, outcomes later in life may differ with the type of victimization experienced in childhood. This makes it evident that not all types of childhood maltreatment are alike and makes it incumbent on practitioners to craft responses that meet particular needs. While practitioners need to be aware that sexually abused children are at greater risk of becoming juvenile runaways, they also need to temper that awareness with the knowledge that these runaways are not necessarily "tracked" into prostitution as adults.

Information from the interview phase of the study is likely to bring further nuances to light. If running away does not necessarily lead to prostitution, it may nonetheless place the victim at risk in ways that are not documented in the arrest record.

The interviews may also shed light on intervening factors that mediate between the experience of victimization in childhood and behavioral outcomes in adulthood. Again, prostitution is an example. Since prostitutes have diverse backgrounds, it is unlikely that any single factor (for example, childhood victimization) explains their entrance into this type of life. While early sexual abuse places a child at increased risk, many other factors play a role, and these factors may emerge in the interviews. If such factors are identified, they would necessarily affect the way practitioners intervene for child victims.

Future directions

Researchers have recently begun to acknowledge that studies of the impact of childhood abuse (including sexual abuse) find substantially large groups of individuals who appear to have experienced little or no long-term negative consequences. There are a number of possible explanations, among them inadequate measurement techniques on the part of the researchers. It is also possible that some factors or characteristics of the abuse incident (less severity, for example), or some characteristics of the child (having effective coping skills, for example) or the child's environment (having a close relationship with a supportive person, for example) may have served as a buffer from the long-term consequences. Protective factors in the lives of abused and neglected children need to be uncovered.

Future studies need to examine cases in which children appear to have overcome, or been protected from, the negative consequences of their early childhood experiences with abuse. The knowledge from such studies would have important implications for developing prevention and treatment programs for children who experience early childhood victimization. These "protective factors" are being explored as part of the study now being conducted by the present researcher.

Notes

1. A summary of this research is in Widom, Cathy Spatz, *The Cycle of Violence,* Research in Brief, Washington, D.C.: U.S. Department of Justice, National Institute of Justice, October 1992. The document can be obtained from the National Criminal Justice Reference Service, Box 6000, Rockville, MD 20849–6000; call 800–851–3420 or order through the Internet at lookncjrs@aspensys.com.

2. A fuller presentation is in Widom, C. S., and Ames, M. A., "Criminal Consequences of Childhood Sexual Victimization," *Child Abuse and Neglect,* 18 (1994):303–318.

3. Browne, A., and Finkelhor, D., "Impact of Sexual Abuse: A Review of the Research," *Psychological Bulletin,* 99 (1986):66–77.

4. Beitchman, J. H., et al., "A Review of the Long-Term Effects of Child Sexual Abuse," *Child Abuse and Neglect,* 16 (1992):101–118.

5. A full description of the research design is in Widom, Cathy Spatz, "Child Abuse, Neglect, and Adult Behavior: Research Design and Findings on Criminality, Violence, and Child Abuse," *American Journal of Orthopsychiatry,* 59 (1989): 355–67.

6. Of the 153 cases of sexual abuse, 40 were processed in juvenile court and 113 in adult criminal court.

7. In calculating the odds, the researcher controlled for the person's sex, race, and age, as these factors may affect the likelihood of being arrested for a crime.

8. See Widom, *Cycle of Violence:* 3.

Findings and conclusions of the research reported here are those of the authors and do not necessarily reflect the official position or policies of the U.S. Department of Justice.

The Police

Police officers are the guardians of our freedoms under the Constitution and the law, and as such they have an awesome task. They are asked to prevent crime, to protect citizens, to arrest wrongdoers, to preserve the peace, to aid the sick, to control juveniles, to control traffic, and to provide emergency services on a moment's notice. They are also asked to be ready to lay down their lives, if necessary.

In recent years the job of the police officer has become even more complex and dangerous; illegal drug use and trafficking is at epidemic levels, racial tensions are explosive, and violent crime continues to increase at alarming rates.

The role of the police in America is a difficult one, and as the police deal with a growing, diverse population, their job becomes more difficult. The need for a more professional, well-trained police officer is obvious.

In the first unit article, "Police and the Quest for Professionalism," Barbara Raffel Price presents a short overview of the problems that police face as they strive for professionalism. Public confidence, respect, and higher education are essential. Price supports community policing as one step toward reaching the goal of professionalism. Organizational stress is the theme of "Reducing Stress: An Organization-Centered Approach." Peter Finn discusses the impact that stress has on police agencies and officers. James Lardner examines changes that have taken place in the New York City Police Department in his article, "Better Cops, Fewer Robbers." "Incorporating Diversity: Police Response to Multicultural Changes in Their Communities," by Brad Bennett, reports on a study done in California concerning how four police agencies responded to demographic changes in their communities.

Next, in "A LEN Interview: Prof. Edwin J. Delattre of Boston University," Professor Delattre discusses the ethics of policing in terms of individual officers, as well as the nature of the organizations in which they serve.

Looking Ahead: Challenge Questions

Is there "community policing" in your community? If not, why not? If so, is it working?

How important do you consider a college education as a requirement for entry into police work? Support your answer.

Should the police be involved in community problems not directly concerned with crime? Explain your response.

What are the pros and cons of outside review of the police?

What strategies can be implemented to deal with organizational stress?

UNIT 3

Police & the Quest for Professionalism

Barbara Raffel Price

Barbara Raffel Price is the Dean of Graduate Studies and a professor of criminal justice at John Jay College of Criminal Justice.

Since the early 1900s, under the leadership of August Vollmer, the father of American policing, law enforcement has been fascinated by the possibilities of professionalism. For the police in those early years, professionalism meant control of their work world with an end to interference from corrupt politicians who appointed unqualified patrolmen and interfered with or controlled hiring, firing and assignment. For Vollmer, professionalism also held a loftier meaning—something he called "scientific policing," which emphasized a style of policing that was detached, objective and, especially, adopted techniques that took advantage of the latest scientific advances in detecting and solving crimes and in approaches to patrolling a community.

Soon after Vollmer appeared on the scene, the police incorporated the term "professionalism" into their public rhetoric. However, policing remained an occupation that had far to go before it would be considered a profession. The principal barrier to professionalism, then as now, is the fact that policing is in one fundamental way unlike any other field striving to professionalize: It has the duty and the right to use coercion, an act that fosters a work culture antithetical to professionalism (which is usually understood to mean service to the client).

Professionalism normally entails:

- A transmittable body of knowledge which is constantly growing and being refined;
- A code of ethics defining relations between members of the profession and the public, including an obligation to render services exclusive of any other considerations;
- High standards for membership, often including higher education and formal training;
- Accountability through peer review and, therefore, continuous evaluation and improvement through research of professional practices;
- At some point in the evolution of the occupation, acknowledgement from outsiders that the occupation is a profession.

Although these demanding criteria arguably present significant obstacles to efficient policing, many continue to believe in and work toward the professionalization of law enforcement. Central to that effort over the years—dating back at least to the Wickersham Commission in 1931—has been an insistence that educational levels of police be raised. More recently, in 1973, the National Commission on Criminal Justice Standards and Goals urged that by 1982, every police department in the United States require four years of college education. In 1995, however, only a relative

handful of departments require recruits to have a college degree. It bears mentioning, too, that most police unions have vehemently opposed education for recruits, as they have other components of professionalization, including peer review and accountability.

Why is professionalism a goal of law enforcement? The most basic answer is that public confidence in the police is essential for order maintenance and stability in the community. When the police are distrusted, government itself is undermined. Professionalism instills confidence and respect because it means to the public that the practitioners have internalized values of service, even altruism, self-control and commitment to high ide-

> *"If there is a future to the professionalization of policing, many believe it rests in pursuing community policing. Others insist that it is an impossible dream."*

als of behavior. Further, professionalism implies higher education. Many have argued that higher education will help police gain an understanding of their role in a democratic society and a fuller comprehension of the responsibilities that come with police power. The President's Crime Commission in 1967 observed that the complexities of policing "dictate that officers posses a high degree of intelligence, education, tact and judgment" and said it was "essential . . . that the requirements to serve in law enforcement reflect the awesome responsibility" facing the personnel selected.

Since the 1960s, when the Federal Government began to assume a major role in upgrading the quality of law enforcement, significant progress has been made, notwithstanding that policing remains fraught with problems. Police are better educated today. Departments are more representative of the communities and populations they serve. Police are more restrained in the use of deadly force. Research on policing, virtually nonexistent in the 1950s, has expanded to a considerable volume generated by universities, private research institutes, nonprofit foundations and Federal agencies. Much more of it is needed.

With the introduction of the patrol car and the two-way radio, the hallmarks of police professionalism were efficiency, as measured by clearance rates, and speed in response to calls. Following the widespread urban unrest of the mid- to late 1960s, law enforcement developed a strategy of community relations that stressed police sensitivity to diverse needs and cultures within the community.

For the past few years, the focus within policing has been directed toward a new, comprehensive strategy called, variously, community policing or problem-oriented policing. In order to work, community policing requires professional police who have acquired nontraditional police skills so that they can involve the community as a co-participant in the control of crime and maintenance of order. Community policing also requires that communities develop consensus as

to what steps should be taken to prevent or reduce crime and it requires cooperation and follow-through by the police and the community.

The question arises as to whether a level of trust sufficient to work with the police exists in those communities that are most crime-ridden. Community policing also raises questions as to whether police have the requisite community organization skills, problem-solving skills, and the ability to mobilize scarce community resources to solve problems.

If there is a future to the professionalization of policing, many in law enforcement believe it rests in pursuing community policing. But others insist that it is an impossible dream—from the community's standpoint there is too little cohesion or ability to respond to police initiatives; from the police standpoint, the requisite skills are difficult to obtain and require mid-management support and facilitation that has, to date, been notably lacking. And then there is the question of availability of resources in the community and their efficacy for solving problems.

About the same time that community policing was taking root around the country, the beating of Rodney King by Los Angeles police was recorded on home video and broadcast worldwide. Other similar incidents of police violence have been noted as well. Public support and trust of the police eroded substantially in the wake of such episodes. Moreover, some have noted the irony of this happening even as advancing professionalism on a variety of fronts (education, organizational structure, ac-

countability and technology) has altered some agencies dramatically within the past decade.

The loss of confidence in the police is due, in part, to the steady increase in the high visibility of crime, including drug abuse, young gangs, organized crime, and terrorism, and the sense—almost certainly false—that we now have a more disorderly and violent society than at any time in our history. Certainly with the abandonment of President Lyndon Johnson's "war on poverty," socioeconomic divisions have widened, and racism continues to be a major source of tension. In this context, the prognosis for community policing, which has been hailed by the police themselves as "smarter policing" and as the best hope yet for the professionalization of policing, is guarded at best.

With police brutality still a significant factor in 1995, it is difficult to claim that professionalism has taken hold in law enforcement. Eradicating the excessive use of force and the scourge of police corruption are the most critical internal issues police face if they are to continue on the long and arduous course toward professionalism. There have been many successes of late for law enforcement, especially in communications technology, forensics, information systems, interagency cooperation, and the development of a commitment to their peers, if not to professional conduct. But until attitudes of the police toward those they serve can be changed, they will continue to make their own jobs more difficult and more dangerous—and professionalism for the police will not come to pass.

Reducing Stress

An Organization-Centered Approach

By PETER FINN, M.A.

People in all walks of life experience, and must find ways to cope with, some degree of stress. However, in the past 25 years, researchers and criminal justice officials have identified stress factors unique to, or more pronounced among, law enforcement officers. Today, law enforcement is widely considered to be among the most stressful occupations, associated with high rates of divorce, alcoholism, suicide, and other emotional and health problems.[1]

Despite the growing understanding of stress factors within the law enforcement profession and enhanced treatment for stress-related problems, many officers feel that law enforcement is more stressful now than ever before. This sentiment can be traced to several factors, including the rise in violent crime during the 1980s and early 1990s; perceived increases in negative publicity, public scrutiny, and lawsuits; fiscal uncertainty; fear of airborne and bloodborne diseases, such as AIDS and tuberculosis; rising racial tensions; and the transition from reactive to problem-oriented policing.

Sources of stress for individual law enforcement officers can be placed into five general categories: issues in the officer's personal life, the pressures of law enforcement work, the attitude of the general public toward police work and officers, the operation of the criminal justice system, and the law enforce-

ment organization itself. Many people perceive the danger and tension of law enforcement work—as dramatized in books, movies, and television shows—to be the most serious sources of stress for officers. In fact, the most common sources of police

officer stress involve the policies and procedures of law enforcement agencies themselves.[2]

This article examines the often-neglected effects that organizational stress has on agencies and officers. It then discusses why managers

From *FBI Law Enforcement Bulletin*, August 1997, pp. 20-26. Reprinted by permission of the U.S. Department of Justice, Federal Bureau of Investigation.

should change stress-inducing policies. Finally, it presents steps that several agencies have taken to reduce organizational stress and thus enhance the productivity and job satisfaction of officers.

TREATING THE SYMPTOM, NOT THE CAUSE

As part of a large-scale study conducted by the National Institute of Justice (NIJ) of programs devoted to reducing police officer stress, researchers interviewed nearly 100 stress-management program directors, law enforcement administrators, mental health providers, union and association officials, officers and their families, and civilians.[3] The respondents agreed that the negative effects of stress on individual officers typically harm agencies as well as officers. As observed by the respondents, the cumulative effects of stress among officers in a department can lead to:

- Impaired officer performance and reduced productivity
- Reduced morale
- Public relations problems
- Labor-management friction
- Civil suits stemming from stress-related shortcomings in personnel performance
- Tardiness and absenteeism
- Increased turnover due to leaves of absence and early retirements because of stress-related problems and disabilities, and
- The added expenses of training and hiring new recruits, as well as paying overtime, when the agency is left short-staffed as a result of turnover.

Most police stress programs and consulting mental health practitioners focus primarily, if not exclusively, on preventing and treating stress among individual officers. However, the "person-centered" approach currently employed by most departments fails to address the un-

> " ...the most common sources of police officer stress involve the policies and procedures of law enforcement agencies themselves. "

Mr. Finn is a senior research assistant at Abt Associates Inc. in Cambridge, Massachusetts, and a special officer with the Belmont, Massachusetts, Police Department.

derlying organizational problems that form the basis of much of the stress experienced by officers.

It stands to reason, then, as one expert in the field suggested, that " ... an organization-centered approach ... identifying the problems the officers have with their work, supervisors, and pay, and making appropriate changes—may well have a greater influence on improving morale."[4] According to the head of the Michigan State Police Behavioral Science Section, the emphasis placed by psychologists and police administrators on person-centered programs has overshadowed the importance of addressing organizational sources of stress.[5]

Unfortunately, stress program staffs and independent practitioners often lack the time to work with management to eliminate the sources of organizational stress. Moreover, few clinicians feel qualified to suggest organizational changes to law enforcement administrators.

At the same time, police administrators might not accept what they perceive to be the intrusion of a mental health professional into department operations. Administrators also may believe that they do not have the time or resources to make the desired changes, or they simply might not agree that organizational changes will reduce officer stress.

Yet, a growing number of agencies have found that even modest modifications in organizational structure can lead to enhanced morale and productivity among line officers. Although some administrators might institute organizational changes simply because they believe it is the right thing to do, there are a host of reasons that should compel reluctant administrators to consider such changes.

ORGANIZATIONAL CHANGE BENEFITS

Enhance the Department's Image

Bad press, public criticism, and legislative scrutiny can be sources of stress for both law enforcement administrators and line officers. Organizational changes that reduce officer stress can improve the department's image simultaneously. Negative publicity resulting from 8 officer suicides in 5 years—3 of them in 1994—prompted the Philadelphia, Pennsylvania, Police Department to create the agency's first stress manager position in 1995. Among other duties, the stress manager examines departmental policies and procedures and recommends ways to make them less stressful.[6]

A newly appointed police chief in a West Coast law enforcement agency decided to remedy years of bad press caused by what many community members considered to be the department's overly paramilitary image. The chief hired an organizational consultant and eventually won new community support by implementing several recommended changes designed to make the department less autocratic.

... even modest modifications in organizational structure can lead to enhanced morale and productivity among line officers.

Save Money

Some departments have documented substantial cost savings resulting from organizational changes. The Mercedez, Texas, Police Department fields 25 sworn officers and serves a city of 14,000 residents. In 1986, the department reorganized to provide an employee development program that included establishing high professional standards, a reward system to promote superior performance, foot patrol assignments, and an increase in the annual in-service training requirement. In the 24 months following these changes, the department's turnover rate fell from 38 percent to 7 percent. Administrators estimate that the reduced turnover has saved the department at least $53,000.[7]

Police administrators understand all too well the costs associated with replacing officers who take early retirement or go on disability. The department not only must pay benefits to departing officers, but it also must pay to recruit, test, hire, train, and equip new officers. In smaller agencies, sudden turnover can result in serious staff shortages that require paying other officers overtime.

Improve Department Morale and Efficiency

Reducing organizational sources of stress should lead naturally to better morale, improved productivity, and, therefore, enhanced overall department efficiency. Even a well-publicized statement from the department's administration recognizing the stress officers experience and expressing support for measures to reduce sources of stress demonstrates management concern about officer well-being. Such pronouncements also help promote the good will necessary to implement change.

IMPLEMENTED CHANGES

Administrators in agencies across the country have implemented significant organizational changes as a way of reducing officer stress. The changes generally affect supervisory style, field training officer programs, critical incident counseling, command support after critical incidents, shift work, and job assignments.

Supervisory Style

One police department has undertaken a comprehensive effort to reduce organizationally generated stress among its 100 sworn officers.[8] A series of stress-related disability retirements prompted the Palo Alto, California, Police Department to commission a study in 1979 to identify sources of stress and suggest options for reducing or eliminating them. The report concluded that the formal and informal organizational structures in the department inhibited effective communication and

created strained relationships among ranks, divisions, and individuals.

As a result, the department hired a management consultant and a mental health clinician to design and implement an 18-month trial program to alleviate organizational stress. Through team building and other methods, the consultant taught department members how to communicate, listen, and solve problems in an orderly, effective manner.

The program proved so successful that it has been continued ever since. It follows a 14-point written plan that serves as a basis for administrators to reduce organizational stress.

First, administrators must identify sources of organizational stress and consult with work units and individual managers to resolve them. For example, the management consultant for the Palo Alto Police Department trained all sergeants in how to prepare for and conduct a performance appraisal and discussed the importance of providing employees with behavior-based feedback in a constructive manner.

In addition, administrators should monitor management decisions with regard to their stress impact, search for implementation methods that minimize the stressful impact, and advise management staff. For example, when the Palo Alto Police Department began to use computer-aided crime analysis to direct patrol and investigative resources toward apprehending career criminals, the consultant designed ways for the department's sworn and civilian personnel to influence and shape the change process.

It is also important to instruct field training officers, supervisors, and managers in communication, problem solving, conflict resolution, and supervisory skills that can minimize stress for employees. At the chief's request, the consultant hired by Palo Alto surveyed each manager on how the chief may have been creating undue stress for them, reported the results to the chief, and recommended changes based on the findings.

Another important step in reducing organizational stress involves training individual managers on stress-inducing practices and events within their units. This training typically results from a manager's request for specific training in problem solving. On occasion, it can be delivered in response to a large number of complaints from line officers, which suggests a management problem.

FTO Programs

A number of departments in California have used a private counselor to train their field training officers (FTOs) in the most productive ways to interact with trainees. The counselor explains to the FTOs how people react when they are criticized and presents the best approaches for offering constructive criticism to recruits who perform poorly. The counselor also tests the FTOs on their supervisory style and presents them with the results so they can see which areas they need to improve. Field training officers who have received the instruction gain a new awareness of the tremendous impact that an FTO program has on the organizational health of a law enforcement agency.

The counselor also advises police executives that they can enhance their departments' FTO programs by designating only officers who volunteer for the program to become training officers. Officers selected to serve as FTOs who have no interest in the assignment often feel that they are being punished. By accepting only volunteers and providing them with supervisory training, departments recognize the tremendous role field training officers play in acculturating new officers. For better or worse, many rookies emulate their FTOs and later use the same helpful or harmful training techniques when they train new officers.

Critical Incident Counseling

The Michigan State Police Behavioral Science Section trains both experienced and new sergeants every year in techniques to manage critical incident stress among officers. The section director designed the training to help sergeants respond in a manner that avoids creating additional stress for officers and reduces the inevitable stress that officers experience from the actual incidents.

During the training, the section director brings in a trooper who has experienced a critical incident and has received counseling through the program. The trooper gives a personal account of what first-line supervisors should—and should not—do when addressing the needs of troopers who require post-incident counseling. The sergeants learn what to expect from an officer who has experienced a critical incident, and the section director explains the warning signs that should alert sergeants that counseling is necessary.

The director of the Behavioral Science Section and another counselor also conduct 2-hour seminars for the agency's executive and command staffs. During this training, the counselors focus on helping managers recognize how their own work styles can impact subordinates. The counselors then suggest ways that managers can motivate their personnel to be more productive.

Command Support After Critical Incidents

The chief executive officer and other commanders of a law enforcement agency should make it a matter of policy to pay hospital visits to every officer shot or involved in a serious accident. This easily implemented policy can have a profound effect not only on the injured officers but also on the department as a whole. According to a veteran police counselor, "The impact of a shooting on the officers involved depends more on the attitude of the depart-

ment toward the officers than on the incident itself."

The commissioner of the Buffalo, New York, Police Department, personally visits every police officer shot while on duty. If he cannot do so, he makes sure that his deputy or another command-level officer goes to provide support.

Command-level staff also can offer assurance and support to family members—including helping with paperwork, finding babysitters, providing telephone numbers for follow-up assistance, and simply spending time with them. Word of the command staff's concern typically spreads through the department grapevine to every officer on the force, instantly improving morale and alleviating stress.

"

. . . when stress impairs an individual's ability to function properly, the sources of that stress must be eliminated or reduced.

"

Shift Schedules

Like many law enforcement agencies, the Michigan State Police used to rotate shifts every 7 days, causing considerable stress for many troopers and their families. As a result, the troopers association received a constant flow of grievances from members complaining of fatigue, eating disorders, and other problems. In an effort to encourage the department to change to a less stressful work schedule, the association asked the department's Behavioral Science Section for any available research that documented the harmful effects of rotating shifts on employee productivity.

The department allowed troopers to determine the frequency of their shift rotation and gave them the option of changing their rotation schedule at least annually. When additional research suggested that all rotating shift work might pose health and safety risks, the command staff included permanent shifts as an option. Today, staff members at each work site choose shifts by majority vote. Many have adopted fixed-shift schedules.

The troopers association succeeded in negotiating the changes, in part, due to the compelling evidence showing the negative effects of shift work on officer productivity. But the department's Behavioral Science Section also helped convince commanders by providing research findings. The president of the troopers association credits the successful resolution of this potentially divisive issue with the fact that the association did not enter into negotiations with the goal of simply winning concessions from the administration. Instead, the association demonstrated to commanders that the department would

benefit from healthier, more productive employees. In other words, by changing the work schedule, the department, as well as the troopers, won.

Job Assignments

The psychologist for the San Antonio, California, Police Department worked with administrators to improve the agency's ability to match officers' capabilities to the needs of their jobs. In convincing administrators of the importance of such an effort, the psychologist argued that stress management should go beyond counseling, that careful selection of job candidates can reduce the stress that arises from a mismatch between the candidate and the job requirements.

The psychologist argued that by performing a "person-job fit analysis" before hiring and placing officers, the department could reduce the need for subsequent mental health treatment for officers ill-equipped to handle the job for which they were hired. Likewise, this preventive approach to mental health would help prospective officers avoid the deep feelings of frustration, disappointment, and self-blame that occur when individuals attempt to perform a job for which they are unsuited.

To determine which skills are necessary for a patrol officer, the psychologist conducted a functional job analysis of the position. He asked a

number of officers to identify the skills required to perform their jobs effectively. The department now uses the skills outlined in the job analysis to select officers for patrol.

The psychologist eventually conducted a functional job analysis of every position in the agency. The department now bases hiring and promotions not only on civil service exams but also on matching individuals' current skill levels with the job requirements for which they are applying. The psychologist also revised the training academy's curriculum to include more blocks on problem solving, critical thinking, and other skills related to preventing and managing stress. The changes in the curriculum involve identifying areas where recruits need expanded training to improve their future on-the-job performance and thereby reduce their levels of stress.

CONCLUSION

Everyone experiences stress. As any stress counselor would explain, a certain degree of stress is essential to a healthy, productive life. However, when stress impairs an individual's ability to function properly, the sources of that stress must be eliminated or reduced.

Likewise, organizations work with a certain degree of naturally occurring stress, generated by the pressures of performing the tasks for

---

Suggestions for Implementing Organizational Change

Consultants provide the following suggestions for implementing any major effort to change organizational policies and procedures in law enforcement agencies.

- The administration should involve a sizable cross-section of the agency's personnel in identifying organizational issues that require attention, designing a prototype program, and hiring program staff
- The chief should endorse and provide support to any initiative
- Commanders should plan for an 18-month or longer trial period

- Commanders should rely on the core start-up group for support and feedback during the initial stages of the program
- Administrators should guarantee program success to all agency levels and work units
- Counselors or outside consultants should expect and encourage the agency and its personnel to take risks and accept some discomfort in the service of growth and positive change.

Adapted from S.E. Walima and E.F. Kirschman, "Health Resource Coordinators: Organizational Consultation Services," The Police Chief, *October 1988, 78–81.*

which the people in the organization are responsible. However, when an organization's policies and procedures themselves become overwhelming sources of stress, those policies and procedures should be reviewed and changed.

With pressures on law enforcement agencies to perform increasingly complex functions with minimized funding levels, police administrators must examine ways to enable officers to perform their responsibilities as efficiently as possible. The steps that a number of law enforcement agencies have taken to reduce organizational sources of stress illustrate that departments can change their policies and procedures in ways that enhance—and certainly do not compromise—their public safety missions. Given the pressures experienced by today's police officers, law enforcement administrators should address the problem of organizational stress by identifying recurring grievances among officers and

working to change the policies that cause them.

Endnotes

1. R.M. Ayres, *Preventing Law Enforcement Stress: The Organization's Role* (Washington, DC: Bureau of Justice Statistics, 1990), 1; C.A. Gruber, "The Relationship of Stress to the Practice of Police Work," *The Police Chief*, February 1980, 16–17; "A Comparative Look at Stress and Strain in Policemen," in *Job Stress and the Police Officer*, ed. W.H. Kroes and J.J. Hurrell (Washington, DC: U.S. Department of Health, Education, and Welfare, 1975), 60; C.D. Spielberger, *The Police Stress Survey: Sources of Stress in Law Enforcement*, Monograph Series Three (Tampa, Florida: Human Resources Institute, 1981), 43.

2. Ibid., Ayres; Ibid., W.H. Kroes and J.J. Hurrell; *see also* J.J. Hurrell, Jr., "Some Organizational Stressors in Police Work and Means for Their Amelioration," in *Psychological Services for Law Enforcement*, ed. J.T. Reese and H.A. Goldstein (Washington, DC: U.S. Department of Justice, Federal Bureau of Investigation, 1986).

3. The principal interviews took place in San Bernardino, California; Erie County, New York; Washington, DC; and throughout the state of Michigan (June–August 1995). Additional telephone interviews were conducted with similar individuals from San Antonio, Texas; Tulsa, Okla-homa; Metro-Dade, Florida; Rochester, New York; and Coventry, Rhode Island (June–August 1995). This research project was supported by the U.S. Department of Justice, National Institute of Justice, Contract OJP-94-C-007. *See* Peter Finn and Julie Esselman Tomz, *Developing a Law Enforcement Stress Program for Officers and Their Families* (Washington, DC: U.S. Government Printing Office, 1997).

4. Supra note 1, Ayres, 9.

5. G. Kaufman, "Law Enforcement Organizational Health Consultation," (paper presented at the Consultation with Police: Problems and Consideration Symposium, American Psychological Association 93rd Annual Convention, Los Angeles, California, August 23–27, 1985).

6. "Tired? Stressed? Burned Out? Panel Seeks Answers for Philadelphia Police Officers," *Law Enforcement News* 22, 1995, 1, 10.

7. J.L. Pape, "Employee Development Programs," *FBI Law Enforcement Bulletin*, September 1990, 20–25.

8. E.F. Kirschman, "Organizational Development," in *Police Managerial Use of Psychology and Psychologists*, ed. H.W. More and P.C. Unsinger (Springfield, Illinois: Charles C. Thomas, 1987), 85–106; S.E. Walima, "Organizational Health in Law Enforcement," in *Psychological Services for Law Enforcement*, ed. J.T. Reese and H.A. Goldstein, (Washington, DC: U.S. Department of Justice, Federal Bureau of Investigation, 1986), 205–214.

Better Cops, Fewer Robbers

As Ean Evers discovers, tougher recruiting and training standards are only the initial changes in New York's Police Department. The rest of the story lies in what happens when rookies hit the streets.

By James Lardner

OVER THE LAST SEVERAL YEARS, NEW YORK CITY HAS been a laboratory for a great law-enforcement experiment, and America now knows the results. It knows, at any rate, that the chances of being robbed or shot have been greatly reduced, and gunfire has become a noteworthy event in neighborhoods where it used to be background music. Far less attention has been paid to the changes wrought inside the agency that has received much of the credit: the New York City Police Department.

A disinterested researcher would probably not have chosen this particular department for the first pilot study of a bold new theory in policing, any more than a nuclear-waste dump would be the obvious place to test a new concept in horticulture. At the beginning of 1994, it was a debilitated and scandal-ridden force whose name conjured up the image of rapacious young cops beating and robbing drug dealers and of superiors who weren't paying much attention to corruption or crime. Administratively, it was a mile-high hierarchy in which an underling strove above all to protect his superiors from embarrassment.

That was then. Now this same department is everybody's favorite exemplar of purposeful efficiency—hailed in the press, in law enforcement, even in such unlikely precincts as the Harvard Business School, where one day last spring three top New York police commanders dispensed advice on how to run a "high performance organization." It would be hard to name an enterprise, public or private, that has climbed so swiftly from ignominy to acclaim.

James Lardner is the author of "Crusader," a book about David Durk, the New York City detective who helped to trigger the 1970–72 Knapp Commission on police corruption.

It is this remarkable transformation that I set out to examine, a year ago, by following a rookie cop through his first months. The idea was to find out, at his side, what the new N.Y.P.D. is like at ground level, how it is seen by the rank and file and how closely the new public image squares with reality in a department where, historically, they have often widely diverged.

I found the department much changed; it would not be going overboard, perhaps, to speak of a change in culture and to discern in it some significant lessons in human and organizational nature. As is often the case in the aftermath of a great achievement, however, the thrill has begun to wear off. The N.Y.P.D.'s metamorphosis was a joint undertaking of labor and management in a rare interval of mutual admiration. Lately, the issue of pay has reared its ugly head again, along with other points of contention less obvious but no less vexing. Names have been called. Threats have been made. Between a hang-tough Mayor and an embittered union, relations are turning stormy, and the moment of breakthrough and the formula for success are clouding over. Even so, the contrast with the early 1990's is sharp.

The archetype of the corrupt cop of that time was a young suburbanite who, prior to being thrown into a drug-ridden neighborhood with a badge and gun, knew little and cared less about the city and its inhabitants. That profile does not fit Ean Evers, the recruit I chose to follow. He comes from Bay Ridge, a largely white middle-class neighborhood of Brooklyn. At 24, he lives with his parents and spends most of his off-duty hours in easy range of his mother's cooking and a network of boyhood friends. He wouldn't trade the satisfactions of life in Bay Ridge, he says, for "anybody's backyard with a pool."

In quest of a more mature crop of recruits, the N.Y.P.D. decided after its last scandal to require 60 college credits

From *The New York Times Magazine,* February 9, 1997, pp. 44-52, 54, 62. © 1997 by James Lardner. Reprinted by permission of Wylie Agency, New York.

or military service. The minimum age was raised from 20 to 22, producing applicants who, besides being more mature, have had more opportunity to reveal any character flaws that might exclude them.

Ean was hired a year and a half ago—before the college or military requirement. He matured, however, along his own path, learning patience from frequent duty as a baby-sitter for six younger siblings and respect for people of different backgrounds from membership on a racially and ethnically scrambled football team at Lafayette High School. He tends to get hot under the collar when he encounters intimations of racism—when, for example, he invited a group of his police academy classmates to join him at a bar in Bay Ridge and the nonwhites among them got the fisheye from some of the regular patrons. He has not forgotten the faces of those patrons.

In an era when size no longer helps land a job as a police officer, Ean is 6 feet, weighs upward of 230 pounds and has Popeye forearms, a powerful neck and a torso constructed along the lines of one of the refrigerators he used to cart around as a porter in apartment buildings. Closer up, the impression of brawn is softened by a layer of baby fat and a smattering of freckles.

His police training began at home. His father, Bobby, spent 20 years in the N.Y.P.D. and was never shy about discussing the job with his family. His dinner-table anecdotes conveyed a relaxed view of the perils facing a cop in the streets; the real scare stories involved the department itself. Bobby (who is of Lithuanian heritage; the name was changed from Evaskevich) is wont to compare it to "Mother Russia," since, he observes: "We have our own trial room where you can get hung. We have our own gulags. We have our own psychiatrist who'll find you nuts."

Nevertheless, two years after Bobby Evers retired in disgust from the N.Y.P.D., Ean entered it, and part of what I hoped to discover in choosing him for a subject was whether he, too, would come to harbor such harsh feelings for his employer.

Tougher training, like tougher recruiting, is one of the department's watchwords these days. Rookies used to spend six months in the academy; now they spend nine, and the curriculum is heavy with lessons in ethics and integrity. Like the other 1,800 recruits who went through the academy with Ean, he got to see—and be repelled by—the filmed testimony of Michael Dowd, the drug-dealing poster boy of the 75th Precinct in East New York. He also got to hear what amounted to a saturation ad campaign concerning the need, and the channels, for reporting such things, as he concluded he would have no trouble doing.

Besides the new emphasis on corruption, the department has been trying to inject more realism into its training. Ean, like most of the recruits I talked to, enjoyed the "fun house" (where the trainees role-play various police situations) and the "verbal judo" classes (where they practice techniques for helping civilians, and themselves, stay

cool). What was hard for him to take was the boot-camp style of discipline that has long prevailed in the academy—the reprimands and demerit cards and the periodic summons to the recruit operations office. There, trainees stand at rigid attention, waiting to be noticed by a superior who may be busy eating a sandwich, while, in Ean's words, "You're afraid you're going to have your head ripped off."

> The minimum age has been raised from 20 to 22, producing applicants who, besides being more mature, have had more opportunity to create a record of any character flaws that might exclude them.

Early in his training, before he had been issued a weapon, he sprained an ankle in gym class. He was then ordered to travel—unarmed but, since there are no lockers at the academy, in full police uniform—from Manhattan to Queens to see a police surgeon. When he got home and his dad debriefed him, Bobby was irate about what he considered an appalling, but typical, manifestation of the brass's mentality: "You put a rookie who doesn't have a gun yet in uniform on a public train by himself, injured, to travel 45 to 50 minutes to go see a doctor in Queens. If you're the employer, what are you telling that kid? What are you telling everybody in that classroom? 'You're nothing but a number!' "

And yet Bobby had not warned Ean away from police work. Indeed, his great satisfaction with his son's decision was plain to see when the family gathered one March afternoon at a restaurant in Bay Ridge to celebrate Ean's academy graduation; he was delighted, too, that Ean had been granted his request to be assigned to the 71st Precinct, Bobby's old command. And if one of Ean's sisters, Kerri, who is 18, follows through on a vague notion of joining the force, Bobby will be equally proud. He will, however, do his best to prepare Kerri, as he has done his best to prepare Ean, for what he considers the key problem of police life: keeping your feelings for the organization separate from your feelings for the job.

THE SEVEN-ONE COVERS MOST OF CROWN Heights, a Brooklyn neighborhood associated in the city's memory with the riots of July 1991, which were a nadir in relations between blacks and Jews—in particular, the Hasidic Jews of the Lubavitch movement, who have their world headquarters on Eastern Parkway. The riots were also a low point in the recent history of the N.Y.P.D., whose anti-riot teams and commanders watched and waited through two days of violence and destruction before intervening.

One reason Bobby recommended the Seven-One to his son was his favorable opinion of its commanding officer, Inspector Joseph Fox. A compact and enthusiastic man of 40, Fox, like others recently entrusted with precinct commands, doesn't spend a lot of time holed up in his office, and no great crisis is required to lure him from his home in Marine Park at the odd hour of the night or weekend—a four-and-a-half-mile trip that he sometimes makes by bicycle.

Like his father, Evers was becoming a harsh judge of some cops—those, for example, who 'carry' jobs—waiting to report that they've finished a case so that they can have their pick of the incoming assignments.

By department policy, rookies get regular doses of field training during their first three months in a precinct, and Fox, unlike many commanders of old, has made a point of using respected street cops as training officers rather than bestowing the job on well-connected, street-weary veterans who see it as a sinecure with weekends off. He tries to get rookies into radio cars quickly, with knowledgeable partners who will spare them the "forget everything you heard in the academy" routine.

Still, the move from academy to the street remains, as always, a jolt. Some things can't be simulated, like doing a traffic stop with, as Ean put it, "people on the stairs, in the windows, on the rooftops, looking out at you," or encountering your first homicide victim—in his case, a man whose face had been semi-obliterated by gunfire in the hallway of an apartment building on Eastern Parkway. Assigned to guard the staircase, Ean had the awkward duty of intercepting a lady friend of the deceased who wanted permission for a farewell caress. "Ma'am, it would be better if you didn't," he replied.

Nor had he been fully prepared, either by the academy or his father, for the vitriol he encountered in the neighboring 67th Precinct in Flatbush one day, after being sent there along with a few dozen other rookies to monitor a protest rally. On a site where a young man wanted for homicide and auto theft had been shot dead by the police a week earlier, a group of citizens had mounted a demonstration demanding, in the words of one of their placards, "White Cops Outta R Hood." Over the course of a long tour of duty that Ean spent in their hood, he was spat at, saw a bottle whiz past his head and heard himself called a "blue-eyed white devil."

His mother, Maureen—an outgoing Irish-American raised in Hell's Kitchen—took this last piece of invective in stride when I mentioned it to her. "Oh, I call him that all the time!" she said, while observing with sly precision that Ean's eyes are gray. Ean himself seemed stunned that people who knew nothing about him beyond the color of his uniform and skin could address him in such a fashion. (Happily, for the street officers, intense collective displays of anti-police sentiment are not as common as in years past.) By checkoff time, his head hurt from the onslaught of epithets. "A few beers, and this day will be forgotten!" he declared.

That evening, he fell asleep in front of the TV set with thoughts of a missing element in his life: an understanding girlfriend. He was watching the 1956 movie "Somebody Up There Likes Me," in which Rocky Graziano (Paul Newman) gets knocked out for the first time, and his wife, listening on the radio, tells a friend: "I didn't marry a man, did I? I married a middleweight."

Slouched on the sofa at the end of a hard day, Ean said to himself, a lucky man, that Rocky Graziano.

His first weeks were a revelation in excitement and, at other times, in idleness—a distinct novelty nowadays in inner-city police work. Crime in the precinct has declined by 25 percent in the past two years, and though precinct commanders like Joe Fox are thrilled with such statistics, the rank and file is more conflicted. Action and adventure, after all, are part of the job's appeal. "Times are different—I'm not going to see all the things my father saw," Ean says. Over the span of his career, he hopes to have a hand in making Crown Heights as safe as, say, Bay Ridge; but well before that happens, he intends to make it his business to get assigned somewhere else.

With quieter streets, cops have more time for the proactive policing that is a cornerstone of the new anti-crime thinking. At roll call, with some regularity, Fox drops in to update his troops on the news from the latest Compstat meetings (where commanders from around the city analyze crime statistics and strategies) and often to bring up some freshly detected crime pattern and order them to zero in on the blocks in question, blanketing them with "C-summonses" (criminal summonses) for "quality-of-life violations."

Among the new techniques, I discovered, are some that have yet to be widely publicized and that tread on the outer boundaries of what are usually understood to be constitutional rights. On a drizzly evening in May, I hung out at Utica Avenue and President Street, one of the busiest corners in the precinct, while Ean and a group of his fellow rookies, supervised by a sergeant, manned a checkpoint, stopping passenger cars more or less at random and livery cabs and unlicensed "dollar vans" on a more frequent basis.

A few drivers protested, but for the most part the operation was met with surprising equanimity—compared, at any rate, to the likely reaction a decade or two ago or the reaction if such tactics were broadly employed in an affluent white neighborhood. In any case, Ean had spent about two hours on the checkpoint—and had a couple of summonses to show for it—when his radio blurted out a man-with-a-gun call at an address on President Street. To my surprise, Ean and another rookie, Thomas Christ, bolted, not even consulting their sergeant before they raced to a rundown apartment building about a block away.

Ean arrived first, entered the lobby and found himself facing three young men, one dressed all in green, per the description given out over the radio. When he ordered the trio against the wall, the man in green made for the exit. A fair amount of pushing, shoving, cursing and yelling ensued, and the noise drew a crowd into the lobby, creating a heart-pumping situation for the two cops until they could establish order and make an arrest.

Although no gun was found, several cops recognized the prisoner when Ean delivered him to the station house, and one reported that he was wanted for shooting at a state trooper. Two months into his street career, Ean was still seeking his first big collar, and it looked like this might be it. But in one of those little reversals that you don't hear much about in cop movies and TV shows, a computer check revealed that the state-trooper business was an old offense, for which the suspect had already served time. That left Ean—so he assumed, anyway—with two charges: disorderly conduct and resisting arrest.

Until recently, it was procedure for a cop who had made an arrest to bring his paperwork to a conference at the District Attorney's office—an arrangement decried by countless studies as a great waste. Now the cop faxes the papers in and consults with the D.A. by phone; but some aspects of the process appear to be eternal. When Ean heard from the D.A.'s office, a young prosecutor on the other end of the line sifted through the facts and rendered her verdict: the suspect's behavior had been fairly typical of young men in such circumstances, she pointed out, and was "not enough" (words countless cops have heard over the years) to support a charge of disorderly conduct. And if not that, then there was no case for resisting arrest either, since there should have been no arrest to resist.

This first brush with the power of lawyers left Ean in a foul mood. "I had to grab him to pat him down," he told me. "He was yelling and screaming and cursing. He shoved me. And she's saying it's all right for a guy to fight with me. You do the right thing, and somebody who sits behind a desk—somebody who's supposed to be on your side—doesn't back you up!"

A WEEK LATER, I ACCOMPANIED EAN AND HIS FATHER to the 71st Precinct Club, which meets one night a month at a Knights of Columbus hall in Flatbush. Young, old and retired cops eat and drink, tell war stories and air grievances. The club offers a smoky diorama of the shifting demographics of the N.Y.P.D. In 1974, women were 2 percent of the department; now they are 15 percent. Hispanics were 3 percent; now they are 17 percent. Blacks

were 8 percent; now they are nearly 14 percent. All these once-invisible groups were much in evidence.

Of course, the department remains far from a cross-section of the city, and even further from a cross-section of Crown Heights. Whites constitute 68 percent of the city's cops but only 10 percent of the precinct's residents, and most of them are Hasidic Jews, a group virtually unrepresented in the police ranks. But the club also provided a glimpse of subtler changes: the sight, for example, of Ean Evers throwing his arm over the shoulders of a series of peers, white, black, Hispanic, male and female.

> This first brush with the power of lawyers left Evers in a foul mood. 'You do the right thing and somebody who sits behind a desk—somebody who's supposed to be on your side—doesn't back you up!'

The conversation added to the feeling of a profession no longer so insular or defensive. Race was a topic on the minds of cops just then (it was late May), because of a well-publicized incident in Westhampton Beach, L.I., in which an off-duty N.Y.P.D. narcotics detective was reported to have viciously beaten a young black man whose main offense was to be with a white woman. This set of facts (revised in subsequent news accounts, which said the detective was acting in concert with a civilian friend and was not in fact the assailant) inspired a good deal of talk, which was distinguished by a remarkable lack of sympathy for him.

"He will go to prison," Bobby Evers said.

"He should," Ean added.

They were sitting at a large table with a group of Bobby's former (and Ean's current) co-workers and with a pitcher of beer that—as in some Biblical miracle—seemed eternally full. One of the other cops at the table leaned over to me and remarked in a whisper that cops are the worst judges of other cops.

A formidable-looking man, large on every axis, Bobby Evers makes his son look average-sized. He also has a booming voice—handy for police work or managing seven children. Bobby drew two lessons from the Westhampton Beach episode. The best remedy, he told his son, was to be careful about the people you hang out with. But if he were an instructor in the academy, he went on, he would prepare recruits for the inevitable occasions when they would find themselves in the company of other police officers who had drunk too much. His counsel, he said, would be along these lines: "You have to understand that you are responsible for their behavior. If you see them

Crime Stoppers

Making the police accountable is one important step. So is going after small crimes— as a way to prevent the big ones.

By DAVID C. ANDERSON

FOR YEARS AMERICA'S ELEVATED CRIME RATE SERVED AS a political Rorschach test. Blame lenience of laws and courts or blame poverty, racism and social neglect. new york's sharp drop in homicides refocuses the debate on a point so simple that it looks radical: crime control begins with the police. In hindsight, it certainly seems obvious. The key to the change, observes Mayor Rudolph W. Giuliani of New York, is recognizing that the Police Department's ultimate role "is to prevent crime as opposed to arresting people who have already committed crime." Why has the obvious proved so hard to grasp?

The history of the American police is a study in management tension: Police officers on the street are more effective if given broad discretion to deal with crime problems peculiar to neighborhoods. Yet chiefs need to know that officers are actually at work and staying out of trouble.

Over the years, crime control lost out to bureaucratic control as police departments centralized authority to curb bribery, political influence, brutality and malingering. In their new book, "Fixing Broken Windows," George L. Kelling and Catherine M. Coles explain that radio cars supplanted foot patrols because it is easier to keep track of officers in cars, not because motor patrols are more effective against crime. Nor does the 911 system, which channels all calls through central headquarters, do much to prevent crime. It reduces response time, but that has little deterrent value—crime victims typically wait 20 minutes or more before calling the police.

Meanwhile, 911 locks patrol officers into a reactive role. During the 1980's, police theorists argued for detaching officers from 911 duty to work on broader crime problems. But such "community policing," or "problem-oriented policing," requires plenty of officers. As municipal budgets tightened, police departments realized that in 911 they had created an enslaving monster: they dared not ignore emergency calls, yet there were never any officers available to do anything else.

Lee Brown, Police Commissioner to Giuliani's predecessor, David Dinkins, deeply appreciated community policing and understood the need for more officers to make it work. To do so, he and Dinkins engineered an ambitious program to expand the force from 25,465 officers to more than 32,000. Giuliani's first Commissioner, William Bratton, harbored larger ambitions. He sought to resolve the historic tension of police management once and for all by giving the precinct police more discretion in their neighborhoods while holding them strictly accountable for results. The thousands of new officers arriving under the Dinkins-Brown plan gave him the resources he needed. Bratton left office last year, but his replacement, Howard Safir, has seen no reason to change course. The police department's new approach boils down to two elements: quality of life and Compstat.

QUALITY OF LIFE Bratton used laws against drinking alcohol on the street, urinating in public and other minor offenses to mount an aggressive patrol strategy that made the police more visible in high-crime areas. Officers now confront people they

David C. Anderson writes frequently about criminal justice.

suspect of minor offenses and demand identification. Those who can produce a driver's license or other government-issued photo ID are sent on their way with summonses—unless computer checks determine that they are subject to outstanding warrants. Those who are, or who cannot produce ID, are searched for weapons and drugs, then taken to the precinct station. Detectives "debrief" them, pressing for information about drug dealing, gun running and other illicit activities in the neighborhood. Such data then become the basis for special operations.

Headquarters commanders have relaxed orders dating to 1970's scandals that took drug- and vice-law enforcement away from precinct patrol officers and turned them over to special units. As a result, the police theorize, potential criminals are less likely to carry weapons and ask for trouble in other ways. "They're taking the handcuffs off the cops," says Inspector Joanne Jaffe, commanding officer of the 33d Precinct.

"The police do stop you," says Whet Wade, who has served a jail term on a gun charge and now attends a program for people coming out of city jails. "So that prevents a lot of people from carrying their guns."

Jason Mercado, another former jail inmate, has felt the effects of the debriefing strategy. Since his release, he says, he has been stopped and searched four times by the police, and in three instances the cops said someone had told them he was carrying a gun. (He was not.)

Andrew Karmen, a John Jay College of Criminal Justice sociologist, offers figures that appear to document the effects of a larger, more aggressive police presence. One of his charts shows a steep decline in murders committed with guns while showing no change in the number of those committed in other ways. Another chart shows a big decline in killings committed outdoors rather than indoors.

COMPSTAT Given the new tactics, how should headquarters maintain control? In New York, information is power. The compilation of crime statistics, precinct by precinct, was traditionally a leisurely process, with reports forwarded by hand to headquarters a few times a year. Now they must be sent in weekly on computer disks. That allows senior managers to analyze the figures and print out timely charts of police and criminal activity all over the city.

The data serve as the basis for the regular Compstat meetings that are probably the most powerful control device ever devised for the police. A hundred uniformed officers and civilians convene twice a week in a war room at police headquarters. "You have every important player from the borough and the precinct," says Safir, who often attends himself. "You have crime stategists from other boroughs; you have probation, parole, corrections, the District Attorney's office. You have the entire criminal justice system in one room figuring out how to reduce crime in a community."

Louis R. Anemone, Chief of Department, arrives for the inquisition armed with sheaves of statistics along with personal profiles of precinct commanders. The commanders, notified 36 hours in advance, are expected to give formal presentations and answer questions about the statistics for their areas. Commanders and their subordinates stand at a lectern while precinct data play across huge screens. Charts track crime reports and arrests by the week, day and hour. Concentrations of drug trafficking, shooting, robbery or burglary illuminate street maps.

"It keeps you focused," Inspector Jane Perlov says. "I review my stats every day. They could call you any day, and you should be ready to go." The stakes are high. Precinct heads who show up unprepared once too often are bounced out of their commands.

Anemone sits across the room, barking questions, offering advice, sometimes granting a word or two of praise. Safir sits to his right, ready to inject questions or comments. In a recent meeting, Anemone roasted a precinct narcotics supervisor named Abner Moore: "It's a tough area, Abner, but are we doing anything on Saturday? Your arrests are low on Saturday. Aren't they selling dope on Saturday?" All eyes shifted to the screens. Sure enough, an unforgiving bar chart showed only a dozen Saturday arrests, less than a fifth the average for the peak day, Monday. "I want you to balance this, Ab," the chief said. "I certainly don't want you setting a pattern where they know you won't arrest them on Saturday."

The directness of communication is extraordinary for the nation's largest police bureaucracy. Before Compstat, "a precinct commander would never really talk to someone like Chief Anemone," Perlov says. "It would go from you through millions of layers till it got up to him. Now we go down there, we're talking to the Chief of Detectives, Chief of Organized Crime, the Chief of Department and the Police Commissioner. That's an incredible thing."

If the new approach adds up to a real breakthrough, however, it leaves open a troubling issue: What the police call quality-of-life enforcement others call harassment. Do safer streets require an unacceptable sacrifice of community relations?

Patrol officers are given strict procedural guidelines for quality-of-life arrests, summonses and debriefings to keep them within the bounds of "stop and frisk" law as defined by the Supreme Court. Even so, young people like Wade and Mercado volunteer stories of being manhandled, even beaten, in situations where, they claim, the abuse was unwarranted. Norman Siegel, executive director of the New York Civil Liberties Union, says that New York's quality-of-life enforcers are playing fast and loose with the constitutional standard. So far, the public apparently does not care. "We did interviews on TV and said, 'If there's anyone who wants to challenge this, we're prepared to challenge it.' I never got a phone call." The issue has historic resonance. Mark Moore, a professor of criminal justice at Harvard, points out that the police de-emphasized low-level enforcement during the late 1960's. Scarce resources, the experts of those days said, should be focused on major crimes rather than low-level offenses.

"Those arguments won the day because the police didn't like doing it anyway," Moore says. "They didn't want to arrest drunks and have them throw up in the back of the car." But, of course, there was another big reason for the change in strategy: the nation had just been through several "long, hot summers" of urban riots, often precipitated by incidents of police abuse. Low-level enforcement, Moore says, "was where all the oppression, the racism got expressed." Safir was concerned enough about abuse of power to announce a "courtesy, professionalism and respect" initiative upon taking over the department. His commanders insist that the Compstat process should work to control police misconduct. But its effectiveness in that area remains to be seen.

For now, however, it is the drop in homicides that commands attention. Homicides peaked in 1990, at a total of 2,262, then began a gradual decline, as Dinkins and Brown began their expansion program. Decline turned to free fall in 1994 with Bratton's radical new administration. Homicides for 1996 totaled 984, an astounding 57 percent below the 1990 figure. Success probably attributable to the new police management deals a serious blow to skeptics used to thinking about crime in broader, more elegant terms. Lately they have advanced three plausible other explanations:

• The crack epidemic of the late 1980's, which contributed to the spread of guns in the hands of kids and generated violence in other ways, began to die a natural death in the early 1990's. More precisely, it caused a "little brother" syndrome: as one generation of teen-agers gave up their lives to drugs and guns, their younger siblings were so traumatized that they vowed never to behave that way themselves. And now it is their turn to inherit the streets.

• The nature of drug marketing changed in a way that has reduced violence. Richard Curtis, a John Jay College anthropologist, argues that during the 1980's crack dealers formed large organizations that naturally generated violence as they transacted business openly on the streets, competed for territory and fought through internal conflicts. Now they are being replaced by smaller operators who do business indoors and who deal only with people they know.

• Crime-prone age groups have declined as part of the population; young people have also been removed from the streets as they left town or were incarcerated, injured or killed. "When you add up the attrition," says Jeffrey Fagan, director of the Center for Violence Research and Prevention at the Columbia University School of Public Health, "you've got a sea change in the composition of people who are at the highest rates of violence."

But while these broader theories might explain the small declines of the Dinkins years, they cannot explain the more recent plunge. With demographics and drug markets, "you're not seeing dramatic change in a short period of time," says Michael J. Farrell, the department's deputy commissioner for policy and planning. "The intervention is much more clear."

Skeptics also seek support in crime figures from other cities, which showed declines in the early 90's. In cities with populations of more than one million, the homicide rate peaked in 1991 at a rate of 33 per 100,000 residents. The rate fell after that, to 21 per 100,000 in 1995. Yet a closer look suggests that New York is driving the national trend rather than following it. New York outdistanced the other big cities: its homicide rate was 29 per 100,000 in 1991; by 1995, it had fallen to 16 per 100,000, a decline of 45 percent. (For 1996, the figure was 13 per 100,000.)

Only three cities saw declines that big: in Houston, killings dropped 48 percent; in San Diego, the figure was 46 percent, and in Dallas, it was 45 percent. But the numbers from those cities are no reason to discount New York's. Dallas has a population less than a quarter that of New York. Comparisons break down with differences in magnitude. The fact that New York has been able to achieve its declines on so huge a scale counts for plenty. To the extent comparisons are valid, police departments in the other three cities behaved similarly to New York's during the four-year period, either expanding the number of officers on the streets, engaging in more aggressive patrolling or both. "The word is out," says Alfred Blumstein of Carnegie Mellon University. "The police can make a difference."

doing something stupid, stop them!" A couple of Bobby's listeners questioned whether this was teachable, but there was general agreement on the underlying principle. As a sinewy sergeant named Jack Lewis put it, "Somebody has to say enough's enough—and it only takes one."

The corruption scandal of the early 1990's prompted the N.Y.P.D. to undertake a serious if belated examination of its personnel practices. The new hiring standards were one result. (Had they been in place all along, the department determined, fully 74 of the 86 cops arrested on graft, drug dealing and other corruption charges in those years would never have been accepted in the first place.) In addition, it became possible, for the first time in memory, for trainees to flunk out of the academy, as roughly 3 percent of Ean's classmates did on one basis or another.

On the way to finding Ean Evers, I interviewed 15 police academy trainees. They were an unscientific sample—but a remarkable one in a force that pays a starting salary of less than $28,000 a year.

Craig Bullard, a physical-fitness buff with his own work-out room for neighborhood kids in the East Bronx, expressed a Jackie-Robinsonesque view of his mission as a young black cop: by the force of his example, he hoped to make others consider the job for themselves. "The only way things are going to change for us is by being on the inside," he told me. Andrew Bershad, raised on Long Island by a Costa Rican mother and a Russian father, was an E.M.T. before becoming a cop, and the two jobs, he said, held essentially the same appeal: "The warm fuzzies—that's what carries you, because the money's no good."

Susan Bohack, the daughter of an artist from New Mexico, formed a desire to be a police officer (and ultimately a detective) while reading Truman Capote's "In Cold Blood" in high school. Against the wishes of her parents, she moved to New York and enrolled at the John Jay College of Criminal Justice. After checking out other career possibilities (and with a less-than-ringing endorsement from her husband, an aspiring Wall Street trader), she took the final plunge, giving up a job as office manager for two Manhattan oncologists, which paid about twice the N.Y.P.D. salary.

Reaching the roof and scanning the rooftops below, Evers caught sight of a man scrambling over a barrier between one roof and the next. 'Give up!' he shouted.

The department is undoubtedly getting a higher caliber of recruit than in the late 80's, when, as Mayor David Dinkin's own anti-corruption panel observed, it appeared that "virtually anyone" could become a New York City cop. From what I've seen, however, more careful recruiting isn't the biggest change that has come over the department since Bobby Evers's day.

When he entered the N.Y.P.D. in 1973, it was still reeling from the Knapp Commission investigation, which had pushed one generation of commanders into retirement while leaving the next generation with an intense distrust of the rank and file. Fear of corruption, brutality or racial incident led headquarters to promulgate a series of "Thou shalt nots," which by the time they had filtered down to the street cops sounded a lot like "Thou shalt not police."

Almost any offense involving drugs, for example, was perceived as off-limits to the uniformed force. "Every working cop knew that if you were involved in too many drug collars, the police department would put your name on a list," Bobby recalls. In Crown Heights, he says, gambling and narcotics joints operated with impunity, offering up a few empty boxes of cereal in a half-hearted attempt to pass themselves off as grocery stores. Gun-toting crack salesmen, one of the biggest threats to public safety in the mid-to-late 1980's, went largely ignored until they made the mistake of killing a cop, Eddie Byrne, in February 1988.

Bobby says he never witnessed any stealing or drug-dealing among his colleagues, though he has no doubts that such things happened. What he did see was "thousands of cops" who habitually avoided radio calls, leaving a small cadre—no more than 20 percent, by his estimate—to do most of the work, and they did it, according to Bobby, with little confidence that the department really valued their dedication.

The transforming moment came at the beginning of 1994, when William Bratton took office as Police Commissioner. With the support of the new mayor, Rudolph W. Giuliani, he let it be known that a cop who saw evidence of a crime was expected to do something—something more, that is, than fill out an "intelligence report" to be sent off into the headquarters void. By his words, by the people he surrounded himself with and by what got punished and rewarded, Bratton established that inaction, not action, was now the easiest way for a cop to get in trouble.

To a beaten-down patrol force, the effect was electric. The message, according to Tommy Goldsmith, Bobby's longtime partner, came down to: "You're a cop, you're an adult—do what you have to do."

In much the same spirit, the department began to shift authority down to the precinct commanders, who became anti-crime kingpins with the right to make changes in deployment and secure their own court orders; many of them, in turn, brought street-level cops into their deliberations. Inspector Fox cites the example of three policewomen in the Seven-One who, on their own initiative, sought permission to stake out a school in civilian clothes—and collared a child molester. Until the last few years, according to Fox, cops would learn about such a problem and have "no connection to the outcome." He told the policewomen, "I never got to do anything like this when I was a young cop."

It took nerve to adopt this approach, and a fresh supply of nerve not to back down when, in April 1994, the 30th Precinct scandal erupted in upper Harlem; 33 cops were eventually convicted of perjury, drug dealing and robbery. In the past, this sort of thing had thrown the department into a bunker mode. Bratton dealt with it forthrightly, but he was determined to be remembered as something more than a mere corruption fighter. Giuliani, for his part, was already well known as a corruption fighter, so he had no need to prove himself in that arena. The best remedy for corruption, he said, was "to give police officers meaningful, active work to do and to have high standards."

ACCORDING TO NO END OF MANAGEMENT-theory books, employees perform better when given responsibility, latitude and respect than in a more traditional command-and-control regime. Bratton, a consumer of this literature, took it seriously and implemented it in, of all places, the N.Y.P.D. The rank and file performed better than many people, including some of their own bosses, might have imagined. Good cops, feeling approval and support as never before, grew more confident and became more of an inspiration to rookies looking for role models.

Most patrol officers in the N.Y.P.D. work fixed tours, and many of the savviest and most energetic gravitate to the midnight shift, whose attractions include a nighttime pay differential and (with manpower at its thinnest) a close sense of camaraderie. For Ean, the first week of midnights (11:15 P.M. to 7:50 A.M.) was exhilarating. He was, he told me, "sitting there like a sponge," soaking up the wisdom of some "awesome cops."

They taught him, among other things, where to respond when you get a burglary call: to some likely getaway route, not to the caller's front door. Another lesson he had not learned in the academy was what to do first with a complainant in a street robbery: get him in the car; tell him, "If you see one of them, let us know," and ask for a description of the suspect he remembers best.

Listening to him describe these insights, I realized that his teachers (one of them Tommy Goldsmith, his father's old partner and now his) were passing along traditions preserved through an era in which they had been widely forgotten. By and large, the lessons had to do with crime fighting or safety, but some, I discovered, were about respect and defusing people's anger. Ean learned, for example, that if he stopped someone matching the description of a suspect and wound up letting him go, he could first ask the radio dispatcher to replay the description. That way, the person would know he had been bothered for a reason.

In some precincts worst hit by corruption, coteries of exceedingly cynical and alienated cops had been leaders and role models. Today, such cops no longer hold their

heads quite so high; dedicated cops hold theirs higher. If it is true, as some have argued, that guns and violence have fallen out of favor among young men of the inner city, it may also be true, among cops, that racism and swagger have become a little less cool.

Like his father, Ean has become a harsh judge of some cops—those, for example, who "carry" jobs, waiting to report that they have finished a case so that they can have their pick of the incoming assignments. Some cops, he has noticed, avoid domestic-dispute calls. Others make a point of getting in and out of them quickly, uttering a few perfunctory words, perhaps, about where a woman might go for an order of protection and then "giving her the slip."

One night in November, Ean and Thomas Fitzgerald, an academy classmate, responded to an assault in Ebbets Field Houses—a housing project on the site where the Dodgers used to play. A woman had been beaten unconscious with a crutch and a broomstick by an ex-boyfriend. They took her to Kings County Hospital and stayed with her for two hours, holding her hand and, after she came out of her stupor, getting an account of the incident and a description of the suspect. The next night, following up on her information, they caught him.

Bobby Evers used to be hassled for taking too long on these jobs. Now, according to Joe Fox, the department no longer cares so much about how quickly assignments are handled. Like Ean, it's more interested in how well they're handled.

Down through the years, of course, many cops have handled domestic disputes, have gone back on the radio to declare them settled and have subsequently discovered that someone had been killed or maimed. "That would hurt me bad severely deep down inside forever," Ean said.

One of the bonds uniting Ean and Fitzgerald is a low opinion of cops who do less than their share of work. For their own part, however, they want all the work they can get—including the calls that other cops have ducked.

"We call ourselves radio whores," Ean told me.

"If central's holding it, we'll take it," Fitzgerald said.

There used to be plenty of excitement to go around. Now, Ean figures, a cop needs to be lucky as well as good, and over the summer and fall it sometimes looked as if the fates were against him. He missed much of the summer after a jogging accident in which a car with a student driver at the wheel ran over his foot. Then he found himself spending a succession of workdays on "fixers," or fixed posts, or guarding sick prisoners at Kings County Hospital. All this was "part of the job," Ean told me. But when I saw him on a fixer, or sitting in the roll-call room waiting to be shipped out somewhere, I noticed his knees bouncing with pent-up nervous energy.

AS THE CITY HAS GROWN CALMER AND THE N.Y.P.D.'s approval ratings have soared, relations between cops and a crime-conscious Mayor have suddenly become volatile. In mid-January, Giuliani put forward a "final" proposal for a five-year contract that would freeze police officers' pay for the first two years (the years they have already worked since the last contract expired), while conferring raises of 3, 4 and 6 percent in the three years to follow. Other municipal unions have accepted the same freeze, and smaller increases. Still, the proposal is widely perceived by cops as a slap in the face since, as a sergeant in the Seven-One told me, "Everybody knows Giuliani's going to be re-elected—and the major reason is not reading scores."

As he spoke, we were standing in front of the station house watching a picket line of about 75 cops. The sergeant, being on duty, could not participate; Ean, processing an assault arrest inside, was in the same boat, though he felt a strong sense of common purpose with his co-workers. The two years of frozen pay had been two years of sharply declining crime. If the Green Bay Packers had been offered a deal like that, he told me a few days later, "you can be sure they wouldn't be in Green Bay anymore."

The demonstration was fairly mild-mannered—certainly nothing like the City Hall protest aimed at Mayor Dinkins in 1992, when cops shouted obscenities with the candidate Giuliani egging them on. Some of them blocked traffic on the Brooklyn Bridge. But there were flashes of potential for something worse for the current demonstration. One of the chants ran: "What do we get? Zero, zero! What should we give? Zero, zero." Indeed, a city-wide ticket slowdown was under way. "What else can we do?" Ean said when I asked him about that. "We can't just walk off the job."

Part of the thrill that ran through the N.Y.P.D. three years ago was the knowledge that a law-enforcement man was Mayor and the Police Department was his favorite city agency. That meant, among other things, immunity from the budget cuts that Giuliani had ordered in virtually every other department. Now, under Bratton's low-profile successor, Howard Safir, the department has launched one of its periodic crackdowns on overtime. This is interpreted as a pay cut by many cops, who have begun to rediscover an old grievance—a sense of being badly underappreciated, even if, as Joe Fox pointed out to me, "a cop stubs his toe and the Mayor's at the hospital."

Some of these feelings have been whipped up by the Patrolmen's Benevolent Association, which has encouraged its members to regard themselves as inherently more deserving than other city workers. The drawn-out contract negotiations for which many cops blame the Mayor were, to a large extent, the doing of the P.B.A. With the help of the State Legislature, it had tried to create an arbitration procedure—ultimately rejected by the courts—that would have used the salaries of cops from around the state as a key yardstick. But beneath these unrealistic notions lie deeper and older complaints.

Patrol has long been termed "the backbone of the department." But when the department wants to reward a patrol officer, it does so with a transfer out of patrol, and

if he fouls up in a higher-prestige assignment, he gets bumped back down to patrol. Although there has long been talk of creating a new rank ("master patrolman," it is called in other cities) to honor outstanding cops who may not have the talent or the inclination to become sergeants or detectives, it hasn't happened. Instead, street cops tend to flee as soon as they qualify for their pensions. "Twenty and gone" remains the unofficial motto of the patrol force.

"The department doesn't care whether you stay or not," says Tommy Goldsmith, and as a case in point, he cites his former partner.

Bobby Evers is well remembered in the Seven-One. Veteran cops and bosses still tell stories about him, like the time he spent a whole day searching for a missing child and found her in a crack house in another precinct; the time he came into the station so wet from a search in the rain that he had to take off his holster and drain the water out of it; the time he personally evicted from the station a cop who had been arrested on burglary charges in the suburbs.

For all his reservations about the department, Bobby hoped to be made a sergeant, and there were those, including Fox, who considered him a natural. In 1991, after 18 years as a cop, he took the sergeant's test, despite new college requirements for sergeants. Some cops, of course, go to college during their spare time. For a cop with seven children and a moonlighting job as super of his building, college would have been a feat. Once the door had been closed, he explained one day over drinks near his security job in a midtown Manhattan office tower, retirement became irresistible because he could virtually double his income. On the other hand, he added matter-of-factly, "It was the worst thing I ever did in my life."

Ean can foresee himself being in the same predicament. College demands a lot of spare time, and "it's hard enough to have any kind of personal life." Besides, a commitment to school "alters the way you do the job," he reasons. What if he were nearing the end of a tour of duty, he asks, and had an opportunity to make a collar, but knew it would mean no sleep on the night before an important exam?

As 1996 drew to a close, his mind was on collars. At dawn on the day before Christmas, coming to the end of an uneventful midnight tour, he and Frank Incerto, a five-year man, got a burglary call on President Street. Their pulses quickened, for the precinct was experiencing a wave of burglaries—more than a dozen in a two-week period. In a few instances, the suspect had made off with expensive jewelry and had become reckless, even scary, committing his burglaries at night when his victims were home.

That particular morning, he had tried to break into two houses on the same block, the second attempt occurring moments before the cops arrived. After following the owner to the rear of his house, Evers and Incerto and two other officers searched the long alley, filled with cans and cats and fences and garages. Within a few minutes, one of the precinct sergeants radioed from the far end of the alley that he had spotted a suspect prying at a window screen of a house on Carroll Street. "He's going onto the roof," the sergeant added, as the suspect scurried upward, window to window.

In the adrenaline rush of dramas like this, cops have an unfortunate habit of converging on the center of action and creating a traffic jam. Ean did something different. He climbed a narrow fire escape to the top of a four-story apartment house on New York Avenue—the tallest building on the block. Reaching the roof and scanning the rooftops below, he caught sight of a man scrambling over a barrier between one roof and the next. As he radioed the other cops, the suspect made a furious dash to get through a security door.

"Give up!" Evers shouted at the top of his lungs.

"I ain't giving up," he shouted back.

By now, the block was hemmed in by scores of cops from the Seven-One and the neighboring Six-Seven, and several had climbed onto the row of connected rooftops. But they needed guidance from Ean, the only cop who could actually see the suspect. And that was still the case when the burglar made a crazy descent to a lower roof in the rear of one of the buildings, followed by a crazier leap to a corrugated-plastic porch roof, which nearly caved in beneath his weight. Then he started kicking at a window screen.

With visions of a possible hostage situation, Evers alerted his fellow cops and scrambled down the fire escape to the alley. He arrived next to the porch in time to see two cops on its flimsy roof, struggling with the man. After subduing and cuffing him, they lowered him into Ean's arms.

Half a dozen cops played a part in the chase and the arrest ("it was a tremendous team effort," Evers said), but the collar got credited to him. He remained at work for the next 16 hours, doing paperwork, collecting witnesses, conferring with the detectives, briefing the inspector and dealing with a prosecutor who had come out to the precinct to "ride" the case. They were 16 delicious hours. "I'm a kid—I really love this stuff," he told me afterward. "This job is a blast!"

Incorporating Diversity

Police Response to Multicultural Changes in Their Communities

BRAD R. BENNETT, D.P.A.

A great demographic change is taking place in the United States, making the population much more multicultural and diverse than it used to be. As with other kinds of social changes, law enforcement agencies must adapt to the population shifts in their communities.

This article discusses the findings of a study undertaken to determine how law enforcement agencies in four California cities responded to demographic changes that took place in their communities between 1980 and 1994. The departments in San Jose, Long Beach, Stockton, and Garden Grove[1] now police cities where African Americans, Asians, and Hispanics represent almost 50 percent of the population, an average of a 17-percent increase in the ethnic population since 1980. The departments have employed a number of strategies to best serve their changing communities.

REPRESENTATION AND INCORPORATION

All four police departments have made concerted efforts to incorporate into their organizations the varied and diverse members of their communities. Through recruiting and hiring strategies, citizen participation, training programs both for employees and community members, community outreach initiatives, and community policing, each department has embraced its diverse community groups.

Recruiting and Hiring

San Jose developed a philosophy that recognized and espouses the value of a diversified work force. This philosophy provided the fundamental ingredient that fostered the attitude necessary to lay the foundation for a successful recruiting and hiring strategy. Many of San Jose's recruiting efforts involve officers as culturally diverse as the applicants they seek. The recruiters seek out potential applicants by attending events, such as festivals and job fairs, frequented by people from a variety of ethnic backgrounds, by advertising in bilingual publications, and by offering incentives to applicants who speak more than one language.

In addition to these fairly traditional approaches, San Jose also developed some unique ways to recruit and promote ethnically diverse employees. The department's program rewards officers with up to 40 hours of paid leave if the individuals they recruit become police officers. The department also helps all officer candidates to overcome obstacles, cultural or otherwise, in preparing for the department's written tests. Mentors from ethnically diverse police officers associations within the department help newly hired officers acclimate to the department.

San Jose's efforts to incorporate representatives of diverse groups do not stop at the entry level. The department continually monitors the composition of special units, such as the detective, gang, training, and personnel units, to ensure that they represent the department and the community. Officers can serve in special units for only 3 years so that all members of the department have an opportunity to do so.

The department also incorporates diversity into its promotional procedures. Recruiting efforts and community relations are enhanced when community members from diverse backgrounds see people similar to themselves in a variety of positions and ranks throughout the department.

Similar to San Jose, the Long Beach, Garden Grove, and Stockton Police Departments have taken steps to recruit and hire personnel who reflect the cultural composition of their communities. Special emphasis has been placed on recruiting Asian applicants because of the large in-

From *FBI Law Enforcement Bulletin*, December 1995, pp. 1-6. Reprinted by permission of the U.S. Department of Justice, Federal Bureau of Investigation.

crease in Asian populations in these communities over the past decade.

All three departments hired individuals specifically to work with the Asian community and to attract more Asian applicants. Community leaders in Long Beach also help by training people within their cultural groups so they can qualify as potential candidates for positions within the police department and in city government in general. In addition, Long Beach established an Asian Affairs Advisory Committee, while Garden Grove works with the City Cultural Cohesiveness Committee to improve its recruiting efforts.

Citizen Participation

All four departments have undertaken successful efforts that bring diverse individuals into their organizations at different levels. These include civilian community service officer, reserve officer, police cadet, Law Enforcement Explorer, and Police Athletic League programs. Such initiatives provide excellent opportunities for police departments to familiarize citizens with agency operations.

These police departments also use a variety of methods for determining the concerns of community members. Forming advisory groups representative of the entire community has proven to be one effective way to establish collaborative relationships with diverse groups. Advisory groups give residents a voice and help them ensure that the department understands their unique needs and serves them in a professional manner. Such groups also prompt police agencies to be more open and responsive to the community.

In addition to forming advisory boards, departments developed neighborhood groups and solicited information through focus groups and citizen surveys. As many agencies move toward a more service-oriented, community-involved approach to policing, it will become increasingly important for the police to try to represent the wide variety of community groups in the ranks of employees and to incorporate the voices of the full range of citizens.

TRAINING

All four police departments conduct training programs to teach employees about the many cultures within their communities. The length of the programs varies tremendously, from a few-hour presentation to a week-long course.

In the two larger departments, San Jose and Long Beach, the programs are components of advanced officer training and are offered only to sworn personnel. The two smaller agencies, Stockton and Garden Grove, provide training to all employees. Most of the programs call on community members to facilitate the training, and the departments have developed rather uncommon approaches to their cultural diversity training.

In San Jose, the police chief sought input from members of the advisory broad to design the cultural diversity training program for the department. Based on their suggestions, the training starts with a segment on change. It addresses a wide range of concerns relevant to individual and organizational change, including understanding the process of change and overcoming resistance. The initial instruction and the discussions that arose from it helped to eliminate many of the barriers that often occur when dealing with new issues, ideas, and approaches.

> " . . . to be responsive to all citizens, police departments must find out what their communities need."

The Long Beach Police Department collaborated with the National Conference of Christians and Jews to develop its 40-hour cultural awareness training course for all department employees. In addition to general topics related to cultural diversity, the program addresses some nontraditional subjects of interest, such as Anglo cultures, the police culture, the homeless, and various religions.

Long Beach also emphasizes cultural diversity awareness in its basic recruit training academy. Recruits received 8 hours of classroom instruction devoted to diversity awareness, and then they spent 16 training hours with citizens from the various ethnic groups within the city. Recruits and citizens thus have an opportunity to interact in a nonconfrontational, positive way.

In addition to cultural awareness training, all four departments encourage or provide training in the various languages spoken within their communities. Bilingual or multilingual officers can be very helpful to their departments and their communities. Unfortunately, as communities become more and more diverse, the number of languages spoken increases as well, and it becomes difficult for agencies to cope. Still, by encouraging all officers to learn other languages, departments can facilitate communication with the full spectrum of community members.

COMMUNITY OUTREACH

To respond to the needs of their diverse communities, the police agencies in the study tried a variety of approaches, including police substations, citizen police academies, and youth programs. Many of these initiatives did not target ethnic neighborhoods in particular; instead, they impacted the police department's responsiveness to all community members.

Police Substations

The San Jose and Garden Grove departments have placed substations in areas where very distinct populations live. Police employees, representatives from other government agencies, and citizen volunteers who speak the residents' languages staff the substations.

Staff members work closely with merchants, apartment complex owners, and residents to ensure police responsiveness to the needs of each community. Especially in large cities, substations provide citizens the opportunity to access needed government services. They also enable government employees to establish personal relationships with community members.

Citizen Police Academies

A number of police departments across the United States have adopted citizen police academies. Through these academies, police agencies seek to educate community members about the roles and responsibilities of police officers and to familiarize the public with the departments and how they work within the community.

San Jose and Garden Grove both have citizen police academies. San Jose includes a wide variety of community members in its classes. Garden Grove requires members of its community policing advisory board to attend the academy to acquaint them with the functions, policies, and operations of the police department.

As noted, to be responsive to all citizens, police departments must find out what their communities need. Similarly, departments also should educate their communities about the functions of the police department, as well as any changes that occur within the department. An open exchange of information between each community and its police department promotes understanding and greater cooperation.

Youth Programs

All four departments have developed youth-centered programs to enhance their relationships with young people in their communities. These programs generally focus on at-risk youth, who often come from culturally diverse backgrounds.

Initiatives include assigning beat officers to schools, conducting educational programs, and sponsoring Police Athletic Leagues. Officers teach Drug and Alcohol Resistance Education (D.A.R.E.), participate in after-school activities, and become involved in the schools as role models, mentors, and counselors.

Involving diverse youth in Law Enforcement Explorer and police cadet programs also has proven advantageous. Youngsters learn self-discipline and often develop improved self-esteem. For students interested in law enforcement careers, these programs expose them to the department and provide them opportunities to learn about policing.

"A common theme became apparent during the study of these four California police departments: Leadership makes a difference."

Through these programs, the departments have focused on getting the police and young people together in positive circumstances. Relationships between police and children have improved tremendously in the schools where officers have been assigned. Young people and officers get involved with each other in positive settings that benefit both groups. Positive contacts made through these programs often translate into improved relationships between officers and the children's families as they interact outside the school environment.

COMMUNITY POLICING

Many members of the law enforcement profession believe that community policing provides the best method for being responsive to and involved in the community. As an organizational philosophy, it promotes a set of values and corresponding procedures that form the basis for police-community interaction to solve problems. Community policing reverses the notion that the police have sole responsibility for maintaining public order, recognizing instead that the community at large is responsible for the conditions that generate crime.

Empowering the community to solve its own problems is the key to making community policing work. This means that the police and members of the community—neighbors, families, individuals, schools, organizations, churches, and businesses—must accept the challenge to assume joint responsibility for the community's safety and well-being.

The four departments studied, similar to many police agencies across the country, have taken steps to implement community policing. Many of the initiatives already described are components of those efforts. Most of the agency personnel interviewed for this study believe that this approach offers the best opportunity for responding effectively to changing and diverse communities. Only by listening to and working with community members can the police determine what needs to be done and how best to do it.

Officers in San Jose, Stockton, and Garden Grove were reassigned from normal patrol duties to specific neighborhoods. These officers formed partnerships with community groups to identify and solve neighborhood problems. The police arranged their priorities based on the problems identified by residents. Some of the strategies employed by these departments for solving community problems included community surveys, meetings, education, and involvement; neighborhood cleanups; citizen patrols; school and youth programs; government and social service involvement; and community empowerment initiatives.

Increased Population Diversity

During the 1980s, 6 million people legally immigrated to the United States. In the previous two decades combined, only 7.4 million immigrants legally entered the country. Census information shows that between 1980 and 1990 the country's population of Asians doubled, from 1.5 percent to 3 percent of the U.S. population. The Hispanic population grew by half, from 6.4 percent to 9 percent of the population by 1990. Despite the rapid growth among immigrant groups, African Americans continue to be the largest minority group in the United States, representing 12.1 percent of the population in 1990.

The diversity of the United States is expected to expand even more. Projections by the U.S. Census Bureau suggest that Asians will continue to be the fastest-growing race in America, reaching 11 percent of the population by the year 2050. Hispanics are expected to eclipse African Americans as the largest minority group by the year 2010 and to increase to 21 percent of the population by 2050. By that year, the number of African Americans probably will rise to 16 percent of the total population, while the number of whites will fall from 75 percent to 53 percent of the population. By 2050, the U.S. population will be divided almost evenly between minorities and non-Hispanic whites.[4]

Source: Chris Swingle, "U.S. Minorities Expected to Grow by 2050," *Democrat and Chronicle*, Rochester, New York, December 1992, 1.

The San Jose, Stockton, Long Beach, and Garden Grove departments are all moving toward implementing community policing departmentwide. These departments believe that to be successful they must involve all stakeholders in tailoring their philosophies and processes to meet the specific needs of their communities. Department employees, as well as community members, must participate in the development of community policing as a law enforcement approach in order for it to be effective. Such participation raises two important sets of expectations—those between individual employees and the police organization and those between the community members and the organization. Police leaders must work to balance these expectations in order to move effectively toward community policing.

To begin this process, the agencies formed internal committees composed of a cross-section of department members to determine the particular approach most suitable for each department. After establishing a general internal philosophy and approach, representatives from the agencies then met with community members to design specific strategies for the various communities within their cities.

Everyone involved in implementing community policing should recognize that it is not a fixed or standardized program. It is not a structured model of policing that can be replicated and transferred from agency to agency with ease. Rather, departments must adopt philosophies and approaches that meet the unique needs of their communities. Only in this way will community policing provide the promised benefits for police departments who want to serve their diverse communities effectively.

LEADERSHIP

A common theme became apparent during the study of these four California police departments: Leadership makes a difference. New leaders in each organization led all four departments in making significant strides toward enhanced responsiveness to their communities. Interviews with department members revealed that what distinguished the new leaders from their predecessors was the ability to translate intentions into realities. Because they could deal effectively with their constituencies both inside and outside the organization, these leaders could turn their visions for their departments into action and reality.[2]

The current leaders reorganized the influence of relationships among the agency, the individual employees, and the community members on organizational responsiveness. The leaders first addressed internal issues, because it is important to attend to employees' needs before addressing the needs of the community. Next, they developed strategies for dealing with police-community relationships.

These strategies reflect both a concern for community problems and a social responsibility that goes beyond law enforcement. They include service dimensions that recognize that crime prevention is a community matter and suggest that the police broaden their approach beyond merely responding to crime. The approaches adopted by the leaders of all four agencies recognize that the police must become more

Ethnic Changes in Total Population

	1980 Ethnic Population	1990 Ethnic Population	Increase
San Jose	36%	50.4%	14.4%
Long Beach	33%	50.5%	17.5%
Stockton	43%	56.0%	13.0%
Garden Grove	22%	45.3%	23.3%

problem-oriented; they must scrutinize problems, obtain as much information as possible from everyone involved or affected, and only then develop solutions.[3]

CONCLUSION

All four agencies set the goal of being responsive to their changing communities. As shown by the various strategies and programs employed by each agency, there are many ways to achieve that goal. Developing positive relationships with young people from diverse backgrounds, actively seeking input on departmental operations from the full spectrum of community members, conducting imaginative police training in the areas of cultural sensitivity and improved communication, and adopting the community policing philosophy moved these agencies toward their goals.

There is no guarantee that every effort to improve police service to a changing and diverse society will be successful. Yet, these four agencies show that imaginative and resourceful moves toward responding to changes in their communities can be made.

The United States historically has been noted for incorporating people from all over the world into a common society. Once again, the country is being called upon to open its arms to people from many backgrounds, and police departments must do their part. By embracing all segments of their communities, agencies can tap into the vast resources of their many members. By drawing on those strengths, the police and the public can work together to make communities safer for everyone.

Endnotes

1. The 1990 census showed the population of these cities as: San Jose, 782,248; Long Beach, 429,423; Stockton, 226,255; and Garden Grove, 149,700.

2. Warren Bennis, "The Artform of Leadership," in *Public Administration in Action*, ed. Robert B. Denhardt and Barry Hammond (Pacific Grove, CA: Brooks/Cole Publishing, 1992), 311–315.

3. Roy Roberg and Jack Kuykendall, *Police Organization and Management, Behavior, Theory, and Processes* (Pacific Grove, CA: Brooks/Cole Publishing, 1990), 48–52.

Law Enforcement News interview
by Marie Simonetti Rosen

"Character" is a word—and a concept—chock full of definitions and naunces. Character is the aggregate of features and traits that form a person's nature. It is also used to describe a body of moral qualities, ethical standards, principles and the like—as in, "a person of character." Edwin J. Delattre, the author of "Character and Cops," has been focusing his attention on the ethics of policing for more than a decade. His interest encompasses not only the individual officer but also the nature of the organizations in which they serve.

Delattre is a professor of philosophy and education and the Dean of the School of Education at Boston University. He received a bachelor's degree from the University of Virginia in 1963 and a Ph.D. from the University of Texas seven years later. He has also written extensively in the areas of education, police ethics, organized crime and gangs. His working life also includes time for service as an adjunct scholar of the American Enterprise Institute for Public Policy Research in Washington.

For Delattre, policing is a higher calling, and the responsibility that goes along with the public trust is an awesome one. He is a strong believer in high standards, from the selection process to leadership. Nowadays, with policing seeming to be placing more emphasis on ethics in their police academies, he has some advice: Don't separate ethics from the main body of education and training; incorporate it into all academy and field training. An ethics course that stands alone is doomed, he says, because recruits will get the impression that *"it has nothing really to do with the rest of their training and responsibilities."* As important, he believes that ethics must be seen to be believed. *"You can talk about ethics from now till doomsday; there's no evidence that any course on ethics ever taught in human history made anybody a better person."*

Given his background in education, it is no surprise that Delattre has strong opinions when it comes to sensitivity training—the type usually imposed in the aftermath of a critical incident. He feels that this type of training often treats officers as if they were patients thereby ruining the possibility of genuine education. *"If you've got some lesson that needs to be taught in the department, the people ought to be treated as students, not as patients as if there were something wrong with them."*

That's not to say, however, that Delattre is opposed to training. To be sure he is a strong proponent of ongoing training—training that is well integrated within the entire department. For starters, he believes that training personnel should be "rolled in and out of the academy" on a regular basis to keep them in touch with [the] street. Field training is also an area that should be strengthened in many departments by selecting officers who have good teaching skills. Academy and in-service training, he states, should not be thought of as separate entities.

Delattre is on the road a lot. He's frequently invited by law enforcement agencies to lecture on police ethics and integrity, and has made such appearances from coast to coast, on behalf of law enforcement organizations in New York, California, Ohio, Rhode Island, Michigan, North Carolina and Florida. He is a regular speaker at the FBI's National Academy and National Police Executive Institute. Those who have had the opportunity to hear him speak are usually left wanting more than ever to go forth and do the right thing. And for Delattre, that's the essence of integrity—doing the right thing even when you know no one else is looking.

A LEN interview with

Prof. Edwin J. Delattre of Boston University

Author of "Character & Cops"

"It's long been recognized in political philosophy and political theory that virtue has a better chance of triumphing if you can get virtue and self-interest on the same side of the ledger, rather than in conflict with each other."

LAW ENFORCEMENT NEWS: You've stated that you are "shocked and alarmed" by educational programs on ethics for police that stress "appearances" and "perceptions" rather than actualities. Could you elaborate?

DELATTRE: When you teach people that perception is everything, or the only thing that matters is how things are perceived by somebody or other, you really denigrate reality. You claim that facts don't matter, that the truth doesn't matter, that evidence doesn't matter, and you end up in a situation where you have to pander to whatever somebody's perception happens to be. I walk into the police academies, and sometimes they have mirrors by the front door, and on top of the mirror is a sign that teaches recruits and others that perception is everything. I recently worked for a department that has great problems of brutality and corruption. In their in-service education programs they begin with a quote that says perception is the only thing.

When an institution supposes that perception is the only reality, it inevitably becomes windblown, because perceptions are fickle. You end up trying to satisfy everybody and not standing for anything. Look at the history in this country of police leaders, precinct commanders and the like who look the other way when there is corruption or brutality on their own watch because they think it's better for their careers if it's not discovered while they're there. They place the perception of a clean operation above the truth and above fidelity to the public trust. When organizations are slavishly adoring of perceptions, they won't stand by

convinced they cannot trust their leader to stand by them in the face of political and media pressure, that agency sows the seeds of its own internal decline. . . .

DELATTRE: Sure. The mission withers because most of us will not put things that matter to us at risk unless we think that people we have a right to trust will back us up.

LEN: Let's say you have a use-of-force situation where there are some questionable aspects to it, and the mayor immediately comes out and says, "Yep, we're going to indict the officer." Or the reverse happens, where an officer really has used excessive force, yet the mayor backs that officer up in the face of public concern. What responsibility do you think the leader of a city or a community has in terms of standing up for reality rather than perception?

DELATTRE: The mayor is not the chief of police, and the mayor is not the district attorney. When the mayor starts making pronouncements about what they're going to do in specific cases, the mayor is behaving as if he or she *were* the chief of police or the

---

"If such a course [on ethics and human dignity] is expected to stand all by itself, it's doomed to failure because then newcomers get the impression that it has nothing really to do with . . . the responsibilities they'll have on a daily basis."

---

their own people, and they won't stand by the public interest either. If an organization tends to treat perception as the only thing to be feared and to be driven by—I've had the experience in some departments of being on the street with cops in a cruiser, and they'll see some potentially volatile situation on the streets, and they'll just say, "I'm not getting involved in that." They know perfectly well that no matter how good a job they do if they stop, it could go south and nobody will back them up. That's what happens when the adoration of perception undermines all respect for reality. And to be teaching people that good policing, good law enforcement and fidelity to the public trust requires a slavish devotion to perception is as dangerous as anything I can imagine teaching. What I said in the preface to the book was, suppose you perceive me as your true and loyal friend, when in fact I'm a hypocrite and a cheat and a liar, and the first chance I get to take advantage of you for my own gratification on a big enough scale, I'm going to take it. Now which matters most, your mistaken perception, or the truth about it?

LEN: Let's look a little further at the idea you mentioned a moment ago that when honorable police are

district attorney. That's imprudent. It's a failure to understand the boundaries of one's own authority and responsibility.

The most important thing is that a police chief or leader who's responsible to a mayor in matters of policy can't run a department by a strategy of pre-emptive capitulation, by just acquiescing in whatever the mayor does, whether the mayor wants to micromanage the department or make all policy statements about internal matters in the department. A chief who will pre-emptively capitulate has just destroyed the possibility of leadership of the department itself. Now, it's obviously a fact that lots of political figures are politically windblown and stand for their own careers more than they stand for the public interest. That doesn't mean that everybody has to bow to their wishes when they're out of bounds. A police chief who says, "Well, whatever the mayor wants," has just thrown away any hope the department has of living up to the public trust.

LEN: Looking back over time, do you feel that more police leaders are losing their nerve when it comes to going against what a mayor wants?

DELATTRE: No, that's not my impression. A lot of the police chiefs, superintendents and commissioners that I know are more than reasonably long on courage. Where something that matters to them might be at risk, I don't find that they routinely capitulate in things that they shouldn't. Obviously, I meet some who do, and sometimes when I'm invited to work with departments, it's because the leadership has gone awry. But as far as the proposition that somehow the police chiefs and commissioners are not standing on the high ground as much as they used to—no, I don't see any evidence of that.

A reflection on society

LEN: The idea of maintaining high standards is central to the work that you've done. You've heartily disagreed with the notion that police wrongdoing can be chalked up to police reflecting the society from which they come. You go on to say that efforts that reduce police education and training to therapy intended to make police sensitive are doomed to failure. Could you explain that?

guage backgrounds, and it's important for them to know things that matter to people, irrespective of color or gender or linguistic or ethnic background. But that's very different from saying, oh, well, it's just a microcosm. The recruitment, training, supervision and accountability are all intended to say that this institution and the people in it bear the public trust. They have the right, the authority and sometimes the duty to abridge individual liberty. For that reason, it just won't do to say that anybody who is a member of society is fit to be here.

Now that doesn't mean that the applicant pools won't reflect the general composition and makeup of the society as a whole. That being said, the department has to be very good at background investigations, job-related relevant considerations in the fitness of people in terms of talent, in terms of accomplishment, in terms of character, habits of behavior and the rest that befit them to accept responsibility that affects profoundly the lives of others, who will also be dependent on them in grim, demanding, challenging services. Now the business of therapy is that therapy treats people as patients. Education treats people as students. If you've got some lesson that needs to be taught in the department, the people ought to be

---

"There are no lessons to be learned from that [O. J. Simpson] trial or the aftermath—there are only old lessons to be remembered."

DELATTRE: The first is what I call the microcosm argument, which holds that you have to expect things like the beating of Rodney King, or the attitudes of Mark Fuhrman and things of that sort, or exhibitions of incompetence by police, because you have all sorts of evils in society as a whole, including incompetence and bigotry and alcohol abuse and drug use and dishonesty and corruption and bribery and racism and sexism—all these ills that humanity has always been afflicted with in one way or another. The argument runs that you have to expect to find these same things in roughly the same proportion in any institution that's part of the society because the institutions are just a microcosm of the society as a whole. That's not true, of course. People generally enter society by being born, but you don't enter a police department by being born. Police departments are selective, and they are authorized and required to be selective precisely so they won't be mere microcosms of the society. It's important for them to be diverse in a variety of ways, including linguistic accomplishments and the ability to communicate with people of different lan-

treated as students, not as patients as if there were something wrong with them. The worst sorts of things that happen in a generic way are that somebody in the department does something wrong as a racist or a sexist or in some other way that does not befit anybody in a position of public trust, and the department immediately treats everybody as though they need therapy, thereby imputing to them attitudes, beliefs and the like that they may not have at all. If you start treating police as patients in need of some cure where you haven't any evidence that that's true at all, you just ruin the possibility of education.

LEN: A recent survey by Law Enforcement News of police department policies regarding applicants' prior drug use seemed to suggest a consensus view that departments would find it all but impossible to recruit if they had policies barring any prior use of drugs at any time in an applicant's past. What are the implications of a dilemma like this?

DELATTRE: It helps to distinguish what's in character for a person from what isn't. All of us were young once, and some of us still are. Gilbert Highet, the great classicist at Columbia, was right to say that many of the problems of the young are attributable to their youth. All of us, I take it, have done things in our youth that we are ashamed of and that we wish we hadn't done. The question is whether behavior that is indifferent to the well-being of others, indifferent to destruction of oneself and the like, is in character for a person or out of character. I mean, that somebody does something once that's out of character is not by any means sufficient grounds to say, well, this person could never be fit to bear a public trust. I don't know whether it's true that applicant pools would be made impossible if everybody were disqualified who had ever used an illegal drug at all. The numbers of people might be considerably reduced, and I don't judge that to be a good thing by any means. I know young men and women who experimented with marijuana, who smoked it a few times, and who then realized that it was inimical to what they aspired to as people and quit. I don't view them as somehow unfit to bear the public trust. They regret what they did. So I don't think anybody should have a formula that says any illegal drug use and you're simply unfit to work here.

Where the drug use has been habitual, long term, or in character for the person, a lot of other very unattractive, unappealing kinds of behavior are also going to be in character for that person. And it seems to me that one wants to be very careful about admitting anyone to public service where indifference to the safety and well-being of others, indifference to the law has been shown to be in character. Obviously the Americans with Disabilities Act says you can't disqualify anyone who has been addicted and has had treatment and is now clean. It's a tremendously unwise feature of law to treat the acquisition of a bad habit as if it were a congenital disability. But even the law doesn't have the implication that, if a person has shown bad habits to be in character, that the person has to be accepted for employment. The risk, of course, is that there are departments where the legal counsel and the leadership of the department are so frightened of ADA that they just don't want to know about histories of prior use, and that's effectively to say, "Well, we're going to require the public to trust people that we don't have any idea whether the people deserve to be trusted." That's a failure of leadership on a grand scale.

LEN: Many departments around the country use psychological tests and background checks to get a suitable recruit. To the extent that departments do not skimp on this process, do you think such testing works?

DELATTRE: My experience is that it can give you pretty much the information you need to find somebody who is obviously and dramatically unqualified and unfit for the responsibilities of the office. I don't

know that they can be relied on for anything much more subtle than that. There are probably people who know better than I do, but I've never seen evidence that they could cut to a finer grain than that. The background investigation conducted by really good investigators, the personal interview conducted by people who know what kinds of attitudes, dispositions and habits, what kinds of judgment and communication are really essential to effective policing—those things strike me as enormously important, even irreplaceable. So does real vigilance in the course on training, not only academy training, but field training and subsequent supervision during a probationary period. Those things have to be done by people who really know what they're doing and who know what to look for, and my experience is that that's a much more refined way of finding out everything you need to know than a mere psychological test.

How to teach ethics

LEN: When it comes to training and ethics, what kind of program would you recommend? Do you think a special course in ethics is the way to go in police academy training?

DELATTRE: It's perfectly all right to have a course devoted to constitutional heritage and the obligations of police under the Constitution, and what an oath of allegiance to the Constitution means in daily life. You can explain the principle of human dignity and how the idea of minimum necessary force follows from it, and so on. But if such a course is expected to stand all by itself, it's doomed to failure because then the newcomers get the impression that it has nothing really to do with the rest of their training and the responsibilities they'll have on a daily basis. They will treat the ethics sessions as irrelevant to what they really know to be policing. There has to be a resonance between what you do in any course on ethics and what's done in all the other courses in programs of education. So, for example, when you explain to people that you're trying to make them competent with respect to policy and practice as it relates, say, to traffic chases, it's worth making the point that when you voluntarily accept responsibilities that affect the lives of others, you also accept the duty to become good at the fulfillment of those responsibilities. This is something you need to know, you need to be competent at it in order to be good at your duties, so that becoming competent in these matters has ethical consequences. That kind of resonance is essential to affecting the culture of the institution and the expectations of the people who work in it in the right way.

The other thing is that ethics has to be seen to be believed. You can talk about ethics till doomsday; there's no evidence that any course on ethics ever taught in human history made anybody a better person. I know lots of philosophers who are very good in all sorts of reasoning about ethical problems and dilemmas, but I wouldn't trust them as far as I could throw them. And it's not just a conceptual matter; it's a matter of disposition, of respect for persons, of not being so focused on your own self-gratification that you're willing to manipulate others and deceive them and the rest. In practice, people are most affected by considerations of ethics when they see people who are just quietly and unassumingly decent, and that matters more than any course in ethics that was ever taught.

LEN: All the time, it seems, events occur that have a national impact on policing—the O. J. Simpson trial being one recent notable example. What changes in policing do you see as a result of that case?

DELATTRE: In the third edition of "Character and Cops" I included a chapter on the O. J. Simpson trial and race, and I asked the question, "What new lessons were there for police to learn from the trial and the verdict and its aftermath?" The conclusion that I reached was that there are no lessons to be learned from that trial or the aftermath—there are only old lessons to be remembered. I go into some detail as to what those lessons are, all of which are known to police who take their work seriously: about fair-minded-

juries that make decisions so fast that the plausibility of deliberation is minimal. No new lessons in this.

The greatest danger, I think, from the trial is the extent to which the media portrayed all of us as if we were mere members of groups, and not individual human beings. It was as if everybody who is one color has to think this, and everybody who's another color has to think that. You end up with this proliferation of stereotypes of people as mere members of groups with no individual responsibility, no individual autonomy, no individual independence of judgment, no real significance as an individual human being. That's inimical to everything the United States is intended, at its best, to serve. It's inimical to the Bill of Rights. It's inimical to the idea that everybody, as an individual, is innocent until proven guilty. In the chapter I urged that we had to be able to recognize individuals as human beings, and not as mere members of groups identified by color or ethnicity or gender or native-language background, and that if the Simpson trial didn't remind us of that, we were losing an opportunity for good reflection on what counts most.

LEN: In that vein, over the past few years policing has experienced a number of reverse discrimination cases in the area of promotions. What are the ethical issues that surround affirmative action goals?

"There are people who claim that the free cup of coffee is a slippery slope, and everybody who starts that way ends up taking bribes. That's perfect nonsense; it isn't true. . . . But it has its risks."

---

ness toward the public; about the imperative for justice that's embedded in the preamble to the Constitution; about the imperative for honesty, not giving false testimony, filing false reports, committing perjury, and so on. What one sees in that trial, as in others, is people in various responsibilities, not just police, who don't take those ideals of justice and honesty and so on very seriously. The trial doesn't teach us anything new about the media and their capacity to be irrational and to act with indifference to the public interest. It doesn't teach us anything new about prosecutors who don't do the homework they ought to do. It doesn't teach us anything new about judges who are not really in control of their own courtrooms. It doesn't teach us anything new about the length of trials of people who are accused of murdering members of their own family. It doesn't teach us anything new about

DELATTRE: I've been concerned about affirmative action as a matter of law and policy for a long time, and I said in the first edition of "Character and Cops" in 1988 that I was opposed to affirmative action because I believed that rights inhere in individuals and not in groups. I feared that the idea of compensatory justice for people who had not suffered any identifiable wrong would produce great and understandable resentments that would hurt institutions intended to serve the public. I also urged that no matter what the law was, whether it supported affirmative action, required affirmative action or not, that when you entered a high calling like policing, you had a duty to make the very best of it under the terms the law allowed, and if you really didn't have the stomach for that, you ought to pick a less demanding line of work. I pointed out at the same time that this is not something about the imputation of bad motives or accusations against people.

Some of the best people I've ever known believe that I'm wrong about affirmative action. In the years since then, some of the authors of affirmative action, like Joseph Califano, have argued that the time for affirmative action has passed. I think they're right about that. So while I insist that departments, in order to serve the public faithfully, need to pursue real diversity, I don't think it ought to be done so that it adversely affects merit. I don't think it has to affect merit adversely in the slightest. If you combine the expectation of rapid expansion of a department with a residency requirement, thereby dramatically limiting your applicant pool, there is, as we've seen in the cities of the United States, a great risk that the standards will be thrown to the winds. But that has nothing to do with anybody's color or anybody's ethnic or gender characteristics; it has to do with limiting the pool dramatically, and then taking people irrespective of color or gender who are simply not fit to bear the public trust. It doesn't matter whether you're white or black or what you are. It seems to me that any kind of wise leader dealing with a diverse public is going to recognize that the mission of the police can't be fulfilled without very good people who are capable of communicating with the public and of being in service and of being welcomed by the public. But my own experience and my own work as a philosopher militates against affirmative action.

Riding a cycle?

LEN: For most people, it would seem, the No. 1 ethical issue in policing is that of corruption. There are those observers who have suggested that police corruption within a department is a cyclical thing—here in New York, for example, it seems to be a 20-year cycle. Would you agree?

DELATTRE: I think that's silly. It may be true that there are major discoveries every 20 years or so. But the things that the Mollen Commission discovered, and that the New York Police Department discovered in the first place that led to the Mollen Commission, they didn't wait 20 years to happen. Some of those things had been going on, and no doubt some of them are still going on. I've worked in investigations and cases of corruption and the falsification of evidence and so on—I worked on one not long ago where from the time it was discovered to the time where it began, there was a span of 11 years. It wasn't that the department was in no way vigilant about those things; it was not all that easy to discover. But the idea that it just explodes into corruption every 20 years or so seems to me nonsense. Some of the patterns in the ways of introducing people into

corruption have been long-standing. Anybody who thinks you're going to take a big institution and that any kind of reform is going to eliminate all the corruption in it and leave no place where the soil is fertile for the growth of corruption, anybody who thinks that doesn't understand human nature and doesn't understand human institutions.

LEN: Do you think police departments do a good job of policing themselves?

DELATTRE: I think some don't. Some of them are awful at it. Some have long histories of not policing themselves at all. Others are assiduous and conscientious at it, irrespective of their size, and, I would infer from my work with them, have very low levels of corruption within them. Nothing that resembles institutionalized corruption. But what have you got, 15,000 police departments in the country? Anybody who tries to generalize about their condition with respect to resistance to corruption, or peer pressure that weighs against corruption rather than in its favor, anybody who tries to generalize about that is at risk, save in one respect. And that is, in most of the departments I've ever worked with, the idea that some substantial majority of the sworn and civilian people were dirty would be just a canard. There's nothing that would have persuaded me to think that with respect to most departments. I've seen a handful that I thought were pretty much dirty through and through, but not many.

LEN: Generally speaking, the corruption of the 1970s was a type that manifested itself around greed. With the '80s and '90s it seemed to change, so that greed went hand in hand with brutality. For example, where in the 70s, an officer may have been paid to look away while a drug dealer or a vice operation conducted business, now the officer might be just as likely [to] beat up the drug dealer in addition to taking his money and drugs. Do you see anything in that?

DELATTRE: In the 21 years I've been working for the police, I've seen it both ways all along, much of it related to selfishness and self-deception. Lots of people who are greedy are able to convince themselves that they're not, and they convince themselves that everybody else is getting some and they're not, and they're making all the sacrifices, and they're underappreciated, underpaid, and so what's the difference if they take a little. They're grass eaters for the most part. Sometimes people are able to deceive themselves by saying, well, I'm dealing out punishment. The criminal justice system doesn't work; the courts don't work, [m]any guys are back on the street before we finish the paperwork, and so I'm not only going to rip them off; I'm going to give them a little dose of what they deserve in addition. But notice that those are tandem kinds of self-deception, and ways of giving oneself power to which one has no right. That doesn't mean that everyone who's capable of self-deception is going to think of it for himself. Once you get things popping up, people of weak or bad character are likely to take on those ways of doing things themselves. I can't remember the first time I saw corruption conjoined with brutality, but it must be at least 15 years ago. I don't think there's anything new about it.

Super vision

LEN: What about the role of supervisory officers when it comes to making sure that there isn't any corruption and that the officers under them are kept at a pretty high level of ethics and integrity?

DELATTRE: Clarity and open ears are the most important things. That is to say, you have to listen to others. You have to be in communication with them and paying attention to them. You have to be explicit about your expectations, rooted in the policies of the

coffee, but look what he does?" You can't self-righteously set an example; you have to be a particular kind of person and hope that others will look to you and say, "Yeah, this person really rings true when he says, 'We don't take, we don't beat up on suspects in custody, we don't falsify reports.' That's just exactly the way the person really is." There's no other way to achieve that that I've ever heard of.

LEN: We know of some departments where police chiefs have sent letters to local chains like 7–11, asking them—not always successfully—not to give free coffee to officers. What can a chief do in terms of dealing with the private sector to stop this[?] Or maybe before we get to that, what makes the idea of free coffee such a big deal?

DELATTRE: Well, there are people who claim that the free cup of coffee is a slippery slope, and everybody who starts that way ends up taking bribes. That's perfect nonsense; it isn't true. I know lots of cops who take a free cup of coffee and don't take a

---

"Sometimes you can show the better light in which internal affairs deserves to be cast by showing how unappealing the alternatives are."

---

department, nothing tongue in cheek. I've seen people beat up suspects in custody when there was no chance that their supervisors didn't know it. You stop them and say, "Wait a minute, what do you think you're doing; this is against the law; it's against policy. Stop right now." They don't care whether it's illegal; they just want the results. Given the slightest impression that that's true is a license for wrongdoing and exceeding one's authority. This doesn't mean fulminating about standards and all that. It means forging a department in which the voice of recruitment, the voice of academy training, the voice of field training, the voice of supervision all the way to the top is one voice, and the ways of behaving are one way of behaving with respect to matters of character and integrity. This is how we do things here; this is how I do things here in the interest of justice and public service that can be trusted. It's not only that the price of freedom is eternal vigilance; it's that the price of decent supervision is paying attention, listening to your people about what they're up against and seeing what you can do to make their responsibilities meetable by them. And it surely requires neither looking the other way nor behaving in ways so that subordinates can say, "Well, he gets all upset when we take a cup of

free meal, and certainly wouldn't take a bribe. But it has its risks. You're in a place, you're likely to go there more often, so they get better protection than others. There are unfairnesses that result from it. There are also public resentments when people see that somebody gets something free, lots of them will realize that they're paying for it. I've encouraged police that if something is free, leave a tip that is the equivalent of the price of the meal. Likewise for the cup of coffee. If you have a cup of coffee, and they won't take the money, leave a tip there for the service person. As far as the chiefs, better than a letter, it seems to me, would be meeting with business people, saying: "Look, here are the effects of giving things to the police free or at a discount. They are not good things for the public interest, and they are not good things for the police department. I'd be grateful if you wouldn't do it. If you persist in it, I'm going to tell my people that they aren't ever to leave their precinct to go to a place that gives discounts or freebies."

But a sense of proportion is required in this. I've worked with departments where things were in pretty good shape, and it made sense to take on gratuities of a modest sort. I've worked in other departments where the problems of corruption and brutality were far greater. A person who takes on the free-cup-of-coffee issue under those circumstances has no sense of proportion. As a leader, you're only likely to have an agenda of four or five things that you have any hope of accomplishing in several years. If you squander your assets on what are relative trifles, given the circumstances of your department, you won't get to any of the major issues. So how far I would press on small-scale gratuities depends very much on the circumstances of the department involved.

Where the rookies meet the road

LEN: You observed earlier how a department has to speak with one voice from recruitment to academy training, in-service training, and all the way up the line. Yet there's always been this phenomenon in policing where a person goes through the academy and learns what to do and how to act, and then they go into the field, and they're told, "Well, that's what the academy says, but, this is how it's really done." What can a department do to bridge that gap?

DELATTRE: I think it's a very good idea to roll people in and out of academy jobs so that they're current on the streets. Yet you have academy faculty, who are so distant from the streets that it will be credible to recruits when FTOs say, "Yeah, you heard that from so-and-so, but so-and-so hasn't been on the streets in 15 years and doesn't know what's going on out here." The recruit is going to listen to the FTO. If you're rolling people in and out of the academy so they're current, if you're bringing people into the academy people whose performance on the street is distinguished, whether of rank or of experience as master officers, talking about the way things should be done on the street and the way they do them, the question of credibility is met head-on and early. The other thing is that FTOs and academy people ought to be meeting together, talking about common purposes. That means that FTOs and academy people have to be very carefully chosen. There are departments where the FTO job is nothing but a 5-percent, 6-percent, 7-percent salary increase, and they don't take into account in any serious way whether the FTO has any skills as a teacher or is particularly deft at anticipating the sorts of things that go wrong in the course of the evolution and maturation of a police officer. Closer ties between supervisors to whom FTOs are accountable and academy supervisors and to both the FTOs and the academy teachers are salutary. But as long as you think of it as two different and distinct enterprises, where you're got the academy and you've got the field, you lose.

LEN: A number of European police systems start with an academy and field training period that is at least two years long. Do you think that might be a good approach for American police to look at?

DELATTRE: I'd welcome it; it puts real flesh on the idea of in-service education and training, and it gives a natural coherence to the academy and the street. There's a sense in which there's more to talk about once the newcomers have been out there a while. It's expensive doing that, and for lots of departments where retirements are a big factor and rapid expansion is a big factor, that would be very hard to accomplish, which means that, however good the idea is, lots of places in this country simply wouldn't be able to do it. But that doesn't forestall them from very good integration of academy and field training and supervision.

Welcome to the family

LEN: In many police departments, the internal affairs unit is treated like a bastard child. In New York City, to cite one example, when they were revamping internal affairs after the Mollen Commission hearings, many good officers opted to retire rather than accept reassignment to Internal Affairs. Is there anything that internal affairs can do, or can anything be done for them, to address this state of affairs?

DELATTRE: It's long been recognized in political philosophy and political theory that virtue has a better chance of triumphing if you can get virtue and self-interest on the same side of the ledger, rather than in conflict with each other. One of the smarter things that the New York City Police Department did was to make internal affairs assignments a gateway to attractive investigative assignments in other areas: organized crime, homicide, and so on. It seems to me that's a good idea. It won't apply that much to people who are eligible to retire and would rather retire than be associated with internal affairs. But it does have a significant prospect for people who are not nearing retirement. That sort of thing seems to me essential.

No matter how conscientiously internal affairs is run, and no matter how fair it is to the personnel in the department, I'm not convinced that it's possible to overcome a certain resistance to internal affairs, or a certain resolve not to be part of it. Most of what I do in talking with police about internal affairs is to say, look, you really have a choice between responsible and conscientious investigations of alleged wrongdoing in your own institution, or letting somebody else do it. And there's a very great risk that the people from the outside who do it, if you don't do it well yourselves, are going to have political ambitions of their own or agendas of their own that are not very compatible with the idea of innocent until proven guilty. You've got to decide which you think is a) likely to yield a better department, and b) likely to yield greater fairness to you. I think that when you cast it in those lights, and say to people look, it's either/or, it's not going to be neither. It's not as though you're going to be spared this, that if you didn't have internal affairs things were somehow going to be better. In terms of the quality of investigations, things are likely to be a good bit worse, and a good bit more public, and with a good bit of irresponsibility thrown into the bargain. So sometimes you can show the better light in which internal affairs deserves to be cast by showing how unappealing the alternatives are.

LEN: At a recent panel discussion, someone in the audience interpreted your work by saying, in essence, that you believe highly ethical officers are born, not made. Your reaction?

DELATTRE: Nothing could be further from the truth. Everything in my work explains that character is second nature, not first nature. Our character is the disposition and habits we acquire by luck, by guidance, by training over time—and some by accident. Nobody's born with habits, but everybody's born a creature of imitation and a creature who will form habits. Indeed, the overwhelming question is what kind of habits and dispositions we acquire, how we think of others, how we think of ourselves, whether we acquire habits and dispositions of justice and temperance and courage and of refusing to manipulate others for our own gratification by deception. Those are all things that are achieved and acquired. I don't know who was representing my work, but for better or worse, the person didn't understand a bit of what my work is about.

Judicial System

The courts are an equal partner in the American justice system. Just as the police have the responsibility of guarding our liberties by enforcing the law, the courts play an important role in defending these liberties by applying the law. The courts are where civilized "wars" are fought, individual rights are protected, and disputes are peacefully settled.

The articles in this unit discuss several issues concerning the judicial process. Ours is an adversary system of justice, and the protagonists, the State, and the defendant are usually represented by counsel.

The lead article, "Adversarial Justice," asserts that the reliance we place in our adversarial trial court system to deliver just decisions is a misguided leap of faith. Author Franklin Strier maintains that the exclusive responsibility for presenting evidence is assigned to attorneys, whose goal is victory, not enlightenment. In "Day of Reckoning," James Collins reported that the trial jury that found Timothy McVeigh guilty in the Oklahoma City bombing trial struggled with great emotion as it prepared to decide his fate.

The views of Judge Harold Rothwax, as expressed in " 'We're in the Fight of Our Lives,' " should provoke vigorous reaction. Rothwax advocates for the elimination of the exclusionary rule and the unanimous jury verdict requirement. Additionally, peremptory challenges should be restricted, according to Rothwax. What is "jury nullification"? Andrew Leipold discusses the nullification decision, which occurs when jurors in a criminal case acquit the defendant, despite their belief that he or she was guilty of the crime charged. Then, Professor James Q. Wilson's "Moral Judgment; A Little Learning," focuses on the use of expert witnesses in court.

Looking Ahead: Challenge Questions

Should the "exclusionary rule" be abandoned? Why or why not?

Is the American jury system in trouble? Defend your answer.

Explain your understanding of "adversarial justice."

In your view, is "jury nullification" ever justified? Why or why not?

ADVERSARIAL JUSTICE

Franklin Strier

Franklin Strier is professor of law at California State University, Dominquez Hills, California, and editor of the Journal of Business and Management. *His newest book is* Reconstructing Justice: An Agenda for Trial Reform *(Greenwood, 1994).*

We take it as axiomatic that our trial courts dispense justice. The very legitimacy of the courts depends on that expectation. Yet the reliance we place in our adversarial trial court system to deliver just decisions is a misguided leap of faith. This is neither a radical nor novel perspective. Consider, for example, this observation by the eminent jurist Karl Llewellyn:

> The adversary trail seems from outside like back-handedness or trickery which approaches a travesty on justice; a dragging, awkward, unreliable machinery at best; at worst, one which is manipulated. In consequence . . . there is not one sole excrescence of trial machinery that will find one sole jot of support from any person in the court except the lawyer.[1]

Several inherent flaws of the adversary trial system support Llewellyn's assessment, but none more forcefully than the system's weakness in exposing the truth. In a trial, justice without truth is serendipitous. Benjamin Disraeli said, "Justice is truth in action." The U.S. Supreme Court has concurred, frequently stating that the central purpose of the trial is the determination of truth. As the O.J. Simpson trial careens fitfully but inexorably to its uncertain denouement, what and how much truth will it reveal? How good is it, or any American trial, at finding the truth? The sobering reality is that our trials, especially jury trials, are decidedly fickle vehicles to the truth. Justice is the casualty.

Paradoxes and false presumptions suffuse the theories and concepts undergirding our trial system. One such presumption is sometimes referred to as the *fight theory*, which holds that truth is best revealed in the courtroom through the clash of opposing views, rather than through investigation by the judge or other neutral third parties. Adversary theory presumes that the personal motivation of attorneys will generate the most assiduous search for favorable evidence. Essentially, this is the legal version of the "invisible hand" theory: Each party pursuing his or her own self-interest will adduce the most favorable evidence and generate the best arguments, yielding the fairest possible trial and a just result. By the same token, statements of the opposition will be vigorously monitored. Because the parties (rather than the judge) control the proceedings, rigorous cross-examination of adverse testimony is assumed.

The problem with the fight theory is that it is neither logically supportable nor empirically verifiable. Federal judge Jerome Frank, former chairman of the SEC and an oft-quoted critic of the adversary system, challenged the fight theory. His premise was simple: "The partisanship of the opposing lawyers blocks the uncovering of vital evidence or leads to a presentation of vital testimony in a way that distorts it."[2] He concluded: "To treat a lawsuit as, above all, a fight, surely cannot be the best way to discover facts. Improvement in fact-finding will necessitate some considerable diminution of the martial spirit in litigation."[3]

Other critics disparage the fight theory. Judge Marvin Frankel, a leader in the movement to give truth a greater value in trials, was shocked by the wanton leap of logic necessary to subscribe to the fight theory. After noting that other truth seekers do not use adversary means, he observed:

> We . . . would fear for our lives if physicians, disagreeing about the cause of our chest pains, sought to resolve the issue by our forms of interrogation, badgering, and other forensics. But for the defendant whose life is at stake—and for the public concerned the defendant is a homicidal menace—this is thought to be the perfect form of inquiry. We live, at any rate, as if we believe this.[4]

Commenting on the implausibility of the truth-from-fight assump-

---

1. Karl Llewellyn, *Jurisprudence: Realism of Theory and Practice* (Chicago: University of Chicago Press, 1962), 446–47.

2. Jerome Frank, *Courts On Trial* (Princeton, N. J.: Princeton University Press, 1949), 81.
3. Frank, *Courts*, 102.
4. Frank, *Courts*, 102.

This article originally appeared in *The World & I*, August 1995, pp. 289–303. Reprinted by permission of *The World & I*, a publication of The Washington Times Corporation. © 1995.

tion, Thurman Arnold wrote in *The Symbols of Government:*

> Bitter partisanship in opposite directions is supposed to bring out the truth. Of course no rational human being would apply such a theory to his own affairs.... Mutual exaggeration of opposing claims violate(s) the whole theory of rational, scientific investigation. Yet in spite of this most obvious fact, the ordinary teacher of law will insist (1) that combat makes for clarity, (2) that heated arguments bring out the truth, and (3) that anyone who doesn't believe this is a loose thinker.[5]

Our use of the fight theory results in a paradox: Trial procedure assigns exclusive responsibility for presenting the evidence to those with no legal or professional obligation to seek the truth—the attorneys. Their goal is victory, not enlightenment. Studies show that attorneys often spend more time trying to hide or distort facts than revealing them. In every trial, at least one attorney usually tries to suppress or cloud unfavorable evidence.

A tenet of the adversary system is that each side's attorney will fight as hard as he can. Thus the attorney's duty of "zealous advocacy" is prescribed in the various professional codes that purport to delineate ethical conduct for attorneys. But this makes adversarial excess endemic to the system. And although we expect attorneys to adhere to the rules of evidence and confine their strategies to the ethical boundaries of the rules, they often bend the rules and stretch the strategies.

PRETRIAL ABUSE

Attorney abuses begin before the trial, during the discovery process. Under discovery, a litigant may request of the opposing party any relevant information (not protected by privilege) which that party has or to which that party has access. One objective was to do away with the element of unfair surprise in a trial. Initially, discovery was hailed as a boon to truth seeking, fairness, and the expedited disposition of cases. No longer. Discovery abuses now constitute the single greatest source of dispute, delay, cost, and trickery in the adversary system. Excessive discovery tactics either bully the opposition into submission or limit and distort the flow of information. Either result defeats the principal purposes for which discovery was designed.

Attorneys often use written interrogatories as tactical weapons by smothering a relatively impecunious adversary with extensive discovery demands and resultant costs. A survey of Chicago litigators found widespread use of another discovery tool, the deposition (direct questioning of a party or witness), as an aggressive weapon. The idea, said one respondent, is to "see if you can get them mad," to put them "through the wringer, through the mud," so that "they are frightened to be a witness and ... are a much worse witness."[6] Responding attorneys employ an equally mischievous array of tactics. These include creating false, diversionary leads; providing the bare minimum of information; and making the acquisition of that information as difficult and expensive as possible.

In criminal cases, the prosecution always has the constitutional duty to disclose exonerating evidence. But many states now make pretrial discovery a "two-way street," requiring that the defense grant similar discovery rights to the prosecution. California is one of the recent states to mandate reciprocal discovery. The intentional breach of this duty by the defense in the Simpson case may bear heavily on the outcome. During his opening statement, defense attorney Johnnie Cochran flagrantly broke the discovery law by referring to intended witnesses and their prospective testimonies without first disclosing their identities and/or statements to the prosecution for discovery. These witnesses, Cochran said, would offer

---

Trial procedure assigns exclusive responsibility for presenting the evidence to those with no legal or professional obligation to seek the truth—the attorneys. Their goal is victory, not enlightenment.

---

testimony exculpating Simpson or casting great doubt upon the prosecution's evidence. Cochran further suggested that the prosecution had hidden this evidence.

The prosecution expostulated convulsively. The government was unaware of some of the new witnesses. How could it hide that of which it was unaware? The other new witnesses were known miscreants or felons and thus were completely unreliable.

When the prosecution asked for sanctions against the defense, Judge Lance Ito found himself in an extremely delicate situation. Some sanctions were clearly in order, yet they could not be so severe as to produce bias against the defendant

---

5. Thurman Arnold, *The Symbols Of Government* (New York: Harcourt, Brace & Co., 1962), 183–85.

6. Wayne Brazil, "Civil Discovery: Lawyers' Views on Its Effectiveness, Its Principal Problems and Abuses," *American Bar Foundation Research Journal* 787 (1980).

and create grounds for appellate reversal. After all, it was the defense attorney, not the defendant, who was the misfeasor in this procedural breach. The judge mulled it over for a day, then imposed two sanctions: First, he granted the prosecution ten minutes of "reopening" statements—in essence, a rebuttal; second, he admonished the jury to disregard the defense counsel's opening statements as they pertained to six of the potential witnesses.

Significantly, the judge did not mention what the testimony of these potential witnesses was to be. Thus, the jury does not know what weight to attach to the admonition. The warning will, therefore, have little corrective impact on the effect of the defense's opening statements (save suggesting to the jury that the defense counsel is somewhat untrustworthy). The ultimate effect of this gambit by the defense may never be known, but it is likely to be an affordable "cost of doing business."

Discovery abuse epitomizes the adversary system. Indeed, some attorneys argue that adversarial professionalism *commands* the use of such devices whenever they offer significant advantages. Whatever the validity of this contention, the intense competitive pressures of the adversary system make resort to obstructionist discovery devices a constant temptation and a common occurrence.

Pretrial adversarial excesses continue during voir dire (jury selection), a fertile area for trial attorneys to ply their trade. Attorneys may dismiss prospective jurors by challenges. Those whose responses to the voir dire questions indicate probable bias are challenged for *cause*. Attorneys may perceive that other prospective jurors would not view their client's case favorably but are not sufficiently biased to challenge for cause. Such individuals can be removed by *peremptory* challenges. Unlike challenges for cause, peremptory challenges require no stated reason by the requesting attorney; however, they are limited in

> *Discovery abuse epitomizes the adversary system. Indeed, some attorneys argue that adversarial professionalism commands the use of such devices whenever they offer significant advantages.*

number—a common number is six for each side. But in cases of serious crimes, the number may be twelve or more. (There were twenty in the Simpson case.) Because of their limited availability, a premium is put on the attorney's skill in using peremptory challenges.

Statute and case law require the panel from which the jury is selected to be drawn from a representative cross section of the community in which the case is filed. To this end, courts use voter registration lists as the primary source for jury panels. Theoretically, the varying views within the community, if represented on the jury, make for vigorous and salutary debate. The hope is that conflicting prejudices will cancel each other out.

By strategic use of peremptory challenges, an attorney tries to assemble a jury receptive to his case. As candid practitioners readily admit, lawyers conduct voir dire not to get unbiased jurors but to get jurors favorably biased. Attorneys also seek competitive advantage by attempting to influence prospective jurors while interviewing them. Their tactics are designed to *create* bias in prospective jurors—via indoctrination, education, and socialization—rather than merely detect it.

Trial advocacy tracts (some even appearing in law school textbooks) are replete with advice on achieving an illegitimate goal: gaining adversarial advantage during voir dire. Several studies support the conclusion that the vast majority of the attorney's efforts during voir dire are indeed undertaken for gaining adversarial advantage rather than screening for bias. For example, one

survey found that over 80 percent of attorneys' time during voir dire was used to indoctrinate prospective jurors. These findings were confirmed by an extensive survey of Los Angeles jurors (hereafter "the Los Angeles survey") that I conducted in 1987–88. (With over 3,800 jurors responding, it was the largest of its kind.)[7] More than one-third of the jurors agreed that "one or both attorneys were trying to persuade me in addition to probing for bias." This suggests that numerous attorneys are using voir dire for inappropriate didactic purposes.

TRUTH CORRUPTION

Once trial begins, tricks by attorneys can escalate—thanks in large part to the bench's historically lax enforcement of professional conduct rules. When infractions occur, they are routinely winked at by judges and bar association ethics committees. As a result, trial lawyers ostensibly enjoy a unique privilege in plying their trade: They are largely unanswerable to society for behavior that would be morally questionable elsewhere. This led the venerable jurist Felix Cohen to lament: "How the edifice of justice can be supported by the efforts of liars at the bar and ex-liars on the bench is one of the paradoxes of legal logic which the man on the street has never solved."

---

7. Franklin Strier, "Through the Jurors' Eyes," *ABA Journal*, October 1988, 78–81.

Space does not permit even a modest catalog of truth-corrupting tactics, but mention of a few common artifices will suffice:

Coaching witnesses. A standard practice is for attorneys to interview their witnesses in preparation for testimony. The practice is known by a variety of sobriquets—"rehearsing," "horse shedding," "prepping," and "sandpapering"—but the most common term is "coaching." The dangers of coaching are substantial: An attorney who knows the testimony of all friendly witnesses can orchestrate a common story that can avoid contradictions. In the course of coaching their witnesses, attorneys suggest "better" answers that, if not clearly contravening the witness' intended answer, subtly but effectively shade, dissemble, or distort the truth. The Simpson prosecutors continued to accuse the defense counsel of coaching those defense witnesses whose changed stories benefited the defendant.

Attorney statements. Judges frequently tell jurors that attorney statements are not evidence. That is not enough. Jurors should also be informed that *attorneys are not under oath and do not have to believe their own statements.* Few jurors appreciate this. That is why attorneys are so effective when they (permissibly) impeach the credibility of witnesses they know to be telling the truth.

Similarly effective is the presumptuous question, one of the more insidious tools in the cross-examining attorney's arsenal. The presumptuous question implies a serious charge against the witness for which the attorney has little or no proof. An example: "Isn't it true that you have accused men of rape before?" Such innuendos are particularly effective against expert witnesses. A recent study found that by merely posing these questions, an attorney could severely diminish an expert's credibility, *even when the witness denied the allegation and his attorney's objection to the charge was*

sustained. This clearly indicates that the presumptuous cross-examination question is a dirty trick that can sway jurors' evaluations of a witness' credibility.

Explanations for the effectiveness of this tactic vary. Communications research suggests people believe that when a speaker offers a premise, he has an evidentiary basis for it. With their pristine mind-sets, jurors assume that the derogatory premise of an attorney's question is supported by information. Another explanation lies in the possible confusion of jurors as to the sources of their information. The longer the trial, the less likely jurors will be able to distinguish information suggested by an attorney's presumptuous question from that imparted by the witness' answer.

Witness abuse. Cross-examining attorneys often regard witnesses as if they were open garbage cans and treat them accordingly. Early in the Simpson trial, for example, the defense resorted to hardball tactics against witnesses. Recall the derisive browbeating of police detectives by defense counsel. And when Simpson's friend, Ron Shipp, testified that O.J. had disclosed his dream of killing Nicole, the defense counsel on cross-examination accused Shipp of being an alcoholic, a deadbeat, an ingrate, and a perfidious grasper who knowingly betrayed his friend to advance his own aspirations as an actor.

Emotional appeals. In the Los Angeles survey, two-fifths of the ju-

rors felt "one or both attorneys were trying harder to distort or selectively hide facts rather than seeking to reveal the truth so the jury could make an informed judgment." Jurors rank ordered the tactics used to accomplish this obfuscation. "Appeals to the emotions of the jurors" and "repeated interruptions and disruptive tactics" came in first and second, respectively.

An emotional appeal to the jury, of course, is the time-honored ploy of the trial attorney with a weak case. How it will "play with the jury" becomes the overarching con-

> *The longer the trial, the less likely jurors will be able to distinguish information suggested by an attorney's presumptuous question from that imparted by the witness' answer.*

sideration in presenting evidence. Surely one of the most emotional moments in the Simpson trial appears to have been skillfully choreographed by the prosecution to have maximum impact on the jury. Assistant District Attorney Christopher Darden questioned Denise Brown, the sister of Nicole Brown Simpson, on the first Friday afternoon of the trial. After recounting O.J.'s past physical abuses of Nicole, Denise dissolved in tears. Darden then immediately asked for and received a recess, knowing that the jurors would carry that last compelling tableau with them over the entire weekend.

Adversarial trials conduce such drama because they are staged like theatrical performances. The show is the action taking place in the arena, bounded on the jury's right by the witness stand and judge's bench, and on the left by the attorneys' tables. Indisputably, the attorneys are the performers. Only they are allowed to walk freely in the arena, to

Adversarial trials are staged like theatrical performances.

and from the witness stand, the bench, and the jury box. They gesture, flail, and point. But mostly they talk: They bluster, blather, harangue, sermonize, and beguile. They laugh, cry, and bristle; they make the jurors laugh, cry, and bristle. Bar associations unabashedly offer "courtroom acting" classes to attorneys that satisfy continuing-education requirements. It is the greatest show in town because it involves real people with real problems and high stakes: prison or freedom; child custody or childlessness; recompense for serious bodily injury or destitution and welfare. Should matters of such consequence be resolved by a process that elevates showmanship over dispassionate and rational inquiry?

Dumb shows. The "repeated interruptions and disruptive tactics" referred to in the Los Angeles survey can come in many forms. Sometimes referred to as "dumb shows," this category consists of indecorous behavior intended to distract or mislead the jury, such as dropping books or making bogus objections. The legendary Clarence Darrow used a novel subterfuge. Before trial, he would insert a nearly invisible wire in his cigar. When his opponent began interrogating a witness, Darrow would smoke the cigar. Eventually, all eyes would follow the cigar ash, which, magically, never dropped.

Changing the story. In the unique, "fact-finding" inquiry that is the trial, attorneys selectively present evidence only to the extent that it furthers their version of the facts. The objective is to craft a credible story for the jury. In developing its story, the Simpson prosecution team chose an interesting strategy. Knowing it had to tarnish an American icon, the prosecution eschewed the conventional wisdom of beginning its case with evidence of the murder in favor of presenting evidence of antecedent wife beating.

Sometimes the attorneys' stories change as the trial progresses. An

Arizona trial judge offers his impression of how this happens:

> The sporting lawyer's concern is whether the story is convincing, whether it adequately meets the opposing story, not whether it is true or false. Thus it is not at all unusual to hear a courtroom story unfold like a novel, changing as the trial proceeds. Sometimes the story becomes clearer, sometimes fuzzier, sometimes contradicted as it is orchestrated by the lawyer-maestros. As one side crafts a story, the other side expresses outrage at the opponent's fiction and responds by fictionalizing its own story. The story is not as dismaying as the attorney's acquiescence in it. In this sort of liar's paradise, truth ceases to be a Heidegerian revelation; instead, trial evidence becomes a progressive sedimentation, with new layers of lies overlaying the original ones.[8]

The defense's story certainly changed in the Simpson trial. Defense counsel Robert Shapiro initially said O.J. was asleep at the alleged time of the murder. Later, defense counsel Johnnie Cochran claimed O.J. was swinging golf clubs in his yard at that time. We can only speculate as to why the story changed. We know the change occurred after the judge ruled that O.J.'s exercise videotape—recorded shortly before the murders—could be shown to the jury. This evidence would obviously refute the claim that O.J. was so racked with arthritis at the time as to be incapable of a double murder with a knife. Once the arthritis claim was dropped, there was no disadvantage in maintaining O.J. was swinging golf clubs at the time of the murder. Further, it helped explain why O.J. was outside his house when he called his girlfriend on his cellular phone.

Partisan expertise. Will technological advances improve trial truth seeking? Even with the advent of more accurate fact-finding techniques such as DNA testing, the adversarial process will continue to subvert the truth by subordinating it to competing values. Peter Sperlich, who writes on the use of scientific evidence, says: "The adversary system maximizes the opportunities to obscure the facts, coopt the experts, and propagandize the judge. . . . The greatest single obstacle to complete and accurate scientific information . . . is the adversary system."[9]

When expert witnesses are pushed into advocacy roles, attorneys and the system corrupt the value of the witness' expertise. Attention is too often focused on the personal characteristics of expert witnesses instead of the quality of their evidence. In a 1987 book compiling papers and comments on social research and the courts, the authors reached consensus on these points: (1) scientists serving as expert witnesses must expect to be used (and misused) for partisan purposes; and (2) the adversary system is not a reliable means of bringing all the relevant scientific data to the adjudicator's attention or of separating valid research from unwarranted conclusions.

With judges being generally passive, the scope of zealous advocacy

---

8. R. J. Gerber, "Victory vs. Truth: The Adversary System and Its Ethics," 19(3) *Arizona State Law Journal* 3, 19 (1987).

9. Peter Sperlich, "Scientific Evidence in the Courts: The Disutility of Adversary Proceedings," *Judicature*, 66(10) (May 1983), 472, 474, 475.

trial tactics is limited only by the often-fertile imaginations of the litigation attorneys. Censuring individual practitioners or even the entire litigation bar for this state of affairs misses the source of the problem. After all, trial lawyers merely play their assigned roles within the adversary system. We should not condemn the attorney for engaging in morally questionable but nevertheless permissible trial tactics. Rather, we should decry the system that sanctions such tactics.

PROBLEMS WITH THE JURY SYSTEM

Any discussion of the adversary system is incomplete without considering the impact of the jury. Juries became enshrined in the Constitution because they were our bulwark during colonial times against the arbitrary and unjust decisions of the local judges appointed by the English Crown. Now we have representative democracy and many other constitutional protections against government encroachment. (Instructively, the courts of most other democracies do not use juries as we know them; none, including England, use them as extensively.) So the primary purpose of the jury is no longer protection against the government. Rather, it is a vehicle to attainment of an ideal: integration of community values, via the perspectives of common citizens, into the administration of justice. To this end, the law seeks juries composed of a representative cross section of the community where the trial is held.

Whether the jury system achieves or even approximates this ideal is highly debatable. Exemptions from service routinely afforded professionals and other potentially competent jurors both dilute the quality of juries and remove the very individuals particularly able to inject the community values that the law seeks. Most important, juries are usually selected partly or fully by the attorneys. It would betray great naïveté to contend that, in any given trial, the trial attorney's allegiance to the ideal of a representative, impartial jury is more than coincidental.

The main focus, however, should not be the jurors themselves. We should instead vet the jury system. Specifically, does current jury procedure facilitate or inhibit the realization of the ideal? And does this procedure make sense within the context of an adversarial trial?

The jury is called the trial's "fact finder." But unlike fact-finding in any other inquiry, the jury does not find, or investigate, any facts. Instead, it is the passive recipient of information, called evidence, introduced by the partisan attorneys. Although no appellate court has ruled that questions from jurors are forbidden, the vast majority of courts do not allow them or do not inform jurors of the right to ask questions. Incredibly, juries enter deliberations without the opportunity to fill in missing information or clarify uncertainties.

The restriction on questions is only the overture to a litany of ill-founded constraints imposed on jurors. No matter how lengthy or complex the evidence, most courts do not allow jurors to take notes or do not advise them of the right if it is permitted. Nor do they permit jurors to see a transcript of the testimony or a notebook of exhibits. Trials operate under the myth of perfect juror recall—yet another blatantly erroneous presumption.

There's more: Our trials litigate everything at once. All evidence on all possible issues is heard in one continuous trial. Evidence on any issue can be introduced at any time between opening and closing statements. No juror-friendly, logical order to the presentation of witnesses or evidence is required. As a consequence of this implausible scheme of "fact-finding," jurors tend to forget evidence or apply it to the wrong issue. Historian Carl Becker's commentary on the jury system resonates with truth: "Trial by jury, as a method of determining facts, is antiquated and inherently absurd—so much so that no lawyer, judge, scholar, prescription-clerk, cook, or mechanic in a garage would ever think for a moment of employing that method for determining the facts in any situation that concerned him."[10]

Being laypersons rather than experts, jurors are frequently overwhelmed by technical or complex evidence. This would include the DNA evidence that expert witnesses hired by the opposing sides "explained" in the Simpson jury. Unfortunately, these experts often compound instead of ease the jury's task: How is a juror to know if the most persuasive expert is the most authoritative? Also troubling is the potential degree to which the experts' hefty fees may flavor their testimonies.

Equally confounding the jury's search for truth is all the relevant evidence that they *cannot* hear. Because nontruth values such as individual dignity and privacy coexist with truth in the philosophical underpinning of our trial system, large gobs of highly probative evidence can be withheld from the fact finder. As illustration, the sanctity of the family dictates that spouses need not reveal spousal communications. The judge also has great discretion to exclude relevant evidence if he believes its probative value is outweighed by the danger of unfairly prejudicing, confusing, or misleading the jury.

But substantially more evidence is kept inadmissible by exclusionary rules based on erroneous presumptions. These exclusions both compromise the search for truth and profoundly beggar the justice of the final decision. For instance, a procedural rule intentionally blindfolds jurors as to whether civil-case defendants carry insurance. (It is presumed that such information would

---

10. Quoted in Frank, *Courts*, 124.

In this sort of liar's paradise, truth ceases to be a Heidegerian revelation; instead, trial evidence becomes a progressive sedimentation, with new layers of lies overlaying the original ones.

unduly influence the jury's award.) The problem is that juries go ahead and make their own assumptions anyway, thereby unwittingly corrupting the decision-making process even more.

Simpson case watchers will note the magnitude of relevant evidence that may be excluded by the granddaddy of all exclusions, the hearsay rule. A historical distrust of jurors' ability to properly discount hearsay forms the basis of the exclusion. Yet no empirical consensus supports this contention. That is why legal scholars since Jeremy Bentham have advocated that hearsay be excluded only when more direct proof is available.

Jury problems in divining the facts pale in comparison with understanding the judge's instruction on the law to be applied. *Most judicial instructions are worthless.* Rather than explain or clarify the law, the judge's instructions usually confuse the jurors with jargon-laden, incomprehensible language. That is because they are worded to avoid appellate reversal, not to educate the jurors. Consequently, jurors commonly deliberate and vote in ignorance of the law, referring instead to their personal values and biases or succumbing to the emotions evoked by the pandering of the attorneys.

Let us pause to reassess the two preeminent features of the adversarial trial. First, we have the partisan opposing attorneys. With the qualified exception of prosecutors, they have no obligation to the truth but do have an overriding professional and financial incentive to do all they can to win within the decidedly loose bounds of zealous advocacy.

Second, we have the lay jury. It cannot independently investigate but must rely exclusively on the staged, colored, and filtered versions of the facts presented by the attorneys.

This relationship profoundly affects trial outcomes. *The adversary and jury systems combine to deliver a witch's brew of trial justice.* Crafty attorneys have long prevailed in contravention of the merits of the cases they tried before juries by employing superior forensic skills or tricks or pandering to the basest of the jurors' emotions. Not only does the legal profession condone these tactics, it instructs in their use through law school courses and practitioner seminars. Over one-third of the Los Angeles survey jurors believed that the outcome of the case they sat on was dictated by a disparity in skills between the opposing attorneys. Two-fifths said the skills disparity was partly or completely responsible for a "wrong" decision with respect to the verdict or size of an award. These findings are unsurprising in light of adversary system theory, which holds that the optimal benefits of the system are realizable only in the presence of a supposition of epic proportions: Opposing litigants will be represented by competent attorneys of roughly equal skills. No more reason exists to believe this myth than to believe that opposing litigants will have roughly equal resources.

The mismatched attorney phenomenon is not entirely random. The wealthier the litigant, the better the available legal representation. I refer not only to better attorneys, but also to more persuasive expert witnesses and to other litigation

support services that help "scientifically" select the most favorably disposed jurors. These factors have certainly benefited wealthy litigants, such as William Kennedy Smith. It is no small curiosity that our legal system espouses equality of treatment (equal justice); yet our trial mechanism, more than any other, skews trial outcomes in favor of the side with the better attorney and more money.

REFORMS

Though failing, the trial system is not irreparable. I list below a few reform proposals.[11] The aim of all of them is to distribute some of the powers now wielded exclusively by attorneys to the judge and jury. As the impartial players in the trial, they are best suited to seek justice; the attorneys are not. Writes University of Chicago law professor Albert Alschuler:

> Although the adversary system may need a watchman, the task need not be assigned to the watched. Lawyers are simply not the appropriate figures to correct the defects of our adversary system. Their hearts will never be in it, and more importantly, it is unfair to both their clients and themselves to require them to serve two masters.[12]

Action from judges is the key to reform. Few people realize how extensive the judge's inherent authority is. All that is required for its exercise is the courage to impose rationality on the system.

If we are going to continue assigning weighty responsibilities to juries for little pay and much disrup-

---

11. For a full discussion of proposed reforms, see Franklin Strier, *Reconstructing Justice: An Agenda for Trial Reform* (Westport, Conn.: Quorum Books, 1994), chapter 7.
12. Albert Alschuler, "The Preservation of Clients' Confidences: One Value among Many or a Categorical Imperative?" 52 *University of Colorado Law Review* 349, 354 (1981).

tion of their lives, let's at least facilitate their task. All exclusionary evidence rules should be reevaluated to test whether their underlying presumptions correspond with reality. If we truly value the jury system, we should dare to embrace the revolutionary notion that jurors can actually be trusted with hearsay and other evidence commonly excluded, if the judge provides appropriate cautionary instructions. On balance, is justice really served by completely barring potentially decisive evidence because some jurors may ignore these instructions? Jurors should also be allowed to ask questions. When attorney incompetence leaves critical questions unasked, thereby threatening a possible miscarriage of justice, the judge should ask the questions.

The judge can order that all evidence on the same issue be presented at the same time by both sides. Imagine how much more lucid and judicable a trial would be with the following procedures. Witnesses with opposing testimony—including expert witnesses—would testify consecutively. Jurors would have a qualified opportunity to ask them questions. If helpful, the judge could call *neutral* expert witnesses to testify. At the end of each day and during deliberations, jurors could retrieve any or all of the testimony plus pictures of the exhibits from computers in the jury room. In order to provide a framework for processing the evidence, written copies of the judge's instructions would be simplified and given to the jurors *before* as well as after hearing the evidence.

Two important reforms should be made in jury selection. First, trial venues should no longer be changed because of pretrial publicity. In the age of mass media and instant communications, everyone hears about a high-profile case immediately.

Deadly riots followed the first Rodney King trial because it had been moved from a minority community to a predominantly white one; the resulting jury had no African Americans. Now it has been bruited about that Los Angeles District Attorney Gil Garcetti moved the Simpson trial from the west side of Los Angeles (predominantly white) to the more mixed downtown area because he felt a conviction by a predominantly white jury would lack credibility. This may be a valid political judgment, but it has little to do with the law. It certainly contravenes the ideal of a jury representing a cross section of the community where the crime occurred.

Many experts believe most trials are won during jury selection. This militates in favor of the second jury selection reform—eliminating peremptory challenges. (Peremptories remove prospective jurors for reasons other than overt bias.) Inevitable disparities in the jury selection skills of attorneys probably skew the final jury more in a particular direction than the full panel from which it has been drawn. Now, the advent of expensive jury consultants gives an unfair advantage to wealthy clientele both in jury selection and in strategy suggestions during trial.

* * *

These and other reforms will be vigorously opposed. Who gains the most by preservation of the status quo? Not the judges. A recent extensive survey I conducted of the California judiciary confirms the earlier findings of a nationwide Harris survey that judges favor many trial reform proposals. Narrowing further the search for the antireform interests, contemplate who is most adversely affected by an obviously projury reform—videotaped testimony. Prerecorded testimony (i.e., before jury selection) would have the following benefits for juries and the quality of trial justice:

• Jurors would not be inconvenienced by interruptions for sidebar conferences, attorney objections, witness delays, and so forth.

• The resulting compression of evidence presentation time would give the jurors a more comprehensive view of the entire case.

• The court no longer need resort to the absurd fiction that jurors can actually follow the judge's instructions to disregard what they have already heard ("unringing the bell").

• All improper attorney questions and bogus objections intended solely for effect could be eliminated from the jury's purview.

Note that by virtue of the last benefit, any inappropriate nonverbal behavior (gestures, facial expressions) by attorneys or their clients could also be eliminated. Is there any remaining doubt as to who wants to keep trial procedure as is?

> *Action from judges is the key to reform. Few people realize how extensive the judge's inherent authority is. All that is required for its exercise is the courage to impose rationality on the system.*

DAY OF RECKONING

The jury that found McVeigh guilty wrestles with emotion and tears as it prepares to decide his fate

By JAMES COLLINS

"If you don't consider what happened in Oklahoma, Tim was a good person."
—MICHAEL FORTIER

When the prosecution's star witness in the Oklahoma City bombing trial made this observation about his close friend Timothy McVeigh a few weeks ago, he provoked gasps and nervous laughter in the courtroom. The remark was absurd—an amazing, morally obtuse Yogi Berra-ism. And yet it serves as a perfect summary of the argument the defense must now make in order to save McVeigh's life.

After the Denver jury found McVeigh guilty last Monday of all 11 crimes with which he had been charged, the case entered the penalty phase, in which the jurors must decide whether McVeigh deserves to be executed. All the offenses—conspiracy to use a weapon of mass destruction, use of a weapon of mass destruction, destruction by an explosive and the murder of eight federal law- enforcement agents—carry the possible penalty of death. Questions about the morality of the death penalty itself are moot, since in order to join the panel, the jurors had to say they were capable of imposing it. Their vote must be unanimous; if it is not, then McVeigh receives a sentence of life in prison without parole. The jury may choose to give him that punishment, but that is the only alternative to death.

The burden for the prosecutors in this phase is to prove beyond a reasonable doubt that McVeigh's crimes involved one or more "aggravating circumstances." If blowing up a building full of people and killing and wounding hundreds of them isn't an aggravating circumstance, it is hard to imagine what would be. Nevertheless, there are certain legal requirements the government must meet. The federal death-penalty statute lists 15 possible aggravating circumstances, and the prosecution is trying to prove that four of these apply—that deaths occurred while McVeigh was committing various felonies,

that he created a grave risk of death to people other than the victims, that he engaged in substantial planning and premeditation and that he killed federal law-enforcement agents. The jury may also consider aggravating circumstances that are not on the statutory list. In this case, the prosecution is attempting to establish that McVeigh caused multiple deaths, that he caused serious physical and emotional injuries, and that his offenses had a severe impact on the victims and the victims' families. Victim-impact tes-

> **Do you think Timothy McVeigh should receive the death penalty?**
>
> **Yes 78%   No 17%**
>
> **Do you think that law-enforcement officials have captured and identified all of the people responsible for the Oklahoma City bombing?**
>
> **Yes 10%   No 77%**
>
> From a telephone poll of 1,024 adultAmericans taken for TIME/CNN on June 4–5 by Yankelovich Partners, Inc. Sampling error is ±3.1%. "Not sures" omitted.

timony is the technical term for the heartbreaking tales that were told in the courtroom last week.

For its part, the defense, led by Stephen Jones, is trying to show that there are "mitigating circumstances." These can include severe mental disturbance, an inability to appreciate the wrongfulness of one's actions, relatively minor participation in the crime and so on. The defense will not attempt to show that any of these apply to McVeigh,

but there is a catch-all provision that allows it to bring in the background, record and character of the defendant. Accordingly, Jones will call witnesses from McVeigh's past with the hope of humanizing him and showing that up until April 19, 1995, he was a decent young man and fine soldier. Richard Burr, a soft-spoken death-penalty expert who is conducting the defense case in the penalty phase, told the jury that McVeigh is a man "who could be your son, who could be your brother, who could be your grandson."

Jurors and spectators sobbed last week as they listened to the witnesses describe the horrors they and others endured. "I saw a body in a blanket," recalled Jerry Flowers, a member of the Oklahoma City police force. "When I opened up the blanket, there was a 5-year-old boy. His face was gone." David William Klaus, whose daughter died in the bombing, told the jury that he and his wife got married on April 19, 1963, but now they celebrate their anniversary on the following day. Struggling to hold back tears, Klaus said, "There's just a huge hole in my heart that's never going to be filled up."

Businessman Mike Lenz recalled that on the day before the bombing, he looked on as his pregnant wife had a sonogram. Lenz saw that the baby was a boy and gave him a name on the spot—Michael James Lenz III. Lenz's wife and the child she was carrying were both killed the next day. "In one fell swoop, I went from being a husband and a daddy to realizing it was all gone," he said. "There was a point when I actually stuck a pistol in my mouth." Policeman Alan Propkop found a wounded baby with a brick lodged in his body; kicking a moving ambulance, he succeeded in making it stop so that the baby could be taken to the hospital.

One after another, the tragic accounts tumbled forth. Cliff Cagle, whose face was mangled by the bomb, was almost hysterical on the stand. "I lost my job, my honor," he said, "and my grandsons have to see me like this!" A surgeon told of resorting to his pocketknife to amputate the leg of Daina Bradley. Sue Mallonee, an epidemiologist, explained the injuries seen in pictures shown to the jury: dozens of lacerations on Fred Kubasta's back; the severed jugular vein, carotid artery and esophagus of Polly Nichols (miraculously, she lived).

Throughout the hearing, U.S. District Judge Richard Matsch had proscribed evidence he considered inflammatory. He wants the jury to make a reasoned decision based on fact, he said, and so he disallowed pictures of the victims' weddings, for example, and ruled that a nine-year-old boy, Clint Seidl, could not testify about the loss of his mother. The boy's "age and innocence," Matsch said, would make his testimony appeal too much to the emotions. But keeping emotions out of the proceeding was impossible, and jurors cried again and again. The prosecution's final witness was Clint's father Glenn, who read a statement written by the boy. "I will," it said "still make my mother Mother's Day and Valentine's Day cards like the other kids."

Of all the people involved in the case, the one who has been most stoical is the defendant. He showed no emotion when the verdicts were read, nor did he react during the testimony of the victims last week. While others wept, he sat at the defense table in his impassive pose, with his chin resting on his hands. Lawyers and spectators were shocked that McVeigh remained so unmoved, and the jury may also have been affected. "McVeigh's demeanor matters," said Larry Pozner, a veteran defense attorney in Denver. "The jurors see everything and forget nothing. The demeanor of Timothy McVeigh will be weighed."

McVeigh has not made it any easier for his lawyers to convince the jury that he is a real human being like them, with blood running through his veins, who deserves a measure of clemency. The most effective way to make this case would be to call McVeigh to the stand, where he could ask for mercy. Simply by talking to the jury, he would become a less cold and anonymous figure. According to sources familiar with the defense, however, McVeigh will not testify.

So the defense lawyers must turn to others to engender sympathy for their client. The first witnesses Burr called were friends of McVeigh's from the Army. "He was outstanding," said José Rodriguez. "He was a quick study and very intelligent." McVeigh's uniform was put on display. Among the decorations was a Bronze Star won for service in the Gulf War. Neighbors from McVeigh's hometown in upstate New York also testified. "He was just a nice kid," said John McDermott. He told how McVeigh baby-sat for his children and collected comic books. Then he broke down, saying, "I like him. I can't imagine him doing something like this."

Sources familiar with the defense tell TIME that the most important witness Burr intends to call is William McVeigh, the defendant's father. He will be put on last and will narrate a short film that he produced with the help of the defense and with the

SCARS AND GHOSTS

No agency in the Murrah building suffered a higher casualty rate than the Federal Employees Credit Union. Seven of its officers and three of six tellers were killed. Another five members were hospitalized with serious injuries, including a woman who suffered more than 40 broken bones and another who had to have a doorstop surgically removed from her head. In all, 18 of the Credit Union's 33 workers died in the explosion. "There were so many funerals you had to pick," says Lisa Johnson. "Some of them were back to back." The only thing worse for survivors of the close-knit group was not being able to attend at all. Patti Hall, a secretary, slipped into a coma after falling debris punctured both her lungs and crushed her legs, knees and ankles. She did not wake for nearly two months. When she came to, the dead had all been buried. Hall, 60, recently got back on her feet, but she knows she will probably never be able to return to work at the relocated agency. She is glad McVeigh has been found guilty but, she says, "I don't think it's going to heal a thing. It won't bring back 18 employees. There isn't anything in the world that's gonna make up for what's been done."

permission of Matsch. The film is about 15 min. long and shows Tim as a child with his family—a regular American kid. McVeigh's mother, who is divorced from his father, will not testify, say sources, because she is not up to it.

The defense also plans to call some of McVeigh's teachers and may introduce his elementary and high school records, copies of which TIME has obtained. "Tim is a very self-confident student," wrote Miss Chrzaszcz, who taught McVeigh in sixth grade. "He works very hard in the classroom. I will miss him very much." Throughout elementary school, McVeigh was described as "cooperative," "friendly," "helpful" and "well liked." In high school he graduated 49th in a class of 177; his IQ was measured at between 119 and 123. Here, the defense will argue, was a boy with a good future, whose life somehow went awry.

Federal law allows the defense to raise any "circumstance of the offense that mitigates against the imposition of the death sentence." Under this provision, Burr hopes to explain to the jury that McVeigh was sincerely motivated by anger over the FBI attack at Waco. In his opening statement, he told the jury, "You will hear that the fire of Waco did keep burning in Mr. McVeigh." Burr plans to play three videotapes about Waco that influenced McVeigh: *The Big Lie, The Waco Incident* and *Day 51*. McVeigh will submit an affidavit concerning his readings about Waco, and the defense will call Dick Reavis, the author of *Ashes of Waco*. Stuart Wright, the editor of *Armageddon at Waco*, will assist the defense on this week's testimony.

It is doubtful, even after all the defense witnesses have testified, that the jurors will feel any more indulgent toward McVeigh or that they will know him any better. He remains a mysterious figure. When he enters the courtroom, he continues to look relaxed and even jocular, until the jury comes in, and then his face goes blank. His only real confidant appears to be Jones. He had a birthday on April 23, when he turned 29; his lawyers gave him two flannel shirts and a box of Peppermint Patties. He spends most of his time in jail reading the piles of mail he receives. He also reads books. Last month it was W. Somerset Maugham's *The Razor's Edge,* and he is now finishing *Man's Fate* by André Malraux. A book about a young man's spiritual quest and one about revolutionaries—McVeigh must be taking both seriously.

If the jury votes for the death penalty, the sentence will not be carried out anytime soon. Both the guilty verdict and the death sentence can be appealed, and this process may take at least three or four years. Should the execution day come, the method will be lethal injection.

McVeigh has evidently agreed to Jones' effort to win him a life sentence, but if he were true to his beliefs, he should welcome the hangman (or hypodermic man). For years, the book he has cherished is *The Turner Diaries,* a fictional account of an uprising by a courageous band of white supremacists. Earl Turner, the hero, does not flinch at the idea of dying for his cause. Indeed, in the book's final pages he joyfully embraces this fate. "Brothers!" he says, addressing an élite group called the Order. "When I entered your ranks for the first time, I consecrated my life to our Order and to the purpose for which it exists. . . . Now I am ready to meet my obligation fully. I offer you my life." The jury may give McVeigh his chance to do the same.
—Reported by Patrick E. Cole/Denver and Kevin Fedarko/Oklahoma City

Timothy McVeigh, found guilty of 11 counts of murder and conspiracy in the 1995 Oklahoma City Bombing, was sentenced to die by lethal injection if his conviction is upheld on appeal. **Ed.**

JURY NULLIFICATION: A Perversion of Justice?

Trial reforms may have to be enacted to reverse the trend of defendants being set free despite convincing evidence of guilt.

by Andrew D. Leipold

CONSIDER the following two cases. In the first, a man helps his terminally ill wife commit suicide. The prosecutor brings criminal charges against him, and the case looks strong. The defendant freely admits he prepared the toxic mix of drugs for his wife, knowing it would kill her. He argues, however, that he acted out of mercy, because his wife was suffering from a ter-

Dr. Leipold is associate professor of law, University of Illinois at Urbana-Champaign.

minal illness and no longer wanted to live in pain. The defendant takes the stand in his own defense at trial and, during his testimony, breaks into tears, saying he loved his wife, but saw no way to help her except by hastening her death. The jurors believe the defendant is sincere and, although they agree that he has violated the criminal law, return a verdict of not guilty.

Case two: A group of men are charged with vandalizing a grocery store. It was owned by immigrants, and there is strong

suspicion that the crime was motivated by the ethnic unrest that has been infecting the community. Although there is compelling evidence linking the defendants to the vandalism, they have the good fortune of being tried by a jury that shares their dislike of immigrants. Jury deliberations are brief, and the defendants walk away free.

These two cases are examples of jury nullification, which occurs when the jurors in a criminal case acquit the defendant, despite their belief that he or she was guilty

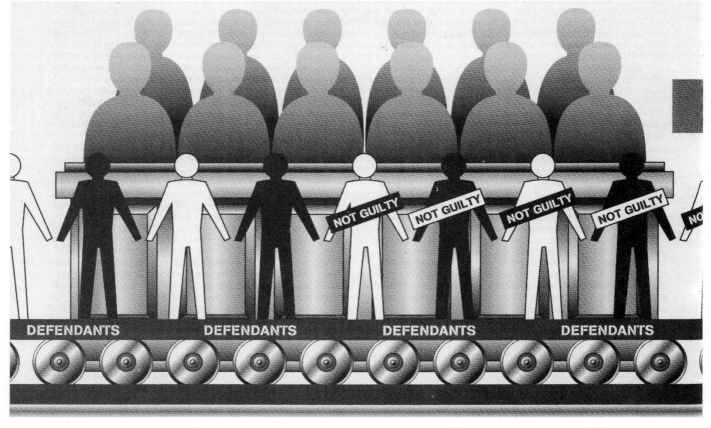

of the crime charged. In every state and Federal court, a jury has the power to decide that, no matter what the law provides and no matter what the evidence proves, a defendant should not be convicted. As the above examples show, sometimes the nullification decision is based on mercy for the defendant, sometimes on dislike for the victim. Juries also have been known to nullify when the defendant engaged in civil disobedience and the jurors agreed with the actions (an environmentalist interfering with logging efforts, for instance) or wanted to send a wake-up call to the police or prosecutor who used questionable methods to gather evidence.

There has been a lot of discussion about jury nullification lately. When juries acquitted O.J. Simpson (in his criminal trial) and the Los Angeles police officers who beat Rodney King, there were loud and sharp claims in newspapers and coffee shops that these verdicts were based on racial prejudice, class bias, an irrational desire to punish the police, or naivete about police practices, not on the evidence presented. A *Yale Law Journal* article, "Racially Based Jury Nullification: Black Power in the Criminal Justice System," by Paul Butler of George Washington University Law School, has helped fuel the debate. He not only recognizes that juries sometimes *do* make decisions that are not based on the evidence, but argues that African-American juries at times *should* use the nullification power when a black defendant is accused of a non-violent crime. These events and discussions have led some people to brink of

despair about juries: "It seems like guilt or innocence doesn't matter anymore," they think. "Today, trials are about politics and about power; the only thing that matters is who is on the jury."

It would be easy to draw this conclusion from watching the nightly news—easy, but wrong. The truth is that juries rarely acquit against the evidence, at least in serious cases. Most jurors are quite sensible and recognize that, if they acquit a factually guilty defendant, they may be turning a dangerous person loose, perhaps into their own neighborhoods. Juries may be merciful, but they are not stupid. More to the point, most garden-variety street crimes don't raise any issues that might lead a jury to nullify. Most crime is intra-racial, so any ethnic kinship a jury might feel for the defendant is blunted by the greater sympathy for the victim. Most crimes also have no political overtones or present obvious examples of police misconduct or prosecutorial overreaching. Perhaps most importantly, the majority of criminal cases never go before a jury. Most criminal charges end in a guilty plea prior to trial, often as a result of an agreement between the prosecutor and defendant. While it is true that prosecutors sometimes offer an attractive plea bargain because they are worried about what a jury will do (what lawyers euphemistically refer to as the "risks of litigation"), instances of nullification are rare enough that most plea agreements probably don't change much.

While the *instances* of jury nullification are small, the problems created by the *existence* of the nullification doctrine are

very large. In an effort to protect the jury's right to acquit for any reason it wants, courts have created an elaborate series of rules that prevent the public from looking behind a verdict to the jury's reasoning. These rules create far more problems for the administration of the criminal law than jury nullification does, yet get relatively little attention.

Let's go back to the second case mentioned above and assume that the jurors considering the vandalism case really want to convict the thugs who committed the crime. What stands in their way now are not any feelings of mercy or spite, but the trial judge. In any trial, a judge is asked to rule on a series of questions about what evidence should be admitted, questions the lawyers can ask, and legal instructions the jury should get at the end of the case. Assume in the vandalism case the judge gives the jury the wrong instruction, misinterpreting the vandalism statute and telling the jury they must make certain findings the law doesn't really require them to make. The jurors go back to deliberate and, duti-

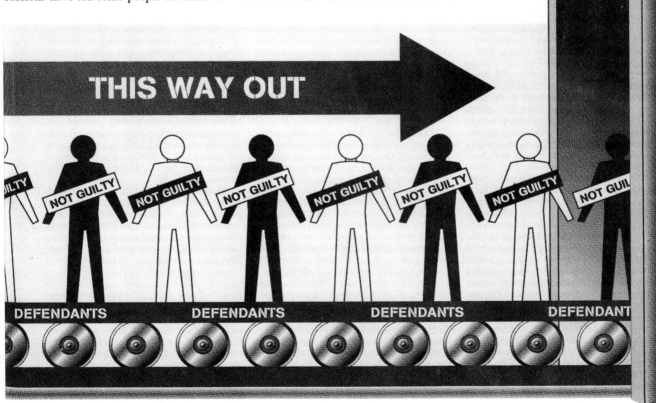

fully following their (faulty) instructions, return a verdict of not guilty.

Most would agree that this was a "bad" verdict—if the jury were given the proper instructions, they probably would have convicted, but because of the error, they let otherwise guilty people go free. This sounds like a perfect case for an appeal, except for one thing: the prosecutor absolutely is barred from asking a higher court to review the jury instructions. Because of the double jeopardy clause of the Constitution ("nor shall any person be subject for the same offense to be twice put in jeopardy of life or limb"), once a jury has returned a verdict of not guilty, the prosecutor is prohibited from bringing the defendant to trial a second time or even asking the court of appeals to consider the errors that were made at trial.

What does this have to do with jury nullification? Simple: I think that the main reason we bar prosecutors from making an appeal from an acquittal is to protect the jury's power to nullify. We are so anxious to preserve the jury's discretion to nullify in the occasional case that we put up with other, probably more numerous, acquittals that are the product of bad legal rulings at trial. This, I would argue, is the real cost of jury nullification—not the convictions that are lost when the jury deliberately acquits against the evidence, but those lost when the jury wants to convict, but erroneously is prevented by the trial court from doing so.

This conclusion—that the ban on government appeals is attributable to our desire to protect the nullification power—seems surprising (and a bit suspicious), because we normally think of the double jeopardy clause as a protection for defendants, to prevent them from being dragged through a trial twice, with all the expense and risk associated with it. While this might make sense as a plain reading of the double jeopardy clause, the Supreme Court never has taken the provision quite that literally. In fact, we allow a prosecutor to put a defendant through more than one trial in all kinds of cases: when the defendant successfully has appealed from a conviction, the government usually can bring him or her to trial a second time; when the first trial results in a hung jury, the prosecution usually can try a defendant again; and when the trial judge declares a mistrial at the defendant's request, he or she usually can be tried a second time (unless the government was trying to provoke a mistrial). Even when the defendant is acquitted by a jury in state court, there is no double jeopardy bar to a second trial in Federal court under the "dual sovereignty doctrine." (Recall that the officers in the Rodney King case were acquitted first in state court, then later convicted on Federal charges.) Despite these exceptions to the double jeopardy clause, the Supreme Court has re-

mained steadfast in its view that a jury acquittal prevents the government from appealing, even to correct pure legal errors like bad jury instructions. When all the explanations for the rule are picked apart and held up to the light, the best explanation is this: We don't allow the government to appeal from an acquittal, no matter how serious the legal errors made at trial, because *maybe*, just maybe, the jurors decided to exercise their power of nullification. If the jury nullified, it would make no sense to allow a government appeal, because the evidence and the legal instructions were irrelevant; the jury decided to acquit for reasons unrelated to the cold legal requirements of guilt. Since juries never explain their verdicts in the courtroom (they just announce "guilty" or "not guilty"), we never really can be sure when one is based on mercy rather than bad legal rulings.

All of this would make great sense if the Constitution gave juries the right to nullify or even if the nullification power were an idea so good that we were willing to put up with the type of "bad" acquittal described above. I believe nullification fails on both fronts: the power is not protected by the Constitution nor does it bring enough social benefits to make the current protected status worth the costs.

The right that isn't

The notion that juries can acquit a defendant for any reason at all is older than our nation. By the late 17th century, English judges had decided that jurors must be left to their own devices and consciences when rendering verdicts, and the idea traveled with the colonists to America. The concept of a supremely powerful jury found a welcome home here. It gave the colonists the power to convict those who misbehaved, while still nullifying the charges against those who broke what many colonists felt were oppressive laws. At the time, the jury's right to "find the law"—to decide for itself what the criminal law should be—was quite logical. Judges often were untrained in the law, making them no better than jurors at interpreting and applying the often-complex common law. As a result, there was a great deal of writing in the decades around the Revolutionary War that seemed to support a "right" of the jury to acquit someone against the evidence.

Yet, if the framers of the Constitution and the Bill of Rights thought that nullification was an important part of the right to trial by jury, they were awfully quiet about it. There is very little in the debates surrounding the drafting or ratification to suggest that they even thought about the issue, much less intended to incorporate it in the Constitution. While the Supreme Court, in construing the constitutional

right to a jury, has been curiously closed-mouthed about the topic, the one time the Court spoke clearly, it decisively stated that a jury's *power* to nullify does not mean that a defendant has the *right* to be tried before a jury with that power. In the 1895 decision of *Sparf and Hansen v. United States,* the Court laid the groundwork for the rule that still prevails in most of the country—judges are not required to tell juries that they have the power to acquit against the evidence nor are they required to let lawyers argue to the jury in favor of nullification. The message is clear—even if courts can't stop juries from nullifying, they are under no legal obligation to help juries exercise the power.

Just because something is not protected constitutionally does not make it a bad idea. In many cases, I think that jury nullification is an excellent concept. If I were on the jury of the man accused of helping his wife commit suicide and I believed he did it out of love for the victim, I would vote to acquit in a heartbeat. Prosecutors are not infallible. At times, they make bad judgments; occasionally, they are mean-spirited; and sometimes, they get so used to the unending stream of bad people and violent acts they miss the human and moral dimension of actions that normally are crimes. So, even if I had the power to prevent all juries from acquitting against the evidence, I probably would not use it.

Nevertheless, jury nullification is a dangerous power, and when any power is left in the hands of an unaccountable group, there is cause for worry. The biggest concern, mentioned above, is that procedural rules now in place—like prohibiting the appeal of acquittals—make jury verdicts less likely to be accurate and fair. There are other difficulties as well:

First, we don't know how the power is used. Because juries almost never explain their verdicts, it is impossible to say how often nullification occurs. Our inability to determine when and why it does also means that we do not know how often juries use this power for good ends rather than evil ones. For every case where a jury acts morally and shows mercy, there may be another where a jury acquits because of hatred toward the victim or favoritism to the defendant. It takes strong faith in human nature to support a doctrine like jury nullification, knowing that the decision to set someone free can be made on a whim or based on prejudice.

In most cases, of course, a decision to nullify will be neither good nor evil; the morality and wisdom of the decision will depend on our individual views. Some will cheer when an abortion clinic protester is acquitted against the evidence, others will despair; some will think justice is done when a man who assaulted a homosexual couple is convicted only of the lowest possible charge (another form of nullification), others will see it as a hateful sign of the times; and many will be shocked when an accused rapist or wife beater is set free because the jury believed that the victim was asking for it. What we think doesn't matter, though. If we want juries with the unreviewable power to acquit when the charges are unfair, we must accept juries that have the power to make decisions others find distasteful and stupid.

Second, juries often don't have enough evidence to make a reasoned nullification decision. Even if we take a kinder view toward juries, there still are reasons to be troubled by the breadth of their discretion. If a jury is to make a reasoned nullification decision, there is certain information it needs to have. Let's say a jury has before it a simple drug possession case by a college-bound high school senior. The evidence looks strong, but the thought of ruining a promising future troubles the jurors. The young man had only a small amount of drugs, looks remorseful, and has a supportive family with him in court. Rather than send another teenager to jail, the jury decides to nullify.

If the jury's perception were accurate, perhaps it made the right call. The problem is what a jury sees might not be the full story. The jurors might not learn that the defendant has had scrapes with the law before, that he is a troublemaker at home and at school, and that, in fact, the police found a load of drugs in the car, which were not introduced at trial because the car was searched illegally. If the jury had known these things, its feelings of mercy quickly might have evaporated. However, there usually will be no evidence introduced of these other facts because they are irrelevant to the technical question of guilt or innocence. Stated differently, because the jury has no right to nullify, evidence that might inform the exercise of that power usually is not admitted at trial, nor are defense lawyers usually permitted to make overt appeals to the nullification power. Juries therefore make the nullification decision in the dark, letting some go free who are not worthy of mercy and convicting some who might be more deserving of it.

Third, encouraging nullification encourages lawlessness. The urge to nullify may tug at our hearts because it is so easy to imagine cases where we would do so ourselves if we were jurors. Consider a woman who is walking alone when she is surrounded by a gang of thugs. The terrified woman brandishes a gun and the gangsters flee, but as they do, she shoots one, causing great bodily harm. In many states, the woman could be prosecuted for assault with a deadly weapon because once the thugs turned and ran, she no longer had the right to use deadly force in self-defense. Yet, many of us would not be troubled with

such legal niceties and would cheerfully acquit if given the chance.

In more reflective moments, though, we should wonder why we let a jury make this decision. We have an elected legislature to pass laws and elected or appointed judges to interpret them. The wisdom of the people's representatives has been that when a person no longer is in danger, he or she may not use force in self-defense. That decision may be right or wrong, but it was arrived at through a legitimate, representative process. Why, then, should the jury be able to ignore that mandate because they sympathize with the woman and detest thugs? The jury is unelected, unaccountable, and has no obligation to think through the effect an acquittal will have on others. Perhaps it will be that thugs will accost fewer women; perhaps the effect will be to blur the line further between legitimate self-defense and vigilantism.

Reasonable people can disagree on the proper reach of the criminal laws. Nevertheless, the place for them to disagree is in public, where the reasons for expansions and contractions of the laws can be scrutinized and debated by those who will be affected by the verdicts juries reach. It is enough that we ask juries to decide whether the defendant before them is guilty of the crime charged. To expect them to make a reasoned decision on the wisdom of the law itself, with virtually none of the information that normally would be required in making such a decision, calls for more wisdom from most juries than fairly can be expected.

A possible solution

There is a way to retain the best features of jury nullification while avoiding some of the problems. If we really want to allow juries to acquit someone against the evidence, we should pass a law making nullification an affirmative defense, much like we do for self-defense, duress, and necessity. (The nullification probably would be classified as an "excuse" rather than a "justification," but in either case, it would serve as a defense to the crime charged.) The statute could be drafted in any way that we wished. It could be a defense, for example, if the defendant reasonably believed that his or her actions were for the benefit of the victim (the mercy killing case), if the harm caused by the defendant's actions were so slight as not to justify punishment (a case of simple marijuana possession for the college-bound high school student), or if the jury believed the defendant already has suffered enough and further punishment would be excessive (a father prosecuted for manslaughter because he failed to strap his child in a car safety seat). A jury would not be required to accept the defense in any of these cases, but, by allowing a defendant to raise an affirmative defense, the

statute would permit the attorneys to submit evidence on the question and the jury to make a more informed decision.

Making nullification an affirmative defense would have two other benefits. First, it would allow judges to make more explicit to the jury that, when the evidence points to guilt, they have the *duty* to convict unless there is a defense. This might help avoid some of the abuses of nullification like that described in case number two above. Second, the focus on nullification might allow some clever lawyer to argue to the Supreme Court that government appeals of acquittals should not be barred by the double jeopardy clause. If I am right that the ban on appeals is explained best by the desire to protect the nullification power and if the power to nullify is not protected by the Constitution—there is little in the historical record to support it— then the government should be able to argue to a court of appeals that the acquittal was based on bad evidence rulings, bad jury instructions, improper defense tactics, or any other legal ground.

I suspect that neither of these things will happen. The rule against appealing from an acquittal is ingrained deeply in constitutional law, and no argument by an academic is likely to change that. Nor do I think there is any danger that states will rush to pass nullification statutes. Broadening the rights of a criminal defendant is not exactly in vogue among politicians, and creating any additional defenses, especially one as open-ended as a nullification defense, would be wildly unpopular with the law- and-order crowd. On the other hand, there are groups, like the Fully Informed Jury Association, that for the last several years have been promoting aggressively the idea of nullification in the legislatures, at shopping malls, and in front of courthouses where potential jurors walk. They argue, at times quite persuasively, that dispersing the criminal justice power into the hands of juries is one way to keep government in check and to ensure that, if bad laws or bad prosecution decisions are made, there will be a backstop that will prevent unjust convictions. As long as we have even modest amounts of mistrust about governments, such efforts will strike a responsive cord.

Whether anything changes or not, jury nullification remains a fascinating and important topic because juries are one of the few institutions that make critically important decisions, yet are almost entirely unaccountable. Understanding how and when they decide to free a person who they believe committed a crime tells us something about how we feel about our laws, prosecutors, police, and the entire justice system. Punishing the guilty and protecting the innocent are among the highest duties of government. Deciding who is to be punished—and who should not—is at the core of those duties. Anything that helps accomplish that task better is worthy of consideration.

'We're In The Fight Of Our Lives'

Bernard Gavzer

At 2 a.m. on Nov. 20, 1990, Leonardo Turriago was pulled over for speeding by two state troopers. They asked if they could look into his van, and Turriago said they could. Inside, the troopers saw a trunk and asked Turriago about it. He sprang open its lock, then ran away. Opening the trunk, the troopers found the body of a man shot five times.

Turriago was quickly caught. In his apartment, police found 11 pounds of cocaine and guns. The suspect told them where to look for the murder weapon, and it was recovered. Turriago was convicted of a second-degree murder and sentenced to 45 years to life.

The defense appealed, saying the troopers had no right to search the van. On June 6, 1996, Turriago's conviction was overturned. A New York appellate court ruled that the police search was not justified and had been coerced.

Criminal Justice in America is in a state of collapse," says Judge Harold J. Rothwax, who has spent 25 years presiding over criminal cases in New York City. "We have formalism and technicalities but little common sense. It's about time America wakes up to the fact that we're in the fight of our lives."

Rothwax believes cases such as Turriago's illustrate that the procedural dotting of every "i" and crossing of every "t" has become more important than the crime's substance. "The bottom line is that criminals are going free," he says. "There is no respect for the truth, and without truth, there can be no justice."

While the search for truth should be the guiding principle of our courts, instead, the judge says, "Our system is a carefully crafted maze, constructed of elaborate and impenetrable barriers to the truth."

Judge Harold Rothwax *has spent 25 years presiding over criminal cases in New York City. What he has seen has convinced him that our courts must be changed if our justice system is to survive.*

A lank and slightly bent man who looks in repose as though he's leaning into the wind, the 65-year-old jurist has detailed his views in a recently published book, *Guilty: The Collapse of Criminal Justice.* Nothing less than sweeping change, he insists, is required to save our system.

Practices we have taken for granted—such as the *Miranda* warning, the right to counsel, even unanimous jury verdicts—need to be reconsidered, says the judge. "You know," Rothwax confided, "more than 80 percent of the people who appear before me are probably guilty of some crime."

Rothwax insists there is a fundamental difference between the investigative and the trial stages of a case. The investigative stage is marked by the notion of probable guilt, he asserts, not the presumption of innocence. "Until a defendant goes on trial, he is probably guilty," the judge says, noting that by the time a person reaches trial he has been deemed "probably guilty" several times.

DEFENDANT	LOCATION

SPECIFIC WARNING REGARDING INTERROGATIONS

1. YOU HAVE THE RIGHT TO REMAIN SILENT.
2. ANYTHING YOU SAY CAN AND WILL BE USED AGAINST YOU IN A COURT OF LAW.
3. YOU HAVE THE RIGHT TO TALK TO A LAWYER AND HAVE HIM PRESENT WITH YOU WHILE YOU ARE BEING QUESTIONED.
4. IF YOU CANNOT AFFORD TO HIRE A LAWYER ONE WILL BE APPOINTED TO REPRESENT YOU BEFORE ANY QUESTIONING, IF YOU WISH ONE.

SIGNATURE OF DEFENDANT	DATE
WITNESS	TIME

REFUSED SIGNATURE   SAN FRANCISCO POLICE DEPARTMENT   PR. 9.1.4

UPI/Bettmann

"When a person is arrested, indicted by a grand jury, held in detention or released on bail, it is all based on probable guilt," Rothwax adds. "Once *on trial*, he is presumed innocent."

A criminal trial *should be a search for the truth. Instead, Judge Rothwax says, "Our system is a maze constructed of elaborate and impenetrable barriers to the truth. . . . Without truth there can be no justice."*

Many of the judge's views have drawn criticism from others in the criminal justice arena. "I think there is a problem with a sitting judge who may think people are guilty before they've been judged guilty," says Norman Reimer, chair of the New York County Lawyers Association's criminal justice section. "In this country you are presumed innocent by everyone and anyone until you are convicted by a jury." Even at the time of arrest? "You absolutely are, beyond any doubt, presumed innocent," says Reimer.

The positions the judge has staked out in what he regards as his crusade to bring sense to the criminal justice system have shocked those who long associated him with strong liberal causes. A lifelong Democrat, Rothwax was a senior defense trial attorney for the Legal Aid Society in New York and a stalwart of the New York Civil Liberties Union early in his career.

"I represented Lenny Bruce and Abbie Hoffman, the Black Panthers and the Vietnam war protesters," he says. "I am today as much a civil libertarian as ever. But that does not mean I must close my eyes to the devastation that has occurred in criminal justice. We have the crime, but where is the justice? It is all tilted in favor of the criminal, and it is time to bring this into balance."

The interests of the victim weigh solidly in Rothwax's courtroom in the Criminal Court Building in Manhattan. However, he is troubled by some decisions of the U.S. Supreme Court, saying: "Its rulings over the last 35 years have made the criminal justice system incomprehensible and unworkable."

Although neither the Supreme Court nor the Courts of Appeals decide the guilt or innocence of a defendant, they do make rulings on the constitutionality of acts by the police and lower courts and thus have a significant impact on our justice system. Key practices of our current system—which have come about as a result of Supreme Court rulings in recent decades—need to be changed, Rothwax believes. Among them are:

• *The Miranda warning:* In New York, Alfio Ferro was arrested in 1975 in connection with a fur robbery that turned into a murder. In the lockup, a detective—without saying a word—dropped some of the stolen furs in front of Ferro's cell. Ferro then made incriminating statements that led to his conviction for second-degree murder.

In 1984, an appellate court overturned the conviction, saying that the detective's action amounted to interrogation and violated Ferro's *Miranda* rights. The *Miranda* warning requires that the suspect be told he has a right to remain silent, that any statement he makes might be used against him and that he has the right to have a lawyer present.

"*Miranda* came about because of abuses such as prolonged custodial interrogation, beatings and starving in order to get a confession," says Rothwax. "I think those abuses have been largely dealt with. Now the police officer is put in the position of telling a suspect in a murder or rape, 'Look, you don't have to tell us anything, and that may be the best thing for you.' And it produces a situation in which a proper confession is thrown out because of the way in which it was read or that it wasn't read at the right time."

Rothwax believes *Miranda* can be replaced by the recording of an arrest and interrogation through videotapes, tape recorders and other technology. This would probably show whether a confession or statement was coerced.

• *The exclusionary rule:* This winter, Federal Judge Harold Baer Jr. refused to admit as evidence 80 pounds of cocaine and heroin obtained in the arrest of a drug courier in the Washington Heights neighborhood of New York City. The evidence was excluded because, said Baer, the police had violated the Fourth Amendment protection against unreasonable search and seizure when they searched the car in which the drugs were found.

The police said their search was proper in view of the fact that they saw men hastily loading bags into an out-of-state car in a high drug area in the middle of the night, and the men ran away when the police approached. Judge Baer, however, said just because the men ran off was no reason to suspect them of a crime. In Washington Heights, the judge said, it was not unusual for even innocent people to flee, because police there were regarded as "corrupt, violent and abusive."

Under a growing chorus of criticism, Judge Baer first reversed himself and then asked that the case to assigned to another judge. It was. Rothwax says this is the sort of muddled episode which arises from the exclusionary rule, producing "truth and justice denied on a technicality."

"The Supreme Court has consistently ruled that evidence seized in violation of the Fourth Amendment *should* be excluded from a criminal trial. But if you read the Fourth Amendment, nowhere does it say that *illegally* obtained evidence *must* be excluded," says Rothwax. "In my view, when you exclude or suppress evidence, you suppress the truth."

Judge Rothwax has a remedy: "Make the exclusionary rule *discretionary* instead of mandatory. If it was at the discretion of the judge, there could be a test of reasonableness. A judge could consider factors such as whether a police officer acted with objective reasonableness and subjective good faith. As it is now, the exclusionary rule is irrational, arbitrary and lacks proportion. No wonder that in 90 percent of exclusionary cases, the police don't know what the law is."

• *The right to counsel:* In 1982, Kenneth West of New York, an alleged drug dealer, was suspected of being involved in killing a man who had taken his parking place. His lawyer, at a police lineup, told the police not to question West in his absence. Nothing came of the case for three years. Then police arrested a former cohort of West who said West had been one of the shooters. The informer secretly taped West talking about the killing. West was convicted, but in 1993 the New York Court of Appeals reversed the conviction, saying the secret taping amounted to questioning him without the presence of counsel.

The right to counsel is provided by the Sixth Amendment. "It is essential there be a right to counsel,' Judge Rothwax says. "But the amendment doesn't say it has to be during police questioning and investigation. As a result of technicalities over this issue of counsel, I have seen murderers go free. Make it clear that the right to a lawyer shouldn't be a factor in the *investigative* stage but only in pre-trial and trial stages."

• *Instructions to the jury:* After closing arguments in the O. J. Simpson murder trial, Judge Ito took great care in telling jurors that Simpson's failure to take the stand in his own defense should in no way be taken to mean anything negative or to draw any other adverse conclusion.

This instruction to the jury occurs in all cases in which the defense asks for it, because a Supreme Court ruling in 1981 that said not to do so amounted to a violation of the Fifth Amendment. (The Fifth Amendment states that no person shall be forced to testify against himself.) "The Fifth Amendment does *not* say that one might not draw reasonable inferences from the silence of a defendant," Judge Rothwax says. "I think we must find a way to return to the standard that existed before, that the judge could tell the jury that the failure to explain could amount to an inability to explain."

The judge would like to see other changes made to the jury system. Among them:

1) *Unanimous jury verdicts should no longer be required.* Why? Rothwax cites a murder case he presided over. "It was an overwhelming case of clear guilt. Yet there was a hung jury. One juror was convinced the defendant was not guilty. How did she know? Well, as she explained it, 'Someone that good-looking could not commit such a crime.' We had to retry the case, and the man was quickly found guilty."

By allowing verdicts to be decided by a vote of 11–1 or 10–2, Rothwax says, there would be a reduced risk that a single juror could cause a retrial or force a compromise in the face of overwhelming evidence of guilt.

2) *Peremptory challenges to prospective jurors should be strictly limited or abolished.* Peremptory challenges allow lawyers to knock someone off the jury without giving any reason. "As we saw in the Simpson case," Rothwax says, "it makes it possible to stack a jury so that the most educated juror is excused, and you end up with a jury that can be manipulated to accept innuendo as evidence."

Judge Rothwax regards the entire conduct of the Simpson trial as an unspeakable insult to the American people, one that left them "feeling wounded and deeply distrustful of the system." He adds: "There was an opportunity to show a vast audience the potential vitality of justice at work. Instead we were assaulted by an obscene circus. We saw proof that the American courtroom is dangerously out of order."

Not everyone agrees with the judge's assessments. "All the arguments Rothwax makes have been addressed and answered in the legal literature," says Yale Kamisar, the Clarence Darrow Distinguished Professor at the University of Michigan and a constitutional scholar. "I think millions of Americans will agree with him, but he has presented a lopsided argument. I think he's wrong."

To sit with Rothwax in court, as this writer did, is to get a sense of his urgency for reform. In three hours, there was a procession of men and women charged with felonies from murder to drug dealing. Rothwax was all business, and he was tough with everyone. After 47 cases had been considered and dealt with, the judge turned to me and asked, with irony, about the defendants we had seen: "Did you notice the huge display of remorse?" There hadn't been any. "That's why," he said, "we are in the fight of our lives."

MORAL JUDGMENT

A Little Learning

*When judges allow 'experts' to exhibit
their private theories in court,
justice is the victim.*

JAMES Q. WILSON

IN 1976 Beverly Ibn-Tamas shot and killed her husband, Yusef, in his medical office in Washington, D.C. She was convicted of second-degree murder and sentenced to spend one to five years in prison. Beverly testified that she had been subjected to repeated beatings and threats during her four-year marriage to Yusef. Other witnesses, including Yusef's first wife, also testified to his violent behavior. Events on the day of the shooting were disputed, but what is clear is that Beverly shot Yusef twice, once from close range. Obviously, however, the jury did not think the crime was premeditated (hence second rather than first degree), and the judge found her a sympathetic defendant (hence the short sentence). Beverly's lawyers appealed, however, claiming that the court had improperly excluded the testimony of Dr. Lenore Walker, a psychologist who described a condition called battered-woman syndrome, and who had frequently served as an expert witness.

A divided appeals court told the trial court to hold an evidentiary hearing on the issue of admitting Dr. Walker's testimony. It did and concluded that Dr. Walker had not established that her methodology was generally accepted by experts in the field. The conviction was upheld. Beverly served one year in prison.

When expert witnesses offer to testify, the judge must rule on the admissibility of their testimony. In doing so, he must answer, among others, these questions: Is the testimony based on facts that are "beyond the ken of the average layman"? Does the expert have sufficient skill and knowledge in this field to make the testimony valuable to the jury? Will the testimony unduly prejudice the jury? The appeals court said that Dr. Walker's testimony might have "enhanced Mrs. Ibn-Tamas's general credibility" and "supported her testimony" that her husband's behavior had led her to believe she was in imminent danger." The court compared Beverly to Patty Hearst, who had argued three years earlier in her trial for bank robbery that expert testimony would "explain the effects kid-

napping, prolonged incarceration, and psychological and physical abuse may have had on the defendant's mental state at the time of the robbery."

Just what could expert testimony have said about this "mental state" that "the average layman" could otherwise not know? The appeals court did not really answer that question, and based on what one can learn from Beverly Ibn-Tamas's trial, the answer in her case seems to be—nothing at all.

A few years later, however, the New Jersey Supreme Court undertook to give an answer in reviewing the case of Gladys Kelly, who had been convicted of reckless manslaughter and sentenced to five years in prison for having stabbed her husband to death with a pair of scissors. Gladys claimed that during their seven-year marriage her husband, Ernest, had abused her. Though some of her claims were disputed, let us assume they were true. On the fatal day they had a fight on the street that began with an argument over money. Ernest pushed Gladys to the ground, but two bystanders separated them. Gladys went off to find her daughter and returned with a pair of scissors. At this point the facts are unclear. The defense claimed that Ernest rushed at Gladys with his hands raised and that she, fearing for her safety, stabbed him. The prosecution claimed that Gladys started the fight, chased Ernest after threatening to kill him, and then stabbed him. The state Supreme Court reversed the conviction because expert testimony by Dr. Lois Veronen about battered-woman syndrome had been excluded.

In reaching this decision, the court drew heavily on amicus briefs filed by the American Civil Liberties Union, the New Jersey Coalition for Battered Women, and the American Psy-

---

Mr. Wilson is James Collins Professor of Management and Public Policy at UCLA and the author of Moral Judgment, *published by Basic Books, a division of HarperCollins Publishers, Inc.*

From *National Review*, June 2, 1997, pp. 37-39. Adapted from *Moral Judgment* by James Q. Wilson. © 1997 by James Q. Wilson. Reprinted by permission of BasicBooks, a division of HarperCollins Publishers, Inc.

chological Association. It discussed the lamentable extent of wife abuse in the United States, complained of the bias against women in the law-enforcement agencies charged with investigating abuse cases, and reviewed the theory of battered-woman syndrome. As interesting as these observations were, they did not address the central issue: whether expert testimony would have aided the jury in reaching its verdict. Since the jury had refused to convict Gladys of murder (instead agreeing on a verdict of reckless manslaughter), it had already accepted a mitigation, no doubt one arising out of her history and circumstances. And since the judge had sentenced her to the minimum term, he also must have understood that there were mitigating factors. The expert testimony, then, had to be designed to aid the jury in deciding that this was justifiable homicide—a case of self-defense.

But what could Dr. Veronen have contributed to that issue? Not that Gladys's fear of being killed by Ernest was reasonable (traditionally a requirement in pleading self-defense); all the facts bearing on that—and they were disputed facts—were already available to the jury. The Supreme Court conceded that. The value it found in the proffered testimony was that it would help dispel two "myths": the first being the "popular misconception" that battered women are "masochistic and actually enjoy their beatings, that they purposely provoke their husbands into violent behavior"; the second, that "women who remain in battering relationships are free to leave their abusers at any time."

As evidence for the first of these myths, the court cited a book by Dr. Walker. But in fact there is no evidence in Dr. Walker's book that the public believes battered women are masochists who enjoy provoking their husbands. Subsequent research has failed to find such evidence.

The second so-called myth raises a serious question that is not easily answered. No doubt many people, hearing of the abuse a woman has endured, ask themselves why she doesn't simply leave. The explanation advanced by Dr. Walker and others is that battered women suffer from "learned helplessness." The phrase was coined by Professor Martin Seligman, a psychologist at the University of Pennsylvania, after studying the behavior of dogs who were confined in harnesses in such a way that they could not escape painful electrical shocks. They soon ceased to struggle, and when presented with a way out they chose not to take it. When the experiment was over, they had to be dragged from their cages. The dogs had lost their will to control their environment. Professor Seligman later described depression in humans as learned helplessness. Dr. Walker asserts that women who have experienced the battering cycle—an increase in marital tension, then a physical attack, followed by a period of loving contrition—become helpless in much the same way as do shocked dogs. They believe they can neither control their environment nor predict the effects of their own behavior. Poverty, concern for their children, and the indifference of police and social-welfare agencies may reinforce this sense of helplessness.

No doubt some battered women (and some women who have never been battered) display these symptoms. But the evidence supporting the view that most battered women feel helpless is sketchy. Mary Ann Dutton, a psychologist deeply sympathetic to the plight of battered women, has written that women exposed to violence and abuse "do not respond similarly" because there is no "singular 'battered-woman profile.' " Some feel psychologically trapped and try to stick it out, others solicit help from friends or call the police; still others resist and fight back. Some go to shelters, some do not. Many of these coping strategies turn out to be ineffective; but, by choosing them, abused women do reveal themselves not to be as passive as shocked dogs in a cage. Some evidence suggests that it is precisely the most severely abused women who are most likely to leave their husbands. We do not yet have good ways of predicting who will leave a relationship and who will remain helplessly trapped within it.

Moreover, killing one's abuser seems quite inconsistent with the theory of learned helplessness. Dr. Seligman's helpless dogs did not bite their abusers, but Dr. Walker's helpless women killed theirs. Dr. Walker's own evidence seems to contradict her conclusions. A helpless woman should feel that her life is governed by external forces rather than by her own choices, but the battered women Dr. Walker studied displayed an internal, not external, locus of control. People who believe that they, and not external forces, govern their lives cannot plausibly be called helpless, especially when in some cases—the women who kill their husbands—they act on that belief.

None of these issues have prevented appellate courts from accepting the view that there is a phenomenon called battered-woman syndrome about which expert testimony will have significant probative value.

THE position that so many judges and legislators have taken is scientifically suspect, philosophically debatable, and legally unnecessary. The science is suspect for a variety of reasons [see "Trial by Expert," *NR,* March 10]; indeed, the problems with bringing social science into the courtrooms are perfectly illustrated by battered-woman syndrome. We do not know what proportion of battered women develop a syndrome (and how many develop the syndrome without being battered), and the evidence for the existence of a syndrome was mostly elicited by interviewers who were predisposed to find it. The American Psychiatric Association has declined to include the syndrome in its *Diagnostic and Statistical Manual (DSM-IV)* despite intense lobbying by its supporters. Dr. Walker herself is an advocate, who displays a tendency to find a "syndrome" where the facts do not support it. When she discovered that many of her women did not display feelings of helplessness and did not have low self-esteem, she expressed surprise and went on to dispute or discount the women's own accounts. She explained that in "reality" these women have no control over their lives, whatever they might say to the contrary; in fact, their denial of helplessness reflects their desire to "gain approval" from Dr. Walker. By 1989, five years after she expressed her surprise at the poor fit between her hypothesis and the data, she had overcome whatever reservations the data had occasioned and now wrote confidently that the "typical battered woman has poor self-image and self-esteem."

Philosophically, it is hard to see why a jury should consider such a syndrome to be an excusing condition if some women (and for all we know, most women) who are battered and who kill their abusers do not suffer from the syndrome. Syndrome sufferers would have the benefit of expert witnesses testifying on their behalf, while equally abused but non-syndrome women would not. Describing a battered woman as some courts have done—as dependent, brainwashed, terror-stricken, or psychologically paralyzed—reproduces rather than eliminates the very stereotypes to which most of us object. Anne Coughlin states it well: the battered-woman claim, designed "ostensibly to refute a variety of misogynist stereotypes," requires accused women "to embrace precisely those insulting stereotypes that the defense was supposed to explode, and it endorses the assumption that women are incapable of the rational self-governance exercised by men." The syn-

> *A jury that is free to acquit a guilty but likable defendant is also free to convict an innocent but detestable one.*

drome defense is, by definition, not available to a woman with a sturdily independent cast of mind and a record of making her own decisions and managing her own affairs. If she kills an abusive mate, she is on her own in claiming self-defense; it is only the passive weak-willed woman who can use the syndrome to bolster her self-defense claim.

Legally, the syndrome may add something to the traditional claim of self-defense, but that something is ill-defined. It is a mistake to say that the old law of self-defense was inherently masculine. As Professor Susan Estrich has pointed out, the rules of self-defense "exist not so much to define manly behavior as to limit manly instincts—in order to preserve human life." It might be manly, she observes, to respond to an insult with deadly force, but it is illegal because the law requires that there be imminent danger of death or grave bodily injury.

It would be difficult to cite or imagine a criminal defense that was applicable solely to a female defendant. Ordinary fair play, to say nothing of the equal-protection clause of the Constitution, suggests that a defense available to one sex be available to both. In February 1989 Paul Kacsmar killed his brother, Francis. At his trial he claimed he acted in self-defense. Paul, a man in his forties, lived with his mother and brother in Pittsburgh. Paul was ill (he had suffered a stroke) and a somewhat wimpy fellow; Francis was a combat veteran who liked to practice judo. They did not get along. Francis thought of himself as the head of the house; Paul resented his claims. There were many arguments over the years and a few fights. Most of the fights involved pushing and shoving, but sometimes punches were thrown, usually by Francis. Paul denied ever being the aggressor and claimed that Francis sometimes threatened to "beat the hell out of him." On the night of the shooting,

Francis accused Paul of not doing his share of the housework. The argument escalated, and Francis hit Paul a few times with his fist. After Paul broke free, he ran to his room, picked up a gun, came back downstairs, and without warning shot the unarmed Francis five times.

Paul was convicted of voluntary manslaughter and sentenced to five to ten years in prison. On appeal, a Pennsylvania superior court reversed his conviction on the grounds that the trial judge had not admitted expert testimony that Paul suffered from "battered-person syndrome." The court reasoned that if a woman could suffer from battered-woman syndrome, a man could suffer from battered-person syndrome. The Pennsylvania court repeated the erroneous cliché that expert testimony on such syndromes can dispel the "myths" that abused people are "masochists who are responsible for the abuse." It did not explain who held such a myth or why anyone would suppose that Kacsmar's jury had entertained it.

When such cases as Gladys Kelly's or Paul Kacsmar's came to the attention of appellate judges cognizant of the problem of abuse, they had two choices: they could reassert the traditional law of self-defense and remind lawyers and trial judges that there were ample ways for getting such a defense to the jurors and clarifying for them the distinctions between justification, excuse, and mitigation; or they could help invent a new standard of personal accountability based on poor social-science research and dubious theorizing and commend it to trial judges and jurors without clarifying its relationship to the law of self-defense or foreseeing its capacity for protean transformation and growth.

THEY chose the latter course. By itself this change might have had little effect, but it was compounded by the willingness of many jurors to judge the motives as well as the actions of defendants. Jurors will judge the moral worthiness of victims despite the fact that the law rests on the proposition that, except for certain conditions (for example, the victim was trying to kill his killer), all lives are of equal moral worth. They will often weigh the motives and character of both victim and defendant and adjust their verdicts accordingly; in extreme cases they will engage in what legal scholars call jury nullification by acquitting a defendant despite overwhelming evidence of guilt. Our sympathy for some defendants may lead us to feel that the jury's refusal to convict despite conclusive evidence is a sign of its humanity. But a jury that is free to acquit a guilty but likable defendant is also free to convict an innocent but detestable one.

Justice is a difficult ideal, vulnerable to attack by benevolence on one side and vengeance on the other. To the extent that the criminal courts allow victims to be put on trial, they foster this siege and allow an affluent defendant to introduce expert witnesses and other evidence that engages the sympathies of jurors while debasing standards of conduct. The law is, or ought to be, a tough master that, by holding us all to a high standard of personal accountability, produces the behavior we wish to see and reduces the opportunity for privilege to corrupt the system.

Juvenile Justice

Although there were variations within specific offense categories, the overall arrest rate for juvenile violent crime remained relatively constant for several decades. Then, in the late 1980s, something changed, bringing more and more juveniles charged with a violent offense into the justice system. The juvenile justice system is a twentieth-century response to the problems of dealing with children in trouble with the law or children who need society's protection.

Juvenile court procedure differs from the procedure in adult courts because juvenile courts were based on the philosophy that their function was to treat and to help, not to punish and to abandon, the offender. Recently, operations of the juvenile court have received criticism, and a number of significant Supreme Court decisions have changed the way the courts must approach the rights of children.

Despite these changes, however, the major thrust of the juvenile justice system remains one of diversion and treatment rather than adjudication and incarceration, although there is a trend toward dealing more punitively with serious juvenile offenders. This unit's opening essay, "Restoring the Balance: Juvenile and Community Justice," proposes an alternative approach to addressing juvenile crime that focuses on the interests of multiple justice clients. This restorative sanctioning model could provide a clear alternative to punishment-centered sanctioning approaches now dominant in juvenile justice and could ultimately redefine the sanctioning function.

Is throwing teens into adult courts—and adult prisons—the best way to deal with juvenile offenders? "Teen Crime" presents the thinking of Congress on this question.

J. David Hawkins advocates using the public health model to curb violence in "Controlling Crime before It Happens: Risk-Focused Prevention." He maintains that it is essential to identify and then eliminate the factors that put youth at risk for violence. The article that follows, "On the Street's of America," gives the reader a glimpse into a youth gang known as Fairview Hawks.

Judges and politicians are debating a solution to violent teenage crime that was once unthinkable: abolishing the system and trying most minors as adults. "With Juvenile Courts in Chaos, Critics Propose Their Demise" sheds light on this debate.

The unit closes by examining a program that uses the power of peer pressure as a positive influence on the lives of youthful troublemakers. "Teen Court" tells how the program works.

Looking Ahead: Challenge Questions

What reform efforts are currently under way in the juvenile justice system?

What are some recent trends in juvenile delinquency? In what ways will the juvenile justice system be affected by these trends?

Is the departure of the juvenile justice system from its original purpose warranted? Why or why not?

What do you think of the "Teen Court" concept? Be specific.

Restoring the Balance: Juvenile and Community Justice

by Gordon Bazemore and Susan E. Day

The problem of crime can no longer be simplified to the problem of the criminal.

Leslie Wilkins

Offender-based control strategies are incomplete, since they take a 'closed system' view of correctional interventions: change the offender and not the community.

James Byrne

In a democratic society, citizens' expectations of government agencies are critically important. Unfortunately, within our juvenile justice system, community needs have been lost in the decade-long debate over the future of the juvenile court and the relative efficacy of punishment versus treatment. A number of politicians and policymakers argue for criminalizing our juvenile justice system through "get tough," adult sentences for juvenile offenders. Some even advocate abolishing the juvenile justice system and its foundation, the independent juvenile court.

On the other hand, many proponents of the juvenile court call for reaffirming the traditional treatment mission. Increasingly, the public and even many juvenile justice professionals perceive that treatment and punishment options are, as one judge aptly put it, "bad choices between sending kids to jail or sending them to the beach."

It is doubtful that either traditional treatment or criminalized retributive models can restore public confidence in the juvenile justice system. Only through extensive, meaningful citizen participation will public expectations and community needs be met. For most juvenile justice systems, achieving this level of involvement will require substantial restructuring.

This article describes an alternative approach to addressing juvenile crime that focuses on the interests of multiple justice clients. Alternatively

Gordon Bazemore is associate professor in the School of Public Administration at Florida Atlantic University. He is currently editing a book on international juvenile justice reform. Dr. Bazemore is principal investigator of a national action research project funded by OJJDP to pilot systemic reform based on restorative justice principles. He has directed several evaluations of juvenile justice, policing, and minority overrepresentation programs.

Susan E. Day is director of the Florida Youth Restoration Project, a community service program for delinquent youth in Palm Beach County, Florida. She serves as program manager for the Balanced and Restorative Justice Project.

From *Juvenile Justice*, December 1996, pp. 3-14. Reprinted by permission of the U.S. Department of Justice, Office of Juvenile Justice and Delinquency Prevention.

referred to as restorative justice, the balanced approach, and balanced and restorative justice (BRJ), this model is viewed by a growing number of juvenile justice professionals as a way to reengage the community in the juvenile justice process.

The Limits of Current Paradigms

Crime should never be the sole or even primary business of the State if real differences are sought in the well-being of individuals, families, and communities. The structure, procedures, and evidentiary rules of the formal criminal justice process coupled with most justice officials' lack of knowledge and connection to (the parties) affected by crime preclude the State from acting alone to achieve transformative changes.

Judge Barry Stuart

Worse still, we fear that even when something does work, it is seen to do so only in the eyes of certain professionals, while 'outside' the system, ordinary citizens are left without a role or voice in the criminal justice process.

John Braithewaite and
Stephen Mugford

If juvenile justice is underfunded, it is also underconceptualized.

Advocates of reaffirming treatment argue that the system is failing because it lacks adequate resources. Critics and defenders of juvenile justice, however, argue that juvenile justice systems have failed to articulate a vision of success. If juvenile justice is underfunded, it is also underconceptualized. As closed-system paradigms, the treatment and retributive models are insular and one-dimensional. They are insular because they are offender-focused and one-dimensional because they fail to address the community's diverse interests.

Although the punitive approach may appease public demand for retribution, it does little to rehabilitate or reintegrate juvenile offenders. Punishment is often used inappropriately, resulting in amply documented negative effects. Ironically, retributive punishment may encourage offenders to focus on themselves rather than on their victims. Even increasing its severity may have little impact if we have miscalculated the extent to which sanctions such as incarceration are experienced as punishment.[1]

In the public mind, punishment is at least somewhat related to offense. In contrast, treatment appears to address only the needs of the offender. Treatment programs often ask little of the offender beyond participating in counseling, remedial services, or recreational programs. Even when such programs "work," they make little difference in the lives of victims of juvenile crime, citizens concerned with the safety of their neighborhoods, or individuals who want young offenders held accountable for their actions.[2]

In fact, both punitive and treatment models focus little attention on the needs of victims and victimized communities. Neither model engages them as clients or as coparticipants in the justice process. Whether treatment or punishment is emphasized, the offender is the passive and solitary recipient of intervention and service. Increasingly reliant on facilities, treatment programs, and professional experts, juvenile justice systems exclude victims and other community members from what could be meaningful roles in sanctioning, rehabilitation, and public safety.

Fortunately, treatment and retributive models are not the only options for juvenile justice. The alternative, a community-oriented system, would involve citizens in setting clear limits on antisocial behavior and determining consequences for offenders. Victims' needs for reparation, validation, and healing would be at the core of a community justice system, which would work toward building crime-resistant communities whose residents feel safe. It would emphasize the need for building relationships and involving youth in work, service, and other roles that facilitate bonding with law-abiding adults. Finally, a community justice system would articulate more meaningful roles in rehabilitating offenders and improving community safety for employers, civic groups, religious communities, families, and other citizens.

Toward Community Juvenile Justice: A Balanced and Restorative Approach

Government is responsible for preserving *order* but the community is responsible for establishing *peace*.

Daniel Van Ness

• In inner-city Pittsburgh, young offenders in an intensive day treatment program solicit input from community organizations about service projects they would like to see completed in the neighborhood. They work with community residents on projects that include home repair and gardening for the elderly, voter registration drives, painting homes and public buildings, and planting and cultivating community gardens.

• In Florida, young offenders sponsored by the Florida Department of Juvenile Justice and supervised by The 100 Black Men of Palm Beach County, Inc., plan and execute projects that serve as shelters for abused, abandoned, and HIV-positive and AIDS-infected infants and children. In Palm Beach County, victim advocates train juvenile justice staff on sensitivity in their interaction with victims and help prepare victim awareness curriculums for youth in residential programs.

• In cities and towns in Pennsylvania, Montana, Minnesota, Australia, and New Zealand, family members and other citizens acquainted with a juvenile offender or victim of a juvenile crime gather to determine the best response to the offense. Held in schools, churches, or other community facilities, these family group conferences are facilitated by a community justice coordinator or police officer and ensure that offenders hear community disapproval of their behavior. Participants develop an new partnership between youth and victim advocates, concerned citizens, and community groups.

The balanced and restorative justice model is centered around community-oriented responses to crime.[3] Jurisdictions implementing it represent a diverse range of urban, suburban, and rural communities. These communities share a common commit-

Punitive and treatment models focus little attention on the needs of victims.

agreement for repairing the damage to victim and community and a plan for reintegrating the offender.

• In Minnesota, Department of Corrections staff collaborate with local police and citizen groups to establish family group conferencing programs and inform the community about offender monitoring and victim support. In Dakota County, a suburb of Minneapolis, retailers and senior citizens whose businesses and homes have been damaged by burglary or vandalism call a crime repair hotline to request a work crew of probationers to repair the damage.

• In Deschutes County, Oregon, offender work crews cut and deliver firewood to senior citizens and worked with a local contractor to build a homeless shelter.

• In more than 150 cities and towns throughout North America, victims and offenders meet with volunteer mediators to develop an agreement for restitution. At these meetings, victims express their feelings about the crime and gain information about the offense.

• In several cities in Montana, college students and other young adults in the Montana Conservation Corps supervise juvenile offenders working on environmental restoration, trail building, and other community service projects. They also serve as mentors.

While many professionals have become demoralized as juvenile justice systems are threatened with extinction, others are seeking to create a ment to restructuring juvenile justice on the basis of a new mission (balanced approach) and a new value framework (restorative justice).

Restorative and Community Justice

From the perspective of restorative justice, the most significant aspect of crime is that it victimizes citizens and communities. The justice system should focus on repairing this harm by ensuring that offenders are held accountable for making amends for the damage and suffering they have caused. The most important issue in a restorative response to crime is not deciding whether to punish or treat offenders. Rather, as Howard Zehr suggests, the three primary questions to be answered are "What is the harm?" "What needs to be done to make it right?" and "Who is responsible?"[4]

A restorative system would help to ensure that offenders make amends to their victims. Juvenile justice cannot do this alone, however. Restorative justice requires that not only government but victims, offenders, and communities be actively involved in the justice process. In fact, some have argued that the health of a community is determined by the extent to which citizens participate in community decisions. An effective justice system strengthens the capacity of communities to respond to crime and empow- ers them to do so. As Judge Barry Stuart notes:

> When members fail to assume responsibility for decisions affecting the community, community life will be characterized by the absence of a collective sense of caring, a lack of respect for diverse values, and ultimately a lack of any sense of belonging. . . . Conflict, if resolved through a process that constructively engages the parties involved, can be a fundamental building ingredient of any relationship. As members increase their ability to resolve disputes creatively, the ability of the community to effectively sanction crime, rehabilitate offenders, and promote public safety increases.[5]

The most unique feature of restorative justice is its elevation of the role of victims in the justice system. Victim rights has become a popular slogan, but victim needs are addressed by the system only after the needs of judges, prosecutors, probation officers, treatment providers, and even offenders are considered. Restorative justice does not define victim rights as the absence of offender rights; it focuses on the needs of victim, community, and offender. To bring balance to the present offender-driven system, however, it is necessary to give priority to victims' needs for physical, material, and emotional healing.

The Balanced Approach Mission

The balanced approach is a back-to-basics mission for juvenile justice that supports a community's need to sanction crime, rehabilitate offenders, and ensure public safety. Toward these ends, it articulates three goals for juvenile justice: accountability, public safety, and competency development (see figure 1).[6] Balance is attainable when administrators ensure that equitable resources are allocated to each goal.

• **Accountability.** Crime is sanctioned most effectively when offenders take responsibility for their crimes and the harm caused to victims, when offenders make amends by restoring losses, and when communities and victims take active roles in the sanctioning process. Because the offender's obligation is defined primarily as an obligation to his victims rather than to the State, accountability cannot be equated with responsiveness to juvenile justice professionals by obeying a curfew, complying with drug screening, or writing an essay. Nor can it be equated with punish-

the mere absence of bad behavior. It should increase the capacity of adults and communities to involve young people in work, service, dispute resolution, community problem solving, and cognitive skills building.

• **Public safety.** Assuring public safety requires more than mere incapacitation. Communities cannot be kept safe simply by locking up offend-

groups to enhance the role of juvenile justice professionals as resources in prevention and positive youth development.

The principle behind BRJ is that justice is best served when victims, offenders, and communities receive equitable attention in the justice process. The needs of one client cannot be met unless the needs of other clients are addressed. Crime severs bonds between victims, offenders, and families. Although offenders must take full responsibility for their acts, the responsibility for restoring mutual respect, understanding, and support among those involved must be shared by the community.

The health of a community is determined by the extent to which citizens participate in community decisions.

ment. It is easier to make offenders take their punishment than it is to get them to take responsibility for their actions.

• **Competency.** The most successful rehabilitation ensures that young offenders make measurable gains in educational, vocational, social, civic, and other competencies that enhance their capacity to function as productive adults. When competency is defined as the capacity to do something well that others value, the standard for achieving success is measured in the community. Competency is not

ers. Locked facilities must be part of any public safety strategy, but they are the least cost-effective component. A balanced strategy invests heavily in strengthening a community's capacity to prevent and control crime. A problem-oriented focus ensures that the time of offenders under supervision in the community is structured around such activities as work, education, and service. Adults, including parents, are assigned clear roles in monitoring offenders. A balanced strategy cultivates new relationships with schools, employers, and other community

Small Changes Yield Large Results

The change at the heart of BRJ is embodied in the community-building interventions described above. BRJ collaborators, including juvenile justice and other service professionals, have discovered that even small changes in how they conduct business can have immediate and lasting effects on the dynamics of community relationships.

Communities in the United States and across the globe are making dramatic policy changes on the basis of restorative priorities. In 1989, New Zealand began requiring that all juvenile offenders over age 14 (except in the most serious cases) be referred to a family group conference in which restorative goals are addressed in meetings that include victims, offenders, support groups, families, policymakers, social workers, and others. The New Zealand law appears to have drastically reduced court workloads and the use of incarceration.[7]

Fourteen States have enacted legislation adopting the balanced approach as the mission of their juvenile justice systems. A number of States have administrative rules or statewide policies that require case managers and other decisionmakers to consider the goals of the balanced approach in dispositional recommendations. In Pennsylvania and Montana, decisionmakers are

Figure 1

Restorative Justice

Competency

Public Safety

Accountability

Table 1
The Participants in a Balanced and Restorative Juvenile Justice System

Crime Victims	Offenders	Citizens, Families, and Community Groups
◆ Receive support, assistance, compensation, information, and services. ◆ Receive restitution or other reparation from the offender. ◆ Are involved and are encouraged to give input at all points in the system as to how the offender will repair the harm done. ◆ Have the opportunity to face the offenders and tell their story. ◆ Feel satisfied with the justice process. ◆ Provide guidance and consultation to juvenile justice professionals on planning and advisory groups.	◆ Complete restitution to their victims. ◆ Provide meaningful service to repay the debt to their communities. ◆ Face the personal harm caused by their crimes by participating in victim offender mediation or other victim awareness programs. ◆ Complete work experience and active and productive tasks that increase skills and improve the community. ◆ Are monitored by community adults as well as juvenile justice providers and supervised to the greatest extent possible in the community. ◆ Improve decisionmaking skills and have opportunities to help others.	◆ Are involved to the greatest extent possible in rehabilitation, community safety initiatives, and holding offenders accountable. ◆ Work with offenders on local community service projects. ◆ Provide support to victims. ◆ Provide support to offenders as mentors, employers, and advocates. ◆ Provide work for offenders to pay restitution to victims and service opportunities that allow offenders to make meaningful contributions to the quality of community life. ◆ Assist families to support the offender in obligation to repair the harm and increase competencies. ◆ Advise courts and corrections and play an active role in disposition.

using balanced approach criteria as funding guidelines and have formed statewide groups to oversee the development of restorative justice efforts.

Balanced and restorative justice cannot be achieved by mandates or legislation alone. As the three jurisdictions that constitute the OJJDP-funded demonstration effort are learning, the new model cannot be implemented overnight. Working with different juvenile justice systems in diverse communities, administrators in Palm Beach County, Florida, Dakota County, Minnesota, and Allegheny County, Pennsylvania, are pursuing varied approaches to systemic change to build a restorative model from the ground up. These administrators have made significant progress but acknowledge that the kind of change envisioned by BRJ is quite different from past practices. This change is especially striking in the model's focus on citizen involvement, including restructuring juvenile justice agencies to more effectively engage the community.

Balanced and Restorative Justice: New Roles for Citizens and Professionals

I'm glad to see somebody is finally trying to instill some responsibility in these kids. I'm happy to help when it's obvious that we're trying to make taxpayers out of these kids, rather than tax liabilities.
                                    Community Member

In the mediation session I learned that the offender was just a little kid and not the threat I thought he was. I also learned he had some needs that weren't being met. . . . For the first time (I've been a victim before), it seemed like someone was responding to my needs and listening to me.
                                    Youth Crime Victim

When I first walked into the conferencing meeting and saw the victim and her friends and then saw my grandfather there I wished I could have gone to jail instead. But once everybody had talked about the crime I began to realize that Mrs. B was really hurt and scared by what I had done. I had to work hard to earn the money to pay her back and to do the community service hours (but the work on the crew was pretty fun) and I thought it was fair after all.
                                    Juvenile Offender

Now I know what my job is really about! As a manager, I have a better sense of how to allocate, or reallocate, our resources. And my staff are getting a better sense of what their role is and how this fits with my vision of what the community's role should be. We know we're really 'out of balance,' but for the first time we have a plan to move forward without chasing every fad and new program that comes along. We can also talk to the community about what we're doing in a way that they understand and want to help.
                        Manager of a Local Juvenile Justice System

As a community justice model, balanced and restorative justice offers a new vision of how victims, offenders, and others can be involved in the juvenile justice process. As table 1 illustrates, this vision is best understood by examining how the model is viewed by its participants.

Balanced and restorative justice is a work in progress. No juvenile justice system is completely balanced or fully restorative. But if juvenile justice systems, including those most committed to the model, fail to meet the standards they have set for community and client involvement, it is not because the model is utopian. It is because administrators are constrained by management protocols designed to deliver services based on the treatment and retributive paradigms.

Figure 2
What's New About the Balanced Approach?

Current System	Balanced and Restorative Justice
Resource Allocation and Staffing Patterns	*New* Values
	New Clients
Programs and Practices	*New* Performance Outcomes
	New Decisionmaking
Performance Outcomes?	*New* Resource Allocation and Staffing Patterns

The innovation of balanced and restorative justice lies in its agenda for restructuring the juvenile justice system to make it community-focused rather than bureaucracy-driven. This agenda demands new values, clients, performance objectives, decisionmaking processes, program priorities, staff roles, and patterns of resource allocation. As figure 2 suggests, while most juvenile justice agencies determine intervention priorities on the basis of current staff roles and resource allocations, juvenile justice managers who adopt the balanced approach mission are committed to making their agencies and systems value- and client-driven and outcome-oriented. Decisions are based on the premise that programs are means to accomplish restorative outcomes that address community needs (see table 2).

From a community justice perspective, the value of a program and the quality of its implementation is gauged in large measure by the extent to which it involves community members at all levels of implementation.

Citizen Involvement and Client Focus

In the total quality management (TQM) movement,[8] the concept of a client involves three components: a recipient of service, a target of intervention and change, and a coparticipant who must have input into the process and be involved to the greatest extent possible in decisionmaking.

The input of each client group is needed to stimulate and maintain community involvement. Currently few citizens are involved at significant levels in juvenile justice because they are seldom asked. Although many professionals would welcome community involvement and may work hard at collaboration and service brokerage, such efforts often fail to include employers, clergy, civic leaders, and neighborhood residents. Too often, juvenile justice agencies are unable to find appropriate roles for community members who are not social service professionals or time to support their efforts. Short-term involvement is often uninteresting because it is not linked to interventions that achieve significant outcomes for offenders or victims. When citizens are asked to participate, it is often on the basis of civic duty rather than personal commitment. As Braithwaite and Mugford observe, citizens are more willing to become involved if they have a personal interest in the offender, victim, or the family.[9]

Crimes typically evoke a community of concern for the victim, the offender, families and friends, and interested citizens and community groups. As the New Zealand experiment with family group conferencing illustrates, these personal communities can be a primary resource in resolving youth crimes. It is around such microcommunities that citizen participation in justice decisionmaking is being built.[10]

BRJ practices and programs invite a high level of citizen participation. Community involvement is never easy, but it is satisfying for citizens to help young offenders make restitution to their victims.

The more active roles for offenders, victims, and community in the juvenile justice process, noted in table 1, have implications for the roles of juvenile justice professionals. The most important and difficult challenge in moving toward balanced and restorative justice will be to alter the job descriptions and professional orientations of juvenile justice staff. For those accustomed to working with offenders individually or in programs and facilities, the role change implied by the need to engage victims and communities may be dramatic. Essentially, this change may be best understood as moving from direct service provider or service broker to community justice facilitator.[11]

As table 3 suggests, the new roles involve juvenile justice professionals in activities with each of the three justice clients. These activities include a variety of efforts to enhance preventive capacity and to help adults provide offenders with opportunities for competency development.

Getting There

Some may say this [movement toward restorative justice] is Utopian. While this may be true, in a climate of failure and irrational extremism in the response to juvenile crime, there may be *nothing so practical as a good Utopia.*

Lode Walgrave

Robert Fulcrum tells the story of a reporter visiting the cathedral in Chartres, France, during the cathedral's construction. Hoping to get a sense of how those working on this magnificent structure understood and experienced their contribution to its completion, the reporter began asking several workmen about their jobs. The first, a stonecutter, said that his job was simply to cut the stone into square blocks for someone else to use in the foundation; the job was monotonous, and he had been doing the same thing day in and day out. Next, the reporter asked a workman who was painting stone blocks on the front of the building about his job. "I just paint these blocks and nothing more," he said. "There is not much to it."

Frustrated that these workmen had little to say about the significance of working on this historical effort, the reporter moved to another part of the building and approached a man carefully cutting stained glass windows. Surely, this man felt that his work was the artistic opportunity of a lifetime. Once again the reporter was disappointed; the man said that he was very tired and somewhat bored with his task. Finally, as he walked out of the cathedral in despair, the reporter passed an elderly woman stooped and working rapidly to clean up the debris left from the stone and glass cutters, painters, and other artisans. He asked what it was that she was doing. Her answer was that she was building the most magnificent cathedral in the history of the world to the glory of God.

As this story illustrates, the key to progress toward restorative justice is viewing small steps as the building blocks of a more effective juvenile justice system.

Will balanced and restorative justice work? BRJ is not a treatment program but a model for system reform. It cannot be assessed by using traditional program evaluation technologies. The success of a restorative justice system should be measured not only by recidivism but also by victim satisfaction, offender accountability, competency development, and public safety.[12] The success of BRJ will depend on the consistency and integrity of implementation, how well its core philosophy is understood,

Table 2
Outcome Measures and Priorities for Practice in the Balanced Approach

Competency Development

Intermediate Outcome

Measures	Priorities for Practice
◆ Proportion of youth on supervision completing successful work experience or employment (quality of experience?). ◆ Proportion of youth on supervision completing meaningful work/service project. ◆ Extent of bonding between youth under supervision and community adults. ◆ Increase in empathy and improvement in skills. ◆ Demonstrated improvement in conflict resolution and anger management. ◆ Measured increase in educational, interpersonal, citizenship, and other competencies.	◆ Structured work experience and employment programs. ◆ Service/active learning. ◆ Cognitive and decisionmaking programs. ◆ Dispute resolution training. ◆ Intergenerational projects. ◆ Cross-age tutoring. ◆ Conservation and environmental awareness.

Accountability

Intermediate Outcome

Measures	Priorities for Practice
◆ Proportion of offenders completing fair and appropriate restitution orders or agreements. ◆ Proportion of victims given input into the process. ◆ Proportion of victims satisfied with the process. ◆ Proportion of offenders showing measured increase in victim awareness and empathy. ◆ Proportion of offenders and victims completing mediation or other resolution and community service. ◆ Proportion of offenders completing meaningful community service projects (number of such projects completed).	◆ Restitution to victims. ◆ Restorative community service. ◆ Victim offender mediation. ◆ Direct service to victims or surrogate victims. ◆ Victim awareness panels or victim offender groups in treatment programs.

Public Safety

Intermediate Outcome

Measures	Priorities for Practice
◆ Proportion of offenders reoffending while under juvenile justice supervision. ◆ Number of citizens involved in preventive and monitoring activities. ◆ Decrease in community fear and increase in understanding of juvenile justice. ◆ Decrease in school violence and increase in school and community-based conflict resolution. ◆ Increase in competency, empathy, and internal controls for offenders under supervision.	◆ Structuring time of offenders being supervised in the community: work experience, community service, and alternative education. ◆ Effective use of natural surveillance and community guardians such as employers, relatives, churches, and mentors. ◆ Continuum of graduated community-based sanctions and surveillance. ◆ Prevention and capacity building in schools and other community groups.

Table 3
New Roles in the Balanced and Restorative Justice Model

The Coparticipants

Victim	Active participant in defining the harm of the crime and shaping the obligations placed on the offender.
Community	Responsible for supporting and assisting victims, holding offenders accountable, and ensuring opportunities for offenders to make amends.
Offender	Active participant in reparation and competency development.

Juvenile Justice Professional

Sanctioning	Facilitate mediation, ensure restoration, develop creative or restorative community service options, engage community members, and educate the community on its role.
Rehabilitation	Develop new roles for young offenders that allow them to practice and demonstrate competency, assess and build on youth and community strengths, and develop community partnerships.
Public Safety	Develop incentives and consequences to ensure offender compliance with supervision objectives, help school and family control and maintain offenders in the community, and develop prevention capacity of local organizations.

---

how effectively it is adapted to local conditions, and whether restorative justice is given a chance. Although restorative justice may not lead to immediate reductions in recidivism, the standard of comparison should be the current system. As a First Nations Community Justice Coordinator in Yukon, Canada, reminds us:

So we make mistakes. Can you—the current system—say you don't make mistakes? . . . If you don't think you do, walk through our community. Every family will have something to teach you. . . . By getting involved, by all of us taking responsibility, it is not that we won't make mistakes, we would be doing it together, as a *community* instead of having it done to us. . . . We need to make *real differences* in the way people act and the way we treat others. . . . Only if we empower them and support them can they break out of this trap.[13]

It is the failure of the current paradigms that has moved some policy-makers toward radical measures to abolish the juvenile justice system. Those who wish to preserve it see balanced and restorative justice as a means to do so by crafting a new system in which juvenile justice reflects community justice.

Notes

1. For commentary on closed-system approaches to community corrections, see J. Byrne, "Reintegrating the Concept of Community in Community Corrections," *Crime and Delinquency* 35 (1989): 471–499; see also A.J. Reiss and M. Tonry, "Why Are Communities Important in Understanding Crime?" *Communities and Crime* (Chicago: University of Chicago Press, 1986). Like treatment, punishment will remain an essential component of any juvenile justice system. However, punitive measures focused primarily on incarceration represent only one limited approach to meeting community needs to sanction crime. For commentary on more educative and expressive approaches to setting tolerance limits for crime, see J. Braithewaite, *Crime, Shame and Reintegration* (Cambridge, England: Cambridge University Press, 1989); L. Wilkins, *Punishment, Crime and Market Forces* (Brookfield, VT: Dartmouth Publishing Company, 1991); G. Bazemore and M. Umbreit, "Rethinking the Sanctioning Function in Juvenile Court: Retributive or Restorative Responses to Youth Crime," *Crime and Delinquency* 41 (1995): 296–316. The counterdeterrent effects of retributive punishment, including stigmatization, weakening bonds, and conventional peer and adult relations, are also well documented. Finally, empirical evidence that criminal justice decisionmakers typically overestimate the perceived punitive effects of incarceration is provided in M. Crouch, "Is Incarceration Really Worse? Analysis of Offenders' Preferences for Prison Over Probation," *Justice Quarterly* 10 (1993): 67–88.

2. The critique of the individual treatment model presented here is not premised on the largely discredited "nothing works" perspective, nor do we question the need for an effective rehabilitative model for juvenile justice. Rather, our criticisms of traditional counseling-based treatment are based primarily upon the very limited context of intervention in most treatment programs and on the deficit assumptions about offenders on which most of these programs are based. A more comprehensive agenda for rehabilitation and reintegration would focus more on relationship building and the development of roles for delinquent youth that allow them to demonstrate competency while forming bonds with conventional peers and adults. A competency development component of such a reintegrative and restorative agenda is outlined in G. Bazemore and P. Cruise, "Reinventing Rehabilitation: Exploring a Competency Development Model for Juvenile Justice Intervention," *Perspectives* 19 (1995): 4; and G. Bazemore and C. Terry, "Developing Delinquent Youth: A Reintegrative Model for Rehabilitation and a New Role for the Juvenile Justice System," *Child Welfare* (forthcoming).

3. Balanced and Restorative Justice (BRJ) is also the title of a national action research project funded through the Technical Assistance and Training Prevention division of the Office of Juvenile Justice and Delinquency Prevention. This project provides national training and information dissemination as well as support and assistance to demonstration projects currently implementing BRJ.

4. H. Zehr, *Changing Lenses: A New Focus for Crime and Justice* (Scottsdale, PA: Herald Press, 1990).

5. Judge B. Stuart, notes from presentation at the annual conference of the Society for Professionals in Dispute Resolution (Toronto, Canada, 1993): 7.

6. In a balanced system, programs and practices aimed at repairing harm to victims should, as Troy Armstrong has phrased it, "resonate with" practices aimed at rehabilitative and public safety objectives. Specifically, holding offenders accountable is a first step in the rehabilitative process. Developing capacities for competent behavior in offenders increases community safety by increasing connectedness and concern for others as well as life skills. Enhanced community safety is often necessary to carry out meaningful community sanction-

ing, offender reintegration, and victim support and restoration. For a detailed discussion of the balanced approach mission, see D. Maloney and G. Bazemore, "Rehabilitating Community Service: Toward Restorative Service in a Balanced Justice System," *Federal Probation* (1994); G. Bazemore, "On Mission Statements and Reform in Juvenile Justice: The Case of the Balanced Approach," *Federal Probation* (1992); G. Bazemore and C. Washington, "Charting the Future of the Juvenile Justice System: Reinventing Mission and Management," *Spectrum: The Journal of State Government* (1995). Table 2 of this paper provides a general summary of how performance objectives on each goal can be measured.

7. F.W.M. McElrae, "Restorative Justice—The New Zealand Youth Court: A Model for Development in Other Courts?" *Journal of Judicial Administration* 4 (1994), Australian Institute of Judicial Administration, Melbourne, Australia.

8. W.E. Deming, *Out of Crisis* (Cambridge, MA: MIT Center for Advanced Engineering, 1986); L. Martin, *Total Quality Management in Organizations* (Newbury Park, CA: Sage, 1993).

9. J. Braithewaite and S. Mugford, "Conditions of Successful Reintegration Ceremonies: Dealing with Juvenile Offenders," *British Journal of Criminology* (1995): 34. The authors give examples of how relatives, friends, and acquaintances of young offenders, victims, and their families become vital resources in restoring and meeting the needs of crime victims while also helping offenders when asked to participate in family group conferences.

10. For a more detailed description of the New Zealand and Australian models of family group conferencing, including research findings and critical concerns about implementation, see G. Maxwell and A. Morris, *Family, Victims, and Culture: Youth Justice in New Zealand* (Wellington, New

Zealand: Social Policy Agency and Victoria University, Institute of Criminology, 1993); C. Alder and J. Wundersitz, *Family Group Conferencing: The Way Forward or Misplaced Optimism?* (Canberra, Australia: Australian Institute of Criminology, 1994); M. Umbreit and S. Stacy, "Family Group Conferencing Comes to the U.S.: A Comparison With Victim Offender Mediation," *Juvenile and Family Court Journal* (forthcoming).

11. The transformation from service provider to the facilitator role is used to describe changes in probation services in the Vermont Department of Corrections' restructuring of the State's probation system through Community Reparative Boards.

12. Answering the question "Does it work?" in a restorative community justice framework must give consideration to improvements in the capacity of community groups and citizens to prevent, sanction, and control crime. For example, the development of community support groups of nonprofessional citizens is generally not viewed as a success outcome, but such measures may be a more critical gauge of long-term community safety than reductions in recidivism of offenders in treatment programs.

13. Rose Couch, Community Justice Coordinator, Quanlin Dun First Nations, Yukon, Canada. As quoted in B. Stuart, "Sentencing Circles: Making 'Real Differences'," monograph, Territorial Court of Yukon, Whitehorse, Yukon, Canada.

Supplemental Reading

Bazemore, G., and M.S. Umbreit. (1995). "Rethinking the Sanctioning Function in Juvenile Court: Retributive or Restorative Responses to Youth Crime." *Crime and Delinquency* 41(3): 296–316. This article proposes restorative justice as an alternative

model for the juvenile courts to address limitations of sanctioning choices inherent in individual treatment and retributive justice paradigms. NCJ 156328

Bazemore, G., and M.S. Umbreit. (1994). *Balanced and Restorative Justice.* Washington, DC: U.S. Department of Justice, Office of Juvenile Justice and Delinquency Prevention. Community supervision of juvenile offenders based on the balanced and restorative justice approach is discussed in this examination of the Balanced and Restorative Justice Project being developed as an outgrowth of the Office of Juvenile Justice and Delinquency Prevention's juvenile restitution training and technical assistance program. NCJ 149727

Cragg. W. (1992). *Practice of Punishment: Towards a Theory of Restorative Justice.* New York: Routledge. This book develops a theory of punishment in which the central function of law is to reduce the need to use force in the resolution of disputes. The author examines traditional approaches to punishment to determine why they have failed to provide a coherent and humane approach to sentencing and corrections. NCJ 143921

Umbreit, M.S. (1995). "Holding Juvenile Offenders Accountable: A Restorative Justice Perspective." *Juvenile and Family Court Journal* 46(2): 31–42. This article defines accountability for juvenile offenders as an intervention strategy within the context of the restorative justice paradigm, in which the meaning of accountability shifts from incurring a debt to society to incurring a responsibility for making amends to the victimized person. NCJ 156121

Umbreit, M.S., R.B. Coates, and B. Kalanj. (1994). *Victim Meets Offender: The Impact of Restorative Justice and Mediation.* Monsey, NY: Willow Tree Press. This book reports findings from a study of victim-offender reconciliation and mediation programs for juvenile offenders in California, Minnesota, New Mexico, and Texas. NCJ 147713

TEEN CRIME

Congress wants to crack down on juvenile offenders. But is throwing teens into adult courts—and adult prisons—the best way?

By RICHARD LACAYO

CONGRESS MADE AN AGREEABLE DIS-covery three years ago. Early in 1994, in an abrupt statistical spike, voters in large numbers started saying that crime was their No. 1 concern. So when the House and Senate passed the omnibus crime bill later that year, people actually noticed. Which is one reason why, in a sluggish political summer, when Washington is competing with Mars and Mike Tyson for some quality time with the rest of America, Congress is going after crime again. In May the House passed a bill that would give $1.6 billion to states that agree to toughen their handling of kids who commit serious felonies, in part by making it easier to try them as adults. Last week the Senate Judiciary Committee was pushing forward on a similar bill, in the hope of bringing it to a vote this month. "People are expecting us to do something about these violent teenagers," committee chairman Orrin Hatch complained as he tried to speed through more than 100 proposed amendments. "We've got to move on this."

In truth, the problem isn't quite as pressing as it was a few years ago. With crime rates dropping, so is juvenile crime. But felonies by kids had exploded over the previous 10 years, a legacy of the crack trade and armed gangs, so the recent decline is still a dip in a high plateau. From 1985 to 1995, juvenile arrests for violent crimes rose 67%. Perhaps a fifth of all violent crimes is the work of teens. "In America today, no population poses a greater threat to public safety than juvenile criminals," says Representative Bill McCollum, the Florida Republican who wrote the House version of the bill.

Some criminologists are also warning that a new wave of "superpredators" will soon hit the streets. In fatherless households and fractured neighborhoods, millions of four- to seven-year-olds, the baby boomers' own mini-boom, are headed for their teens.

So Congress wants to make it easier to try juveniles accused of violent crimes as adults—and to incarcerate them in adult prisons. Under both the Senate bill and the House bill, states that want the federal dollars would have to make prosecutors and not judges the ones who decide whether a teenager charged with a serious violent felony or drug offense should be tried as an adult. To demonstrate that crimes really do carry punishments, states would also have to impose a rising scale of "graduated sanctions" for all juvenile offenses, beginning with the first, and keep adult-style criminal records on juvenile offenders. Under the present system, most such records are often closed, meaning prosecutors can't learn whether an accused youth is a repeat offender. "The juvenile justice system isn't working," says McCollum. "This bill puts consequences back into the law."

Over the past five years, however, every state except Hawaii has decided to allow some kids to be tried in adult criminal courts. Altogether, some 12,300 youths are prosecuted as adults each year in state

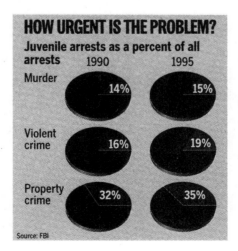

HOW URGENT IS THE PROBLEM?

Juvenile arrests as a percent of all arrests

	1990	1995
Murder	14%	15%
Violent crime	16%	19%
Property crime	32%	35%

Source: FBI

courts. That is about 9% of all juveniles arrested for violent crimes and a 70% increase over the number who were tried as adults a decade ago. But if the bills become law, those numbers would climb further. Child-welfare advocates say that would effectively dissolve the separate system of justice for kids that dates to 1899, when Chicago established the nation's first juvenile court.

Supporters of the bills say they correct a problem created in 1974, when new legislation channeled nearly all young offenders to the juvenile system. What isn't clear is whether moving young criminals back to adult courts has much impact on crime. According to a recent study by the liberal National Center for Initiatives and Alternatives, Connecticut has the highest juvenile-to-adult transfer rate and Colorado the lowest, yet their youth-crime rates are the same. Since the 1970s, New York has been automatically trying as adults kids 16 and older charged with serious crimes. In the same period, its juvenile crime rates doubled.

The politics of juvenile crime can also get complicated. Republicans are unhappy over polls that show that a majority of Americans believe Democrats are just as capable of handling crime. But while Americans have largely soured on the idea of rehabilitation for adult offenders—even some liberal criminologists have conceded that the most ruthless teen felons must be locked up—polls also show most people to be less sure that children can't be turned back. "I'm afraid this bill will gobble up some juveniles who do not really fit the most extreme category," says Democrat Joseph Biden of Delaware, the former chairman of the Senate Judiciary Committee.

One area in which Republicans could be getting out ahead of the public mood is in the provisions that would imprison kids with adults, though not in the same cells. While reportedly 8,000 teens are already housed

How to Start a Cease-Fire: Learning from Boston

IT IS NINE O'CLOCK ON A GAMY SUMMER NIGHT, AND BILL STEWART is on curfew patrol. The probation officer bounds up the stairs of a Dorchester triple-decker apartment building to check on a boy who was once caught with marijuana. The boy must be home between the hours of 7 p.m. and 7 a.m., seven days a week, under a system of court-ordered curfews of young offenders, each curfew set individually by a judge. There had been worrisome signs of gang involvement in this case. A week ago, someone fired a shotgun blast into the second-floor porch, and the boy's parents still have pellets in their arms and legs.

The kid, who just turned 17, is home. So are his older brother, two of his friends—and a bag of marijuana. "Three strikes and you're in," says Stewart. Jail, that is. Two plainclothes policemen who accompany Stewart confiscate the bag and run background checks on the boy's friends. When Stewart visits the apartment the next night to make sure the kid is still honoring the curfew and to search the place, he finds on the wall of a closet the roster of the Argyle Street Ballers, a small gang that sells drugs. "Now we know the players," he explains. "Now we can put the weight on them."

Stewart is not alone in putting weight on potential juvenile offenders in Boston. The city's Operation Night Light, which began in 1992, and Operation Cease-Fire, which emerged last year, have unleashed desk-bound probation officers in a drive coordinated with other law-enforcement agencies to keep drugs and weapons off the streets. The joint operations, part of a larger collaborative effort, have led to one startling result. Last week Boston completed its second year without anyone under 17 being killed by a firearm. No other American city with a population over half a million can match this record. "Boston is the first city in the country to interrupt the cycle of violence that began with crack," concludes David Kennedy, senior researcher at Harvard's Program in Criminal Justice Policy and Management.

In the early '90s, Dorchester, Roxbury and Mattapan were war zones, teeming with guns. Since the Dorchester district court first began imposing curfews in 1991, the city's gangs can no longer hang with impunity on crack corners at midnight.

Operation Cease-Fire is not just a police operation. It involves more than a dozen agencies, including the U.S. Attorney, the Drug Enforcement Administration and the Bureau of Alcohol, Tobacco and Firearms, the Suffolk County District Attorney as well as the Ten Point Coalition, a network of 43 black churches in the city. Says the Rev. Eugene Rivers, co-founder of the Ten Point Coalition: "The streets are much safer. The collaboration between the black churches and the police has produced results unseen in any other city." The two groups are now quietly working together to clear up scores of unsolved homicides.

Before Cease-Fire, federal and local law enforcement communicated like the Hatfields and the McCoys. "We were ordered not to notify the Boston police," says Michael Hennessey, a lieutenant in the school police, "because it would make the school administrators look bad."

No longer. Today everyone sees everyone else's intelligence. U.S. Attorney Donald Stern gets a copy of each report on a gun charge from the Boston police department. Stern in turn uses federal indictments to help take down Boston's most dangerous youths. All data are fed into the computers of the Youth Violence Task Force, an élite 65-person unit that tracks and targets gang activity. "We made threats directly to gang members and then delivered on it," says Police Commissioner Paul Evans. A case in point is the Intervale Posse, for years one of the most vicious gangs in the city. Despite repeated warnings from state and federal authorities, Intervale continued to terrorize its Dorchester neighborhood. Cease-Fire struck at dawn last August, arresting 24 gang members; 15 were brought down with federal warrants. "They are the teeth of the whole thing," notes David Singletary, an officer with the Youth Violence Task Force, as he cruises Dorchester one night with his partner, Kenny Israel, talking to street kids. "Once you say 'federal time,' it's a different ball game. You can end up doing your time in Leavenworth, and there is no parole."

Last week Attorney General Janet Reno praised the Boston project, and the Detroit police department sent officers to learn more about the experience. Detroit's executive deputy chief Benny Napoleon was impressed by the level of interagency coordination. "They're all at the table at the same time, consistently. We would see greater results from trying to duplicate the ways they do it."

No one in Boston, though, is getting cocky. "If we let up, the homicides could come right back again," warns Sergeant Kathleen Johnston, who is responsible for safety in the Boston public schools. "They are like a chronic disease." —*By Sam Allis/Boston*

with adults, federal rules require "sight and sound" separation, meaning juveniles cannot be within reach of adults. Some corrections officials say that requires a pointless division of facilities used by both populations—for instance, two exercise areas when one could be shared. The Senate bill would override the complexities of the sight-and-sound rule by imposing a "no physical contact" provision, which means that the same facilities could be used. But juvenile advocates say that breaking down the barriers would make kids prey to rape and other forms of abuse. Kids held for truancy, the most common reason for juvenile arrest, would be morsels for the older guys. "Children commit suicide eight times as often in jails as they do in juvenile-detention facilities," says Mark Soler, head of the Washington-based Youth Law Center.

The White House has proposed its own bill that puts more emphasis on money for crime-prevention measures, such as keeping schools open in the afternoon from 3 to 6, when almost half of juvenile crimes take place. While the Senate would allow states to use as much as 40% of the federal money they get for prevention programs, the House would require them to spend it all on law enforcement. The White House wants to require safety locks on guns to prevent kids from accidentally shooting other kids, a provision opposed by the National Rifle Association. "A juvenile-crime bill should crack down on gangs and guns," says senior adviser Rahm Emanuel. "If it doesn't do that, it is a juvenile-crime bill in name only."

Just naming the legislation has caused a fight. When McCollum introduced his House version last year, he called it the Violent Youth Predator Act. Insisting that "predator" was dehumanizing hype, Democrats demanded a change. McCollum backed off and called it the Juvenile Crime Control Act. But this isn't just a fight over crime. It's also a fight over which party is tougher on crime. In that one, harsh words can be as tempting as harsh sentences.

—*Reported by Sally B. Donnelly/Washington*

Controlling Crime Before It Happens: Risk-Focused Prevention

J. David Hawkins

Traditionally, the juvenile justice system has employed sanctions, treatment, and rehabilitation to change problem behaviors after they have occurred. Advocates of a prevention-based approach to crime control invite the scorn of critics who believe prevention amounts to little more than "feel good" activities. Yet the practitioner—the probation officer confronted daily with young people in trouble—is often aware of the need for effective prevention. As a probation officer in the early 1970's working with delinquent teenagers, I found myself asking, "Couldn't we have prevented these youngsters from getting to this point? Couldn't we have interceded before they were criminally referred to the courts?"

Once they have experienced the reinforcing properties of drugs and are convinced of crime's profitability, young people are difficult to turn around. Once invested in the culture of crime, they reject the virtues attributed to school and family, for reasons that are all too clear. For them, school is not a place of attachment and learning, but of alienation and failure; family is not a source of love and support, but of unremitting conflict.

Dealing with these youths as a probation officer, I saw my job as something akin to operating an expensive ambulance service at the bottom of a cliff. The probation staff were the emergency team patching up those who fell over the edge. Many of us who have worked in juvenile corrections have come to realize that to keep young people from falling in the first place, a barrier is needed at the top of the cliff. In short, we believe that prevention is more effective and less costly than treatment after the fact. David Mitchell, chief judge of the juvenile court for Baltimore County, once observed, "It is of no value for the court to work miracles in rehabilitation if there are no opportunities for the child in the community. Until we deal with the environment in which they live, whatever we do in the courts is irrelevant."

Effective prevention based on the public health model

In prevention, where action precedes the commission of crime, it is wise to heed the admonition that guides physicians: "Above all, do no harm." Hard work and good intentions, by themselves, are not enough to ensure that a program to prevent violence or substance abuse will succeed, let alone that it will not make things worse.

Early prevention efforts in the "War on Drugs" serve to illustrate this point. Well-meaning people were concerned about substance abuse and decided to do something about it by introducing prevention programs in the schools. They collected information, pictures, and even samples of illicit drugs, took these materials to the schools, and showed them to students; they talked about the behavioral and health effects of drugs and warned of the risks associated with their use. Contrary to intention and expectation, these drug information programs failed to reduce or eliminate drug use and, in some instances, actually led to its increase.[1] The real lesson learned in the schools was that information, which is neutral, can be employed to the wrong end, producing more harm than good. These early prevention workers had not envisioned drug information in the context of a comprehensive prevention strategy.

Increasingly, the preventive approach used in public health is being recognized as appropriate for use as part of a criminal justice strategy.[2] It

From the *National Institute of Justice Journal*, August 1995, pp. 10–18. Reprinted by permission of the U.S. Department of Justice, Office of Justice Programs.

is instructive to review an example of how the model has been applied to disease control. Seeking to prevent cardiovascular disease, researchers in the field of public health first identified risk factors; that is, the factors whose presence increased a person's chances of contracting the disease: tobacco use, high-fat diet, sedentary lifestyle, high levels of stress, and family history of heart disease. Equally important, they determined that certain protective factors (e.g., aerobic exercise or relaxation techniques) helped prevent the development of heart problems.

These public health researchers were concerned with halting the onset of heart disease in order to avoid risky, invasive, and costly interventions, such as angioplasty or bypass surgery, after the disease had taken hold. Their goal was to reduce or counter the identified risk factors for heart disease in the population at large; their strategy was to launch a massive public advocacy campaign, conducted in multiple venues (e.g., the media, government, corporations, schools), aimed at elimination of "at risk" behaviors (and the attitudes supporting them). If risk could not be avoided altogether, the campaign could at least promote those behaviors and attitudes that reduce risk of heart disease. Proof that this two-pronged strategy has been effective is in the numbers: a 45-percent decrease in the incidence of cardiovascular disease, due in large measure to risk-focused prevention.[3] Application of the same prevention principles to reduce the risks associated with problem behaviors in teenagers, including violence, can work as well.

Identifying risk factors for violence

Using the public health model to reduce violence in America's communities calls for first identifying the factors that put young people at risk for violence in order to reduce or eliminate these factors and strengthen the protective factors that buffer the effects of exposure to risk. Over the

past few years, longitudinal research (that is, studies that follow youngsters from the early years of their lives into adulthood) has identified factors associated with neighborhoods and communities, the family, the schools, and peer groups, as well as factors residing in the individual that increase the probability of violence during adolescence and young adulthood. These factors, presented in exhibit 1, also have been shown to increase the probability of other health and behavior problems, including substance abuse, delinquency, teen pregnancy, and dropping out of school. It is important to note that only factors identified in *two or more* of these longitudinal studies to increase the probability of the checked health or behavior problem have been included in the exhibit. Although future research may reveal, for example, that alienation and rebelliousness place an individual at risk of violent behavior, consistent evidence does not yet exist to support this hypothesis.

In neighborhoods. Five risk factors arising from the community environment are known to increase the probability that a young person will engage in violence:

• *Availability of guns.* The United States has one of the highest rates of criminal violence in the world, and firearms are implicated in a great number of these crimes. In recent years, reports of gun-toting youths in inner-city schools and of violent incidents involving handguns in school environs have created mounting concern. Given the lethality of firearms, the increased likelihood of conflict escalating into homicide when guns are present, and the strong association between availability of firearms and homicide rates, a teenager having ready access to firearms through family, friends, or a source on the street is at increased risk of violence.

• *Community laws/norms favorable to crime.* Community norms are communicated through laws, written policies, informal social practices, and adult expectations of young people. Sometimes social practices send conflicting messages: for example,

schools and parents may promote "just say no" themes while alcohol and substance abuse are acceptable practices in the community. Community attitudes also influence law enforcement. An example is the enforcement of laws that regulate firearms sales. These laws have reduced violent crime, but the effect is small and diminishes as time passes. A number of studies suggest that the reasons are community norms that include lack of proactive monitoring or enforcement, as well as the availability of firearms from jurisdictions having no legal prohibitions on sales or illegal access. Other laws related to reductions in violent crime, especially crime involving firearms, include laws governing penalties for licensing violations and for using a firearm in the commission of a crime.

• *Media portrayals of violence.* The highly charged public debate over whether portrayals of violence in the media adversely affect children continues. Yet research over the past 3 decades demonstrates a clear correlation between depictions of violence and the development of aggressive and violent behavior. Exposure to media violence also teaches violent problem-solving strategies and appears to alter children's attitudes and sensitivity to violence.

• *Low neighborhood attachment/community disorganization.* Indifference to cleanliness and orderliness, high rates of vandalism, little surveillance of public places by neighborhood residents, absence of parental involvement in schools, and low rates of voter participation are indicative of low neighborhood attachment. The less homogeneous a community in terms of race, class, religion, or mix of industrial to residential areas, the less connected its residents may feel to the overall community and the more difficult it is to establish clear community goals and identity. Higher rates of drug problems, juvenile delinquency, and violence occur in such places.

• *Extreme economic deprivation.* Children who live in deteriorating neighborhoods characterized by extreme poverty are more likely to develop problems with delinquency, teen pregnancy, dropping out of school, and violence. If such children also have behavior and adjustment problems early in life, they are also more likely to have problems with drugs as they mature. The rate of poverty is disproportionately higher for African American, Native American, or Hispanic children than for white children; thus, children are differentially exposed to risk depending on their racial or cultural backgrounds.

In families. Obviously, the home environment, family dynamics, and parental stability play a major role in shaping children. Three risk factors for violence are associated with the family constellation: poor family management practices, including the absence of clear expectations and standards for children's behavior, excessively severe or inconsistent punishment, and parental failure to monitor their children's activities, whereabouts, or friends; family conflict, either between parents or between parents and children, which enhances the risk for all of the problem behaviors; and favorable parental attitudes and involvement in violent behavior, which increases the risk that children witnessing such displays will themselves become violent.

At school. Two indicators of risk for violence are associated with a child's experiences at school. Antisocial behavior of early onset (that is, aggressiveness in grades K–3, sometimes combined with isolation or withdrawal or sometimes combined with hyperactivity or attention-deficit disorder) is more frequently found in boys than girls and places the child at increased risk for problems, including violence, during adolescence. The risk factor also includes persistent antisocial behavior first exhibited in adolescence, such as skipping school, getting into fights, and misbehaving in class. Young people of both genders who engage in these behaviors during early adolescence are at increased risk for drug abuse, juvenile delinquency, violence, dropping out of school, and teen pregnancy. Academic failure, if it occurs in the late elementary grades and beyond, is a second school-related risk factor that is likely to result in violence and other problem behaviors. Specifically, it is the *experience* of failure that appears to escalate the risk, rather than ability per se.

In peer groups and within the individual. If youngsters associate with peers who engage in problem behaviors (for example, drug abuse,

---

Exhibit 1. **Risk Factors and Their Association With Behavior Problems in Adolescents**

Risk Factors	Adolescent Problem Behaviors				
	Substance Abuse	Delinquency	Teen Pregnancy	School Drop-Out	Violence
Community					
Availability of Drugs	✓				
Availability of Firearms		✓			✓
Community Laws and Norms Favorable Toward Drug Use, Firearms, and Crime	✓	✓			✓
Media Portrayals of Violence					✓
Transitions and Mobility	✓	✓		✓	
Low Neighborhood Attachment and Community Disorganization	✓	✓			✓
Extreme Economic Deprivation	✓	✓	✓	✓	✓
Family					
Family History of the Problem Behavior	✓	✓	✓	✓	
Family Management Problems	✓	✓	✓	✓	✓
Family Conflict	✓	✓	✓	✓	✓
Favorable Parental Attitudes and Involvement in the Problem Behavior	✓	✓			✓
School					
Early and Persistent Antisocial Behavior	✓	✓	✓	✓	✓
Academic Failure Beginning in Elementary School	✓	✓	✓	✓	✓
Lack of Commitment to School	✓	✓	✓	✓	
Individual/Peer					
Alienation and Rebelliousness	✓	✓		✓	
Friends Who Engage in a Problem Behavior	✓	✓	✓	✓	✓
Favorable Attitudes Toward the Problem Behavior	✓	✓	✓	✓	
Early Initiation of the Problem Behavior	✓	✓	✓	✓	✓
Constitutional Factors	✓	✓			✓

delinquency, violence, sexual activity, or dropping out of school), they are much more likely to do the same. Further, the earlier in their lives that young people become involved in these kinds of experiences—or take their first drink of alcohol or smoke their first marijuana cigarette—the greater is the likelihood of prolonged, serious, and chronic involvement in health and behavior problems. Even when a young person comes from a well-managed family and is not burdened with other risk factors, associating with friends who engage in problem behaviors greatly increases the child's risk. In addition, certain constitutional factors—those that may have a biological or physiological basis—appear to increase a young person's risk. Examples of constitutional factors include lack of impulse control, sensation seeking, and low harm avoidance.

Protective factors

It is well known that some youngsters, even though they are exposed to multiple risk factors, do not succumb to violent, antisocial behavior. Research indicates that protective factors reduce the impact of negative risk factors by providing positive ways for an individual to respond to these risks. Three categories of protective factors have been identified:[4]

• Individual characteristics: A resilient temperament and positive social orientation.

• Bonding: Positive relationships with family members, teachers, or other adults.

• Healthy beliefs and clear standards: Beliefs in children's competence to succeed in school and avoid drugs and crime coupled with establishing clear expectations and rules governing their behavior.

Individual characteristics. Youths who seem able to cope more successfully than others with risk factors appear resilient: they are able to bounce back in the face of change or adversity; they experience less frustration in the face of obstacles and do not give up easily. They are also good-natured, enjoy social interaction, and elicit positive attention from others. Gender is another factor. Given equal exposure to risks, girls are less likely than boys to develop violent behavioral problems in adolescence. Finally, intelligence protects against certain problem behaviors, such as delinquency and dropping out of school, although it does not protect against substance abuse. Such individual characteristics enhance the likelihood that children will identify opportunities to make a personal contribution, develop the skills necessary to follow through successfully, and receive recognition for their efforts. However, these individual protective factors—resilient temperament, positive social orientation, gender, and intelligence—are innate and are extremely difficult to change.

Bonding. Several studies have revealed that children raised in environments in which they are exposed to multiple risk factors have nevertheless become productive, contributing members of the community. In interviews with these young people, they invariably note that someone took an interest in them. Some adult in the community—whether a parent, an aunt, a grandmother, a teacher, a youth worker, a minister, a businessperson—established a bond of affection and cared enough to reach out. Research has shown that the protective factor of bonding with positive, prosocial family members, teachers, or other significant adults or peers can be strengthened by preventive intervention.

Healthy beliefs and clear standards. When the adults with whom young people bond have healthy beliefs and well-defined standards of behavior, these serve as protection against the onset of health and behavior problems in those youngsters. Examples of healthy beliefs include believing it is best for children to be free of drugs and crime and to do well in school. Examples of well-defined standards include clear, consistent family prohibitions against drug and alcohol use, demands for good performance in school, and disapproval of problem behaviors. When a young person bonds to those who hold healthy beliefs and set clear standards, the two protective factors are reinforcing; they work in tandem by providing a model on which to base behavior and the motivation to practice approved behavior so that the bond is not jeopardized. Both bonding and healthy beliefs/clear standards mediate the relationship between a young person and the social environment, including community, family, schools, and peer groups; these protective factors can be encouraged and strengthened.

The preconditions of bonding. Bonding may take place with a caregiver, a family member or other significant adult, or it may represent an attachment to a social group. For bonding to occur, however, three conditions must be met. The first is the *opportunity for active involvement.* People become bonded to a family, a school class, or a community because they are given the chance to participate in the life of the group. In a classroom where the teacher calls on only the students in the front who raise their hands, the others are denied an opportunity for active involvement; as a result they may lose their commitment to education. The situation is similar in a family where the 13- or 14-year-old uses the home as a hotel—essentially a place to sleep—but has no responsibilities in the family. Youngsters need to be given the chance to contribute, in ways commensurate with their level of development, to life in the family, in the classroom, and in the wider community.

The opportunity to become involved is not enough, however. A second condition of effective bonding is *having the skills needed* to succeed once involvement gets underway. Young people need to be taught the skills without which they will be unable to pursue opportunities effectively. Examples of skills that have been shown to protect children include good cognitive skills, such as problem-solving and reading abilities, and good social skills, including com-

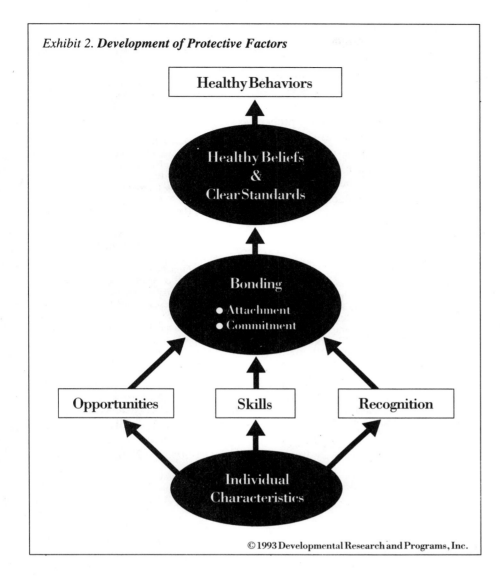

Exhibit 2. Development of Protective Factors

Healthy Behaviors

Healthy Beliefs & Clear Standards

Bonding
- Attachment
- Commitment

Opportunities **Skills** **Recognition**

Individual Characteristics

© 1993 Developmental Research and Programs, Inc.

munication, assertiveness, and the ability to ask for support. The third condition of bonding is *a consistent system of recognition or reinforcement for skillful performance.* Young people often receive little or no recognition for doing the right thing. The focus is on what they have done wrong; much less frequently are their accomplishments acknowledged. The efforts they put forth, the challenges they face, and the contributions they make should be celebrated in personally and culturally accepted ways.

Thus, along with opportunities and access to skills, recognition or appreciation provides an incentive for continued contribution and is a necessary condition for enabling young people to form close attachments to their

communities, schools, and families. Exhibit 2 shows how protective factors are developed and how they influence one another.

Community guidelines for preventive intervention

In designing preventive interventions for the 1990's and beyond, community leaders should keep in mind some key principles. The first is that prevention strategies should focus on *known* risk factors. Once communities identify the risk factors they need to address, the prevention program developed in response should be targeted to reducing those factors and to en-

hancing protective factors. Another guideline is that intervention should be planned to coincide with the point in a child's development that is optimal for achieving the desired outcome. Thus, prevention interventions need to be geared to the *appropriate developmental stages* of the child. If behavior problems at age 4, 5, and 6 are known to be associated with substance abuse and delinquency later in life, this means all youngsters should be taught in the early elementary grades the skills they need to manage and control their impulses in order to get along with others.

Allied to the principle of intervention at the appropriate stage is *early intervention,* necessary to prevent behavior problems from stabilizing and becoming entrenched. Ideally, prevention begins before the child is born to ensure that low-income mothers and other adult caregivers have the skills they need to nurture children. These skills will equip them to understand that a crying baby is not a bad baby who needs to be spanked or disciplined. Prenatal care, home visits to low-income single mothers, and caregiver training in nurturing skills can significantly reduce child abuse. Studies show that more than a fourfold reduction in child abuse is achievable by home visitation before birth and during the first few months of infancy.[5]

Prevention programs need to reach those who are at high risk by virtue of exposure to *multiple risk factors.* These multiple risks require multiple strategies that also are sensitive to the cultural diversity that characterizes many communities.

Commitment to risk-focused prevention programs arises only when there is buy-in by the community; that is, when the programs are felt to be "owned and operated" by the community. This sense of proprietorship evolves when all the various stakeholders in the community—the key leaders through the grassroots members—come together representing their diverse interests and develop a strategy for how to implement risk-focused prevention. The

"Communities That Care" approach is one such strategy.

Implications for criminal justice

The inclusion of prevention as a central element of criminal justice policy and practice is emblematic of a new emphasis reflecting the realization that enforcement alone is not enough to reduce youth violence. This realization reflects the recognition that, in spite of geometrically increasing investments in enforcement, the courts, and corrections, violent crime, especially among young people, has continued to rise over the past decade.

For criminal justice, the orientation to prevention means establishing partnerships with other organizations, groups, and agencies in the community to identify and reduce risks for crime and violence and to strengthen protective factors that inhibit violence in the community. Community policing represents a clear example of this shift in criminal justice from an exclusive focus on the "back end"—after the crime has been committed. Integral to the intervention process is the involvement of the community and of social service and other agencies at the "front end"—working in tandem with law enforcement to identify problems and design strategies to solve them. In refining its role, criminal justice is taking on a much greater challenge than in the past, but doing so holds the promise of reducing crime in the long term.

Notes

1. Stuart, R.B., "Teaching Facts About Drugs: Pushing or Preventing?" *Journal of Educational Psychology* 37 (1974): 98–201; and Weaver, S. C. and F. S. Tennant, "Effectiveness of Drug Education Programs for Secondary School Students," *American Journal of Psychiatry* 130 (1973): 812–814.
2. See, for example, William DeJong's *Preventing Interpersonal Violence Among Youth: An Introduction to School, Community, and Mass Media Strategies,* Issues and Practices, Washington, D.C.: U.S. Department of Justice, National Institute of Justice, August 1994: 12–15.
3. From a speech delivered at the National Academy of Sciences in January 1994, by Kenneth I. Shine, M.D., President of the National Institute of Medicine.
4. See Hawkins, J. D., R. F. Catalano, and J. M. Miller, "Risk and Protective Factors for Alcohol and Other Drug Problems in Adolescence and Early Childhood: Implications for Substance Abuse Prevention," *Psychological Bulletin* 112 (1992): 64–105; Werner, E. E. and R. S. Smith, *Overcoming the Odds: High Risk Children From Birth to Adulthood,* New York: Cornell University Press, 1992; and Rutter, M., "Resilience in the Face of Adversity: Protective Factors and Resistance to Psychiatric Disorder," *British Journal of Psychiatry* 147 (1987): 598–611.
5. Olds, David L., C. R. Henderson, Jr., R. Chamberlin, and R. Tatelbaum, "Preventing Child Abuse and Neglect: A Randomized Trial of Nurse Home Visitation," *Pediatrics* 78 (1986): 65–78.
6. For information about the Communities That Care comprehensive community prevention planning approach, contact Developmental Research and Programs, 130 Nickerson Street, Suite 107, Seattle, WA 98109. Phone: (800) 736-2630; Fax: (206) 286-1462.

J. David Hawkins teaches social work at the University of Washington in Seattle and directs the University's Social Development Research Group.

Children at Risk

On the Streets of America

Kids have only a slight chance of getting off the street when most of the people they know are criminals, gang members, and drug addicts.

Mark S. Fleisher

Riddled by pellets from a 12 gauge shotgun, a broken street light fixture lies atop debris at the side of the street. "About seven last night, a guy fixed it and put in a new light," says Rick (pseudonyms are used), a member of a youth gang known as the Fairview Hawks. "And now look at it." He points to the thick shards of glass next to the light pole where the lamp once illuminated a segment of Fairview, a narrow, north-south street traversing rolling hills in a residential area of a midwestern city.

A working-class neighborhood, the Fairview district consists of small wood-frame houses nestled under the branches of old trees. Although less than ten minutes from

Anthropologist **Mark S. Fleisher** studied the culture and language of the Hesquiat Indians of British Columbia and the Clallam Indians of Washington State before changing his focus to street criminals and youth gangs. An associate professor of criminal justice sciences at Illinois State University, Fleisher is the author of *Warehousing Violence* (Sage Publications, 1989) and *Beggars and Thieves: Lives of Urban Street Criminals* (University of Wisconsin Press, 1995).

major freeways to the east and the downtown businesses to the west, this area has virtually no condominiums, strip malls, movie theaters, or restaurants—no white-collar families that support urban growth. Except for the police, utility workers, and letter carriers, few outsiders cruise up and down Fairview. In part that's because the Fairview Hawks loom over the physical and social landscape. The gang consists of some seventy blacks, whites, and Latinos, about three-fourths of them male, ranging in age from the early teens to early twenties.

Fairview Hawks control an area of about ten square blocks between 57th and 61st streets, which run east-west. "The corner of 60th and Fairview is ours!" asserts G-Love, who by virtue of her age (nineteen) and her status as a founding member has assumed the informal role of one of the gang's leaders. Like gangs, or "sets," in other urban and rural areas, Fairview Hawks demark their territory with graffiti and protect it with violence. Spray paint on houses, garages, sidewalks, and driveways all around the neighborhood are signs of ownership: "FH" for Fairview Hawks and a dollar sign, which indicates a love of money. Green is the Fairview Hawks' color. "I love money, and money's green," says G-Love.

Even though they are engaged in unlawful activities and have been called a gang by outsiders, the Fairview Hawks don't think of themselves that way. "We're a family," says seventeen-year-old Poodle (sometimes known as Poodle Bitch, because of her occasionally irascible temperament). "We ain't no gang," asserts fifteen-year-old Renée. "A clique, that's what we are. I call us a cliquilation." She smiles, proud of her linguistic creativity.

And certainly the Fairview Hawks are not an example of a drug gang, a group of street criminals (most often adults with criminal histories) whose main enterprise is to sell drugs and who use violence to protect or expand their drug-selling territory. Instead, this type of gang fills the social needs of its members, whose early family lives left them alienated, emotionally unstable, and without educational aspirations.

The Fairview Hawks formed a few years ago, partly to counter harassment from North, a gang from the city's north side. G-Love says she and Fat Sal, TJ, Buck, Sweet Pea, and Frosty were sitting on her front porch and decided to transform themselves from a bunch of neighborhood kids into a clique with a color and graffiti. Others soon joined. About twenty members get together every day; Caramel, eighteen, calls this the "everyday group." But on weekend nights and at times when Fairview Hawks experience trouble from other gangs, the group expands quickly.

Many Fairview Hawks started out as members of other city gangs. "Everyone's chillin' with their own set, but they're down with Fairview," says Caramel, who—along with G-Love, Afro, Brawn, and Vinny—held membership in various Crip sets. Others, including Ann, Chucky D, Jenny, Lucky, and Green Bean (he's tall, thin and wears green clothing) were Latin Counts. Most gangs in the city categorize themselves as Crips or Bloods, using gang names that originated in Los Angeles about 1970 and spread around America. The names are often used by youngsters who have no knowledge of, or social affiliation with, the Los Angeles originals. The two types of gangs are customarily archenemies, but Fairview Hawks who identify themselves as Crips or Bloods get along well, by virtue of sharing a

neighborhood and growing up together (many of them are brothers, sisters, or cousins).

Nearly all the gang members are school age, but they don't attend school. Most have been arrested a number of times for truancy, violent crimes, or drug dealing while others have been suspended for carrying weapons in school and for recurrent misbehavior. G-Love and Sweet Pea say that when they started elementary school, they didn't get along with anyone there, hated the teachers, didn't want to listen to orders, and ran away to the street. By the eleventh grade, both had dropped out and preferred the company of youngsters on the street to those in the playground. "Kids on the street were like me," notes G-Love.

Daily life for street kids is simple, often boring, and relatively free from the stresses that affect mainstream adolescents.

Daily life for these street kids is simple, often boring, and relatively free from the stresses that affect mainstream adolescents. When school kids are running around the neighborhood on early morning paper routes, waiting for the school bus, attending algebra and chemistry class, doing homework, practicing team sports, heading off to part-time jobs, and worrying about scores on college entrance exams and picking a college, Fairview Hawks are asleep, numbing themselves with drugs, or just hanging out.

The gang has four "chill spots," or houses where the kids are permitted to hang out. G-Love's mother's house is the biggest, most popular spot. Up the street, kids chill at Tonya's and rely on her for support. "Tonya—she's a mom, she's got kids and everything—is like the mom of the family," says Caramel. "She's close to Dan, TJ, Chucky D, and Kirk. She is the one that all the boys write and call from prison. If any of us go to jail, we always call Tonya's house." Caramel laughs.

The day begins sometime between one and three in the afternoon. Sleeping all morning and most of the afternoon is a regular practice because these teen-agers don't go to sleep until three or four A.M. They don't have to awaken early because they've all quit school and only a few have jobs. And those who do get jobs usually quit within weeks. Between four and six in the afternoon, the everyday group starts to congregate around G-Love's front porch; a few go inside to watch TV or play video games.

Before long, someone walks a few blocks to a gas station convenience store on 61st and buys some forty-ounce bottles of malt liquor or beer. Then someone rolls a joint (marijuana cigarette) or prepares a blunt (a hollowed-out, blunt-tipped cigar filled with marijuana). Or someone lights up what they call a "dank stick"—a cigarette dipped in formaldehyde that's been cut, or thinned, with nail polish remover or even wood alcohol or brake fluid. Smokers of dank become high instantly: legs weaken and bodies sag lifelessly. Sweet Pea says, "It makes you not think about none of your problems at all."

The kids chat and gossip and listen to music. On some weekend evenings, they may move into someone's house and dance to rap music. Boys may toss a football up and down Fairview in front of G-Love's house or play basketball at a public park a few blocks away. Less often, gang members go swimming in a public pool, attend a movie, or go wading in a large public fountain that's a few miles away. Favorite pastimes are dominoes and craps—they love to gamble.

G-Love says they usually don't go looking for trouble unless they're really "messed up" (drunk and/or high on drugs) and have a car. Nevertheless, violence is a fact of life and includes drive-by and walk-by shootings. Although they weren't the intended victims, Caramel and G-Love were injured during a walk-by shooting one August evening. They were sitting in G-Love's car, just around the block from her mother's house, when a North gunman fired an SKS assault rifle at them for "two or three minutes," according to Caramel. A number of Fairview boys at the scene were unhurt, but G-Love was hit in the face and back by fragments of shattered glass or metal, and Caramel was hit in the foot by a bullet and received other wounds. G-Love managed to drive the car away from the scene. Shootings like this one are an "ongoing process," explains Caramel. "They'd shoot at our friends, so we'd get mad and retaliate back on them, then they'd get mad and retaliate back on us."

I watched one afternoon as gang members prepared for battle, having spotted several members of North a few blocks west of Fairview and 60th. Hostile words and threats were exchanged, and boys emerged from houses along Fairview and dashed toward a high spot on the hill next to G-Love's, a vantage point from which to fire down on enemy gang members driving below. Weapons appeared from hiding spots: shotguns, high-powered rifles, an assault weapon, a semiautomatic weapon, and powerful handguns. "It's some funny shit, man," declared a young warrior. "I'm gonna jump right out in the middle of the street. It's the Fourth of July!" Another exclaimed, "I'm ready to rock 'n' roll. I'm ready to ride." They darted back and forth along the ridge, seemingly oblivious of their own exposure to danger.

The street can be dangerous, but most of these teen-agers were first exposed to violence at home.

According to several Fairview Hawks, quite a few of the gang members have been wounded or killed by firearms during the year. A twenty-five-year-old man was shot in the chest four to six times by unknown killers. A twenty-three-year old was murdered by North gang members, two years to the day after his brother was killed by Bloods. A sixteen-year-old was shot accidentally, and his fifteen-year-old brother was shot by a rival; both survived. A seventeen-year-old boy was shot in the head by a rival and now sits permanently in a wheelchair. A fourteen-year-old boy was accidentally shot in the head by his best friend as they handled a .45 caliber handgun. A thirteen-year-old girl survived being shot in the chest with a .38 handgun by North. A sixteen-year-old was shot in the arm with a 12 gauge shotgun at close range in a drive-by shooting on Fairview. Two seventeen-year-old boys survived being shot at by rivals. Gang-related tragedy hits the families of these kids, too.

"Violence doesn't scare me. I'm used to it. It's normal," says Poodle in a matter-of-fact voice. "I seen shootings and drive-bys." Fist fights don't frighten her either. Indeed, she was arrested for assault after punching her mother in the face during a court hearing. ("We used to get into fist fights at home, too.") But Caramel says, "My biggest fear is watching all my friends die. I don't want to fear dying. I don't want to die violently. It'll all get better someday. I wish it would all stop."

Life in the Fairview district can be dangerous, but most of these teen-agers were first exposed to violence at home. In years of research in prisons and jails and on street corners in Seattle and other cities, I have interviewed and hung out with hundreds of gang members and adult street criminals, ranging in age from the late preteens to nearly seventy. The families they were born into usually offered only fragile and undependable social ties, with children bound only weakly to their parents or other adults who helped raise them (stepparents, aunts, uncles, cousins, grandparents).

Most commonly, the parents are alcoholics, and many use other drugs as well, such as marijuana, heroin, and cocaine. Many fathers are criminals, often drug dealers. Mothers, and sometimes grandmothers, engage in criminal activities with their husbands, brothers, sons, and nephews. Even women who do not participate in crime are active consumers of the money and goods obtained illegally. Parents fight with each other and beat their sons and daughters. In many cases, men sexually molest their sons, daughters, or stepchildren. Mothers of these children are passive bystanders who pretend not to know—fearful, they say, that they might be beaten themselves or have their supply of drugs cut off.

As the children mature, the neglect and the emotional and physical abuse heaped on them persist. Eventually they pull away, abandon their homes, and embrace street life with a calamitous zest. Enjoying the freedom of living by their own rules, they set off on a life of drug and alcohol addiction, personal irresponsibility, an inability to form meaningful social attachments, an incapacity to sort important aspects of their lives from unimportant ones, impulsive behavior, aggression to relieve stress, and no sense of lifelong priorities. Many of these damaged adolescents feel as if the course of their lives is outside their control. When confronted with the facts about their drug and alcohol use, dim future, violent behavior, and lack of education, they often respond, "It's just who I am."

Fairview Hawks, like young gang members I've studied in many other cities, usually are the products of particularly destructive family experiences. Institutionalization is also common in their backgrounds. Caramel recounts a series of seven placements in residential treatment programs, hospitals, and juvenile detention facilities, from when she was age ten to seventeen, including nearly a year in a state hospital at age thirteen. She says they told her she had "an anger problem and a chemical imbalance." During her last commitment to a treatment facility, Caramel met G-Love, who also was a patient.

Street kids are unlikely to get help unless they are sentenced to prison. And it isn't the worst thing that can happen to them.

G-Love says she smoked her first joint when she was eight, and by age twelve she drank and smoked "bud" (marijuana) every day, gambled, enjoyed an occasional street fight, and stole cars. After a car theft when she was twelve years old, G-Love was remanded by a juvenile court judge to a thirty-day psychiatric evaluation. But she rebelled, and a month turned into four years in custody. "I hated the matrons," she says with a scowl, and "I fought them, jumped them, beat them whenever I could, and I ran away. But they kept bringing me back." G-Love adjusted slowly and learned to live with counseling, planned recreation, good food, and a clean bed.

These kids are unlikely to get help unless they are convicted of a felony and sentenced to prison. And ironically, prison isn't the worst thing that can happen to them. In fact, it is a way of insuring that they will stay alive, get treatment for addictions to alcohol and other drugs, receive a moderate level of education, and obtain medical and psychological or psychiatric care. Most prisons, despite exaggerated stereotypes, are cleaner and safer

Sitting in classrooms studying, commuting to work, and paying taxes aren't attractive alternatives.

than inner-city neighborhoods. In prison, there are no drive-by shootings.

Whether so-called rehabilitation programs can be considered successful depends on who is evaluating the programs. Educated people, among them those whose incomes depend on the existence of such programs, often claim that education and job training will stop crime and offer street criminals lawful opportunities. My years of street ethnography show a different picture: Persistent criminals, as well as gang members, are living a life style they have chosen. They don't fear the criminal justice system, and in the end, most reject attempts to force them into a way of life they neither want nor understand. Sitting in classrooms studying, commuting to and from work, spending forty or more hours a week behind a desk, and paying taxes aren't attractive alternatives to the street criminals and gang members I've known.

Fairview Hawks and kids like them usually are raised by parents for whom school has no meaning. School is just a place to hang out with fellow gang members. And a close look at household life shows that the parents of gang members often discourage children's school attendance, because the school day and homework take time away from selling drugs or stolen property, thus reducing household income and the amount of cash that mom or dad can spend on drugs and alcohol. And even if the children are educated, who will hire them?

Some gang members and adult street criminals do find a way to get off the street and into a lawful life style. Grass-roots organizations that reach people on street corners and in gang neighborhoods are a more effective intervention tool than expensive, bureaucracy-laden government programs. The Fairview Hawks are more likely to get help from people who aren't afraid of going into the inner city, having once lived on the street themselves.

Flaco, in his mid-forties, used to work for a neighborhood organization and is now setting up his own project. He is the first bilingual Latino to become a certified drug and alcohol counselor in the state. He even received a certificate of recognition from the Points of Light Foundation inspired by President Bush. But for many years, his life consisted of drugs, crime, gangs, and prison.

Born in Nogales, Mexico, and raised in Tucson, Arizona, Flaco lived until the age of nine with his mother and stepfather. Then his mother was hospitalized and his stepfather was unable to care adequately for Flaco and his six brothers. His mother's relatives offered

"My brothers were chosen, but no one wanted me. 'OK,' I thought, 'if no one wants me, I don't want nobody.' "

to care for the children, but they only wanted Flaco's brothers. He was left on his own. "I remember the conversation where my brothers were chosen, but no one wanted me. 'OK,' I thought, 'if no one wants me, I don't want nobody.' "

Flaco soon began sniffing glue and gas fumes; by age ten, he was regularly smoking weed; by age twelve or thirteen, he was a member of a gang in south Tucson. He shot (injected) heroin for the first time at age fifteen. For the next two decades, his life was dominated by heroin. "If God made anything better than heroin," says Flaco, "he kept it for himself."

At age twenty, Flaco was imprisoned in the maximum security unit at the Arizona State Prison for selling heroin, among other charges, and within a year, he became associated with one of America's most infamous prison gangs, known for its violence and drug distribution inside prison walls. For nearly fourteen years, Flaco lived by the sword and the syringe. "I felt closer to the guys in prison than to my own family. Sometimes I forgot I had a family. I never got a visit, and I lost all contact with the world."

On September 1, 1985, Flaco was released. At age thirty-three, he didn't know how to live on the outside. "My [criminal] behavior and attitude kept me alive all along, and now they expected me to get rid of all that. I didn't know if I could make it." Flaco decided to stay drug free for twelve months, just to see what the world looked like. He has managed to stay drug free ever since.

Unfortunately, kinds have only a slight chance of getting off the street when the majority of the people they know—including their own brothers, sisters, cousins, mothers, and fathers—are active criminals, gang members, and drug addicts. Supportive, intimate ties are optional on the street, where relationships exist in the moment and people are responsible only for themselves. As a field researcher studying adult street criminals and young gang members, I found that reciprocity and frequent contact were vital to sustain open relationships. But I learned to limit my natural urge to get personally involved. "I am a street ethnographer," I told myself, "an observer, not a cop, social worker, or surrogate father."

But watching adults destroy their lives with drugs and alcohol and criminal behavior was easier to endure than watching adolescents do the same things. Adults, I told myself, have control over their own lives. If a thirty-five-year-old street criminal chooses to shoot heroin, that is entirely his decision. But I watched teen-agers pollute themselves with alcohol, marijuana, and dank, and no adults seemed to care about this drug abuse. Every day I spent with the Fairview Hawks brought me disturbing dreams. I knew that many of these youngsters had committed serious crimes, but many of them had not, yet all were trying to survive as best they could, alone on the street, without community members rescuing them.

One thing I learned from studying Fairview Hawks is this: These youngsters would probably not be alcoholics, drug addicts, gang members, and convicted felons if their parents or other adults truly cared about them. And this is the most painful thing I have learned on the streets.

Books to Read

Beggars and Thieves: Lives of Urban Street Criminals, *by Mark S. Fleisher (University of Wisconsin Press, 1995)*

The American Street Gang: Its Nature, Prevalence, and Control, *by Malcolm W. Klein (Oxford University Press, 1995)*

With Juvenile Courts in Chaos, Critics Propose Their Demise

JUSTICE BESIEGED

By FOX BUTTERFIELD

CHICAGO—The nation's juvenile courts, long a troubled backwater of the criminal justice system, have been so overwhelmed by the increase in violent teen-age crime and the breakdown of the family that judges and politicians are debating a solution that was once unthinkable: abolishing the system and trying most minors as adults.

The crisis began building a decade ago, when prosecutors responded to the growth in high-profile youth crime by pushing for the trials of greater numbers of children, dramatically raising caseloads.

But the courts have become so choked that by all accounts they are even less effective than before, with more juveniles prosecuted but fewer convicted and no evidence of a drop in rearrest rates for those who go to prison.

The resulting situation angers people across the political spectrum, from those who believe the juvenile court is too lenient, to those who feel it fails to prevent troubled children from becoming ensnared in a life of crime.

In interviews around the country, judges, probation officers, prosecutors and defense lawyers described a juvenile court system in perhaps the worst chaos of its history.

In Chicago, where the first juvenile court was created in 1899, judges today preside over assembly-line justice, hearing an average of 60 cases a day, about six minutes per case. In New Orleans, public defenders have to represent their poor clients with no office, no telephone, no court records and little chance to discuss the case before trial. In New York, where the recent case of Malcolm Shabazz—who admitted setting the fire that killed his grandmother, Malcolm X's widow—focused new attention on Family Court, some officials say it is time to junk the system.

Almost everywhere, with juvenile courts starved for money, record-keeping is so primitive that often the judge, the prosecutor and the defense attorney have different records on the same defendant, making an accurate assessment of the case impossible. And because the courts cannot afford their own warrant squads, young defendants sometimes fail to show up for trial or simply skip out of the courtroom with virtual impunity.

Despite calls for tougher justice, the overcrowding and lack of resources mean that only a small percentage of the young people who move through the juvenile justice system are imprisoned, although there are other forms of punishment, the most common of which is probation.

Of the 1,555,200 delinquency cases referred by the police to prosecutors nationwide in 1994, 855,200, or just over half, resulted in what in adult criminal courts would be called indictments, said Jeffrey Butts, at the National Center for Juvenile Justice. Of these, Mr. Butts said, 495,000 defendants were found guilty.

In turn, 141,300 of these cases resulted in a juvenile's being incarcerated. That is 9 percent of those originally sent to prosecutors by the police.

By contrast, in adult criminal court, which is explicitly intended to be punitive, 90 percent to 95 percent of defendants who have been indicted plead guilty in a plea bargain, often as a way to win a lighter punishment. The philosophy of juvenile court traditionally was to rehabilitate rather than punish young offenders, a premise that has come under attack in recent years.

Congress is poised to pass legislation, backed by President Clinton, that would provide Federal grants to states that sharply increase the number of young people they try in adult court. The legislation, already passed by the House and likely to be adopted soon by the Senate, would further undermine the authority of the juvenile court at a time when many specialists predict there will be a new wave of youth crime, as the number of teen-agers increases by 15 percent in the next decade.

"The Family Court is bankrupt," said Peter Reinharz, chief of New York City's juvenile prosecution unit. "It's time to sell everything off and start over."

Mr. Reinharz is a longtime critic of the juvenile court, but even its staunchest defenders are now troubled by what they see.

"It is no longer just the chronic problems that have long plagued the court, like overcrowding and making do with less," said Bart Lubow, a senior associate of the Annie E. Casey Foundation who has studied juvenile courts around the nation. "Now there's a crisis of confidence, since the very notion that has been its cornerstone, that children are different from adults and therefore need to be treated differently, is in question."

Among the issues swirling in the nation's 3,000 juvenile courts are the following:

• As pressure to get tough on young criminals has increased, the number of juveniles arrested who are prosecuted in court has climbed to 55 percent in 1994 from 45 percent in 1985.

But the percentage of young people convicted has not kept pace, rising to 33 percent in 1994 from 31 percent a decade earlier.

In Chicago, the figures show an even more dramatic effect of overloading the system. The Cook County State's Attorney has increased the number of juveniles he prosecutes to 85 percent of all those sent to him by the police, but about 70 percent of these cases are dismissed for lack of evidence or the failure of witnesses to appear, according to a new study by the Children and Family Justice Center of

the Northwestern University School of Law.

"This is the dirty little secret of Cook County," said David Reed, the lead author of the report. "You have lots more cases but almost the same number of judges and prosecutors, and they can only do so much work and prove a certain number guilty. So all these kids are brought in on criminal charges and then most are let go. It fosters cynicism about the court, makes the public and crime victims mad and teaches young people that justice is a joke."

• With an angry public demanding harsher punishments, it is becoming increasingly difficult for judges to differentiate between defendants who may have committed a youthful indiscretion and those who are on their way to a lifetime of crime. The distinction is critical. Almost 60 percent of those teenagers sent to juvenile court for the first time never return. But every time a young person is sent back to court, his likelihood of being arrested again increases until recidivism rates reach 75 percent by a fifth appearance, said Howard Snyder, of the National Center for Juvenile Justice.

• Despite a rush by legislators in all 50 states over the past decade to pass laws trying young people in adult court, there is no evidence that being convicted in adult court or sentenced to adult prison is more effective in reducing youth crime than the juvenile justice route. A new study of 5,476 juvenile criminals in Florida, which followed them from their arrest in 1987 through 1994, concluded that those tried as adults committed new crimes sooner after their release from prison, and perpetrated more serious and violent crimes, than those tried as juveniles.

Charles Frazier, a sociology professor at the University of Florida and a co-author of the report, said that keeping young people in the juvenile justice system works better because juvenile institutions provide more education and psychological treatment for inmates, helping offenders rehabilitate themselves. By

contrast, adult prisons now are more punitive and have largely abandoned trying to change criminals' behavior.

"Ultimately, you are going to release all these people back into the community, and the juvenile justice system does a better job of reclaiming them," Professor Frazier said.

19th-Century Origin
Firmly but Gently Disciplining Youths

The criticism of the juvenile court misses a fundamental point, some specialists believe. With the breakdown of the family, can any court system, juvenile or adult, do the job society once did: instill discipline and values in children, punish them if they are bad and then help redeem them?

"The juvenile court was set up 100 years ago, in a very different America, to help cure kids of immigrant families with manageable problems, like truancy, petty thefts and fighting," said Jeffrey Fagan, the director of the Center for Violence Research and Prevention at Columbia University.

As envisioned by the pioneering social worker, Jane Addams, the juvenile court was to be a surrogate parent and the judge a kindly doctor, seeking to understand the social conditions that had led the child astray, the way a doctor would study a disease. This paternalism was reflected in the informality of the courtroom, with the judge sitting at an ordinary table, not behind a bench, and wearing only street clothes, not a robe.

The court's guiding principle was to do what was "in the best interest of the child," not to protect the community or insure the child's constitutional rights. So punishments were kept light, since children were thought to still be in the process of forming their personalities, and thus more amenable to reform than adults. And all proceedings and records were kept confidential.

An antiseptic nomenclature was even invented to avoid stigmatizing children. A boy was "taken into custody," not arrested. He had a "petition of delinquency" drawn against him, rather than being charged. And there were no convictions, only "adjudications," and no sentences, only "placements."

But today, poverty, joblessness and violent teen-age crime seem far worse than they were in the 1890's, often making the court's customs appear a quaint anachronism.

Also, as a result, Professor Fagan said, "The juvenile court can no longer do what it was set up to do. It certainly can't do what the public expects it to do, control juvenile crime."

Statistics only hint at the magnitude of the troubles the court is asked to resolve.

Since 1960, the number of delinquency cases handled by juvenile courts nationwide has risen almost four times, to 1.55 million in 1994. During the same period, the number of cases involving abused or neglected children, which are also handled by juvenile courts, has increased five times faster than even the delinquency cases, said Mr. Butts of the National Center for Juvenile Justice. And these abused and neglected children are often the very ones who become delinquents.

Among delinquency cases, violent crimes are rising the fastest. From 1985 to 1994, juvenile crimes involving weapons soared 156 per-

cent, murders jumped 144 percent and aggravated assaults were up 134 percent. Property crimes were up 25 percent.

A Case in Point
In a Chicago Court, Beating the System

Perhaps the most revealing place to see the troubles is in Chicago, home to the nation's oldest and largest juvenile court. The Chicago court is not the best; that may be in Louisville, San Jose or Oakland, where the judges command wide respect. Nor is it the most beleaguered; that distinction may belong to Baltimore or New Orleans. Cook County is just a good example of what goes on in a high-volume juvenile court.

A tiny 13-year-old defendant, so short he could barely see Judge William Hibbler seated behind the bench, was on trial for murder.

The defendant—who will remain unidentified in accordance with the court's rules of confidentiality—was wearing an Atlanta Braves baseball jacket, and he looked more like a team mascot than a hardened criminal. But the teen-ager was charged with first-degree murder for shooting a man who was trying to buy crack cocaine.

At an even younger age, he was arrested for armed robbery and burglary, though without being sent to prison. This time, after his arrest for murder, he had been allowed to return home because the court had failed to give him a hearing within the 36-hour limit specified for juveniles.

While free awaiting trial for murder, he had stolen a car.

Neither his mother nor father was in court. His father had died of alcohol poisoning; his mother, a crack addict, was in a boot camp on a drug charge.

Judge Hibbler, the presiding judge of the delinquency division of the Cook County Juvenile Court, wore a black robe, a small sign of how the court has shifted from its original

The Juvenile Caseload: A Closer Look

THE DELINQUENCY CASELOAD HAS SURGED...
Estimated number of delinquency cases handled in juvenile courts around the country. A youth may be involved in more than one case.

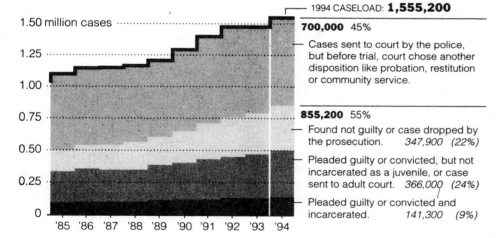

— 1994 CASELOAD: **1,555,200**

700,000 45%
Cases sent to court by the police, but before trial, court chose another disposition like probation, restitution or community service.

855,200 55%
Found not guilty or case dropped by the prosecution. *347,900 (22%)*
Pleaded guilty or convicted, but not incarcerated as a juvenile, or case sent to adult court. *366,000 (24%)*
Pleaded guilty or convicted and incarcerated. *141,300 (9%)*

...ESPECIALLY FOR SERIOUS CRIMES...
Change in cases for selected crimes.

VIOLENT CRIME*	CASES IN 1994	CHANGE SINCE '85
Murder	3,000	+144%
Aggravated assault	85,300	134
Robbery	37,000	53
Forcible rape	5,400	25
OTHER SERIOUS CRIME		
Weapons offenses	48,800	+156%
Simple assault	177,700	91

*The four crimes in the F.B.I.'s violent crime index.

...REFLECTING MORE ARRESTS
Arrests per 100,000 for violent crimes.*

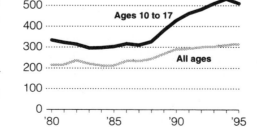

Sources: National Center for Juvenile Justice; Office of Juvenile Justice and Delinquency Prevention, F.B.I.

The New York Times

informality and evolved, in the judge's phrase, into more of a "mini criminal court."

The courtroom is inside the Cook County Juvenile Center, a modern structure a block long and eight stories high that from the outside looks more like an office building than a courthouse with a juvenile jail attached. The building was recently reconstructed as part of an effort to reverse the turmoil overtaking juvenile court.

Inside, however, the waiting rooms are still painted a dingy brown and are jammed with largely black and Hispanic families, many of them holding crying babies. In the men's rooms the toilets are broken and the metal mirrors are scrawled with graffiti.

These dilapidated conditions, said Mr. Lubow of the Casey Foundation, "basically say to the families and kids who come to juvenile court that we don't take them seriously, that we value them less as people."

Now, after talking with his lawyer, the youth begrudgingly confessed to murder as part of a plea bargain. Judge Hibbler then solemnly ordered that he "be committed to the Illinois Department of Corrections, Juvenile Division, till 21 years of age."

The boy smirked. He knew he had beaten the system again. He could be free in as little as five years. Without the plea bargain, he could have been transferred to adult court and faced a minimum sentence of 20 years.

It was the kind of case that infuriates conservatives and others, suggesting that juvenile court is little more than a revolving door.

But it was also the kind of case that makes children's rights advocates argue that juvenile court is failing to help young people from troubled families by intervening early enough to prevent them from becoming ensnared in a life of crime.

Even many judges themselves, who are often the only defenders of the juvenile court, concur that the court is foundering. But the judges

tend to blame the politicians who have passed laws to try more teenagers in adult courts.

"There is a crisis," Judge Hibbler acknowledged. But, he contended, "Children don't stop being children just because they commit a crime, and calling for an end of the juvenile court is the same as saying we should do away with grammar schools and junior high schools and just put everyone in college."

Clogging the Courts
Convictions Flat As Caseload Soars

In the traditional juvenile court, probation officers played a key role.

They presided at what is still widely called "intake," or arraignment in adult terms. After the police decided which juveniles to send to court—usually about half were dismissed with the equivalent of a parking ticket—the probation officers would screen out children whose crimes were petty or who had no record. Nationwide, they filtered out about half the cases referred by the police.

But in Chicago in the late 1980's, in response to the epidemic of crack cocaine and the rise of teen-age gun violence, Richard M. Daley, then the Cook County State's Attorney, wrestled this power away from the court probation department. To appear tough on crime, he began prosecuting 97 percent of the cases forwarded to him by the police, according to an analysis by The Chicago Sun-Times.

Mr. Daley is now mayor of Chicago, and that figure is down to 85 percent, the State's Attorney's office says.

But Bernardine Dohrn, the director of the Children and Family Justice Center at Northwestern University, said that prosecuting such a high proportion of cases has overwhelmed the court, resulting in about 70 percent of the cases filed by the State's Attorney being dropped before trial.

A new study by Ms. Dohrn's center has found that while the number of delinquency cases heard each month has more than tripled in the last decade, the number of convictions has remained almost flat.

"They are clogging the system," Ms. Dohrn said, "and when you do this wholesale, you drive kids into the system who don't belong there and you don't find the kids who aren't in school and are getting into serious trouble. They are able to pass through for a long time without being stopped. So it's a double whammy, and dangerous."

Probation officers are also supposed to enforce the most commonly used punishment in juvenile court, probation—a court order requiring a young person to go to school or find a job and obey a home curfew the rest of the day.

But no one likes probation: not judges, who want more innovative alternatives; not the offenders, who chafe at the loss of freedom, and not the police or prosecutors, who regard probation as a farce. Worst of all, probation further undercuts the credibility of the court.

For judges, probation is part of a terrible dilemma. "I really have only two major choices," said Glenda Hatchett, the presiding judge of the Fulton County Juvenile Court in Atlanta.

"I can place these kids in incarceration, where they will learn to become better criminals, or I can send them home on probation, back to where they got in trouble in the first place," Judge Hatchett said.

Because governments have always regarded the juvenile court as a "poor stepchild" of the criminal justice system, Judge Hatchett said, there isn't money for the kinds of programs she believes would help, by reaching at-risk children and their parents when the children are 4, 5 or 6 years old, before it is too late.

Shifting Roles

Probation Officers Become Enforcers

Laura Donnelly is a Chicago probation officer with a master's degree in social work.

That makes her part of a vanishing breed, because today more and more probation officers have degrees in criminal justice. The change reflects the transition of the juvenile court from its origins in social welfare, treating the best interests of the child, to a criminal justice agency.

Ms. Donnelly has a caseload of 45 youths whom she visits a few times a month at home, school or work to make sure they are where they are supposed to be. Three of her clients have disappeared completely. She is confident she could find them, if she had enough time, which she does not.

She could also get a court-ordered arrest warrant, but the juvenile court cannot afford its own warrant squad, and police officers she knows are reluctant to spend time looking for children on warrants, unless the person is arrested on a new charge.

"A lot of officers don't want to waste their time on kiddie court when the judge is going to release the kid anyway," she said.

Ms. Donnelly stopped by a house on Chicago's South Side where one of her clients lived with his grandmother and 13 cousins, since his mother was a crack addict who couldn't be found. A husky 16-year-old, the boy was on probation for selling crack and was confined to his home 24 hours a day unless accompanied by his grandmother.

A charge of auto theft had been dropped when he repeatedly failed to appear for trial and the witnesses in the case tired of going to court without any result. That is a common way for young defendants to win.

Ms. Donnelly reminded the boy that he had another court date in

two days, relating to a charge of theft and battery incurred while he was supposed to have been confined to home. He had forgotten about the appearance.

It was another day's work for Ms. Donnelly. "These kids have had nothing but chaos in their lives," she said. "That's what we have to overcome, to give them as much structure and consistency as we can."

"But how," she asked, "do you replace the absence of the family?" Sometimes she thinks the only answer is to move in herself. But she knows that would not work either.

A Move for Change

Young Suspects In Adult Courts

All these troubles have sparked a growing movement to drastically restructure and perhaps abolish the juvenile court.

Leading the charge are conservative politicians who have passed laws in all 50 states allowing juveniles to be tried in adult court and sent to adult prison.

In Illinois a person under 17 may be tried in adult court for crimes including murder, carjacking and armed robbery as well as possession of drugs or weapons within 1,000 feet of a school or housing project, a provision that disproportionately affects minorities. Illinois also has a version for juveniles of the "three strikes and you're out" law.

Congress is poised to pass the most Draconian law yet, with provisions for $1.5 billion in Federal grants to states that try larger number[s] of young people in adult court and making 14-year-olds subject to trial in Federal court if they commit certain felonies.

"It's the end of the juvenile court," said Ira Schwartz, dean of the School of Social Work at the University of Pennsylvania. "All you would have left is a court for lar-

ceny." Such a truncated court would not be financially viable and would probably be scrapped, he suggested.

At the same time, some left-wing legal scholars have also called for abolishing the juvenile court, though for very different reasons. Barry Feld, a professor of law at the University of Minnesota, believes that young people often fail to get adequate legal representation in juvenile court and would fare better in adult court, where they would be more likely to be assigned decent lawyers.

Under his plan, as a further protective measure, juveniles in adult court would be given a "youth discount," or lighter sentences, depending on their age.

Some children's advocates who in the past championed the juvenile court have begun urging still another solution—that the court scale back its judicial role and transfer its functions to community groups or social service agencies that would provide better treatment for young people in trouble.

In the rush to try juveniles in adult courts, some critical questions go unasked. For example, are 13- and 14-year olds really competent to stand trial like adults?

Often such young defendants cannot tell a coherent story to help defend themselves, said Thomas Grisso, a psychiatry professor at the University of Massachusetts Medical Center. What then should the court do? Wait till they are more mature?

As a result of all this ferment, Mr. Schwartz said, "What we have right now in the juvenile court is chaos, with every state moving piecemeal on its own." A century after the creation of the juvenile court, he said, "Unless we take it more seriously, what we are headed for is its abolition by default."

Teen Court

By SHARON J. ZEHNER

Newspaper headlines and television broadcasts have chronicled the ominously sharp rise in juvenile crime that occurred during the past several years. While everyone agrees that rising levels of juvenile crime represent a serious threat to the quality of life in communities around the country, little consensus exists regarding the best way to respond to this profound problem.

The debate, no doubt, will continue for years to come. However, some promising programs already have proven effective in curtailing youth crime. Among these is Teen Court, a program that uses the undeniable power of peer pressure as a positive, rather than negative, force to help convince youthful troublemakers that crime yields serious consequences. Teen Court also provides law enforcement agencies a unique opportunity to help guide at-risk youths away from crime at a time when they are particularly impressionable.

In states where Teen Court is in place, youths who complete the program re-offend at a much lower rate than do youths tried and sentenced in juvenile courts.[1] The program also represents a cost-effective alternative to traditional court processing because Teen Court relies largely on volunteers. While Teen Court is not designed to replace municipal juvenile courts, it does offer a highly structured and effective means to guide some youths away from trouble by showing them that criminal activity has both immediate and long-term consequences.

Background

From its relatively inauspicious beginnings in rural Texas 20 year ago, Teen Court—also known as Youth Court and Peer Court in various parts of the country—has grown into a nationwide network of programs, each uniquely tailored to meet the needs of its hometown community. Today, 250 Teen Court programs exist in 30 states.

The central feature of the Teen Court approach is that youthful first-time offenders charged with a misdemeanor offense receive judgment from their peers. During Teen Court hearings, teenage volunteers act as court clerks, bailiffs, and jurors, as well as attorneys for the prosecution and defense.

Defendants may receive a wide range of sentences, mirroring both the criminal and punitive sanctions handed down in juvenile and adult courts. Defendants must complete their sentences within 30 days. Those who do not meet the terms in this time frame are remanded to juvenile court.

Approximately 20 distinct Teen Court programs currently operate in the State of Florida. This article focuses on the program in Bay County, which includes Panama City and several smaller municipalities. Most

Ms. Zehner is the Director of Bay County Teen Court in Panama City, Florida.

> " Teen Court combines elements of the criminal justice system with volunteers to address a pressing community problem. "

From *FBI Law Enforcement Bulletin*, March 1997, pp. 1-7. Reprinted by permission of the U.S. Department of Justice, Federal Bureau of Investigation.

of the features and principles discussed, however, apply to Teen Court programs in place throughout the country.

The Process

On any given Tuesday evening in Panama City, six or seven juvenile defendants nervously pace the hallways of the Juvenile Court Building as they await their Teen Court hearings. Inside the courtroom, the Teen Court director and her staff coordinate the activities of over 20 students volunteering for the evening. The student defense attorneys, all of whom are in high school, have just 1 hour to meet with their clients and prepare a defense strategy.

While the hands of the defense attorneys are somewhat tied—all Teen Court defendants must plead guilty in order to participate in the program—the student lawyers focus on their clients' character, grades, school behavior, attitude, and any mitigating circumstances that jurors should consider when they debate possible sentences. Across the hall, student prosecuting attorneys use the hour to prepare their cases. Volunteer adult attorneys roam among the prosecution and defense teams, offering advice as needed.

Meanwhile, the director's staff sits in the main courtroom, answering questions, collecting essays and apology letters from previous defendants, and selecting the juries for this evening's hearings. Each jury consists of student volunteers and defendants who are currently serving their sentences. An equitable mix of jurors is important, given the tendency of some defendant-jurors to impose harsh sentences on the defendants whom they judge. Student volunteers do not share that philosophy. Because a unanimous verdict is required before juries can stop deliberations, the jurors learn to compromise and build a consensus when arriving at a sentence.

Just before 5 p.m., the student attorneys, as well as their clients and parents, return to the main court-room to await the arrival of the judge. A Bay County Administrative Juvenile Judge initiated the Bay County Teen Court program in Panama City several years ago. Today, this judge and several circuit and county judges volunteer to sit on the bench each week.

Announced by the bailiff, who is a member of the Bay County Sheriff's Explorer's Program, the judge leads the court through the Pledge of Allegiance and a moment of silence. All present then recite the Teen Court Oath of Confidentiality, pledging to " . . . keep secret all said proceedings" held in their presence. The sensitive nature of the cases discussed in Teen Court and the fact that the defendants are juveniles dictate that the oath be strictly enforced and adhered to by all volunteers and members of the program staff.

From this point, the Teen Court session proceeds like any other court hearing. The bailiff swears in the members of the jury and announces the first case. Both sets of attorneys then make opening statements.

Following the statements and any initial appeals from the defense or prosecution teams, the student clerk swears in the defendant, who takes the stand. The prosecution and defense attorneys then question the defendant and can request the opportunity to cross-examine the defendant or redirect questions, following questioning from the opposing counsel. At the conclusion of the testimony, the attorneys make closing statements and sentencing recommendations. The judge then dismisses the jury, accompanied by an adult volunteer, to deliberate.

While in the jury room, the jury selects a foreperson who leads the jurors in a discussion of the evidence and facts presented by both sides. Simultaneously in the main court-room, a second set of attorneys begins its case with another defendant. At the conclusion of the second hearing, the jury from the first hearing returns to the courtroom to deliver its sentence. As it does so, the jury from the second hearing is es-corted out of the courtroom and the process begins anew.

Once the verdict has been delivered, the judge calls the defendant and the defendant's parents to the bench for instructions. The judge reminds the youth that participating in the Teen Court process is a privilege and that failure to complete the court's sanctions will result in the case being transferred to juvenile court. The judge then informs the parents that they are responsible for reporting all infractions to the Teen Court director.

Immediately after the courtroom proceeding, the juvenile and parents meet with uniformed officers from the Panama City Police Department's community services division, who explain the terms of the sanctions. These officers, trained in the intricacies of the Teen Court program, can answer specific questions concerning the terms of the sentencing contract.

> " . . . each youth must complete a 7-hour workday supervised by the Panama City Police Department's community services division."

The officers develop deadlines for each of the juvenile's sanctions and provide the youth with a community service contract. Once the paperwork is signed, the family is released, and the juvenile's 30 days begin counting down.

Sanctions and Counseling

The Teen Court philosophy takes a two-track approach to sentencing. Defendants receive sanctions designed to punish their misdeeds. The program also mandates that defendants and their parents participate in counseling to help them understand the

Teen Court process and appreciate the potentially far-reaching consequences of antisocial and criminal behavior.

Sanctions and criminal cases heard in Bay County Teen Court can range from a prescribed number of community service hours, to curfews, to monetary restitution for victims. In addition to any other sanction imposed, each youth must complete a 7-hour workday supervised by the Panama City Police Department's community services division. During these workdays, the juveniles complete a variety of tasks, ranging from cleaning playgrounds in local housing complexes to scrubbing bathrooms and floors at the building used for the police department's after-school program for underprivileged children.

Defendants primarily complete community service hours at several area middle and high school sites after school, 3 days a week, and on Saturdays. Youths have painted the inside and outside of two local high schools, cleared away rubble from a demolished building at the Humane Society, decorated a police department float for the annual Christmas parade, and sorted Christmas toys for needy children.

Each defendant also must serve on a jury, ensuring a constant pool of jurors for future defendants. As with all participants of the Teen Court program, defendant-jurors must observe a strict dress code—no shorts, message T-shirts, short skirts, etc.—and must remain inside the courtroom for the duration of the session.

If the defendant's sentence involves restitution of any type, payment must be made to the Teen Court office within 30 days of sentencing. Typical restitution claims involve medical bills for battery victims and reimbursement for stolen goods.

Teen Court defendants also can be required to write letters of apology to their victims, as well as to

their own parents. To strengthen the impact of this sentence, the youths often must deliver the apologies in person.

Defendants also can be sentenced to write detailed essays, up to 5 pages in length, on topics relating to the crimes they committed. A typical paper might be titled "How Stealing Affects the Economy." Defendants caught dealing drugs often are sentenced to write essays about drugs and the importance of resisting peer pressure.

Youths placed on curfew or house arrest must be available to answer random telephone calls from the Teen Court director. Juveniles on house arrest may leave their homes only to go to school, work, church, or court, unless physically accompanied by a parent.

All families must attend a 3-hour session with the staff of Anchorage Children's Home, one of the county's social service agencies. The counseling session focuses on helping families understand, and cope with, the Teen Court process. At the conclusion of the mandatory session, the defendants and their parents view a videotape titled *Life Inside*. The video provides a realistic view of life in correctional institutions and features narration by inmates sentenced to state prisons for drug convictions or violent felonies.

> ## "Law enforcement officers receive notification of the sanctions imposed on the youths they referred to Teen Court."

Defendants then tour a local jail. The video and brief onsite tours generally get the intended message across to younger, less-hardened defendants. For those who require a stronger message, Teen Court worked with the Bay County Sher-

iff's Office Boot Camp to accommodate a 2-hour tour of the facility.

Defendants touring the boot camp spend the first hour walking through the facility and learning about the inmates' rigorous daily schedules. Afterwards, defendants line up in the dormitory area, where several drill instructors subject them to an hour of "in your face" shock incarceration. Previously supplied with notes detailing each defendant's behavior and attitude problems, the volunteer instructors seek to break down the youths' defense systems. Nearly all defendants emerge from this exercise visibly upset, including street-smart teens who repeatedly declared themselves unreachable.

Monitoring

The director and an assistant monitor all active Teen Court cases on a daily basis. If a juvenile misses a deadline for community service hours or written sanctions, the director immediately issues a warning letter, giving the defendant 10 days to rectify the situation. Juveniles who do not comply with the terms of the warning have their Teen Court cases closed and referred to juvenile court. Likewise, defendants placed on house arrest or given a curfew remain subject to random calls from the Teen Court director for the duration of their sentences.

Violators are immediately removed from the Teen Court program and their cases referred to juvenile court. The same is true for defendants who fail random drug tests.

Law enforcement officers receive notification of the sanctions imposed on the youths they referred to Teen Court. The Teen Court office elicits officers' opinions regarding the sentences imposed and asks the officers to provide a monthly critique of the program. The office also advises officers when a referred defendant completes the program or when a juvenile is removed for noncompliance.

Results

At the conclusion of their 30-day allotment to fulfill the terms of their sentences, juveniles have either completed the program or have been removed from it. Those who complete the program are invited to the Teen Court office to destroy their referring affidavits and can resume their lives without a criminal record.

Approximately 40 percent of the defendants who complete Bay County's program accept the standing invitation to return to the program as court volunteers. Those who do not complete the program hear from the Florida Department of Juvenile Justice regarding an impending appearance in juvenile court.

Nationally, nearly 95 percent of the juveniles accepted into Teen Court complete the program and do not re-offend within a 12-month period.[2] Bay County's figures mirror the national success rate with more than 90 percent of juveniles referred completing the program and less than 10 percent of defendants re-offending within the 12-month, postcompletion tracking period.[3]

Low recidivism rates are matched by the fiscal soundness of Teen Court. Typically, communities spend about $3,000 to process a child through the juvenile court system, from arrest to probation. On average, it costs less than $300 to process a child through Teen Court.

Although low recidivism rates and cost-effectiveness make Teen Court a viable supplement to the existing juvenile court system in many communities, the real measure of success is the degree to which the lives of defendants are changed by the Teen Court process. While completing their sentences, defendants often bring notes to the Teen Court office, written by appreciative teachers and school administrators, commending the students for their good behavior and improved grades. For many of the students, these notes represent the first successes of their young lives. Just a taste of genuine praise is all many of these youths need to help convince them to make serious life-enhancing decisions about their attitudes and behavior.

Parents of former defendants also voice overwhelming support for the program. In Bay County, the Teen Court office mails parents an evaluation form when their child has completed his or her prescribed sanctions. In recent surveys, 78 percent of responding parents rate the program "very effective," compared to 14 percent who rate the program "somewhat effective." Only eight percent of the respondents report that the program did not help their child.

Cooperation

Teen Court cannot operate successfully in a vacuum. A partnership among law enforcement, the judiciary, and the school system must exist for Teen Court to work as it is designed.

To ensure a quality partnership from the outset, the judge who initiated the Bay County program began with a volunteer board of directors comprised of stakeholders in juvenile justice issues from throughout the community. Currently, the Teen Court board consists of attorneys, business people, teachers, law enforcement officers, and concerned citizens, as well as representatives from the state attorney's office and the Florida Department of Juvenile Justice.

The Law Enforcement Role

For local law enforcement officers in Bay County, cooperation with Teen Court is a rewarding experience. Involvement with Teen Court furthers agencies' community policing efforts, while it gives officers the opportunity to be part of a solution to juvenile crime.

Currently, all officers in the Panama City Police Department receive basic instruction about the Teen Court program. Personnel from all units—including detective squads—are encouraged to refer first-time juvenile offenders who meet the program's requirements to Teen Court.

Officers in the department's community services division, as well as school resource officers from the Bay County Sheriff's Department, receive more specialized training concerning the terms of Teen Court contracts. Upon observing several Teen Court trials, the officers and deputies can then begin guiding defendants through the intricacies of their individual contracts. After reviewing the contract terms with defendants and their parents, the law enforcement officers act as informal mentors, periodically checking with the defendants to ensure they are working to complete their sentences.

Referral Criteria

In Bay County, juveniles can be referred to Teen Court by a law enforcement officer, school resource officer, school administrator, juvenile judge, state attorney, or representative of the Department of Juvenile Justice. To qualify for the Teen Court program, a juvenile must:

- Be between the ages of 11 and 16
- Be charged with a misdemeanor
- Not have a prior record
- Pay restitution for any stolen property not returned to victims
- Admit guilt and, with the consent of a parent or guardian, waive the right to a speedy trial.

Since its inception in May 1994, the Bay County Teen Court program has been embraced by local law enforcement administrators and line officers alike. Administrators value the opportunity it provides for the area's young people to see law enforcement in a positive, rather than negative, light. By having the option of referring first-time offenders to Teen Court instead of juvenile court, officers can give youthful wrongdoers a chance to make amends—and help guide them through the process—without saddling them with a juvenile record.

By interacting with the defendants as they fulfill their community service hours, officers have a chance to serve as positive role models for at-risk young people. Often, this constructive interaction proves enough to convince troubled youths that law enforcement officers are not out to get them. More important, some of the defendants adopt more positive outlooks as a direct result of interaction with the officers. For law enforcement officers conditioned to seeing negative outcomes, few results could be as rewarding as seeing young people turn their lives around and turn their backs on lives of crime.

Direct Referral

The Bay County Teen Court is one of the few in the State of Florida that receives cases through direct referrals from law enforcement officers. The direct referral system calls for officers in the field to judge the suitability of a particular juvenile for the program.

"Low recidivism rates are matched by the fiscal soundness of Teen Court."

If the officer believes that a young person is a first offender, then the of-

Sanctions

All defendants in Bay County, Florida, Teen Court must:

- Participate in 1 to 4 Teen Court juries
- Perform 10 to 50 hours of community service
- Pay financial restitution to victims

In addition, sanctions could include one or any combination of the following:

- Apology letters to victims and parents
- Essays, up to 5 pages long, relating to the crime
- A curfew of 5 p.m. for up to 30 days
- House arrest for up to 30 days
- A tour of the Bay County Jail
- A tour of the Bay County Sheriff's Office Boot Camp
- Drug and alcohol counseling
- Driver's license suspension

ficer can refer the case directly to the Teen Court office, bypassing the juvenile justice system entirely. Once the child has been transported to the jail and fingerprinted—if the offense warrants this process—the youth's case file, including the affidavit, witness statements, etc., is placed in a box at the police department. The Teen Court office checks this box daily.

The director also checks with the Department of Juvenile Justice to ensure that the juvenile is, in fact, a first-time offender. Youths who qual-

ify for the program are sent an appointment letter putting the Teen Court process into motion.

Often, defendants appear in court within 3 weeks of their arrest. The brief waiting period is particularly helpful when sentencing very young offenders who have a tendency to forget why they are being punished.

Referral of youths to Teen Court reduces the workload of the overburdened Department of Juvenile Justice. The Bay County program reduces the juvenile court caseload by more than 250 cases a year. Diverting first-time offenders charged with misdemeanors to Teen Court enables the department's case managers to work more closely with multiple offenders and those youths charged with felonies.

The direct referral system also helps reduce duplication of services because only one intake interview is conducted. If the Teen Court director discovers that a juvenile referred to the program is not a first-time offender, the youth's original affidavit simply is forwarded to the Department of Juvenile Justice and the standard juvenile court process is put into motion.

Conclusion

The rising level of criminal activity committed by young people is a complex problem, fueled by many contributing factors. Institutions working alone—whether schools, law enforcement, or the courts—will have limited impact in addressing the problem. Yet, together, they can make a difference. Communities that develop an integrated approach to resolving the issues that surround youth crime enhance their chances of reducing juvenile crime levels.

Teen Court combines elements of the criminal justice system with volunteers to address a pressing community problem. The program succeeds for two reasons. It uses peer pressure to reinforce the negative consequences of crime, and it creates a structured environment for law enforcement, the courts, and the community to intervene before first-time offenders become hardened criminals. While Teen Court cannot replace juvenile court, communities searching for solutions to the vexing problem of youth crime might find that it offers a valuable complement to the existing approach to juvenile justice.

Endnotes

1. Tracy Godwin, with David Steinhart and Betsy Fulton, "Peer Justice and Youth Empowerment: An Implementation Guide for Teen Court Programs," in partnership with the U.S. Department of Justice, the U.S. Department of Transportation, and the American Probation and Parole Association, (Washington, DC: U.S. Government Printing Office, 1996).

2. Ibid.

3. Ibid. However, it should be noted that juveniles referred to juvenile courts have committed more serious crimes than defendants referred to Teen Court.

Punishment and Corrections

In the American system of criminal justice, the term "corrections" has a special meaning. It designates programs and agencies that have legal authority over the custody or supervision of persons who have been convicted of a criminal act by the courts. The correctional process begins with the sentencing of the convicted offender. The predominant sentencing pattern in the United States encourages maximum judicial discretion and offers a range of alternatives from probation (supervised, conditional freedom within the community), through imprisonment, to the death penalty.

Selections in this unit focus on the current condition of the U.S. penal system and the effects that sentencing, probation, imprisonment, and parole have on the rehabilitation of criminals.

In the lead essay, "Can We Break the Pattern of the Criminal Lifestyle?" Mark Fleisher argues that the nation *can* afford to build more and more prisons. He asserts it is cheaper to house persistent criminals in prison than it is to release them every few years, then to arrest and convict them again to pay for the damage they left behind. Professor John DiIulio Jr. maintains it is time to support serious efforts at making probation and parole effective community correctional strategies. His ideas are found in "Reinventing Parole and Probation."

"Eddie Ellis at Large" is the story of a man who spent 23 years in New York State's toughest prisons for a crime he did not commit. Released several years ago, he has worked vigorously to effect change in his own community and in the justice system. Probation officers frequently face decisions that place the needs of offenders in direct conflict with the welfare of society. "Ethical Considerations in Probation Practice" sheds light on this dilemma and asserts that probation officers can benefit from a firm foundation in ethics.

In the next article, Nicole Gaouette reports that the numbers of women entering prison are growing rapidly.

They are part of an influx of women filling America's prisons at a rate that eclipses the male incarceration rate. "Prisons Grapple with Rapid Influx of Women—and Mothers" also points out that most of these prisoners are incarcerated for nonviolent, drug-related crimes that are now drawing harsher sentences.

Is segregation of inmates into race groups a good idea? Prison officials and politicians think that it is. Their contention is that separating inmates by race boosts safety and control and is just being practical. "To Keep Peace, Prisons Allow Race to Rule," explores this issue and suggests that there may be other unintended outcomes.

The article that follows, "The Color of Justice," points out that there are more nonwhite men on death row then their Caucasian counterparts, according to the numbers. Is the disparity due to racial discrimination or to some other not-so-black-and-white issues? The results of the study reported in "What Works? What Matters? Recidivism among Probationers in North Carolina" suggest correctional intervention may make a difference in *some* cases.

The concluding report, prepared by the Death Penalty Information Center, points out that the number of executions in 1996 was the second highest since 1976.

Looking Ahead: Challenge Questions

What issues and trends are most likely to be faced by corrections administrators at the close of this century?

What are some of the reasons for overcrowding in our nation's prisons?

Why have prisons become so violent and difficult to manage in recent years?

Discuss reasons for favoring and for opposing the death penalty.

CAN WE BREAK THE PATTERN OF THE
CRIMINAL LIFESTYLE?

". . . Keeping violent inmates imprisoned will reduce the number of victims and lower the cost of street crime."

Mark S. Fleisher

CRIME CONTROL policies are failing, despite optimistic statistics to the contrary. Crime control refers to the use of imprisonment as punishment for unlawful acts committed and a deterrent to their commission, as well as rehabilitation programs that include, but aren't limited to, education, vocational training, and treatment for alcoholism and drug addiction. Policymakers who pander for votes by alleging that getting tough on criminals will curb street crime are wrong. These threats have little effect on behavior-hardened street criminals.

During my years of research among "hard-core" adolescent delinquents and persistent adult criminals who cycle between sidewalks and cellhouses, we hung out together on street corners and in alleys and bars, missions and flophouses, jail and prison cells, and places where drugs were sold. This research, funded by the U.S. Census Bureau and Harry Frank Guggenheim Foundation, revealed that these criminals do not want to find legal jobs and stop using alcohol and drugs. Moreover, they do not interpret their lifestyles as lawful citizens do.

Persistent criminals see an unlawful lifestyle as relatively carefree and morally acceptable. Living a lawful lifestyle, however, would force them to relinquish the freedom of social irresponsibility. These criminals have little interest in society's rules and have learned to use the criminal justice system to their advantage. To them, prisons are sanctuaries that deliver social, medical,

Dr. Fleisher, Law & Justice Editor of USA Today, *is associate professor of criminal justice sciences, Illinois State University, Normal, and the author of* Beggars and Thieves: Lives of Urban Street Criminals.

and recreational services. A system of effective crime control measures can be developed, but to do that, policymakers must learn more about the lives of street criminals.

The lives of persistent criminals have a trajectory or path which has its inception in early life. I call this trajectory a "street lifecycle." It has four sequential stages, each one linked to and establishing the conditions for the next.

My subjects' childhood homes were angry places. They were born into families where parents were alcoholics, most smoked marijuana, and many used heroin or cocaine. Fathers were criminals, often drug dealers. Mothers (and sometimes grandmothers) were involved directly in criminal activities with their husbands, brothers, sons, and nephews. Sometimes, these women were passive observers, but they always were active consumers of the money and goods brought about by crime.

Parents usually did not get along well with each other, especially when they were drunk. Women were beaten by their mates' fists or slashed with a knife; men were cut by knives wielded by women. Fathers and mothers assaulted their sons and daughters. Children were whipped with belts, punched with fists, slapped with hands, and kicked. I have witnessed mothers striking their sons and daughters repeatedly with heavy leather straps, then looking at me and saying, "It's for their own good."

In these homes, no one read to their children; no one cautioned them about the dangers of alcohol and drugs; no one said school was important; no one encouraged youngsters to read; no one bought school supplies; no one encouraged kids to write stories; no one helped children with arithmetic; and no one cared.

In their teenage years, these youngsters abandoned home life for street life. At first, they stayed away for a few days or a week,

but as they adjusted and became part of the street's action, stints away from home grew longer and longer, until these youths never returned. They wandered city neighborhoods and banded together into loosely knit social groups (gangs), which afforded them some modicum of safety and protection, but at the same time exposed youngsters to drugs and violence and cut them off from social relationships to children and adults who might have helped them. By junior high school, nearly all were chronic truants and drug addicts, indulging freely in alcohol, marijuana, crack cocaine, heroin, or a combination of these drugs. They apprenticed at burglary, car theft, drug selling, pimping, and armed robbery—occupations that soon landed them in juvenile detention and then, as adults, in prison.

For adolescent and young adult criminals, a stint in prison often proved an acceptable alternative, offering them goods and services unavailable on the street. Prison is stable and provides plenty of food, a clean bed, recreation, and access to medical and dental services. State and Federal spending on inmate medical care exceeds $3,000 per inmate annually. Research shows that most inmates leave prison healthier than when they entered. Social life in prison is good, too. Some inmates continue criminal activity, such as drug dealing, while others just "lay up" and enjoy the safety and pleasures of not hustling for money and food every day.

Eventually, the easy life inside ends. Nearly all prison inmates are released and go back to home neighborhoods. As criminals age, they return to find that social ties have been broken from years in prison. Going home gets harder. Some former street companions still are behind bars, others were killed on the street, and some have died from drug overdoses, developed AIDS, or become ill from chronic alcoholism

Member of Fremont Hustlers, a Kansas City, Mo., gang, examines progress of germination of marijuana plant seeds. Plastic cake container becomes a mini-greenhouse for seeds placed on a moistened paper towel within it. Once the seeds sprout, they are planted in a marijuana "garden" until they are ready to harvest.

There is only one sure way to protect battered and neglected youngsters. They must be placed permanently in small residential homes funded and regulated by the Federal government. Local foster care programs may be well-meaning, but they often are poorly funded, suffer from inadequate administrative oversight, and do not provide stable, long-term homes for children. A system of Federal residential homes can be effective with adequate funding, well-trained adults, and high-quality care.

Kids deserve safe and stable places to live. Such residential homes must receive line-item Federal funding, with firm financial support from states. These facilities never must become pawns in political battles. Church groups, volunteer organizations, schools, and other community agencies can assist by identifying at-risk youngsters of all ages and developing community facilities for them. Decreasing the escalation of socially destructive behavior means ending child abuse. Protecting children is not just another remedy for breaking the street lifecycle—it is the *only* remedy. Everything else is very expensive damage control.

The cost of these residential homes is paltry compared to the annual price of crime and victimization. One study estimates health care costs associated with violent acts over a three-year period were approximately $179,000,000,000. America must be intolerant of interpersonal violence by keeping offenders in prisons for very long terms. Discontinuing "second chances" and keeping violent inmates imprisoned will reduce the number of victims and lower the cost of street crime.

Let us stop apologizing for imprisoning violent criminals. Research shows it is cheaper to house persistent criminals in prison than it is to release them every few years, then to arrest and convict them again and to pay for the damage they left behind. What is more, the nation can afford to build more and more prisons. State and Federal expenditures on adult correctional facilities nearly always are less than four percent of total budgetary expenditures. Ironically, spending money on prisons boosts the economy. The cost of prison construction and the annual operating budgets of correctional facilities are paid to contractors and staff members who spend salaries on shopping, vacations, houses, cars, etc.

If more and more prisons are to be built, they must be used in a more cost-effective manner. Operating budgets can be cut by examining rehabilitation costs. The centerpiece of criminal justice rehabilitation is education. Taxpayers are told that educated inmates will change their lifestyles. If alcoholics and drug addicts were treated for addictions and understood the destructiveness of alcohol and drugs, they would

and/or hepatitis. They must compete against younger, more active criminals for the street's limited bounty. The harshness of street life never ends. Many aging hustlers prefer to return to the secure world of prison; others panhandle and commit petty crimes to support chronic alcohol and drug habits. These men and women sleep on cardboard boxes on concrete sidewalks, in empty cars and abandoned buildings, and under bushes in city parks.

Decades of research in social science have shown that intimate face-to-face interactions in early life are crucial in the molding of an individual's basic personality, the formation and perpetuation of attitudes toward the world, and the determination of socially acceptable behavior and personal self-control. Adolescent behavior is the single most important indicator of bad parenting. A 15-year-old runaway girl in Kansas City, Mo., understood the link between parenting and street crime: "My mother's six kids are drug addicts, alcoholics, runaways, violent, and gangbangers. What kind of mother do you think she was?"

Where were the parents of the teenage boys and girls I watched prostitute themselves to earn cash for drugs and alcohol? At two in the morning, I was the only adult among adolescent gang members. No parents kept these children out of harm's way.

There are mothers and fathers who are awful parents, and no amount of scapegoating, expensive family therapy, and excuses can compensate for the damage inflicted on kids by years of parental abuse and neglect. To transform violent and drug-addicted, neglectful parents into loving and kind caretakers would be as expensive and risky as rehabilitating the deviant youngsters reared by them. There are no documented cases of family therapy programs that can transform hundreds, if not thousands, of brutal parents into kinder and gentler mothers and fathers. Would you allow your children to be cared for by a former cocaine addict and convicted felon? How much tax revenue are you willing to invest in high-risk programs for people with proven histories of violence toward kids? What will be the return on your investment?

stop drinking and using drugs and the crime linked to substance abuse would end. If delinquents and adult criminals received vocational training, they would find legitimate jobs and stop selling drugs, firearms, and stolen property. Criminals sentenced to prison would learn a "lesson" and, when released, acquire a job and live a lawful lifestyle. The education model of social change assumes, of course, that criminals gladly would meet society's lawful expectations once given a chance to do so. That is a foolish assumption, though.

Education as a remedy for a criminal lifestyle for the most part has been a failed experiment in social engineering, but this lack of success has not dulled its popularity. Government administrators design, implement, and oversee education-based crime control programs and, when they fail, bureaucrats report "modest success" and request more money for improved, expanded, and intensified initiatives.

Before diverting another dime of tax revenue to education-based programs, taxpayers should demand proof they have economic value. The public needs an answer to this question: How many former state and Federal inmates who were recipients of education-based programs filed a Federal and/or state income tax return within one, three, five, or 10 years after release? A similar question should be asked of community-based rehabilitation programs. These data should be easily obtainable. Inmates and probationers should have a Social Security number, which could be checked against state and Federal income tax databases.

If taxpayers do not break even on the cost of rehabilitation programs, the bureaucracies that support them must be pared down and the money invested in worthwhile projects. These might encompass rehabilitating dilapidated schools, buying computer equipment for children who stay in school, providing low-interest loans to college students, and rebuilding inner cities.

Work is the standard community activity everywhere in America. We should expect no less from prisoners. In *Warehousing Violence,* I showed that, in a maximum-security Federal penitentiary—the United States Penitentiary (USP) at Lompoc, Calif.—skilled administrators transformed a prison into a revenue-generating "factory." Products created by inmate employees in Federal Prison Industry (Unicor) were valuable commodities that garnered revenue which exceeded the USP Lompoc's annual operating budget by about $25,000,000.

Three female members of Fremont Hustlers. G-Love (left), one of the gang's founders, and Cara (center) were shot in 1994 by a 15-year-old member of the Northeast Gangstas, wielding an Ak-47 and looking for someone to kill. Rosa (right) became a mother in 1996. (The father is the marijuana grower shown on the previous page.) Three years earlier, she had been shot in the chest by a .38 caliber handgun fired by a Northeast Gangsta.

What is more, the inmates said that monthly salaries earned in Unicor, which averaged about $220 each, markedly improved their quality of life. Inmates shopped at the commissary for name-brand products and favorite snacks and in early evening could be seen walking on the prison compound, eating quarts of ice cream. This lifestyle, said many of the prisoners, "beats sleeping under bridges."

The benefits of inmate work do not end there. The Federal prison system's financial responsibility program requires convicts to pay court-ordered child support, alimony, and court-imposed fines. The more they earn, the more they pay. State correctional agencies have caught on. Oregon Prison Industries manufactures a line of clothes, "Prison Blues," and exports them to Italy, Japan, and other countries. California prison industries export prisoner-made clothing to Japan and Malaysia. State inmate workers earn $6–8 an hour, and their wages are garnisheed for room, board, and restitution.

Every inmate should have a full-time job manufacturing valuable goods or supporting the production of those items. American union leaders fuss about inmate labor taking away union jobs. What are the alternatives? The nation can spend billions more tax dollars on prison construction and operating budgets with little financial relief in sight, or develop prison-based industrial programs that reduce the cost of Federal and state imprisonment. Realistically, those who are locked behind secure walls and fences can't do many jobs available to free citizens, but inmate workers may be the lower-paid, low-skill American labor force that is needed to compete against Third World workers. If the skills of imprisoned felons displace union workers, the latter ought to seek more education and get better jobs.

There are felons who do not need to be imprisoned. Offenders whose past behavior does not include arrests and/or convictions for sex and/or violent crimes may pose little threat to lawful citizens. Convicted, nonviolent felons should toil for 40 hours a week on community work details, fixing roads, painting houses, picking up rubbish and sweeping streets, and performing other community work, all under the watchful eye of supervisors. Work is rehabilitating; rehabilitation is work.

J O H N   J .   D I I U L I O ,   J R .

REINVENTING PAROLE and PROBATION

A LOCK-'EM-UP HARD-LINER MAKES THE CASE FOR PROBATION

No one—at least no one in elite policy-wonk circles—is a bigger fan of incarcerating known, adjudicated adult and juvenile criminals than I am. No one has written more over the years about the cost-effectiveness of incarceration as measured both in terms of its crime-reduction value and in terms of doing justice. Still, when it comes to the search for rational, workable crime policies, it's time to admit that the brain-dead law-and-order right is no better than the soft-in-the-head anti-incarceration left. More and more conservatives now favor abolishing parole, sharply curtailing probation, imprisoning every adult felon for his or her entire term, and warehousing juvenile offenders in adult jails. The prudent response, however, is not to abolish probation and parole, but to reinvent them.

First, let's get crystal clear on the grim facts about crime, prisons, probation, and parole. Be giddy about recent drops in national crime rates if you wish, but each year Americans still suffer some 40 million criminal victimizations; about a quarter of these are violent crimes. Only about 1 in 100 crimes actually results in anyone getting caught, convicted, and sentenced to prison. Most felony defendants are repeat offenders; yet most felony defendants are sentenced not to prison but to probation.

Likewise, a half-dozen studies prove beyond a reasonable doubt what every veteran policeman knows: most prisoners are *not* petty, nonviolent thieves or mere first-time, low-level drug offenders. Yet most of these hardened criminals are still

John J. DiIulio Jr., is the Douglas Dillon nonresident senior fellow in the Brookings Governmental Studies program and professor of politics and public affairs at Princeton University.

paroled well before they have served out their latest sentence behind bars. On any given day in America, there are three convicted adult criminals out on probation or parole for every one in prison—and many of these are indistinguishable (in terms of their violent and repeat criminal histories) from those who remain in prison. As for juvenile offenders, between 1989 and 1993 the number of adjudicated juvenile cases that resulted in probation rose by 17 percent. The number of probation cases involving a "person offense"—such as homicide, rape, robbery, or assault—soared by 45 percent.

Literally dozens of careful studies document that probation and parole are, to put it mildly, failing to protect the public. Nearly half of all state prisoners in 1991 had committed their latest crimes while out on probation or parole. While formally "under supervision" in the community, their "violations" included more than 13,000 murders, some 39,000 robberies, and tens of thousands of other crimes. More than a quarter of all felons charged with gun crimes in 1992 were out on probation and parole. Here, too, what's true for the revolving-door adult system is even more true for the no-fault juvenile system. In many cities, for example, most cases involving violent older teen thugs who get referred to adult court result in probation. Kids plea bargain too.

GETTING WHAT WE PAY FOR

Why are the adult and juvenile probation systems so poor, and what, realistically, can be done to improve them—soon?

A big part of the answer is that we spend next to nothing on the systems, and get about what we pay for. Take adult probation. Joan R. Petersilia, former director of RAND's criminal-justice research program, has calculated that we currently spend about $200 per probationer for supervision. "It is no wonder," she notes, "that recidivism rates are so high." Likewise, Patrick A. Langan, a statistician with the U.S. Justice Department, has found that more than 90 percent of probationers are supposed to get substance abuse counseling, pay victim restitution, or meet other requirements. But about half do not comply with the terms of their probation. Probation sanctions, he concludes, "are not rigorously enforced."

But how could they be properly supervised by overworked, underpaid probation officers with scores of cases to manage? As Petersilia argues, even probationers who are categorized as high-risk offenders receive little direct, face-to-face oversight. If "probationers are growing in number and are increasingly more serious offenders," she advises, "then they are in need of more supervision, not less. But less is exactly what they have been getting over the past decade."

Ditto for juvenile probation. Over half of street-level juvenile probation officers earn less than $30,000 a year. In big cities, the probation caseload of serious and violent juvenile cases has increased rapidly. In a national survey, probation officers admitted that their average urban caseloads were at least 25 percent higher than they should be.

To reinvent probation, we will need to reinvest in it. More money, more agents, and closer supervision are just the first phase. Equally important is the type of creative and critical thinking represented by Boston's probation chief Ronald P. Corbett. Among other innovations, Corbett has teamed local probation officers with local police officers. Patrolling the streets together, they have cut crime. Corbett has also got probation officers to work with inner-city clergy on a wide range of crime control and prevention initiatives.

In Philadelphia, the district attorney's office has developed a no-nonsense program in which volunteers from the neighborhoods where the juveniles committed their crimes hear the cases, set terms, and monitor compliance. Run for the district attorney's office by veteran probation officer Mike Cleary, the citywide program boasts an 80 percent success rate, costs little to administer, and holds kids (including hundreds of juvenile felony offenders) accountable.

"The value of Philly's program," observes former New Jersey Superior Court Judge Daniel R. Coburn, "is that it separates the minnows from the sharks, then holds the minnows accountable and hence less likely to become sharks, let alone become the predatory Great Whites we must incarcerate." He should know. Coburn pioneered two major and highly successful programs in New Jersey. One is the state's Enforcement Court, which goes after people who remain on probation because they failed to pay fines and restitution, collects the money, restores the trust of crime victims, and brings literally millions of dollars into state coffers that can be used to beef up other justice programs. The other is the Sheriffs Labor As-

sistance Program (SLAP), which puts low-level criminals to work cleaning up parks, painting public buildings, helping out in nursing homes, and more. "Fail to do exactly what you're required to do on SLAP," Coburn declares, "and you get slam—as in, see you in jail for sure."

HOPE FOR PAROLE TOO?

Admittedly, parole is a tougher reinvention nut to crack. In the late 1980s, I myself had expressed hopes that intensive-supervision parole programs could protect the public and its purse. But the best studies of intensive-supervision programs for high-risk parolees soon found that the programs cut neither recidivism nor costs. So for the last several years I have argued in favor of some types of "three strikes and you're out" laws.

And I continue to strongly favor a no-parole policy for some categories of violent and chronic criminals.

But the most interesting parole-reinvention idea I've encountered to date comes from Martin Horn, formerly head of New York State's parole authority and now commissioner of prisons in Pennsylvania. As Horn argues, in most cases there is relatively little that parole agents can do to keep an offender who is determined to commit new crimes from committing them. The flip side is that parolees who want to go straight often can make it if they are literate, civil, and can stay off drugs, remain sober, and get a job. But parole agents often waste time chasing the bad guys rather than helping the good. And in many states, the laws perversely limit a parole agent's discretion. For example, I've heard many agents complain of having to revoke the parole of guys who failed a drug test but who were not, in the agent's best judgment, doing anything more than getting high. As one agent confided, "A parolee of mine is ok and is looking for a job. He pees in a bottle and comes up dirty, and I have to send him back inside. But a real predator I know is using, selling, and almost certainly doing other crimes. He stays on the streets unless I catch him red-handed—and I won't. It's insane."

Horn's radical notion is to reinvent parole on the basis of a "personal responsibility" model. A released prisoner would be given the equivalent of a parole services voucher. For a fixed period of time—say, two years—he can use the voucher to seek education, job training, drug treatment, or other services from state-selected providers. If he wants to help himself, he can. If not, he's on his own. Do a new crime during this period—bite the hand that is offering you a way to help yourself—and you do the time for the crime, plus a year or two.

It's time to get behind serious efforts to reinvent probation and parole, and time to debate fresh ideas. After all, we are not going to put every convicted adult and juvenile felon behind bars and keep him or her there—nor should we.

> WE ARE NOT GOING TO PUT EVERY CONVICTED FELON BEHIND BARS AND KEEP HIM OR HER THERE—NOR SHOULD WE.

MAN OF THE YEAR

EDDIE ELLIS AT LARGE

Former Black Panther Eddie Ellis spent 23 years in New York State's toughest prisons for a crime he did not commit. Released just three years ago, he hit the streets running and hasn't stopped since, taking the organizational skills he honed in prison back to his community, where he works ceaselessly to help those who suffer most from America's latest economic boom: the prison business. Prison Life salutes Eddie Ellis for his tireless efforts to make desperately needed changes in his own community and in the justice system at large.

Pam Widener

The Negro race, like all races, is going to be saved by its exceptional men.
W.E.B. Du Bois

With his usual red-faced exuberance and borderline Hell's Angel demeanor, this evening's moderator, activist-lawyer and William Kunstler protégé Ron Kuby never for a moment lets us forget why we have gathered. We are in the Puffin Room, a small gallery in downtown Manhattan hung with hauntingly beautiful art created by and for political prisoners the world over, a large number of whom are in the US. The panel is *The Politics of Incarceration*.

"Just imagine," Kuby says, "that there was some sort of disease that hit one white high school student in four. And what this disease did was it robbed these young white people of three, four, five, ten years, 20 years of their youth—their most productive years. Some of them it would cripple, and some of them it would kill. First it hit one in four young white high school students. And then one in three. And then finally people predicted this plague would hit one in two. You know what would happen in this country. There would be outrage.

Hundreds of billions of dollars would be spent to cure this problem; no expense would be spared.

"That's the reality of what happens when white people are afflicted. As those of us here tonight know, when African-Americans and Latinos and when poor people generally are afflicted, the system is much different.

"I want to introduce to you a man," he continues, "who has suffered tremendously, and in his suffering has given incredible things to a generation of young people this country is trying to destroy. A man who is truly one of society's unsung heroes."

Enter Eddie Ellis. He is a tall, lean, dignified man in his early 50s, bespectacled, with soft white hair and a white-speckled moustache. He looks his age, but has the bearing of a wise village elder. Nothing about him suggests he spent 23 years in prison. He seems calm, at ease, grounded in thought. Yet there is an energy hovering with studied patience behind his eyes and there is a constant purse to his lips, making them seem like a floodgate about to give from the intellectual pressure behind them.

"It is a tremendous honor and a pleasure to be asked to speak here," he

says, "particularly in the company of such distinguished panelists. Indeed, I think that we've come a long, long way for just being asked."

His voice is distinctive. Once you hear it you'll recognize it in a heartbeat, even from several rooms away. It is the first of countless times I will hear Eddie refer to himself as "we," and I will come to understand that it's a reflection of his community-based world view.

"Unfortunately," he continues, "I have—since I got out of prison, which has been about three years—a set, prepared speech that I normally give. And over the three years I've gotten fairly good at delivering it." Laughter. "When I spoke to Ron Kuby about what I would talk on tonight, of course I had in mind my set speech. And he asked me to deviate from that speech. He said that the other presenters—the other illustrious presenters—would be using all of the material that I had in my set speech." Laughter. "Which they did." More laughter. "So I'm left here with this set speech that everybody else has already spoken about."

In the last three years, the set speech Eddie emerged from prison with has evolved into at least four versions, each

Photo by Chris Cozzone.

"From the plantations to the projects to the prisons.

I think that somewhat describes the journey that African Americans have taken in this country."

of which can be customized on the spot to meet any occasion. His habit is to scribble a list of key words on whatever piece of paper is nearest while the other guests are speaking. When his turn comes, he speaks off the cuff, waving the piece of paper as though conducting his own symphony, consulting it only occasionally to make sure he hasn't left anything out, which is highly unlikely.

"The title of the speech," says Eddie slowly, pausing between each phrase and dragging his s's like snakes, "is From the Plantations to the Projects to the Prisons.

"And I think that somewhat describes the journey that African-Americans have taken in this country. We went from a plantation . . . to a project . . . to a prison."

THE WAR COMES HOME

The same sense of outrage and urgency that dissidents took to the streets in the '60s to protest the war in Vietnam now drives countless seminars, conferences, lectures, marches and rallies throughout the nation and across the

World Wide Web in response to the tragic failure of the War on Crime. In 1990, the debate was significantly stirred when The Sentencing Project, a non-profit research organization in Washington, D.C., released a report called *Young Black Men and the Criminal Justice System: A Growing National Problem.* The report revealed that almost one in four African-American males in the age group 20–29 was under some form of criminal justice supervision on any given day; in prison or jail, on probation or parole.

The Project's update in October 1995, *Young Black Men and the Criminal Justice System: Five Years Later,* revealed an even more outrageous situation: the numbers were up to one out of three young black men now under some form of criminal justice supervision, with predictions that the number would increase to one in two in the next several years. Already in some cities, like Baltimore, the number was more than one in two.

The report documented the cost of criminal justice control for these nearly one million young black males at about

$6 billion a year; and went on to say that African-American women are the fastest growing prison population, rising 78 percent between 1989 and 1994. The number of black women incarcerated for drug offenses increased 828 percent from 1986 to 1991; African-Americans and Hispanics constitute almost 90 percent of offenders sentenced to state prison for drug possession.

"It would behoove us," the report admonished, "to learn from the mistakes of recent years and to begin implementing a strategy that will insure that the next generation of children will face a future filled with greater opportunity and promise."

In the months following the report, a new war has ensued. Special interest groups bent on building more prisons and prosecuting that "next generation of children"—already labeled "super-predators"—as adults to insure that the new human warehouses are well stocked, are up against community-based organizations working to stop them before the bottom of the pyramid erupts. It's a war being waged on our own soil, and if the prison expansion lobby isn't halted by the millennium, The Sentencing Project's year 2000 report may very well be called *Slave Times,* and none of us will be able to afford it.

"Very soon," Eddie says, "we will see prison colonies all over this country that feed the local economies. And very soon we're going to run out of inner-city people to put in these prisons. And I think at that point all of us will be in some serious, very serious trouble."

As staggering as The Sentencing Project's findings were, the disproportionate rate of Black male incarceration is nothing new. African-Americans have been over-represented in prisons since the beginning of the American penitentiary system in 1790. During the period of Reconstruction following the Civil War (1865–66), Southern states enacted the Black Codes as a system of social control. Blacks who were unemployed or without a permanent residence were declared vagrants; they could be arrested and fined and, if unable to pay, be bound for terms of labor. By 1878, just five years after emancipation, Blacks represented 33 percent of the American prison population and 95 percent of most prison populations in the South. Black prisoners were separated from white prisoners and subjected to more brutal and inhumane conditions than those suffered under slavery. During the 1880s, the death rate of Black prisoners was as high as 25 percent in some states—even while the disproportionate number of blacks in prison continued to grow.

"Prior to 1954," wrote noted '60s prisoner Eldridge Cleaver, "we lived in an atmosphere of Novocain. Negroes found it necessary, in order to maintain whatever sanity they could, to remain somewhat aloof and detached from 'the problem.' We accepted indignities and the mechanics of the apparatus of oppression without reacting by sitting-in or holding mass demonstrations."

In the prisons, Blacks were severely punished for protesting their condition. They had no political or legal influence, and no opportunity to complain or press charges against their white jailers. They lived with the constant threat and fear of lynching. Black prisoners were frequently taken from jails and hanged with the support and assistance of law enforcement officials.

In the late '50s, mirroring the attitudes and activities in the communities, black prisoners began to protest segregation and discrimination. Black Muslims initiated the prison protest movement, first by challenging discriminatory treatment of Muslims, and later expanding the struggle to include the constitutional rights of all prisoners.

The late '60s and early '70s saw the birth of radical urban political movements. The burgeoning Black and Latino prison populations, many of whom were involved in radical movements such as the Black Panther Party and the Young Lords, began to apply their urban philosophies to the prison struggle. Black prisoners argued that they should be considered political prisoners; whether or not their crimes were political, their condition derived from political, economic and legal inequality.

Also in the '60s, the FBI began their infamous COINTELPRO operation, a systematic attack on organizations like the Panthers and other radical groups. Eddie Ellis was one of scores of leading Panthers targeted by COINTELPRO. The illegal operation decimated the Panthers with 768 arrests and almost five million dollars in bail bonds between 1967 and 1969. Thirty-eight Panthers were killed.

AMERICA AFTER ATTICA

Born and raised in Harlem, by 1966 Eddie was 25 years old and director of community relations for the New York City branch of the Black Panthers Party. In 1969, as part of COINTELPRO, he was arrested and accused of killing a man he'd never seen before, had no connection to, and no motive for killing. There was no physical evidence linking him to the crime. He was sentenced to 25-years-to-life and wound up at Attica penitentiary in New York State.

"I was convicted," Eddie says, "on the testimony of two police officers who got on the stand and perjured themselves—said that they actually saw me shoot this individual."

To this day, Eddie maintains that evidence exists which can exonerate him, but the New York City Police Department and the FBI refuse to turn the records over on the basis that it would compromise national security. A more likely reason is that in the few incidents where records have been made available—most prominently in the case of Dhoruba Bin Wahad—they exposed illegal covert operations specifically designed to pervert the criminal justice system and use it to remove people with undesirable political views.

Dhoruba Bin Wahad, like Eddie, was a Black Panther convicted of murder and sentenced to 25-to-life. It took him three years of his prison time just to read through the 300,000 pages of documents turned over to him under the Freedom of Information Act, but eventually he discovered that the FBI had withheld evidence and "disappeared" witnesses, leaving Dhoruba in no position to mount a credible defense. In 1990, after serving 19 years, his conviction was reversed and he was released.

Several other political prisoners—some still incarcerated, some finally released after serving their entire sentences—continue to argue their cases. Eddie, though he spent every moment of his 25-year bid working toward his exoneration and release, has never been inclined to dwell on his own case. He's too busy moving forward.

"Attica was one of the most brutal, oppressive and racist prisons that I have ever been in," Eddie remembers. "There was no rehabilitation taking place, there was no education. There was nothing going on except brutality and racism. And it was this brutality and oppression which ultimately led the guys to rebel."

In September, 1971, the growing revolutionary consciousness erupted at Attica. At the first signs of revolt, the school where Eddie was working was sealed off and abandoned by the guards, who joined forces to repel the prisoners back through B-Block and C-Block to D-Block, where the standoff took place. Eddie was locked down in C-Block, with a window overlooking the D-Block yard.

"The day they took the prison back," he recalls, "was the day I witnessed state-sponsored murder. That was a definitive turning point, not just for me, but for criminal justice in America. Attica was a watershed."

In what still stands as America's deadliest prison revolt, 32 prisoners and 11 state employees were killed.

"After Attica, there was a tremendous spotlight focused on the criminal justice system and on the prison system. The 19 demands made by the brothers at Attica ultimately became the groundwork for a minimal set of standards by which prisons would be run."

THE THINK TANK

In the wake of the Attica rebellion, a number of political prisoners from throughout the state were transferred to Green Haven prison near Poughkeepsie, New York. Most of these prisoners shared a background of political activism and consciousness raising, and they were concerned with trying to make sense of the prison experience: what they were doing there, what the purpose of prison was, and how they could best prepare themselves and other prisoners to return to their communities.

By the time Eddie arrived at Green Haven, he had already been in five of New York's 13 prisons. There are now close to 70 prisons in the state.

"Every prison I was in," he says, "I seemed to know everyone, they seemed to be very familiar to me. People who came from the neighborhood. And if I didn't know them personally, some friend of mine knew them. We discovered that we knew almost everyone in the prison system. Which seemed to suggest that the pool from which prisoners come is a very small pool."

Under the "guiding intellectual spirit" of Papa Rage, a/k/a Larry White, who had been transferred to Green Haven as a leader of the 1970 Auburn prison rebellion, and energized by the creative mindset of Senior Chaplain Ed Muller, a group of prisoners—mostly lifers—formed a "think tank" to begin investigating just how small that pool was. They soon discovered that over 75 percent (the figure is closer to 80 percent now) of all the people in the New York State prison system come from just seven neighborhoods in New York City: Harlem, the Lower East Side, the South Bronx, Bedford Stuyvesant, Brownsville, East New York, and South Jamaica.

How is it, they asked, that in a state as large as New York, with 150 assembly districts, just 18 of them produce such a disproportionate number of people in the prison system?

"If you look at those seven communities," says Eddie, "you find some common characteristics. One of them, of course, is that they're populated by people who are of African-American and Latino descent. You find social conditions that by every possible measure—health care, housing, family structure, substance abuse, employment, education—rank at the very bottom in the state."

As Eddie explains it, people born and raised in inner-city areas where basic social institutions that should support and sustain their lives are dysfunctional develop a different way of seeing themselves and a skewed world view.

"We call it a 'crime-generative attitude.' And that attitude basically says that I'm living in a society where my community has been written off, relegated to the back of the bus . . . and so consequently I have to get mine; I have to do what I can do for myself; and I have to do it however I have to do it.

"By the time children get to be eight or nine years old, they've already formulated some very concrete ideas about themselves, about the world, about law enforcement, about what's acceptable and what's not acceptable. And in communities such as this, where unemployment is as high as it is, people automatically gravitate towards income generation that is marginal at best, and in the worse case scenario is criminal, so-called.

"One of the first things that happens in prison," he continues, "is you become very isolated. You begin to feel that the prison experience is a total experience in which you are totally powerless. And that feeling of powerlessness on the part of prisoners, I think, feeds a feeling of powerfulness on the part of the administrators and the guards. And that power relationship is the relationship that dominates the entire time that people are in prison."

Over the next 10–15 years, the Think Tank's five core members—Larry White, Cardell Shaird, Charles Gale (all of whom are still locked up), Lawrence Hayes and Eddie Ellis—continued to analyze the umbilical relationship between the communities and prison. They began to publish papers, using what they described as a Nontraditional Approach to Criminal and Social Justice, emphasizing that the fundamental solution to crime, violence and drugs lies in the community and that the relationship between prisoners and the communities should be enhanced.

"It's an analysis based in fact," says Eddie. "It's a fact that close to 90 percent of all the people in the New York prison system are either Black or Latino. It's a fact that over three quarters of them come from seven neighborhoods in New York City. It's a fact that approximately 90–95 percent of everybody who is in the prison system will one day

come out. And it's a fact that over 90 percent of the people who come out go back to the same communities they lived in prior to going in."

The Think Tank did a study of the New York State prison population between 1940 and 1990 and discovered that most of the prisoners in 1940 were Irish, Italian, German and Jewish, and up until the 1960s the rate of recidivism was relatively low. The reason, they found, was that the white prisoners got vocational training and were welcomed into union positions when they got out of prison. But as the minority prison population grew, the job market for released convicts shrank, and so the notion of rehabilitation was discredited.

The Nontraditional Approach says that education in prison can no longer be based in a white, middle class, Eurocentric foundation, but must be rooted in African-American/Latino value systems.

In the tolerance for reform that followed Attica, the prisoners at Green Haven began to develop programs they could suggest to state prison authorities. Among the ideas that were ultimately co-opted from prisoner proposals were prerelease centers, regular phone calls, and special trailers for weekend family visits. Under an umbrella prison organization, Political Action Committee (PAC), they developed model programs, such as The Resurrection Study Group, that teach prisoners individual and civic responsibilities and prepare them to return to their communities committed to educating young people before they too get into trouble. The programs teach Afrocentric values, history, economics, politics, and belief systems designed to build self-esteem, enhance self-confidence, and encourage constructive social attitudes.

The Green Haven think tank was instrumental in implementing the first prison baccalaureate program in the state in 1973, and, by 1982, the first masters degree program.

"I spent most of my time in prison in some degree program," says Eddie. "And the other portion of the time I spent developing programs and teaching various kinds of educational classes." Eddie went into prison a college dropout and came out holding associates degrees in liberal arts and in paralegal studies, a B.S. in business administration, and a masters degree in theology.

"If I had more time," he says, "I probably would have gotten more."

He credits one man in particular, Marist College professor Lou Howard, with helping to develop his command of language.

"He had a drill," says Eddie. "I still remember it—A parts and B parts—you've got to know them backwards and forwards, you've got to be able to diagram sentences and pick out the verb and the preposition, and understand the relationship of adjective to adverb. It was almost paramilitary the way the guy drilled it into us. But most of us really needed that kind of approach to education, and certainly to the English language."

Professor Howard remembers not so much what he taught Eddie as what he learned from him.

"I think we assessed Eddie's progress," he told me recently from his office at Manhattan Borough Community College, where, at age 71, he continues his language drills, "by the extent to which he could help me to see that a particular author had written something that was relevant to some social problem." For an entire semester, the two studied world literature together in private, one-on-one classes. Eddie had enrolled in a course that wasn't actually being offered, and Howard had shown up to teach it anyway. Eddie remembers it as the most rigorous—20 books in 12 weeks—and the most enriching of his career.

"It was incredible," he says. "For a whole semester I was immersed in the classics. It really broadened my scope, gave me a whole other dimension—experiences I would not have gotten otherwise."

Prisoners, prison administrators, and even politicians know that lack of education is largely what lands people in prison in the first place. A 1994 study by the federal Bureau of Prisons found that the more education a person receives in prison, the less likely he is to return to prison. Yet an amendment to the 1994 crime bill banned federal grants to prisoners for post-secondary education, and in June, 1995, prisons throughout the nation faced the painful reality of commemorating their last college graduation ceremonies. The amendment was sponsored and pushed by a handful of politicians who claimed, falsely, that prisoners were receiving a significant amount of federal money that should rightfully go to more deserving students on the outside. In fact, prisoners received about 6 cents of every 10 program dollars, and no qualifying student on the outside would have been denied a grant, regardless of how many prisoner applicants there were.

At Green Haven, where higher education in New York prisons had been conceived 23 years earlier, the last graduation was an especially charged occasion.

"This ceremony," said graduate and prisoner Mario Andre in his valedictorian speech, "marks the end of a 23-year relationship between Marist College and this prison. Like many other efforts at engineering a more just and equitable society in this country, it, along with college programs for prisoners all over America, has fallen victim to a chilling wind that at the moment is blowing uncompromisingly hard to the political right."

Former prisoner Latif Islam reminded the graduates and their families that there was a time when young men entering the system were immediately taken under the wings of prisoner-scholars like Eddie Ellis and shown something in themselves they hadn't seen before.

"Maybe," said Latif, in a practiced speech-maker's voice with a hint of street in it, "we need to begin to see something in those brothers who are not here tonight enjoying this. Maybe we need to begin to see something in them that they don't see in themselves. Don't let this adversity knock us down. Don't let it stop us. Make this degree your teaching degree."

During slavery, when literate slaves risked losing their fingers—the penalty for breaking the illiteracy law—to pass their knowledge on to the others, a tradition developed in African-American scholarship: a Black scholar owes the rest of the Black community a commitment to service. W.E.B. Du Bois canonized the commitment at the beginning of this century in *The Talented Tenth,* and today, the grandchildren of the talented tenth, scholars like Cornel West and Henry Louis Gates, Jr., are vociferously keeping that commitment alive and in the mainstream. In *The Future of the Race,* published earlier this year, Gates and West explore the paradox of the largest black middle class ever coexisting today with one of the largest black underclasses. In the last quarter of a century, the size of the black middle class—primarily because of expanded opportunities afforded by gains in civil rights—has quadrupled, while the size of the black underclass has grown disproportionately as well. In 1995, 45 percent of all black children were born at, or beneath, the poverty line.

"If it is the best of times for the black middle class," writes Gates and West, "it is the worst of times for an equally large segment of our community."

When Eddie Ellis entered prison in 1969, West and Gates were entering the "first-generation Ivy" Black student bodies at Harvard and Yale. While Eddie was helping to create Afrocentric programs in the New York prison system, Gates and West were helping to establish African-American Studies as an academic field at universities throughout the country. The underlying premises of *The Future of the Race* are that American society has failed to protect the basic, ostensibly inalienable rights of its people—equal access to eduction, adequate housing, affordable medical care, and, finally, equal economic opportunity, "equal access, indeed, to hope itself"—and that the leadership of the African-American community has a special responsibility to attend to these rights and to "design, promote, lobby, and agitate for bold and imaginative remedies to the conditions of inequality and injustice." The underlying premise of the Think Tank's Nontraditional Approach is that these failed social institutions (education, housing, medical care, economic opportunity)—and hope itself—are directly responsible for generating crime and imprisonment, and that prisons must be converted from "warehouses for the living dead" into universities that teach self-identity, sense of community, commitment to social change and empowerment. And that it is the special responsibility of those who have been imprisoned to attend to these rights and agitate for reform.

NEIGHBORHOOD DEFENDER

Eddie Ellis sits in his office at the Neighborhood Defender Service of Harlem on 125th Street. Below, beyond the floor-to-ceiling window of the second floor office, the pride and tragedy of this legendary boulevard bustles by as Eddie regales me with another breathless marathon sentence.

"So what I'm saying is that in these communities, there are these crime-generative factors that produce a certain kind of an attitude, and if you live in a community you acquire that attitude, and you begin to act it out. Now, if that's true—and we work on the assumption that it's true—then the prescription for law enforcement that deals specifically with criminal behavior, that is, the identification, apprehension, conviction, sentencing and incarceration of so-called criminals, that approach is doomed to fail, because the people who are involved in this criminal behavior because of larger, systemic, socioeconomic reasons."

Looking down at the stream of activity in the street, I think about how extraordinary it must be for Eddie to be in this office every day—to be on this block—to be in this village of Harlem.

"All the time I was in prison," he had told me, "the 23 years I was in prison, I just thought about and worked towards one thing, and that was coming out."

Twenty-six years later he's the Coordinator of Community Education for the Neighborhood Defender Service of Harlem, an agency set up in 1990 by the Vera Institute for Justice to provide free, high-quality legal defense to residents of Harlem and East Harlem who are accused of crimes but cannot afford to hire private lawyers.

One of the many distinctions between NDS and other legal defenders is the degree to which it maintains a close connection with the community. Unlike most public defenders, they don't get appointed to cases, which means that if nobody calls them for help, they go out of business. Part of Eddie's job is making sure the community knows the service is available. Most people who get into trouble with the police don't know that they can call a lawyer. Most people, even if they know what their rights are, do not know how to exercise them in a moment of crisis. Eddie works to educate the community about how to respond if they or somebody they care about is arrested; how to avoid confrontation with police; how to avoid making the legal trouble worse than it is.

When designing NDS, Vera Institute Director Christopher Stone drew primarily on his experience as a Yale Law School student in the early 1980s—not his time at the school, but the time he spent working in prison. In 1980, as a first year law student, he helped develop a program eventually known as PACT,

or Project for a Calculated Transition, that brought Yale law students to Green Haven prison for discussion groups. In the classes, students kept prisoners—mostly lifers—up to date on current law, and prisoners lectured students about prison and crime in the streets.

From these early discussion groups at Green Haven, Stone gained valuable insights that helped him meet his goal of designing a truly helpful, client-oriented public defender.

Though he wasn't working closely with Eddie, Stone met him on several occasions over the two-and-a-half years he visited Green Haven. He remembers being particularly impressed with how smart and organized Eddie was at editing and publishing the Green Haven newspaper; and at how little he focused on his own case.

"A lot of the more sophisticated lifers," says Stone, "had figured out that it wasn't the first thing they should talk about. But it was rare that I'd meet someone who over time wouldn't find a way to bring up his case and ask for help. Eddie was always focused on the people, on organizing."

About a year after NDS was formed, a staff member came into Stone's office to ask him if he would add his signature to a petition to urge the release—or work-release—of a prisoner by the name of Eddie Ellis. Although Stone hadn't seen Eddie in almost ten years, he recognized the picture of him immediately.

"Does he have a job?" he asked, "because a job is probably more important than an extra signature on this petition." When he discovered that there was in fact no job waiting for Eddie, Stone created one for him.

"Most guys," he says, "when they get out, if they have a job at all, they're lucky to have a manual labor job. And those things are hard—tough hours, occasional work, low pay. It's really hard."

Having not only a job, but a job with an organization that understood where he was coming from, what his own needs were, and that meshed with his personal gifts and interests, has probably made all the difference in the world for Eddie.

As much as Stone was doing Eddie a favor, it felt more like he was repaying a debt.

"The men at Green Haven," Stone says, "really taught me a huge amount, and it influenced the work I've done in my life a lot. Being able to create that

job for Eddie felt like we were giving him something he deserved. He did a lot for other people along the way, long before he ever got out of prison."

Anyone who's ever had any kind of involvement with the prison system knows that there is prison time and there is freeworld time, and the two are entirely different. In prison, no matter how much you try to maintain your connections to the outside world, it's ultimately impossible to hold onto the big picture. Even Eddie, who was known for how able he was to keep up with things while he was locked up, was stunned when he got out.

"He just couldn't believe it," says Stone. "He couldn't believe what happened to Harlem. He couldn't believe the way the kids were acting, he couldn't believe the music, he couldn't believe life in the streets."

One of the things that carried Eddie through 23 years in prison was a tireless fascination with the world—an ability to keep learning and to keep moving forward. He came out of prison convinced that community education should be based in an Afrocentric curriculum, and within a few months, he was able to incorporate it into a much broader political view of the world and how rich and diverse it is.

"It's a rare gift," says Stone, "and it's why he's so good at what he does. And it's why the connection between what he does for a job—education and outreach work for NDS—and what he does as an avocation with his political work in the community, is such a nice mix. He manages to use the connections in his life—his time in, his time out, his politics, his profession, his skills—in a powerful way to advance the causes he's interested in."

Eddie's avocation in his work as cofounder and president of the Community Justice Center a few blocks east of NDS on 125th Street. One of the things the Think Tank resolved was that they needed to develop an organization in the street that could carry out the work—the research, publishing papers, policy advocacy and development—as well as continue to create innovative programs for prisoners and analyze existing programs to determine their efficiency and cost-effectiveness. Shortly after Eddie's release, he helped set up this outside arm. The uniqueness of CJC is that is is operated entirely by prisoners and ex-prisoners, and the Board of Directors, with one or two exceptions, is comprised of people in prison.

Just as the Nontraditional Approach provides an analysis of the prison population and determines what kinds of programs that specific population needs, the Community Justice Center strives to determine and define what changes people in inner-city communities want to see in the criminal justice system.

"One of the big problems," Eddie maintains, "is that someone else always gets to speak for us. The academicians speak for us, the professional penologists speak for us, the law enforcement people speak for us, the politicians speak for us, the media speak for us. We haven't really heard from the people in our communities." CJC holds forums and conferences all over the state in predominantly black and Latino and poor communities to get a sense of what the leadership, the community-based organizations, the clergy and the elected officials want to see the criminal justice system do, so that they'll be able to make specific recommendations to the Legislature and the governor.

Thanks largely to Eddie's unusual organizational capacity, the CJC has a dozen major programs in action or development, including Operation Cease Fire, their major youth program; a Food Services Program which works with disabled veterans; a Post-Release Program; a Drug Elimination Program, which works with the Housing and Urban Development Corporation to rid drugs from public housing developments; a Work Study Program which unites City University students with recently-released prisoners; a rally to commemorate the 25th anniversary of the insurrection at Attica; an educational and vocational skills program for adolescents on Rikers Island; a voter education and registration campaign called Operation Big Prison Vote, which will soon be in every county jail in the state; and their most ambitious undertaking, the Uptown Development Project, a multi-million dollar plan initiated and run by prisoners to rebuild four square blocks of land in northern Harlem into a model community with commercial businesses, public housing for special-needs populations and state-of-the-art educational & entertainment complex.

Because of their expertise and education, the CJC is fast becoming one of the DOC's most valuable resources. Soon they will work exclusively on a consulting basis, hired by state offices such as HUD, Corrections, Parole and Probation, to solve problems that up to now have been unsolvable, largely because, according to Eddie, "the perspective has not been as good as it could be."

"Eddie is a real force for progress," says Stone. "He never stops working, moving the ball forward. And as a result, he brings people who are working with him forward. It's very rare. Not just for people who've been inside, it's very rare among humanity."

"There's a group of men who formerly were incarcerated in many prisons throughout the state of New York," Eddie says, "who made a commitment while we were in prison that once we got out of prison, we would try to do something to assist our brothers and sisters who were still in prison to come out; but even more importantly, begin to try to make some fundamental changes in the society out here so that many of our younger brothers and sisters will not ultimately have to go in."

THE REAL WAR ON CRIME

On a clear April morning, I'm driving toward Rikers Island to teach when Eddie's unmistakable tenor torrent comes sailing into my car over the WBAI airwaves.

There's something immensely appropriate about listening to WBAI New York on your way to jail. No other station devotes so much air time to prison issues, prison voices, and to the direct relationship between the street and the yard. No other station gets so many calls from concerned mothers needing advice on how to keep their sons from being arrested or killed.

Brother Shine, the station's resident recovering prisoner and producer of most of the prison shows, is broadcasting a speech Eddie delivered a few days earlier at Medgar Evers College in Brooklyn.

"Over the last few months," Eddie says, "I have been rapidly coming to the conclusion that we seem to be stuck in what Martin Luther King used to call the 'paralysis of analysis.' That is to say, we become paralyzed by analyzing and re-analyzing and discussing and re-discussing these issues over and over again. And while I agree that there is a need to share information and fellowship and to be able to feed off one another's posi-tive energy, I think at some point we have to make some distinctions, we have to draw some lines, we have to come to terms with the fact that while we're analyzing this problem, it's getting worse and worse.

"What we have here, essentially," he continues, "is a serious assault and attack on poor people all over America, and people of color in particular: Latinos and people of African descent. And depending on where you line up in the spectrum, sometimes you can see this war and sometimes you can't. And the serious problem for most of us is that we don't even know that we're in a war. And because we don't know that we're in a war, we're losing the battle very rapidly."

Twenty-three years down, this man never lost the ability to see himself—to see us all—in a larger historical perspective.

"Some people take the position," he says, "and I think I stand with them, that from the point that Europe invaded Africa we've been at war. Sometimes it's a hot war, sometimes it's a cold war, sometimes it's more overt than others, but at least since then we've been at war. Our organization has an analysis, and we say that we've simply moved from the pyramids to the plantation to the projects to the prisons. That has been the sojourn of African people: from the pyramids to the plantation to the projects to the prisons."

In 23 years, he never lost the ability to expand his world view.

"We look at what's going on in New York City. The mayor has declared war on the so-called 'quality of life' type crime. I'm not really sure what that means or what that is, but I know that [the] ultimate effect of it is that young Black and Latino men and women are now being arrested for things that they normally would not have been arrested for.

"We know for a fact that young truants—juveniles—are being picked up by the police, in some cases fingerprinted and photographed. We heard this morning about the kinds of abuses police brutality brings. We know that the police department has been picking up young men, school age, and putting them in line-ups without authorization from their parents.

"There's a war going on. This is not accidental, this is not coincidental, this doesn't just happen in a vacuum."

Crabs in a Barrel

It's about as difficult for a young white female to get to Rikers Island as it is easy for a young black male. It takes three passes and one guard trailer just to get to the Control Building.

I exit the Control Building. Two turnstiles, one DOC bus, a metal detector and five iron gates later—I arrive in the classroom in the catacombs of one of Rikers 10 jails.

On any given day, there are about 20,000 people at Rikers. Thirteen are in my writing class. I know how slim their chances will be. When they are released, just getting home from Queens Plaza, where the DOC bus will leave them at 4:30 in the morning—after 10 hours in a small, overcrowded, stinking bullpen—will be an unlikely victory. Not buying a quart of beer from Brothers & Son Deli will be the first thing not likely to happen. Not picking up as many cracks as $4.00 can buy from the dealer who greets the bus every morning is also a low odd. The flow between Rikers and the street is constant and seamless.

Clarence, a student this term, has been one of two things for most of his life: high in the street or sobering in jail. The sober mester wears on and the drugs in Clarence's system wear off, he has become more frustrated with his situation, with the disunity in his community, with his own shame at being unconscious all these years, and with the unconsciousness of the men around him.

"Crabs in a barrel," he says now, "pulling each other down." He tells us that this awakening occurs every time he's in jail, but then when he leaves, his Master (drugs) takes over again. This time feels different: he finally understands the futility of complaining; he finally feels compelled to take responsibility for his own life. Unfortunately, he also feels compelled to preach it to the others, who are growing increasingly tired of it. Listening to him sermonize to the young, headstrong guys in the class is heartbreaking—mostly because they don't want to hear him.

This morning, Clarence's recitation of his epic *Master Plan*, about how the Black community has been divided to be at war with itself, sends some of the younger guys off on a violence tangent, wanting to shoot leaders and blow up buildings.

All Kevin knows is that he has no power and no voice, and

"If you feel so helpless because your leaders were killed," Clarence yells despairingly, "you need to learn what they knew so you can continue the struggle!"

periods are filled with sudden clarity and hope, but mostly with remorse over a wasted and offensive life. He is weary, but still has the trickster's gleam in his eye. I imagine he'd frighten me in the street, and I'm not easily frightened.

As it turns out, Clarence is a wandering bard. Scores of poems, all in his head. Long, rhyming histories and morality tales. Sometimes I think he must have written the verse long ago, before the drugs took over, and that the lyrics resurface during his straight times. Or I imagine he creates the poems constantly, whether he's straight or high, but only cares enough to recite them when he is sobering in jail.

At the other end of the spectrum is Kevin, one of the younger students, a bright-eyed bundle of conflict crying out in subtle ways to be saved while demanding overtly to be killed. He's the sort of kid I imagined when I read Cornel West's description in *Race Matters* of "the nihilism that increasingly pervades black communities . . . a numbing detachment from others and a self-destructive disposition toward the world." Only there's something trying to shine through in Kevin. His eyes tell me that, his eyes and the fact that he shows up every day.

Kevin has a lot to say, but it's nearly impossible for him to speak. The language just isn't there for him. He makes all the motions—he even raises his hand politely when he wants to offer something—but what comes out is a muffled, halting, nearly aborted effort. Usually, he manages to get a key word out so that we can all finish his thoughts for him. Clarence, being a trickster, can sometimes get Kevin to elucidate—and he can always get him to smile—by pretending to be deaf in one ear.

An ongoing debate about victimhood and empowerment has dominated our class all semester. The men have a deeply ingrained belief in conspiracy theories and none has enough education to argue his way out of feeling oppressed and enraged. As the se-

that talking and marching don't seem to get anyone anywhere.

"Guns," he says. "Bombs. Blow up all—just—everything. Total—"

I wish Eddie Ellis were here. Kevin needs to meet a man who understands his rage, who has taken arms for it, served legendary time for it, and is now more powerfully able to avenge it—with his mind.

After class, moving past streams of brown and black men in green uniforms strutting in haphazard single-file from mess hall to yard, I catch up with Kevin.

"Listen," I say. "I've been meeting a lot of these men lately." He's listening. "Guys who were leaders in the Black Panther Party and who were targeted by the government and locked up and—"

"Those were, they—" he waves a hand to indicate total destruction. "*Set up.*"

"Totally shafted," I agree. "But I gotta tell you, these guys are doing some powerful things now. These are the men who are going to be making the changes you want to see. A lot of these men are coming out now after doing 20, 25 years. They're coming out committed to fighting. And they're the ones who can do it. Because they know *everything*. They just spent half their lives in prison, no one knows as much as they do—"

Kevin nods, respectful of that kind of time in.

"Yeah," he nods, "they know."

"Not only do they know the system," I say. "While they were locked up, they got educated. They got college degrees. Masters degrees. They got as many degrees as they could. There's nothing these guys don't know. They stand a better chance of making changes than anyone."

Kevin nods some more and looks sideways at me.

"You mean," he says, "you actually met some of these brothers?"—*PW*

Hearing Eddie's voice on the airwaves makes me consider just how profound and far-reaching his accomplishments have been.

In addition to his normal workload, his calendar includes countless speaking engagements at high schools, colleges, churches and community centers, talk show appearances, lectures to parole boards, presentation of proposals to the Department of Corrections, and lobbying the State Legislature in Albany. He has become a primary source for local papers, radio and television. There simply isn't anything happening in the criminal justice system—and particularly in the New York prison system—that Eddie isn't aware of or involved in.

He serves as a member of the National Criminal Justice Commission, a diverse, nonpartisan group of about 40 citizens, scholars, criminal justice experts and community leaders from across the nation who originally came together two years ago to assess the state of crime policy in America. The result of their efforts, a report called *The Real War on Crime*, published earlier this year, provides the most definitive analysis of crime and punishment in the United States since the 1968 Kerner Commission report on civil disorder. It offers solutions for reducing violence and provides a set of recommendations that will fundamentally reform the criminal justice system and begin to cure its deep afflictions.

The Real War on Crime concludes that the criminal justice system is in crisis. Although the prison population has tripled and law enforcement expenditures have quadrupled since 1980, citizens in record numbers report that they feel unsafe in their homes and on the streets while crime rates have remained virtually unchanged. In order to fund jails and prisons, state and local governments have been forced to divert money from education, health care, job programs and community development. Moreover, our practices and policies have helped set the nation back on the same "separate and unequal" racial divide the Kerner Commission observed more than a quarter of a century ago. The rate of incarceration for African-Americans is six times the rate for whites, "a fact that has much to do with

discrimination," the report states, "as it does with rates of crime."

The very first, and most critical, recommendation the Commission makes is that "all states—absent some demonstrated urgent need—should impose a three-year moratorium on new prison construction."

The most effective campaign for this recommendation, at least in New York State, has been launched by the Community Justice Center. Their latest program, the Prison Moratorium Project, has united community-based organizations throughout the state to lobby for a halt to prison construction over the next five years, and to establish an "Alternative Budget" to re-allocate the $900 million dollars Governor Pataki currently proposes for building three new maximum-security prisons and creating an additional 4,300 cells.

Based on proposals for criminal justice change and changes in the juvenile justice law (trying 13-year-olds as adults and moving 16-year-olds into enhanced penalties), Pataki anticipates needing 10,000 new cells between now and the year 2000 to accommodate the new prisoners coming in.

"And we don't have to ask what those people are going to look like," Eddie tells the students at Medgar Evers. "And we don't have to ask where they're coming from. What we need to do is we need to begin to stop the process.

"We're asking everyone in this audience to join us in calling for a moratorium on prison construction for the next five years.

"We believe that the linchpin of social policy in America is built upon the construction and the maintenance and the development of this prison-industrial complex. And if we do not bring it to a halt—or in the worst-case scenario slow it down—we've got a serious problem on our hands. This is what we intend to do."

The applause ringing through my car speakers begins to subside, but Eddie is not finished.

"Frederick Douglas," he begins again softly, "used to say that power concedes nothing without demand. And Marcus Garvey said that world history is never kind to weak people. And part of the reason that we're in this quandary, part of the reason that we're in this problem,

part of the reason that we're even here today at Medgar Evers talking about this issue, has to do with our weakness, has to do with our disunity, has to do with the fact that although we're all warriors in a battle, we don't have a strategic plan.

"We say that if we can do this, we can begin to formulate the beginnings of another movement. A movement that may have as profound and deep ramifications as the human rights movement of the '60s and the anti-war movement in the '70s.

"We're in the beginnings right now, we think, of the development of a movement that will have major implications—socially, politically, economically, educationally, recreationally, religiously. A movement that must, at this time, begin its forward assault on those forces that are assaulting us.

"We say that we will begin this movement—and we're in the process of beginning this movement—from this day forward."

Twenty-five years ago, Eddie Ellis survived the watershed Attica revolt. In its aftermath, he and a handful of other prisoners initiated a wave of reforms in the prison system, critical reforms that sought to enable prisoners to make the positive changes in themselves that ultimately would impact on the communities they came from. Eddie and his peers identified the vital relationship between prisoners, their neighborhoods and the conditions that create criminal behavior.

In just the past few years, short-sighted politicians have wiped out post-Attica prison reforms and assured the perpetuation of the root causes of crime—lack of education, few job opportunities and poverty—and thus ensured the continued boom in the prison-industrial complex.

Eddie now stands at the center of another maelstrom. The war has spilled out onto the streets. Men like Eddie Ellis, who lived through Attica and decades of life in some of America's worst prisons, know how to deal with this kind of ignorance.

We need to listen to Eddie Ellis, I think yet again as the applause subsides. He knows. He's been there.

And now he's out of the cage.

Ethical Considerations in Probation Practice

by Marylouise E. Jones, Department of Psychology, Research Unit and Arthur J. Lurigio, Department of Criminal Justice, Research Unit, Loyola University Chicago (IL)

Editor's Note: Portions of this paper were presented at APPA's 21st Annual Training Institute, July 1996, Chicago, Illinois.

Probation officers frequently face decisions that place the needs of offenders in direct conflict with the welfare of society. In making such decisions, they can benefit from a firm foundation in ethics. Recent books have highlighted the importance of ethics for criminal justice professionals (Braswell, McCarthy, & McCarthy, 1991; Pollock-Byrne, 1994; Souryal, 1992). For example, Pollock-Byrne (1994) notes that within the criminal justice system, there is a variety of moral dilemmas, including "questions of responsibility and excuse, the limits of the state's right to control the individual, the ethical use of force, and the appropriate use of discretion" (p. 200). Ethical issues in probation practice, however, have been largely ignored (Brown, 1989).

Criminal justice is a young discipline, far more concerned with crime control than with philosophy. Most probation practitioners have not been exposed adequately to the philosophy of justice or to any serious or formal study of ethics. Courses in ethics and justice usually are not required for criminal justice degrees—the most common degree among probation officers—or included in probation officers' training curricula. Nonetheless, ethical issues in community corrections are significant and complex. These issues are common to other professions. But criminal justice agents, including probation officers, can be distinguished from other professionals in terms of the broad ethical nature and ramifications of their decisions.

Criminal justice professionals often render decisions on behalf of society as a whole. These judgments entail a far greater responsibility than the decisions of many other professionals and are not just inci-

dentally, but are primarily, moral decisions (Sherman, 1992). For example, when a police officer decides to arrest a person or when a judge decides to release a person on bail, the decision has significant ethical and moral implications.

Upholding the social order is a fundamental obligation of the criminal justice system (Souryal, 1992). Social order focuses on the rights and welfare of individuals and of society at large. Laws and sanctions are designed to ensure that everyone has the freedom to pursue their interests and activities without undue fear or threat of victimization. Difficulties arise when the needs of individuals conflict with those of the broader community. For example, locking up someone who is a neighborhood nuisance may alleviate the misery of a few persons while infringing on an individual's freedoms and fundamental rights. Balancing individual rights with society's well-being begs the question of how much social control (i.e., laws and punishments) is needed to maintain an orderly society. Striking such a balance forces criminal justice practitioners to reconcile the welfare of their clients with the welfare of society.

Ethics and Probation Officer Discretion

Community corrections practitioners experience ethical challenges because of the formidable task of weighing an offender's welfare against the welfare of society. The basic rationale of probation is that society is willing to take a chance on offenders who are able to conform to its rules. Probationers are allowed to remain in the community as long as they adhere to the court-ordered conditions of release. If they violate the conditions of release,

which constitutes their contract with society, probation may be revoked and they may be subsequently incarcerated.

When probation began, and throughout most of its early history, its purposes were primarily altruistic, as probation caseloads comprised mostly lower-risk property and first-time offenders. There were fewer offenders with developmental disabilities, psychological disturbances or drug addictions, and fewer offenders convicted of violent crimes and other felonies. With changes in the size and seriousness of probation caseloads, balancing offenders' welfare with the safety and protection of the community has now become the ethical imperative of probation.

Ethical decisions in probation are made within less rigidly defined contexts than are found in other criminal justice domains. Probation officers exercise considerable discretion in handling their caseloads. They typically have a lot of flexibility with regard to scheduling their time and structuring their activities. Probation officer discretion is an important aspect of supervision. Many probation officers do not automatically submit violation petitions after they discover offenders' infractions. In fact, some may give offenders second and third chances before initiating the revocation process. Probation officer discretion also plays a critical role in determining the nature of these officers' reports to judges (Souryal, 1992). Probation officers can sway judicial decisions by portraying probationers in different lights. Probation officers' judgments are especially influential in presentence investigations. Because probation officers' recommendations in presentence investigations often are adopted by judges (Abadinsky, 1996), ethical decisions affecting the way they present information are significant and can have serious consequences for offenders.

From *Perspectives*, Summer 1997, pp. 26-32. © 1997 by The Council of State Governments. Reprinted by permission of the American Probation and Parole Association.

Offenders' performance on probation is affected by officers' ability to broker suitable employment or treatment services. Outcomes also are affected by officers' handling of probation infractions and their interest in clients' rehabilitation and reintegration. However, probation officers' success with clients may be hampered for

that the morality of an action is judged in terms of its consequences. A moral action produces good results, that is, it increases pleasure and decreases pain; an immoral action produces bad or harmful results, that is, it decreases pleasure and increases pain. Simply put, cheating, stealing and murder are all wrong because of their bad

the pleasure of one. The greatest good for the greatest number creates the context for community. The proportionality of pain and pleasure must be judged in this context.

Utilitarianism calculus is illustrated by the following example. A probationer misses a report date in order to take care of his children. Adhering to a zero tolerance policy for nonreporting, his probation officer files a petition to have him violated. The probationer then is convicted of a violation and is sentenced to jail. Consequently, the probationer cannot provide for his family while he is incarcerated and his relationship with his officer is strained. Should the probation officer have filed a petition to violate him? Following the principles of utilitarianism, the officer should have weighed the possible pain of the probationer against the possible pain inflicted on the community if the probationer does not follow rules. If the probationer presented little threat to society, a utilitarian would maintain that the probation officer was wrong to violate him.

Moral principals have lost their distinctiveness. For modern man, absolute right and absolute wrong are a matter of what the majority is doing. Right and wrong are relative to likes and dislikes and the customs of a particular community. We have unconsciously applied Einstein's theory of relativity, which properly described the physical universe, to the moral and ethical realm."

—Martin Luther King Jr.

a number of reasons over which they have little control. High caseloads, long work hours, lack of training and the absence of clear goals can all interfere with the quality of services (Whitehead, 1996). Furthermore, probation officers cannot always depend on the public support or resources that they need to do their jobs effectively (Wehmhoefer, 1993). The constant interplay of intra- and extra-agency factors that influence officers' effectiveness and the fact that probation officers are often the final arbiters for many caseload decisions require their judgments and activities to be grounded firmly in basic ethical principles.

Foundation of Ethics

Normative ethics is the study of right and wrong. In particular, normative ethics tries to discover the fundamental aspects of all ethical judgments. For example, lying, cheating, stealing, raping and killing generally are considered wrong. If so, what is the common characteristic of all these actions? One of the most preeminent figures in the history of Western philosophy, Socrates, searched for the universal principle that is common to all just or virtuous actions.

Utilitarianism

An ethical theory that attempts to describe universal moral principles is utilitarianism, developed by Jeremy Benthem and John Stuart Mill. Utilitarianism posits

or harmful consequences. According to Benthem, "An action . . . conforms to the principle of utility . . . when the tendency it has to augment the happiness of the community is greater that any it has to diminish it" (Dewey & Hurlbutt, 1977, p. 227). Charity and benevolence are moral actions because they produce beneficial consequences. Thus, Benthem contended that all human actions are motivated by the desire to increase pleasure or decrease pain. He argued that a person's motivation does not determine the rightness or wrongness of given action. Even if the motivation for an action is to increase pleasure (which is good), the result of that action may inflict pain on a large number of people. Such an action must be regarded as bad because of its outcomes, not because of the original intentions of the actor.

A central question when weighing the correctness or goodness of actions in utilitarianism is, "Whose happiness or pleasure is paramount?" According to utilitarianism, all parties affected by an action should be considered. Therefore, both the happiness of the individual and that of the community should be calculated in determining the goodness of a particular action. The morally correct action is the one that produces the greatest good for the greatest number of people. Presumably, the pleasure of one individual does not outweigh the pleasure of an entire community. For example, stealing makes a thief feel good. But the thief's victims may suffer sadness, anger, fear and physical and emotional distress as a result of the thief's actions. In this instance, the pain of many outweighs

Deontological Ethics

Immanuel Kant, a proponent of deontological ethics, believed that by focusing solely on consequences, utilitarianism misses something even more basic to morality, namely, goodwill or the intention to do what is right. For Kant, the key to morality is human intention, not consequences. An act is right if it is motivated by the goodwill or intentions of an actor regardless of whether the action achieves positive consequences. Right actions arise from virtues such as honesty, loyalty and respect for the law (Dewey & Hurlbutt, 1977). Wrong actions arise out of selfish or malicious motives.

Consider the following scenario involving two probation officers working in the same department: One probation officer files a violation of probation petition against a probationer who missed last month's payment of restitution. He does so to teach the probationer the importance of obeying the rules of the court and to deter future rule breaking. The other violates a probationer who missed his last payment of restitution because the probationer belongs to a racial group that the probation officer is prejudiced against.

Kant would have argued that there is a fundamental moral difference between the first and the second probation officers' actions, despite the fact that the consequences of the two cases are identical. In the utilitarian view, because the ends of both officers' actions are the same, they have the same moral value. Nonetheless, from Kant's perspective, there is still a moral difference. The first probation officer acted morally in order to instruct the probationer and to help him to avoid future difficulties. In contrast, the second probation officer was motivated by prejudice. For Kant, although the second probation officer engaged in the same action as his colleague, he filed the petition for the wrong reason so his action has no moral worth. In short, he did the right thing for the wrong reason.

Kant's principle of morality contains a categorical imperative: People have the unconditional duty to behave morally. Kant's belief is that people should do only what they would permit others to do. In our example, the categorical imperative is that a probation officer who chooses a particular response to deal with a probationer's rule breaking must believe that the response would be the same one chosen by other probation officers and that it would apply to all probationers in the same situation.

Another formulation of Kant's categorical imperative focuses on the belief that human beings have intrinsic value and that they ought to be treated with respect. Within this formulation, probationers should never be regarded as objects, that is, used to prove that one is "tough on crime" or to demonstrate the punitiveness of a particular sanction. Because probation officers constantly must weigh the needs of individual offenders against those of society, they may have difficulty satisfying the moral imperative.

Problems with both utilitarianism and deontological ethics complicate moral decisions. Utilitarianism has trouble dealing with situations involving the maximum pleasure for the majority at the expense of the minority. For example, a large group enslaves a small group so that the large group can gain certain comforts and benefits from the servitude of a few. Utilitarianism holds that the suffering of a few is outweighed by the pleasure of the many. Nonetheless, regardless of the pleasurable consequences for some, slavery and oppression are patently wrong, just as hurting or exploiting others is inherently unjust.

Similarly, Kant's moral theory has no way to deal with conflicting motives. For example, a probation officer is required to keep probationers' records confidential. But when a probationer with a prior conviction for a sexual offense applies for a job as a janitor in a school, the probation officer may fear for the safety of students and school staff. Does the probation officer reveal confidential information to the potential employer or protect the confidentiality of the probationer? Kantian theory offers no solution to this predicament. The utilitarian would weigh the harm done by revealing the information against the potential harm that may arise from not doing so. Much more harm could result from failing to warn an employer of possible dangers.

Common Ethical Dilemmas of Probation Officers

In the moral dilemmas facing probation officers, it is not always clear what effects an officer's actions may have for offenders or society. The probation officer who does not violate probationers for failing drug tests may be either facilitating their success or enabling their addictive behaviors. Probation officers may promise services to clients without any guarantee that these services will ever be offered. Promising probationers possible employment may be helpful in motivating them to fulfill probation requirements but may demoralize them when jobs never become available.

Probation officers also may be forced to weigh the needs of particular clients against those of other probationers. Because of severely limited treatment resources, such as for substance abuse, the probation officer who enrolls a probationer in a program may prevent another person—perhaps one more likely to succeed in the program—from getting treatment (Duffee & Carlson, 1996; Silverman, 1993). Similarly, a probation officer may interact with agencies that might be reluctant to accept other clients from the officer's caseload if particular clients fail in their programs.

Besides balancing societal and offender needs, probation officers also belong to the wider criminal justice system, which imposes expectations that affect ethical decision making (Silverman, 1993). These demands may come in the forms of sentencing requirements, administrative exigencies or peer pressures. Whistle blowing against the probation administration may be another area of ethical concern for officers if they perceive that their agencies' practices are interfering with the rights and well-being of their clients (Rosecrance, 1988). Administrators may be more willing to cover up inadequacies rather than to allow the undesirable practices of their departments to come to light. Officers must weigh loyalty to their profession and colleagues against the harm that may ensue if they permit unethical practices to continue. As Pollock-Byrne (1994) noted, "All criminal justice professionals are more likely to operate in an ethical manner when they believe in the validity and justness of the system that employs them."

As discussed earlier in the context of Kant's theory, probation officers can be confronted with ethical dilemmas relating to confidentiality. For example, an offender enters into a romantic relationship with a person who is not aware of his previous convictions for domestic violence. Is it the duty of the officer to keep this information confidential or to inform the offender's partner out of concern for her safety? Confidentiality issues become even more difficult with juvenile probationers (Goldsmith, 1988).

Confidentiality issues also arise when probation officers come in contact with offenders' families. With more severe programs, for example, home confinement and intensive probation supervision, offenders' punishments spill onto the lives of others. Von Hirsch (1990) suggested that concern for the rights of others has been overlooked in community corrections. For example, he pointed out that home visits may shame or demean offenders because of the presence of unconvicted third-party witnesses whose sense of privacy is diminished. Confidentiality issues can arise yet again when probation officers are concerned with the well-being of crime victims (Whitehead, 1996). Issues concerning the confidentiality of an offender's whereabouts vs. informing a victim who might be at risk again from that offender are often under probation officer discretion.

> ## "Integrity without knowledge is weak and useless, and knowledge without integrity is dangerous and dreadful."
>
> —Samuel Johnson

Other circumstances may place professional ethics in conflict with personal ethics. For example, probation officers may not agree with their clients' choices (e.g., the decision to have an abortion) or they may condone—either explicitly or implicitly—illegal behaviors (e.g., recreational drug use) (Pollock-Byrne, 1994).

Most probation sentences require offenders to report to a probation site, but there may be instances when doing so is not in probationers' best interests (Close & Meier, 1995). Such cases include probationers who may be too ill or physically handicapped to travel. In addition, probationers in gangs may be placed at risk if they have to travel through rivals' neighborhoods to report to their officers.

Finally, ethical issues may arise out of the unequal relationship between probation officers and their clients. Probation officers may misuse their power (Pollock-Byrne, 1994). Concerns with the misuse of force come into play even more so when probation officers carry weapons and work in stricter surveillance programs. According to Sherman (1992), "Force is the essence of criminal justice. . . . The decisions of whether to use force, how much to use and under what conditions are confronted by police officers, juries, judges, prison officials and probation and parole officers" (p. 17).

Typology of Probation Officers

What are probation officers supposed to do when faced with the kinds of dilemmas described here? Whom should they be serving? How can they maximize benefits for offenders and minimize harm to society? A well-known typology of probation officers helps to illuminate the ethical postures that officers may assume (e.g., Klockars, 1972; Souryal, 1992). Each of these probation officer types acts out of a particular ethical principle or a set of principles. Not every officer fits into one type. Rather, most officers represent a combination of types, and those within a type may not always behave the same way. In addition, no type is considered completely ethical or unethical. Such determinations require knowledge of the context in which actions take place (Souryal, 1992).

Punitive Officers

The first type of officer is the punitive or law enforcement practitioner who always places society's interests above clients' interests. "This type underscores a dogmatic, utilitarianism view that seeks to maximize goodness through serving the largest number of beneficiaries—community members" (Souryal, 1992, p. 366). Controlling offenders and enforcing the conditions of probation are the main goals of these officers. They file petitions to violate probationers no matter what the circumstances in order to uphold all the rules and regulations of probation.

The relationship between probation officers and offenders is distant and built on only the conditions of the sentence. Their interactions are frequent, formal and brief. Punitive officers are detached from offenders and depersonalize them. They have little concern for probationers or their families. Whether probationers complete their sentences successfully is of minor importance to punitive or law enforcement practitioners. As Souryal (1992) notes, "In this model, recognition of the true purpose of supervision, of the obligation to assist a fellow human being in distress, or of fidelity to the ethics of treatment is all but ignored" (p. 366).

The punitive officer is concerned with preserving community safety by controlling probationers. Probation is viewed as a privilege, not as a right. Probationers are perceived as criminals who should be closely supervised, a danger from whom society must be protected. The punitive officer frequently reminds offenders that probation will be revoked, without exception, if conditions are violated. This style of supervision emphasizes firmness, legal authority and rule abidance. Interaction between the rule enforcer and probationers tends to be formal, official and largely a manifestation of "one upmanship" on the part of the officer. Punitive officers uphold the law for its own sake, irrespective of whether the best interests of probationers have been satisfied.

Punitive officers attempt to protect society by monitoring offenders and making sure that they adhere to the conditions of release. By ignoring probationers' needs, however, such officers may bring more harm to the community. Although offenders may comply with the conditions of probation, they may not be able to reintegrate successfully into society because they lack the services or skills to do so. Society may be harmed by these probationers in the future.

Welfare Officers

The welfare/therapeutic practitioner or social worker is the second type. Probation officers in this category focus on offender treatment and rehabilitation. Even if clients violate the conditions of probation, their welfare outweighs the possible harm to the larger community. Probation officers concentrate their energies on "advocating, brokering, educating, enabling, and mediating" for their clients (Souryal, 1992, pp. 366–367). Offenders' needs are crucial. Officers of this type attempt to broker services such as employment, housing and psychological counseling for their clients. They treat clients with care and respect.

Welfare/therapeutic officers attempt to rehabilitate offenders and reintegrate them into the community, and they view the conditions of probation as ways to facilitate offenders' progress. Probation is a time for problem solving. Social-work oriented offi-

---

Table 1

American Probation and Parole Association's Code of Ethics

1. I will render professional service to the justice system and the community at large in effecting the social adjustment of the offender.

2. I will uphold the law with dignity, displaying an awareness of my responsibility to offenders while recognizing the right of the public to be safe-guarded from criminal activity.

3. I will strive to be objective in the performance of my duties, recognizing the inalienable right of all persons, appreciating the inherent worth of the individual, and respecting those confidences which can be reposed in me.

4. I will conduct my personal life with decorum, neither accepting nor granting favors in connection with my office.

5. I will cooperate with my co-workers and related agencies and will continually strive to improve my professional competence through the seeking and sharing of knowledge and understanding.

6. I will distinguish clearly, in public, between my statements and actions as an individual and as a representative of my profession.

7. I will encourage policy, procedures and personnel practices which will enable others to conduct themselves in accordance with the values, goals and objectives of the American Probation and Parole Association.

8. I recognize my office as a symbol of public faith and I accept it as a public trust to be held as long as I am true to the ethics of the American Probation and Parole Association.

9. I will constantly strive to achieve these objectives and ideals, dedicating myself to my chosen profession.

cers cultivate close relationships with offenders in order to formulate a suitable treatment plan that will assist offenders in avoiding future crimes and in making their lives more productive. Officers in this category assume that individuals are fundamentally good and will choose noncriminal behaviors and life styles once they are

> *"The ethic of care recognizes individuals' basic rights and values but it does not elevate them above society's.*

helped to understand themselves. This self-knowledge will promote personal growth and unnecessary prosocial attitudes. Within this framework, offenders are seen as emotionally disturbed, victims of circumstances or socially disadvantaged.

Welfare/therapeutic officers' actions are noble from the viewpoint of Kant's model because of the sincere and benevolent motivations behind their actions. However, these officers may be inclined to "rescue" clients by finding resources for them without allowing clients to make mistakes and learn how to acquire necessary services. "Finally, there is a danger of becoming too personally involved with clients, a situation that may lead to considerable disappointment and frustration for the practitioner" (Souryal, 1992, p. 367).

Passive Officers

The third type of officer, the passive time saver or civil servant, cares about neither clients' needs nor the welfare of the community. The only persons these probation officers care about are themselves. Practitioners of this type see the greatest good in inactivity and avoidance of work. They merely manage their caseloads, viewing their work as meaningless. They may be employees who do not define themselves as service providers or professionals. Or they may have once belonged to one of the aforementioned probation officer types but have become burned-out and are waiting for promotion or retirement. Or they may simply be amoral.

Probation officers who adopt the role of civil servant invest in their jobs a modicum of effort and personal commitment. Civil servants concentrate on maintaining or advancing their positions within the agency and find no law enforcing or casework vo-

cation in probation. Instead, this type of officer works within the probation bureaucracy and concentrates on retirement, pension or entry into another field such as law or police work. Consistent work attendance, proper and prompt completion of paperwork, and the kind of self-enhancement that results in salary increases are characteristic of the time saver. Their job performance contributes to the smooth flow of office functioning; however, all responsibilities are met minimally and mechanically. Although contact with offenders is regular, civil servants attempt to minimize personal interactions with them. Civil servants' duties, as they perceive them, are advising probationers about their failure to obey rules, apprising the court of offenders' criminal behaviors and observing probationer progress as opposed to initiating client changes.

Synthetic Officers

The final type of role identification of probation officers incorporates both the treatment and control components of probation. Synthetic or combined officers' supervisory styles reflect the desire to satisfy the basic orientations of the rule enforcer

and social worker. In doing so, these officers are, perhaps unknowingly, coming to grips with the probation officer's fundamental quandary: reconciling the conflicting tensions arising from the legal and social services dimensions of probation work. Synthetic officers integrate monitoring and rehabilitation by evaluating each case to determine which particular strategy will best protect community safety and meet the offender's needs. This type of officer is most likely to develop working relationships with community resource agencies and local police departments. They understand the complexity of probationers' difficulties and acknowledge the inherent limitations in working through these problems.

In the combined type, practitioners see the highest good in the middle ground between the welfare of their clients and the protection of the community. Although offender control is important, these probation officers also try hard to obtain client services. Practitioners of this type are both humanitarian and justice-oriented. Their decisions are based on the view that offenders' interests are critical. As we noted earlier, their decisions are made on a case-by-case basis; sometimes, the welfare of the individual is secondary to the com-

---

Table 2

Federal Probation Officers' Association Code of Ethics

As a Federal Probation Officer, I am dedicated to rendering professional service to the courts, the parole authorities, and the community at large in effecting the social adjustment of the offender.

I will conduct my personal life with decorum, will neither accept nor grant favors in connection with my office, and will put loyalty to moral principles above personal consideration.

I will uphold the law with dignity and with complete awareness of the prestige and stature of the judicial system of which I am a part. I will be ever cognizant of my responsibility to the community which I serve.

I will strive to be objective in the performance of my duties; respect the inalienable rights of all persons; appreciate the inherent worth of the individual; and hold inviolate those confidences which can be reposed in me.

I will cooperate with my fellow workers and related agencies and will continually attempt to improve my professional standards through seeking of knowledge and understanding.

I recognize my office as a symbol of public faith and I accept it as a public trust to be held as long as I am true to the ethics of the Federal Probation Service. I will constantly strive to achieve these objectives and ideals, dedicating myself to my chosen profession.

Source: Close and Meier (1995)

munity's and vice versa. Because of this, such probation officers must be attuned closely to the basic ethical principles underpinning their actions. In practice, they are probably the most ethical of all the probation officer types.

What about probation officers who are inclined to act according to a certain type but are prevented by their current work environments from doing so? For example, officers may be inclined toward the welfare/therapeutic model. However, because of the constraints of large caseloads, lack of resources and agency expectations, they are prevented from being more social work-oriented with their clients. Similarly, punitive officers may want to impose harsh penalties on probationers to keep them in line but are prevented from doing so because of judges' decisions. Hence, probation officers also are influenced by the contexts in which they work. The greater the degree of discontinuity between officer type and department culture, the more likely it is that officers will become frustrated, cynical and at risk of becoming passive time savers. The best situation is one in which officer type and department culture are congruent.

Conclusions

Probation officers should be aware of basic ethical principles (Braswell, 1996). Specifically they should be guided by the ethic of care, the central goal of which is to reintegrate individuals into the community (Pollock-Bryne, 1994). Such a posture embodies the belief that probationers are human beings no matter what types of crimes they have committed. The ethic of care recognizes individuals' basic rights and values but it does not elevate them above society's. Within all relationships, a continual re-evaluation of needs, responsibilities and rights must occur to insure that the well-being of all parties is promoted. Therefore, ethical probation officers must be ready to override the needs of offenders who pose a serious threat to the welfare of the community.

Probation officers will be able to make competent moral decisions better by examining the values and motivations underlying their actions. They must work out of a combined model of enforcement and treatment. Such a challenge can be met by adhering to basic ethical principles. In making ethical decisions, probation officers can receive guidance from the American Probation and Parole Association's and the Federal Probation Officers' Association's codes of ethics (see Tables 1 and 2). In addition, officers can enroll in recently developed training sessions on professional ethics (Wehmhoefer, 1993). The wider network of staff within probation departments, including fellow officers, supervisors and chiefs, also can encourage and support officers' ethical decisions and give them a forum to air ethical concerns and problems. The continually changing nature of probation supervision will create new ethical questions for practitioners (Silverman, 1993). A basic grounding in ethics is necessary in fulfilling probation's goal of serving both offenders and the community.

References

Abadinsky, H., Probation and Parole: *Theory and Practice*. Englewood Cliffs, NJ: Prentice-Hall, 1996.

Braswell, M. C., *Criminal Justice: An Ethic for the Future*. In M. C. Braswell, B. R. McCarthy, and B. J. McCarthy eds., *Justice, Crime and Ethics*, pp. 399–411. Cincinnati,OH: Anderson Publishing Company, 1996.

Braswell, M. C.; McCarthy, B. R; and McCarthy, B. J. eds. *Justice, Crime and Ethics*. Cincinnati, OH: Anderson Publishing Company, 1994.

Brown, P. W., Ethics: Right or Wrong [Book Review]. Federal Probation, 53, 82(1989).

Camp, C. G., and Camp, G. M.. *Corrections Year 1994: Probation and Parole*. South Salem, NY: Criminal Justice Institute, 1994.

Close, D., & Meier, N., *Morality in Criminal Justice: An Introduction to Ethics*. Belmont, CA: Wadsworth Publishing Company, 1995.

Dewey, R. E., and Hurlbutt, R. H., eds., *An Introduction to Ethics*. New York: Macmillan, 1977.

Duffee, D. E., and Carlson, B. E., "Competing Value Premises for the Provision of Drug Treatment to Probationers," *Crime and Delinquency*, 42(1977):574.

Goldsmith, H. R., "The Role of the Juvenile Probation Officer Regarding the Adolescent Sex Offender and Related Issues," *Journal of Offender Counseling, Services & Rehabilitation*, 12(1988):115–122.

Klockars, J. P, *The Reality of the Probation Officers' Dilemma*. Federal Probation, 36(1972)18–29.

Pollock, J. M., *Ethics in Crime and Justice: Dilemmas and Decisions*, 2nd ed. Belmont, CA: Wadsworth Publishing Company, 1994.

Rosecrance, J., "Maintaining the Myth of Individualized Justice: Probation Presentence Reports," *Justice Quarterly*, 5 (1988):235–256.

Sherman, L., "Learning Police Ethics," *Criminal Justice Ethics*, 1(1992):10–19.

Silverman, M., "Ethical Issues in the Field of Probation," *International Journal of Offender Therapy and Comparative Criminology*, 37(1993):85–94.

Souryal, S. S., *Ethics in Criminal Justice: In Search of the Truth*. Cincinnati, OH: Anderson Publishing Co., 1992.

Von Hirsh, A., "The Ethics of Community-Based Sanctions," *Crime and Delinquency*, 36(1990):162–173.

Whemhoefer, R. A., "Ethics in the Probation and Parole Profession: A Vision for the Future," *Perspectives*, 17(1993):8–9.

Whitehead, J. T., *Ethical Issues in Probation and Parole*. In M. C. Braswell, B. R. McCarthy, and B. J. McCarthy, eds. *Justice, Crime and Ethics*, pp. 243–260. Cincinnati, OH: Anderson Publishing Company 1996.

Prisons Grapple With Rapid Influx of Women—and Mothers

By Nicole Gaouette

Staff writer of The Christian Science Monitor

DAWN RING misses her kids. She and a few other women sitting in a small classroom have drawn battered desks into a tight circle to talk. As with mothers everywhere, the conversation often comes back to their children.

Mary and Dorothea worry about their daughters, who are misbehaving; Rose shows off a dog-eared baseball card featuring her son at bat; Dawn talks with quiet pride about her twins, a boy and girl who share her freckles and sandy coloring.

But this is no PTA meeting. The classroom is theirs, not their kids', and they aren't here voluntarily. Murder, prostitution, drugs, and fraud have brought these women to a Rhode Island prison where they are serving sentences of months or, in some cases, years.

They are part of an influx of women filling America's prisons at a rate that eclipses the male incarceration rate. More than two-thirds of the 137,000 women behind bars are mothers, often single parents. Most are incarcerated for nonviolent, drug-related crimes that are now drawing harsher sentences.

The trend shows no signs of slowing, and evidence suggests America's justice system is woefully unprepared to deal with this new society of female prisoners, who present thorny family, health, and rehabilitation problems that male inmates don't have.

As states overhaul their welfare systems and prison-rehabilitation programs fail to keep pace with the growing inmate population, many experts believe the problems associated with women in prison will grow. And the repercussions

of this female juggernaut, experts say, will be felt far beyond prison walls. They point in particular to the children of inmates, who are far more likely than other children to end up in the juvenile-justice system or in prison.

"We're creating a never-ending society of dysfunctionality," says Mary Ann Farkas, a criminologist at Marquette University in Milwaukee. "There are a lot of angry children separated from mom."

An explosion in incarceration

The US has the second-highest incarceration rate in the world, and while women represent just 6.3 percent of those behind bars, their numbers are growing rapidly. The female prison population jumped 6.4 percent between July 1995 and July 1996, according to the Bureau of Justice Statistics, an arm of the US Department of Justice. In jails, which hold people for no more than a year, the average growth rate is even higher: an annual 10.2 percent for women since 1985, versus 6.1 percent for men.

"To say female incarceration is rising is an understatement," says Emily Edwards, director of Cleveland's Women's Re-entry Resource Network. "It's exploding."

Why the increase now? Sociologists offer a slew of reasons. The women in Dawn's group, who didn't want their

ROBERT HARBISON—STAFF

PROUD MOTHER: *Patricia, sharing a photo of her daughter, Amber, is in Massachusetts's Framingham prison for the fifth time. She says the drug treatment program helps, but the 'biggest problem is having no support when I leave.'*

last names used, have firsthand experience with many of them: from improved surveillance in retail stores to the growing numbers of poor women to changing attitudes toward female incarceration. Once sent to reformatories, women are now expected to do hard time.

But all the experts agree there's one major factor: mandatory drug-sentencing laws. Such laws impose fixed prison terms for drug offenses and have been the biggest force behind the rocketing female incarceration rate, they say.

Figures from the Washington-based Sentencing Project show 1 in 3 women in state prisons is there on drug-related charges, surging from 1 in 10 in 1979. The current rate for men is 1 in 5.

At the Massachusetts Correctional Institute at Framingham, a sprawling compound where Massachusetts women

PRISON LIFE: *Dawn has been an inmate at this Cranston, R.I., women's facility three times. The former heroin addict, prostitute, and mother says she has been offered no real rehabilitative help. 'I'm not talking about parenting classes, I'm talking about reality. We leave here, what are we gonna do?'*

numerous beatings, will tell you her alcoholism and drug addiction contributed to the events of that night.

Thirty-six percent of the 221 women at the Rhode Island facility are there on drug charges, but staff worker, Sister Teresa Foley, contends the numbers can be misleading. "It's often masked. A woman might be picked up on prostitution charges, but why are they hooking? Or shoplifting, or writing bad checks?"

Dawn is a case in point. She's serving a year for prostitution—she prefers the word loitering—but was working to feed a voracious hunger for heroin. "I was spending about $350 a day," she remembers. A stocky woman with wavy hair and kohl-rimmed hazel eyes, Dawn is brusque but open.

"On a good day, it took three hours to earn enough," she says, "I did more robbing than loitering, but I gotta loiter to get in the car." She's clean now, but one way or another, the drugs have

were once sent for talking back to their husbands, records show 85 percent of inmates have a substance-abuse problem. The other 15 percent, the staff quips, are lying.

Drugs have made their mark in the Rhode Island prison's classroom, too. Dorothea, a tough-talking, wiry woman, is there for dealing cocaine. Rose, who killed her common-law husband after brought Dawn back to prison three times.

A different set of needs

Addressing the multiple problems of incarcerated women has always been difficult. Now, as rising populations strain prison budgets and staff even further, the situation is drawing scrutiny.

The US Department of Justice is investigating reports of sexual harassment and sexual abuse at prisons in Alabama as well as Michigan, which is one of 11 state prisons singled out in a recent Human Rights Watch (HRW) report. Class-action suits have drawn attention to harassment in other states, including Georgia, where three women's prisons have opened since 1989.

As more women enter prison, overcrowding compounds problems like sexual harassment, as it becomes more difficult to supervise staff. It can also strain resources for inmates' medical, psychological, or educational needs.

California boasts the world's two largest women's prisons, yet in late 1995 its facilities were operating at 60 percent to almost 100 percent overcapacity, according to HRW. Those conditions spurred inmates to sue, alleging that overcrowding limited access to everything from toilets—the women say they had to urinate in the stairwells—to education. And two of the state's prisons face suits that allege medical care so negligent it led to inmate deaths.

In 1993, Ohio and Virginia were among five states that didn't provide yearly health checkups, according to a survey of 49 correctional systems. Connecticut didn't offer pre- or post-natal care, though it reported 20 pregnant inmates. Gynecological care isn't available in Alabama and Georgia, though education is, as it is in every other state.

Critics say even education programs don't make the grade when it comes to helping women support themselves and their kids on release. Some experts attribute this failing to outmoded ideas of what women should learn. "In male institutions, you'll have 10 to 14 programs—computers, electrical training," says Dr. Farkas of Marquette University. "In a women's institution, you're lucky to have three, and they're more likely to be cosmetology and cooking."

Others see the inadequacy of services as a matter of money. "So much money goes into basic operating costs that it's harder to find funding to help prison-

CHANGING VIEWS: *Before and after self-portraits decorate the walls of the drug-treatment wing at the Rhode Island women's prison. The program tries to help women identify why they use drugs. Currently, about 30 women are enrolled.*

ers," explains Jenni Gainsborough of the American Civil Liberties Union (ACLU). "The sheer increase in numbers is overwhelming systems that were just adequate before."

Programs are often based on those designed for men, yet women present different, some say tougher, challenges. As a Framingham staffer observes, "you're not likely to find a male inmate who's HIV-positive, drug-addicted, and pregnant."

Those traits would be layered on top of a more common profile. "These women are often their children's primary caregivers," says Phyllis Coontz, a University of Pittsburgh professor of criminal justice. Most have low self-esteem and few skills, she adds, and two-thirds to three-quarters are physical- or sexual-abuse victims. Abuse can often lead to incarceration, experts say, as many women turn to crime when they run away.

While much of this description fits the women in Dawn's circle, Dawn herself downplays similarities. She's kicked the drugs, her ex-husband has the kids, and self-esteem isn't her problem, she says. She might not have finished high school, but she has smarts.

But press a little harder and Dawn, usually chatty, is noticeably more subdued. It turns out she spent her high school years being shuffled between foster homes or taking care of two younger brothers while her mother drank. "We lived with her, but she was never there." When she was, there were beatings and abuse, "but it wasn't her fault, it was the pills." Though Dawn didn't turn to drugs until she was 21, adolescence took its toll. "I was more grown up than I should have been," she says quietly, and declares the subject closed.

Deciding where tax dollars go

Rehabilitation is a contentious issue. Some critics point to studies with male inmates that have shown it to be an "ab-

ject failure and at best marginally successful," says Mike Rushford, of the Criminal Legal Justice Foundation in Sacramento, Calif. Others argue there's no need for society to pay any more for criminals. Advocates for women inmates counter that men and women react to rehab differently. Criminologists like Farkas say neglecting it just leaves women locked in a criminal cycle that will ultimately cost the public more.

But as prisons struggle with greater intake, just offering rehabilitation will become more difficult. A recent study on MCI Framingham stated that as the population quadrupled between 1980 and 1989, programs failed to keep pace to such a degree that some 73 percent of addicted inmates were denied drug treatment in 1995. While warden Kathy Chmiele resolutely defends Framingham's services, only 130 of the 600 women incarcerated there can receive drug treatment at any given time. "The programs are very basic, but they're good," says Patricia Douglas, who is on her fifth stint in Framingham. "The biggest problem is having no support when I leave."

Most prison programs concentrate on extensive group and individual counseling to help addicts understand the reasons for their addiction and better control it. But critics say tax dollars shouldn't be spent to help curb voluntary behaviors.

It's a charge the women in Dawn's circle resent. "Let them be in our shoes for a minute," Mary says angrily. But the group, dressed in regulation blues, is split about how helpful general rehab programs are.

Only Rose says the experience has changed her: "I learned enough not to get involved in abusive relationships from the battered-women's program." Dorothea sees the change as an incremental, ongoing process. "You come in here enough times, you get enough knowledge not to come back," she says.

But Dawn, whose third stay here will end soon, is scathing. "As far as rehabilitation goes, there's none at all," she says. "I'm not talking about parenting classes, I'm talking about reality. We leave here, what are we gonna do?" Like Dawn, many women convicts come back more than once: In 1994, 20 percent of women in prison were repeat offenders, the Bureau of Justice Statistics says.

As at Framingham, women in the Rhode Island prison's drug-treatment program are more positive about rehabilitation than those in the general prison population. That divide might be due to the greater resources applied to drug programs, and to the fact that inmates in drug-treatment programs often must apply to get in, and demonstrate a readiness to change.

High walls, watchful eyes

The Rhode Island prison, formerly a mental institution, is a collection of sturdy red-brick buildings just off a main road in Cranston. Despite the glittering concertina wire that hems one structure in, the complex has the open feel of a campus. Behind the walls though, there's no mistaking the correctional atmosphere. Narrow halls begin and end with barred doorways, and uniformed guards of both sexes are everywhere, as are cameras, discreetly suspended from the ceiling.

"It's a little like being 'Big Sister,'" jokes Warden Roberta Richman of the bank of video screens in her office. From here, she can watch inmates throughout the prison, focusing closely enough to read the small print on posters.

Day-to-day life on the inside, Dawn says, is like "day camp from hell." After the rehab programs, the occasional softball game on the grounds, there is only the claustrophobic monotony of long days punctuated by five daily "counts," when each woman stands by her bed to be checked present.

While women's prisons are generally less violent, more cooperative, and less racially charged than men's, there are still dangers. Sexual coercion is rife, experts say, and violence is growing. Still, Dawn is lucky. Rhode Island, criminologists say, has one of the nation's best women's prisons.

'Being separated from your children is the most hardest truth,' say Dorothea, an inmate at the Rhode Island Department of Corrections Women's Facility in Cranston. She hasn't seen her children since her prison term began more than three months ago.

An empty stroller

On the warden's screens, black-and-white images flicker: women working in the kitchen; talking in therapy; unpacking junk-food orders from the outside world. One shot shows a still, sun-filled room scattered with toys. In its center, casting a long shadow, is an empty stroller.

Most incarcerated mothers say separation from their children is their No. 1 stress factor. Seventy-five percent of these children go to foster homes or relatives other than the natural father, and prisons are usually located in rural areas that are hard to reach for families with few resources. (The California Institute for Women, for example, is five hours away from Los Angeles, the closest city.) As a result, just 9 percent of women in state prisons get visits from their minor children, according to a National Criminal Justice Commission report.

"Being separated from your children is the most hardest truth," Dorothea says to a chorus of agreement. Rose's parents bring her son, and Dawn's ex-husband drives the twins over every Saturday, but they're fortunate. Dorothea hasn't seen her children, who are with her mother, since her prison term began almost 3½ months ago.

Some facilities provide busing from nearby urban centers to facilitate visits, but corrections officials say the difference between visiting rooms at a male and female facility is still striking. "When you lock a man up, the family unit usually stays intact," Ms. Richman says. "When you lock a woman up, you're destroying families."

This family disintegration, many experts say, is one of the greatest dangers of the current incarceration boom. They say children of inmates suffer negative effects that include traumatic stress, aggression, and withdrawal, and can lead to more serious dysfunctional behavior. These children are five times as likely to be imprisoned as other children, and more than half the inmates currently in the juvenile-justice system have a parent in prison, according to JusticeWorks, a Brooklyn-based nonprofit.

Some observers argue that separation from a criminal mother is often in a child's best interests. "If your own child is not an incentive to be responsible, what is?" asks Mr. Rushford, of the Criminal Legal Justice Foundation. "A lot of these women are immature, have drug problems. I suspect they're failing as parents to begin with."

Those who argue for minimizing mother-child separation with nonviolent offenders worry that with the current shift away from family reunification to foster care and adoption, more incarcerated mothers will lose their children to care that wouldn't necessarily be better. Many fear welfare reform will exacerbate the trend.

This has less to do with the retrenchment of services than with a stipulation that requires that after Aug. 22, 1996, those convicted of drug crimes—one-third of female inmates—are no longer eligible for welfare benefits upon release.

Many former welfare recipients are successfully moving into jobs, according to initial reports. But advocates insist this legislation will make it harder for inmates, especially those who've had minimal rehab or training, to succeed on release.

They describe a typical ex-convict with few skills, children to support, and a record that bars her from many jobs. If her child is in foster care, she must have work and an apartment to win them back.

"How do you . . . support yourself?" asks Richman. Many, like Farkas, fear women will turn to the answer Rhode Island staffer Sister Foley supplies. "There are two ways," she says, "crime and prostitution."

A Prison Portrait

■ The female prison population rose by 6.4 percent from July 1995 to July 1996.

■ The female jail population has grown by 10.2 percent a year since 1985.

ONE OF MANY: Audry, an inmate in Framingham, Mass.

■ 80 percent of women in prison are serving sentences for nonviolent offenses.

■ In 1991, 1 in 3 women in state prisons was there on drug-related charges, up from 1 in 10 in 1986.

■ Two-thirds of women in state or federal prisons are mothers of dependent children.

■ Only 9 percent of women in state prisons get visits from their minor children.

■ Children of inmates are 5 times as likely to be imprisoned as other children.

■ More than half the children in the juvenile justice system have a parent in prison.

■ More than 40 percent of women prisoners were physically or sexually abused before incarceration.

Sources: Bureau of Justice, The Sentencing Project, JusticeWorks Community, National Criminal Justice Commission.

Alternatives to incarceration

Most proposed alternatives to incarceration focus on reducing the cost to children—and to society—by putting nonviolent drug offenders in halfway houses or day-reporting centers, where they can get treatment, see their children, and even work.

Critics, like Rushford, are hesitant to fully embrace the idea. "Maybe you can rehabilitate some of them, but they have to make that choice," he says. "I think it's all about screening."

Nevertheless, it's a policy that's advocated by many in corrections, Richman included. "We're talking about policy that's exorbitantly expensive," she says of incarceration, explaining that women are far more expensive to imprison than men. Foster care can cost the state an annual $20,000 per child, and women often need more expensive care. "Why should it cost us $45,000 a year to incarcerate . . . a shoplifter and substance abuser?" she asks.

There are halfway houses for women and their children already operating in some states, including the Women's Re-entry Resource Network in Cleveland. "Treatment costs a lot less than a jail cell every year," says Ms. Edwards, the director. "And it doesn't have an intergenerational cost to the children involved."

Some prisons have adopted the strategy. The Bedford Hills Correction Center in Bedford Hills, N.Y., has a nursery program where children up to 18 months old can live with their mothers. Inmates' role as mother is a significant one," says warden Elaine Lord. "We want to enable that relationship."

Shirley Cloyes, who runs Mothers in Prison, Children in Crisis, has been pushing to make alternatives to prison the norm for nonviolent drug offenders. Her group is starting a grass-roots campaign to repeal mandatory drug-sentencing laws and start a "drug mule" bill that would address the situations of women tricked into smuggling drugs. "Alternatives have been on the books for 20 years," she says. "But they've been underutilized and underfunded."

Those in the field express varying degrees of concern about the future. Some, like Ms. Gainsborough of the ACLU, argue that so long as drugs are seen as a criminal and not a social health problem, female incarceration will continue to skyrocket.

"I see a slow response," says Marquette's Farkas. "But we need more halfway houses and shelters . . . and we'll definitely need more with welfare reform."

Dawn isn't going to wait that long. Upon release, she will head to North Carolina, where her mother lives. "If I stay here, I'll be be back [in prison], or I'll be dead," she says. If she stays clean for a year, she'll get custody of the twins. "I'm going to try and find a job and get along with my mom," she says. "Maybe get a place and a nice guy." She pauses, thinking about the ideas. "That sounds kinda good."

To Keep Peace, Prisons Allow Race to Rule

By Daniel B. Wood

Staff writer of The Christian Science Monitor

LOS ANGELES

MARC MADOW, who spent 17 months in a California prison, says strict segregation of inmates into race groups has unintentionally turned state prisons into factories of racism.

Prison officials and politicians say separating inmates by race boosts safety and control—and is just being practical.

Justice experts say the story is a window into prisons in every state, reflecting the consequences of bulging populations and soaring gang activity.

From entry to exit, nearly every activity—sleep, exercise, and meals—is determined by race. In one California prison, even weight-lifting equipment is labeled "B" for black, "W" for white, or "L" for Latino to avoid fights over it.

These conditions divide inmates and foster a racism that persists after release, says Mr. Madow, who was convicted of writing bad checks. "I thought segregation was dead, but there it was, as vivid as an Alabama lunch counter in the '50s."

But the reasons for such policies are clear, observers say. "It's not a matter of prejudice or stereotyping," says Robert McNamara, a criminologist at Furman University in Greenville, S.C. "If [wardens] didn't put them with their own kind, they might not last a day."

Now out of prison and off parole, Madow, an antiques dealer, is trying to raise public consciousness about institutions that are nominally "correctional," but that in practice may breed the worse qualities of human intolerance, prejudice, and bigotry.

"They were teaching us not to get along and telling us it was OK not to get along," he recalls. "I watched men come in who were racially neutral but who left walking the walk and talking the talk of hatred and fanaticism."

Upon arrival, inmates are divided into four racial categories—white, African-American, Hispanic/Latino, and "other". All nonwhites are then subdivided according to gang—Bloods or Crips for African-Americans—or geographic criteria, such as northern or southern Hispanic.

'I watched men come in who were racially neutral but left [with] fanaticism.'

—*Marc Madow*

This practice is pernicious, says Madow, because those who claim no group are forced to choose one. They develop racial affiliations that continue in prison days and beyond.

"If you live in prison for five to 10 years as a Crip or a Blood, that is your 'jacket' when you leave," he says. "You adopt a dress, a loyalty. And members of both gangs know who you are from that day forward."

These segregation practices are ones that prison officials nationwide "have both allowed and been forced into by the increased populations and violence of US prisons," says Paul Cromwell, a criminal justice professor at Wichita State University.

The coast-to-coast rise of gang activity since 1975 has been tough on prisons, he adds, because such affiliations by inmates not only transcend prison barriers, they become more important on the inside.

"The public may be rightly horrified by such segregation measures, but they have become an increasingly common fact of life," says Professor Cromwell.

From 1985 to 1996, the US state prison population nearly tripled, from 462,284 to 1,076,625. Over that period, the rise of Hispanic populations has changed the power balance of ethnic gangs, experts say. Big-name gangs like Black Guerrilla Family have been displaced by Mexican and California gangs such as the Brown Mafia.

Life on the inside

Race identification in prisons is crucial because of a need for protection, says Madow. When major fights occur between people of different races—a weekly occurrence, he says—all members of each race must join in. Anyone who balks is roughed up or even killed by his own kind.

"All self worth in prison is generated by respect, racial or otherwise," he says, "because inmates have been stripped of everything else—jobs, family, money, clothes, lifestyle."

Replacing those is what Madow calls "pigment think"—a conscious effort by both prison officials and inmates to maintain control by identifying each individual as part of a racial group.

"Inmates dramatically outnumber guards, so [the prison] has a vested interest in keeping the inmate population divided against itself rather than [against] them. Guards need to channel any kind of unrest away from themselves and onto another group."

They also need to prevent racial flare-ups to begin with. For this reason, each race has its own barber who uses his clippers only on members of one race.

Each race is also assigned a certain number of beds. If one bed becomes vacant, no member of another race can occupy it—even if a shortage of beds forces other races to use overflow facilities in the prison gym.

Although no formal divisions of eating facilities are enforced, inmates regularly segregate themselves. Unstated rules prohibit blacks and whites from exchanging food, candy, or cigarettes.

Surviving without a group

Madow's story is confirmed by a fellow inmate, probation violator Aristotle Zylexio Starchild, a Pacific Islander from Papua New Guinea. Because of his dark skin, he was advised to dorm with the African-American inmates but refused, opting to be designated "other."

"Within hours I was visited by Bloods who said I could get messed up, even killed for making that decision," Mr. Starchild recalls.

As for Madow, he was able to sidestep gang affiliation because of his age—at 42, nearly twice the prison average, by being college educated, and by

being in the one race, white, for which there were no subgroups. "The whites are all thrown together—Aryan brotherhood, attorneys, and bikers—so there is no immediate subgroup to go to war with," he says.

Now that he is out, he still avoids physical and eye contact with other races and doesn't start conversations or share with those of other ethnic groups.

Youth especially at risk

Youth fare even worse, Starchild and Madow aver.

A typical scenario, they say, is that of a young black man serving seven months for a DUI (driving under the influence). "He went from nice kid to hard-nosed monster with tattoos, baggy pants, and attitude," Starchild says.

Prison officials admit that attempts to prevent such episodes through counseling don't often work.

"It is very difficult for a young, naive first-termer coming into prison to resist the pressures of other inmates," says Jerry Underwood, spokesman for the California State Prison at Jamestown, where Madow served from August 1992 to Nov. 1993.

The state has tried to quell gang activity by sending leaders to other prisons. But this only spawned more activity.

Madow's assessment gets no argument from state officials. "It's a fact of prison life," says Underwood. "These people are felons who will prey on anyone weaker than themselves. Our over-

riding concern is that they don't violate the safety and security of other inmates."

Safety vs. civil rights

Maintaining control can require measures that seem extreme from the outside. But inmates forfeit some rights, experts say, including the right to bear arms. And while they still have the right to be free of racially-discriminating patterns in housing and treatment, scholars say another civil right takes precedence: the right to live.

"Courts know prisons are being asked to run their facilities with meager sources and bulging populations," says Robert Pugsley, law professor at Southwestern School of Law here. So their tactics "are met with friendly judicial reception."

But this hasn't stopped Madow, who has taken his case to both Amnesty International, which says a 1998 campaign on human rights will examine the issue, and to California legislators who have welcomed his views but promised no action.

"Madow is absolutely correct in his assessment, but I don't know what the answer is," says California Assemblyman Roderick Wright (D), of Los Angeles, who sits on the Assembly budget committee, which oversees corrections.

Just because no one yet knows the solution is not a reason to suppress the problem, counters Madow.

"The first step to correcting the situation," he says, "is for the public to understand that there *is* a problem."

THE COLOR OF JUSTICE

When the question of equal treatment for people of all colors is discussed, it makes some capital punishment scholars see red.

JOHN H. TRUMBO

John H. Trumbo is a reporter and columnist for the daily Auburn Journal in Placer County, Calif. He covers primarily law enforcement and courts.

The fact that there are more non-white men on death row than their Caucasian counterparts is a fact supported by the numbers. The real question is that: Is the disparity due to racial discrimination or some other not-so-black-and-white issues?

It appears that a defendant who has enough money to hire a high-priced lawyer has better odds of beating the death row rap.

If black men who are accused of killing white victims are prime candidates for death row, then why isn't O. J. Simpson facing the ultimate punishment?

And why aren't there more women on death row? It's discrimination, but a closer look at the numbers will show it has nothing to do with color.

Racial discrimination on death row has become a familiar refrain among public defenders and nonprofit organizations dedicated to protecting the rights of condemned men and women. But there may be bigger, less well-defined factors that determine who gets a cell on death row and who doesn't.

Organizations whose focus includes death row issues have sprung up from San Francisco to Washington, D.C., ever since civil rights became a national outcry three decades ago. Not surprisingly, many southern states are home to the most active of these organizations.

"Everyone would concede there is racial discrimination," says Clive Stafford Smith of the Louisiana Crisis Assistance Center in New Orleans. "Debate is absurd. Who could pretend it doesn't have an impact?" he said.

A look at the statistics seems to support Smith's contention.

The Death Penalty Information Center in Washington, D.C., reports that 65 blacks have been executed for murders of whites since 1976, compared to one white person executed for the death of a black victim. However, a look at the race of victims for capital cases shows whites are way ahead of blacks—85 percent to 11 percent. Hispanic victims make up 2 percent and Asians represent 1 percent.

When you remove the racial aspects, the statistical portrait shifts dramatically. From 1976 to 1991, there were 157 executions in the United States. Ninety-four of them were Caucasians and 63 were African-Americans. That is 59.9 percent white and 40.1 percent black, which is almost a perfect match to the ratio of white and black people who occupy the nearly 2,500 death row cells in this country.

If we are to assume that Smith is correct and racial discrimination is significant, then who is to blame?

Americans can blame the decision-makers, says Smith. Like many death penalty defense lawyers, Smith believes that racial bias occurs at every step in the criminal justice process—from the time the officer flicks on the red light for a traffic stop to that moment when the jury foreperson declares that the maximum penalty should be imposed.

Justice Comes With a Price

The first problem, says Smith, is for a death row candidate to get an adequate defense.

"Often, you have a bunch of town drunks representing people who don't have a lot of money," Smith said. In 10 years of wrangling with death penalty cases at the Louisiana Crisis Assistance Center, Smith says death penalty case defendants almost never have hired attorneys to represent them. He can recall only two cases out of 200 in the past decade where the hapless defendants have had hired attorneys.

"And those," he says wryly, "were $5,000 lawyers here in Louisiana who were no better than public defenders."

It appears, then, that a defendant who has enough money to hire a high-priced lawyer has better odds of beating the death row rap.

For example, Smith was not surprised when the Los Angeles District Attorney's Office chose not to pursue the death penalty with O. J. Simpson.

Even though he is black, Simpson is also rich—and that is a different kind of color issue. Some would call it green.

It's simple, Smith says. Prosecutors are less inclined to press for capital punishment when the defense is well-financed. "They (Simpson's prosecutors) aren't charging the death penalty because they won't get it. His defense is too well equipped," Smith said.

Prosecutor Bill Murray, who is black and number two in the San Joaquin County District Attorney's Office in Stockton, Calif., doesn't buy into the poverty factor in death row cases.

"That's not accurate in this country," Murray said. "We don't spare the expense for court-appointed or public defenders." He says even the middle-class defendants who can afford their own attorneys by mortgaging everything they own still end up on death row if they deserve it.

Murray believes Simpson escaped the death penalty phase for the simple reason that there is too much positive history with the defendant. "That case is not strong factually, and there are too many mitigating circumstances on the positive things he's done in his life. They would have been crazy to seek the death penalty on Simpson because the jury may not return that verdict," Murray said.

That argument flies in the face of a quote from U.S. Supreme Court Justice William O. Douglas, who in 1972, observed there were no examples of the wealthy on death row in America.

"One searches our chronicles in vain for the execution of any member of the affluent strata of this society," Justice Douglas wrote.

More recently, Associated Press Writer Bob Egelko reported that there appears to be a direct relationship between dollars and death row.

According to his September 1994 report, every one of the 384 men and four women awaiting execution as of July 1, 1994, was poor enough to qualify for a lawyer at state expense.

Atlanta lawyer Stephen Bright concurs.

"The death penalty is for poor people," said Bright, who serves as the director of the Southern Center for Human Rights in Atlanta and has handled capital cases for 15 years.

"Unlike most of my clients, whose IQs are in the high 60s or low 70s, you're talking about people (rich defendants) who have their lives together, who have the ability to make money.... You would think those would be the cold, calculated murderers most fit for the death penalty. But the death penalty is for poor people," Bright told the Associated Press.

The Gender Debate

Actually, statistics show that death row is for men who, for the most part, are poor, have never married and didn't complete high school. As of 1994, 98.5 percent of death row inmates in this country were men.

This in itself indicates discrimination, albeit in favor of women, says Smith. Since society still sees women as fairer and less violent than men, women who are accused of murders where there are special circumstances that could lead to the death penalty often obtain an escape route that is not available to them.

A typical, little-known case in nearly all-white, upper-middle class Placer County, Calif., illustrates the point.

Aaron S. Harper, 25, was found guilty of a first-degree, lying-in-wait murder of a white man in July 1994. Harper, who is black, faced the death penalty but ended up with life in prison without the possibility of parole.

Trial testimony showed that Harper agreed to do the February 1993 murder as a favor for

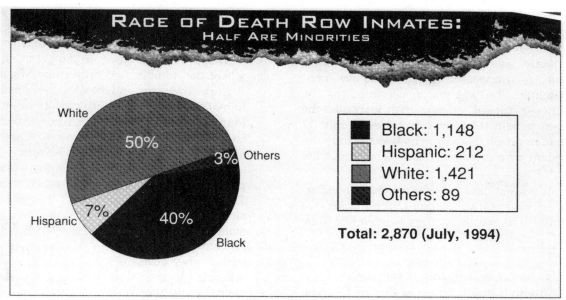

RACE OF DEATH ROW INMATES:
HALF ARE MINORITIES

White 50%
3% Others
Hispanic 7%
40% Black

Black: 1,148
Hispanic: 212
White: 1,421
Others: 89

Total: 2,870 (July, 1994)

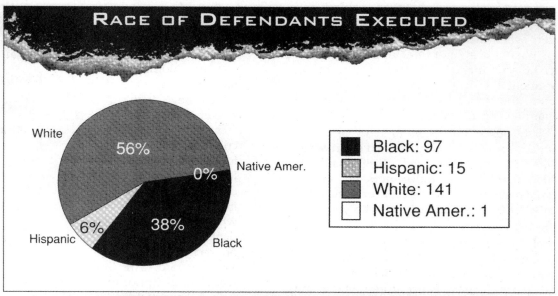

RACE OF DEFENDANTS EXECUTED

White 56%
0% Native Amer.
Hispanic 6%
38% Black

Black: 97
Hispanic: 15
White: 141
Native Amer.: 1

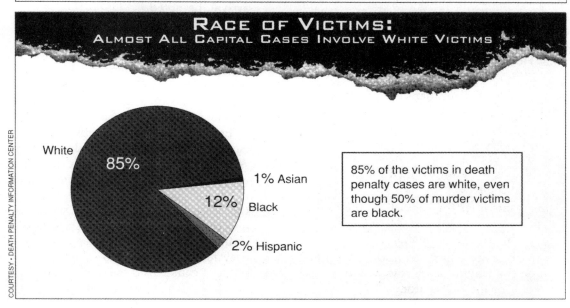

RACE OF VICTIMS:
ALMOST ALL CAPITAL CASES INVOLVE WHITE VICTIMS

White 85%
1% Asian
12% Black
2% Hispanic

85% of the victims in death penalty cases are white, even though 50% of murder victims are black.

COURTESY • DEATH PENALTY INFORMATION CENTER

a white woman, Trina Werly. She wanted revenge on her former boyfriend, whom she believed had molested their young daughter.

Werly was tried for murder and found guilty of a lesser charge of voluntary manslaughter. She was the mastermind of the crime—a capital offense that warrants the death penalty—but expects to serve only 12 years in prison. Harper, who was the only defendant who faced the death penalty, got life in prison.

"It's sexist, and women are the beneficiaries of discrimination, but I don't think we should start executing more women just to be fair," Smith said.

Racial Bias Seen at Every Level

Although Bright observes that in Georgia, 65 percent of all murder victims are black and most perpetrators are black, discrimination enters when there is a white victim. And, he says, there are at least three opportunities for racial discrimination that play a role in bringing about the death penalty: the race of the victim, the skin color of the prosecutor and racial makeup of the jury.

First, police investigators tend to invest "huge responses of resources and effort when white victims are involved," Bright said. He added that Georgia prosecutors go for the death penalty in 70 percent of interracial crime. "It becomes an issue of who you kill," Bright noted.

Take the example of Jerry Walker, who made the mistake of killing the son of a white brigadier general from Fort Benning, Ga., in 1991. It was a convenience store robbery, and the jury gave Walker death, partly, Bright believes, because the victim and his family had the politically-correct skin color and social status. However, Walker was re-sentenced to life in 1993.

Or, consider the murder case of black defendant John Michael Davis who went to death row in 1985 after the district attorney in Georgia's Muscogee County asked the stepfather of the young, white female victim if he wanted Davis to be imprisoned for life or get the electric chair.

Three years after the conviction, the grateful stepfather contributed $5,000 to the district attorney's judgeship campaign.

A second factor which can lead to discrimination on the way to death row, Bright notes, is the color of the prosecutor.

"In a lot of places in the country, a white person is the one who is making the decision to pursue the death penalty," he said.

That's not the case in Stockton, Calif., where the number two prosecutor Murray is African-American and has the responsibility to make final calls on death penalty cases. "As long as I've been here, race has not been an issue," said Murray, who came to California after being a prosecutor in New York.

Typically, any case which has death penalty potential goes through a two-tier process. There is a general discussion on the merits among staff, then one person—in Stockton it is Murray—makes the decision on whether or not to seek capital punishment.

But Murray acknowledges that biases may exist in other parts of the country.

"The southern states have a different situation which they haven't quite shaken," he said.

Even though racial discrimination doesn't appear to be an issue in his San Joaquin County now, they do have three cases pending in federal courts in which the black defendants are appealing based on racial discrimination, Murray said. All three were handled prior to his arrival, he noted.

The third factor—the color of the jury—can also make a difference, said Bright.

> Since 1977, only two California death row inmates have seen the inside of th[e] gas chamber at San Quentin State Prison. There are 397 California inmates still awaiting execution—149 of whom are black.

William Henry Hance, a black man who was executed in Georgia in March 1994, was given the death penalty by a jury composed of one African-American and 11 Caucasians.

Ensuring there is a racially color-blind jury isn't that easy. Often in predominantly black Atlanta, said Bright, the black defendants are accused of killing white victims in predominately white neighborhoods. Consequently, the trials are in those mostly white counties, and the jury pools contain few non-whites.

In such situations, it becomes relatively easy for a prosecutor to excuse a black juror without cause. And even when good cause is required, Bright said, any attorney "with

EXECUTIONS BY RACE — BY STATE
(1977-1994)

STATE	B	H	I	W	Count
AL	7	0	0	3	10
AR	2	0	0	7	9
AZ	0	0	0	3	3
CA	0	0	0	2	2
DE	2	0	1	1	4
FL	11	0	0	22	33
GA	12	0	0	6	18
ID	0	0	0	1	1
IL	0	0	0	2	2
IN	1	0	0	2	3
LA	9	0	0	12	21
MD	0	0	0	1	1
MO	5	0	0	6	11
MS	3	0	0	1	4
NC	0	0	0	6	6
NE	1	0	0	0	1
NV	0	0	0	5	5
OK	1	0	0	2	3
SC	0	0	0	4	4
TX	29	15	0	41	85
UT	2	0	0	2	4
VA	14	0	0	10	24
WA	0	0	0	2	2
WY	0	0	0	1	1
Count:	**99**	**15**	**1**	**142**	**257**

K. WILLIAM HAYES/CAPITAL PUNISHMENT STUDY

> "The system is nothing to write home about, especially when it deals with the question of who should live and who should die."
>
> —Stephen Bright, Director, Southern Center for Human Rights

brains can come up with another reason that isn't race-related."

Bright likes to make an example of Ocmulgee County (Ga.) District Attorney Joe Briley, who has sought the death penalty in 30 cases. Twenty-four of those were black defendants, and in 20 cases, Briley used 169 jury strikes against black citizens and only 19 against white citizens.

In cases where victims were white, Briley exercised 94 percent of his jury strikes against black jurors, Bright said.

There are other examples from Bright's files, including a district attorney in Hinds County, Miss., whose public policy is to "get rid of as many" black jurors as possible. And there's documented evidence in Chambers County, Ala., that a prosecutor there ranked prospective jurors as "strong," "medium," "weak," and "black."

Murray acknowledges the problem with trying to obtain an unbiased jury.

"Selecting jurors is not a perfect process. You just can't control them," he said.

Even with all the opportunities for racial bias to occur, Murray has noticed a safety net that exists on death penalty issues because of human nature.

"People just aren't all that anxious to render death verdicts," he said. "If anything, in this state jurors are going the other way," Murray said.

An Act of Racial Justice

The Racial Justice Act, which proponents tried to include in President Clinton's Crime Bill, would have been a small step toward bringing accountability for racial disparity, Bright said.

"It was a very watered-down remedy and would not have been that effective. It would have just forced the prosecutors to come up with other reasons to put non-whites on death row," he said, even though he was one of its early supporters.

Watered-down or not, Stockton prosecutor Murray is relieved that the Racial Justice Act was rejected.

"It would have been a nightmare for district attorneys," he said, noting that a quota or statistical basis for determining death row cases would be impossible because the Supreme Court has already decided pure statistics are not enough to prove racial bias.

The case that triggered the Supreme Court decision involved Warren McCleskey of Georgia, who was executed September 1991 for shooting a white police officer. His defense referred to a study, conducted by the National Association for the Advancement of Colored People (NAACP), which indicated that blacks who killed whites were more likely to receive the death penalty than whites who killed whites. A review of the NAACP study by an expert methodologist showed that black-on-white murders—including the McCleskey case—often involved other aggravating elements like armed robbery.

The 1987 Supreme Court decision followed the logic represented with Georgia's homicide statistics, which showed that 67 percent of black-on-white killings involved armed robbery, compared with 7 percent of black-on-black killings.

Rep. Don Edwards, D-Calif., told the Wall Street Journal in July 1994 that the Racial Justice Act was an attempt to root out bias among decision-makers on death sentencing.

"Decision-makers in death sentencing—like those in other endeavors, such as voting, employment or jury selection—rarely, if ever, admit that they are racially biased," said Edwards, who at the time, was chairman of the House Civil and Constitutional Rights Committee.

According to the National Center for Policy Analysis in Dallas, the racial makeup of murderers indicates no great disparity nationally for the percentage of blacks on death row (42 percent) and the percentage charged with homicide (48 percent).

In July 1991, Bright testified before the House Subcommittee on Civil and Constitutional Rights. "We make significant public policy decisions based upon a finding that a smoker is 1.7 times more likely to die of heart disease than a nonsmoker," he said, "but we ignore the fact that in Georgia, a person accused of murdering a white person is 4.3 times more likely to be sentenced to death than a person accused of murdering a black (person)."

Bright noted that prosecutors' decisions on who will face the death penalty are highly subjective, and there are no statewide standards that govern when the death penalty is sought.

Mississippi, for example, can impose the death penalty for forcible rape of a person under 14 years old. And in Montana, a state prison inmate who has a prior homicide conviction, or been previously declared a persistent felony offender, can be executed for a deliberate attempted homicide, aggravated assault or aggravated kidnapping.

"The system is nothing to write home about, especially when it deals with the question of who should live and who should die," Bright said.

What Works? What Matters? Recidivism among Probationers in North Carolina

by Mark Jones, Ph.D., and Darrell L. Ross, Ph.D., East Carolina University, Criminal Justice Program (NC)

The phrase "what works" has been associated with several areas of criminal justice policy, but corrections in particular. Since Robert Martinson's (1974) report on prison rehabilitation painted a very bleak picture of correctional intervention's effectiveness, at least 60 articles or books, as well as numerous technical reports and conference papers, have addressed that question with regard to some aspect of criminal justice. Policy makers and legislators constantly search for what works in probation, parole, intermediate sanctions and prison.

Defining and measuring what works is problematic. Traditionally, community corrections administrators and researchers have used low recidivism as a principle measure of success. Feeley and Simon (1992) suggested that high recidivism can be viewed as a success in the sense that programs that catch individuals breaking the law, or the rules, are insuring public safety. Los Angeles County Probation Chief Barry Nidorf (1995) suggested that low recidivism be abandoned as a measuring stick of program effectiveness. In an article describing crime victims as the "Conscience of Community Corrections," Sinclair (1997) stated that the fixation on recidivism as-

sures "an aura of failure by measuring . . . the ignorant one dimensional, win-lose dichotomy of offender recidivism" (Sinclair 1997; 12).

Sinclair's point that community corrections is about more than guarding against recidivism is well taken by the authors, both of whom are former probation officers, one in Georgia and one in Michigan. Nevertheless, recidivism remains one measure by which many community corrections programs are evaluated. Many policy makers hope that corrections officials can devise the right program that will not only prevent recidivism while under supervision, but that such a program will be the permanent baptismal cure that will cause an offender to "sin no more."

In North Carolina, the General Assembly requires the Sentencing and Policy Advisory Commission to examine recidivism among the state's community-based correction programs. The time frame for our study was fiscal year 1992-93, or July 1, 1992, through June 30, 1993. The General Assembly mandated that offenders be tracked for recidivism, and the legislation defined recidivism as rearrest within two years or more after assignment to a program or release from prison.[1]

The term "recidivism" can be defined many ways, and any definition is problematic. For instance, the definition used in this study—fingerprinted rearrest within two years or more—did not include:

1) crimes committed but not reported to law enforcement;

2) crimes reported to law enforcement that did not result in an arrest;

3) crimes committed in other states, unless the crime resulted in extradition from North Carolina to that state;

4) crimes other than those requiring fingerprinting; and[2]

5) crimes that should have been fingerprinted and reported to DCI by local law enforcement agencies but were not.

Such a definition of recidivism also assumes that each fingerprinted arrestee is guilty of the offense with which he/she has been charged, which is not always true. Many arrests eventually result in acquittal, dismissal or reduction of charges.

Despite these shortcomings, the working definition of recidivism is the most useful for a study of this kind, given the improved sophistication of information systems in criminal justice agencies. While the definition for the current study no doubt resulted in isolated inaccuracies, it

Table 1

Recidivism of Program Participants

Program	Number of Participants in Study	Number of Participants Rearrested	Program Impact on Recidivism
Regular Probation	18,966	4,362(23%)	No significant relation to recidivism.
Intensive Probation	2,088	1,274(61%)	Correlated with property, drug, and "other" rearrests.
Electronic House Arrest	1,254	839(67%)	Slight association with property rearrests.
IMPACT (boot camp)	340	175(52%)	No significant relation to recidivism.
Special Probation	2,105	842(40%)	No significant relation to recidivism.
Community Service	7,302	1,658(23%)	No significant relation to recidivism.
TASC	563	196(35)	No significant relation to recidivism.
Community Penalty	252	86(34)	Correlated with avoiding for violent and drug offenses.

provides some overall indicators of recidivism among the programs examined.

The study included: Community Penalties Program[3] (COMPEN), Treatment Alternatives to Street Crime[4] (TASC), Community Service Work Program[5], regular probation, regular parole, intensive probation" intensive parole, electronic house arrest, "special probation" or split sentence, and the Intensive Motivational Program of Alternative Correctional Treatment (IMPACT), or "boot camp" program.

Our objective was to examine which characteristics were associated with whether a person was rearrested, and if he/she was arrested, for what type of offense. In addition to participation in a correctional program or sanction, the following characteristics were included in the analysis on all individuals:
1) age,
2) race,
3) gender,
4) marital status,
5) county size,
6) whether the person pled guilty,
7) whether the person had a monetary condition (over $100) attached as a condition of release or probation,
8) current offense, and
9) number of prior arrests.

The information contained in the client assessment instrument also was included. This included the score recorded by the classifying officer on the following items:
1) number of address changes in the past year,
2) age at first conviction,
3) past alcohol problems,
4) past drug addiction,
5) probationer attitude,
6) employment stability,
7) financial situation,
8) types of friends/associates,
9) educational attainment,
10) prior periods of probation/parole supervision, and
11) prior or current weapons convictions.

Frequencies and means were used to develop a preliminary assessment of the performances (in terms of rearrests) of the program participants. These simple, "univariate," descriptive statistics do not necessarily provide accurate indicators of characteristics that with rear distinguish program participants or identify characteristics associated with recidivism. Table 1 includes the number of offenders rearrested within the various programs. It also includes the impact that participation in a program had on recidivism, when the other factors mentioned earlier were taken into account.

In order to develop a more accurate measure of what factors were associated with rearrest, we used a form of multivariate (more than one variable) analysis called logistic regression. Logistic regression allowed us to examine whether a particular program, or a personal characteristic (independent variable) was a significant correlate of committing a new offense.

There were four logistic regression models conducted. Each of the models measured indicators, or predictors, of four outcomes: rearrest for a violent or sexual offense; rearrest for a property offense; rearrest for a drug offense; and rearrest for other types of offenses not included in categories two, three or four. We did not include rearrests for probation or parole violations, nonfelonious traffic offenses, or civil actions, such as failure to appear in court.

Most of the offenders participated in more than one program. For instance, an offender could have participated in TASC, Community Penalties, IMPACT, regular probation, electronic house arrest, intensive probation and community service, all on one sentence. Plus, the offender could have been ordered to pay a fine, court costs or restitution as a condition of the sentence. We controlled for participation in other programs in the logistic regression models.

Most of the programs had no significant effect on being rearrested or avoiding rearrest. The exceptions included intensive probation, which was a significant indicator of being rearrested for property, drug and other offenses. Even though electronic house arrest had a higher percentage of its participants rearrested, its impact on recidivism, when all factors were taken into account, was only slight. COMPEN was the only program that seemed to have an effect on avoiding rearrest.

Table 2 contains a summary of the other variables and their correlation with recidivism. Personal factors like age, race, substance abuse history, gender, education level, prior weapons convictions, and current offense were more important correlates of recidivism than was participation in a program. Some of the client assessment and personal variables were included in the analysis, but were not associated significantly with being rearrested or avoiding rearrest. Those variables were: number of address changes in the past year, employment, marital status and types of friends or associates.

Implications

While North Carolina policy makers and program practitioners cannot claim that their programs were the magic bullet needed to "cure" criminal behavior, neither should they despair to a great extent. Rearrest, or avoiding rearrest, for those in Regular Probation, IMPACT (boot camp), Special Probation, Community service and TASC, seems more dependent on personal factors than on the program.

The high recidivism rates and correlation with recidivism for Intensive Probation and Electronic House Arrest should be cause for concern. While we do not intend to act as apologists or defenders of those programs, we think that several factors should be considered when evaluating these two programs. Intensive probation was designed as a prison alternative. Therefore, it is reasonable to assume that the program would attract a high-risk clientele. These individuals stood a greater chance of recidivating than regular probationers; such was and always has been the nature of the program.

Officers who supervise intensive probationers sometimes report the names of their clients to local law enforcement officials. We are not suggesting that law enforcement unfairly targets these individuals, but being put on a list of people to watch increases the likelihood of being arrested by those doing the watching. North Carolina's Intensive Probation program uses a team approach to supervision. The team is composed of a probation officer who is responsible for supervising the case and at least one surveillance officer, whose primary responsibility is making field visits. Many of the surveillance officers who assist intensive probation officers, especially those hired in the early 1980s and early 1990s, had law enforcement experience, quite often in the same jurisdiction where they worked as a surveillance officer. This also increased the closeness of the relationship between intensive probation teams and law enforcement.

Between 1988 and 1992, North Carolina experienced the greatest percentage increase in crime rate of any state in the nation Morgan et al. 1994). During this time, North Carolina was experiencing a tremendous prison and court docket crowding crisis. Intensive probation served as an outlet for this backlog, since it and EHA-probation were designed to divert offenders from being incarcerated.

The study reported here was part of a larger study that included released prisoners in addition to participants in the programs mentioned in this article. When the author of the original study presented the findings from the larger study before the Justice and Public Safety Appropriations Subcommittee of the North Carolina House of Representatives, one legislator questioned the utility of pouring money into intensive probation. The first author reminded this legislator that though recidivism for the program was high, it was only slightly higher than that of prisoners who were either paroled, or prisoners who "maxed out," that is, served all of their time and were released into the community with no supervision. The author's words to the legislator were "pick your poison." Either continue to use intensive probation and hope that future rearrests and incarceration can be avoided, or go to the expense of incarcerating these same individuals and expect similar recidivism outcomes once they are released with no way to monitor

Table 2

Other Characteristics' Impact on Recidivism

Characteristic	Relation to Recidivism
Age	Being young was associated weakly with rearrest for violent offenses.
Age at first conviction	Being 17–23 when first convicted was associated with avoiding rearrest for drug offenses.
Alcohol Problem	Having no alcohol problem was associated with avoiding rearrest for drug offenses.
Attitude	Being "unwilling to accept responsibility" was associated with avoiding rearrest for other offenses. Having a receptive or extremely negative attitude was insignificant.
Race	Being African-American was associated with rearrest for violent, drug and property offenses, in that order. Race was not a factor with regard to other offenses.
Gender	Being male was associated with rearrest for violent, property; drug and other offenses.
Education	Being classified as a high school graduate, or an enrolled student, was associated with rearrest for violent and property offenses. Both high school graduates and those with some high school were likely to avoid rearrest for drug offenses.
Financial Situation	Having "no known difficulty" was associated with avoiding rearrest for drug offenses.
Monetary Condition as Part of Sentence	Monetary conditions were associated with avoiding rearrests for violent offenses, drug offenses and other offenses.
Past Drug Problems	Past problems was associated with rearrest for property and drug offenses.
Plea of guilty	Having pled guilty was associated with rearrest for drug offenses.
County size	Being from suburban vs. rural counties was associated with rearrest for drug offenses.
Prior/current weapons conviction	Prior convictions were associated with rearrest for violent, property and drug offenses.
Current Offense	Being under sentence for "other" felonies was associated strongly with avoiding rearrest for property; drug and other offenses. Being under sentence for drug felonies and drug misdemeanors was correlated with avoiding rearrest for drug offenses. Being under sentence for a drug felony was associated with avoiding rearrest for "other" offenses.
Prior Arrest Record	In several cases, having numerous prior arrests was associated with avoiding rearrest. This probably was due to "aging out." As offenders aged, they were less likely to be arrested than younger people, even if the older people had more serious prior records.
Prior probation/ parole supervision	Prior supervision associated with rearrest for "other" offenses.

them or quickly respond to their violations of the law.

The punitive, or surveillance-oriented programs included in the study were either insignificant in relation to recidivism or were associated with being rearrested. The

only program that seemed to impact future criminal activity positively on an aggregate level was Community Penalties. Just as high recidivism for intensive probation could be due to factors not controlled for in our analysis, the low recidivism associated with COMPEN also may have been due to other unknown factors. However, with the rehabilitative ideal having fallen into disrepute over the past three decades, we think it is worth noting that the one program that was associated with avoiding rearrest, at least for violent and drug offenses, was a program that emphasizes a rehabilitative ideal.

While we have discussed the statistically significant findings from our study, we think there is one statistically insignificant finding that merits some attention. Regular probation, often described as a "slap-on-the-wrist" punishment, has been maligned in numerous studies and books as a danger to public safety. Some people under regular probation supervision do commit crimes, both while under supervision, and after being released from probation. Such occurrences always are regrettable and sometimes are tragic. In our study, regular probation, along with community service, had the lowest recidivism of any program. Our multivariate analysis indicated that participation in regular probation was inconsequential in terms of being rearrested or avoiding rearrest.

This slap-on-the-wrist punishment does not appear to pose the danger suggested by at least two prominent writings. The California-based RAND study released in the 1980's suggested that felony probation (our study included felons and misdemeanors) posed a threat to public safety (Petersilia et al. 1985). William Bennett et al.'s (1996) *Body Count* provides some interesting insights on the causes of crime (moral poverty) and suggestions on combating drug abuse. However, though *Body Count's* authors use some empirical and generalizable evidence in their criticisms of community corrections, they also have joined the chorus of condemning regular probation largely by anecdote, rather than by the more rigorous means used in our study.

Conclusion

Our original questions in this article were, what works, and what matters? Though we cannot draw definitive conclusions regarding what works or what does not work in terms of program intervention,

we can draw some inference about what matters. What seems to matter more than program assignment can be found by examining the information in Table 2.

Note some of the characteristics associated with recidivism: youth, gender, prior alcohol or drug problems, being African-American and being from a large county. Our findings partially support Samuel Walker's (1994) position that crime is not a justice system problem. Our results suggest that correctional intervention may make a difference in some cases. Our results also indicate that the problems of young, black males in densely populated areas cannot be fixed simply by creating a new program or the aboliting an existing one.

References

Bennett, William J., John J. Dilulio Jr. and John P Walters. *Body Count: Moral Poverty . . . and How to Win America's War Against Crime and Drugs.* New York: Simon and Schuster (1996).

Clarke, Stevens H. and Anita L. Harrison. *Recidivism of Criminal Offenders Assigned to Community Correctional Programs or Released from Prison in North Carolina in 1989.* Chapel Hill, NC: Institute of Government (1992).

Feeley, Malcolm M. and Jonathan Simon. "The New Penology: Notes on the Emerging Strategy of Corrections and Its Implications." *Criminology* 30 (4): 449–474 (1992).

Martinson, Robert. "What Works-Questions and Answers About Prison Reform." *The Public Interest* 35: 22–54 (1974).

Morgan, Kathleen O'Leary, Scott Morgan and Neal Quitno (eds.). *Crime State Rankings 1994.* Lawrence, KS: Morgan Quitno Corporation (1994).

Nidorf, Barry J. "Recidivism-Let's Get Rid of It." *Perspectives* 19(1): 6–10(1995).

Petersilia, Joan, Susan Turner and Joyce Peterson. *Granting Felons Probation: Public Risks and Alternatives.* Santa Monica, CA: RAND Corporation (1985).

Sinclair, Jim. "Victims of Crime: The Conscience of Community Corrections." *Perspectives* (Winter): 12–14 (1997).

Walker, Samuel. *Sense and Nonsense about Crime and Drugs: A Policy Guide,* Third Edition. Belmont, CA: Wadsworth Publishing (1994).

Endnotes

1. Chapter 507, Section 21.2, 1995 Session of the North Carolina General Assembly.
2. According to Clarke and Harrison (1992), everyone arrested for felonies in North Carolina must be fingerprinted and those prints must be sent to the State Bureau of Investigation's Division of Criminal Information. The senior resident Superior Court judge develops a plan indicating that misdemeanor arrests are submitted to the DCI. Generally, those arrested for traffic offenses, except serious offenses such as hit and run, and driving while impaired, are not fingerprinted, and most of those that are fingerprinted are not submitted to the DCI.
3. COMPEN targets convicted misdemeanants and felons who are eligible for a nonprison punishment and who are facing an imminent and substantial threat of imprisonment. COMPEN officials prepare detailed community penalty plans for presentation to the sentencing judge by the defendant's attorney, or at the request of the sentencing judge.
4. COMPEN is unique in that it is not a postadjudicatory program. COMPEN also contracts and arranges services with public or private agencies and monitors offender compliance with the recommended course of treatment. COMPEN plans often involve some combination of programs including intensive supervision, community service and substance abuse treatment.
5. The primary target group for TASC is drug dependent offenders. TASC programs work with both pre and post adjudicated individuals. Only post adjudicated offenders were included here. TASC coordinators initially screen offenders for substance abuse, then link them to appropriate treatment resources and monitor treatment progress. Approximately one-third of TASC clients are in pretrial status.
6. TASC coordinators are in frequent contact with treatment specialists, and periodic progress reports are submitted to the client's probation officer by TASC officials. TASC clients are required to have at least one monthly contact with their caseworker. Periodic urinalysis screening is required. The program typically lasts four to six months.
7. We should note that our study did not include misdemeanor traffic offenders, which includes the vast majority of drunk drivers. Since drunk drivers compose a large number of the community service population, the impact of community service work could not be assessed with much accuracy in this study.

The Death Penalty in 1996: Year End Report

Executions in 1996 Second Highest Since 1976

The overall pace of executions in the United States remained high in 1996 and the prospects for the future are for even greater numbers of people put to death each year. As of December 17, there were 45 executions, mostly by lethal injection. This represents a slight drop

laws designed to speed up executions. Some of these new laws created a legal logjam as courts considered the constitutionality of the curtailed appeal process.

Texas, the nation's leader in executions for many years, virtually stopped executions this year pending

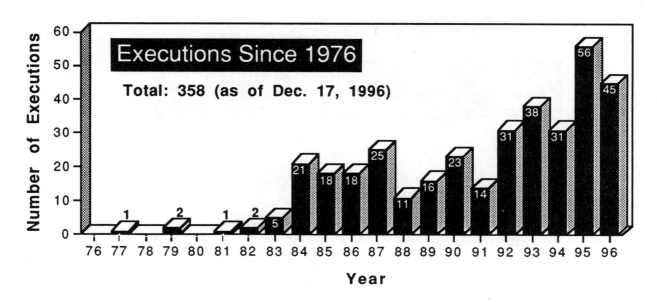

from last year when 56 executions represented the highest number since capital punishment was reinstated in 1976. The 20% decrease in executions this year was probably due to the passage of numerous federal and state

resolution of a challenge to the state's new appeal laws. Once that matter is resolved, Texas will likely renew and even accelerate its frequent executions. On the federal level, Congress passed the Antiterrorism and Effective

The Death Penalty in 1996: Year End Report, December 1996, pp. 1-7. Reprinted by permission of the Death Penalty Information Center.

Death Penalty Act of 1996 which will make it increasingly difficult for even innocent defendants on death row to secure federal review. Congress also eliminated all money for the death penalty resource centers which had been overseeing a major portion of death penalty appeals. Both of these pieces of legislation will result in less thorough representation for those on death row.

This year, the five states with the largest death rows (California, Texas, Florida, Pennsylvania and Illinois) together were responsible for only 8 executions. But these same states have over 1,500 people on death row, indicating that the likelihood for increased executions in the near future is great.

out this year, only 4 involved the murder of a black victim, even though blacks are murdered as often as whites in the U.S. (one additional case involved black and white victims). No white person was executed this year for the murder of a black person, while ten black men were executed for crimes involving white victims. This sends a message that black lives are worth less than white lives. Since the death penalty was reinstated, 90 black men have been executed for the murder of a white victim, while only 4 white men have been executed for the murder of a black victim.

In Kentucky, a recent study found that none of the people on that state's death row were there for the mur-

States With Most Executions Since 1976		States With Highest Per Capita Execution Rate (per 100,000 pop. since 1976)		States With Most Executions in 1996	
Texas	107	Delaware	1.20	Virginia	8
Florida	38	Texas	0.63	South Carolina	6
Virginia	37	Virginia	0.60	Missouri	6
Missouri	23	Louisiana	0.55	Delaware	3
Louisiana	23	Arkansas	0.51	Texas	3

Racial Disparities Even More Prominent

Although the number of people executed varies from year to year, the typical death row inmate remains the same. He is likely to be a poor man who never graduated from high school. He is likely to be a member of a minority. And with only rare exceptions, he has been convicted of murdering a white person. Almost all of the executions this year involved a case with a white victim in the underlying murder. Of the 45 executions carried

der of a black person, despite the fact that there have been over 1,000 blacks murdered in Kentucky since the death penalty was reinstated. Legislation to prevent further racial injustice failed by one vote in the state legislature.

The federal death penalty continues to be targeted mainly at minorities. Almost 80% of those for whom the federal government sought the death penalty under either the "drug kingpin law" of 1988 or the 1994 Crime Bill have been black or Hispanic.

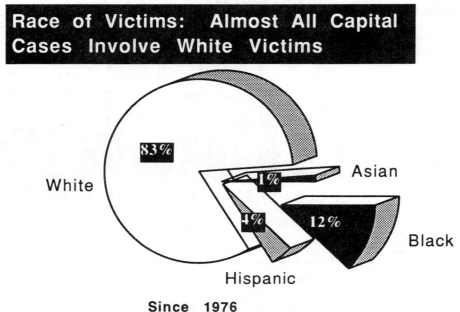

Race of Victims: Almost All Capital Cases Involve White Victims

White 83%

Asian 1%

Hispanic 4%

Black 12%

Since 1976

Death Penalty Reality Often Differs from Expectations

Many of those executed in 1996 did not fit the stereotype of death row inmates as repeat killers who stalk strangers. In fact, many of the cases this year involved murders by close acquaintances of the victim:

- **William Flamer** was executed in Delaware for killing his aunt and uncle.
- **Jeffrey Paul Sloan** was executed in Missouri for murdering his brother and was suspected of killing other family members.
- **James Clark** was executed in Delaware for killing his adoptive parents.
- **Joseph Savino** was executed in Virginia for the murder of his male lover when the relationship went sour.
- **Fred Kornahrens** was executed in South Carolina for killing his ex-wife, her father and her 10-year-old stepson. Kornahrens said he went out of control when his marriage broke up.
- **Emmett Nave** was executed in Missouri for murdering his landlady after confrontations about his apartment.
- **Thomas Battle** was put to death in Missouri for the murder of an 82-year-old neighbor who had befriended him.
- **William Frank Parker** was executed in Arkansas for murdering the parents of his former wife. He also shot his wife, but she survived.
- **Joe Gonzales** was executed in Texas only ten months after his conviction for murdering his former boss. Gonzales acted as his own attorney and waived his appeals.
- **Richard Zeitvogel** was executed in Missouri for the murder of a fellow prisoner. The prosecution said he murdered because he *wanted to be placed on death row.*

The most prominent capital case involving family members has been evolving this year in Delaware, the nation's per capita leader in executions. When 18-year-olds Amy Grossberg and Brian Peterson were accused of murdering their newborn infant, Delaware immediately announced that it would seek the death penalty against both of them, without full knowledge of their mental state or other crucial information.

Election Year Politics

This year was an election year, and the death penalty was the focus of both highly publicized punitive legislation and campaigns demanding swifter executions. Bob Dole campaigned in front of California's death row and criticized President Clinton's appointment of judges as soft on crime. Clinton responded by emphasizing his commitment to less federal review for death row inmates. Congress cutback the opportunity for federal habeas corpus and completely defunded the death penalty resource centers. States, too, pushed for more executions. Virginia, Pennsylvania and Ohio, for example, set multiple execution dates for defendants who had not yet completed their normal appeal. This manipulation of execution dates puts additional burdens on the justice system, since every death warrant results in litigation over a stay of execution, independent of the appeal arising from errors in the case.

Electoral races in which the death penalty played a prominent role produced mixed results, with some candidates surviving attacks based on their reservations about capital punishment. Sen. John Kerry of Massachusetts was re-elected in the face of Gov. William Weld's attack on his opposition to the death penalty. In California, Representatives Vic Fazio and Walter Capps were elected to the U.S. House of Representatives, even after extreme accusations that attempted to align them with the murderer of young Polly Klass.

Politicization of judicial selection intensified. One of the latest victims was Tennessee Supreme Court Justice Penny White. White lost her position on the court after a single death penalty decision in which she *upheld* the conviction of a death row inmate, but joined a decision by other justices overturning the death sentence. A conservative anti-tax group mounted a successful campaign against White, erroneously charging her of being weak on crime because of this single decision.

Twenty Years of Capital Punishment

This year marked the 20th anniversary of the Supreme Court's decision in Gregg v. Georgia upholding the constitutionality of the death penalty under newly passed statutes. However, many of the problems which the Court had identified in the application of earlier capital punishment laws, such as its arbitrariness, racial discrimination and the potential for fatal mistakes, still remain.

Innocence: Four more inmates were released from death row in 1996 after charges against them were dropped: Verneal Jimerson (Illinois), Dennis Williams (Illinois), Roberto Miranda (Nev.) and Troy Lee Jones (Calif.). This brings the total number of death row inmates released since 1973 because of evidence of their innocence to 66. In addition, two other death row inmates had their sentences commuted to life because of strong doubts about their guilt: Donald Paradis (Idaho) and Joseph Payne (Virginia). At least four other death row inmates (Joseph Spaziano (Fla.), Donald Gunsby (Fla.), Kerry Max Cook (Tex.) and Lloyd Schlup (Mo.) had their convictions overturned in 1996 and will either be retried or permanently freed from death row.

Prosecutors Indicted: In Illinois, three former prosecutors (one of whom is now a state circuit judge) were indicted for obstructing justice in the mistaken death penalty prosecution of Rolando Cruz and Alejandro Hernandez. Cruz and Hernandez were released in late 1995 after spending years on death row for a crime they did not commit. The indictments allege that the prosecutors and police officers knowingly presented false information and proceeded with the case against individuals whom they should have known were innocent.

Volunteers: An unusually high number of inmates gave up their appeals this year, thereby "volunteering" for execution. Ten of the 45 people executed this year waived their remaining appeals, including three in South Carolina. (Forty-seven of the 358 persons executed since 1976 have waived their appeals.) The isolated and demeaning conditions on death row, coupled with discouragement over an ever narrower appeal process and the lack of representation, seems to be leading more inmates to take part in state-assisted suicide.

Methods of Execution: One man was executed by a firing squad (John Taylor in Utah) and one man was hung (Billy Bailey in Delaware). Seven people were executed in the electric chair, and the remainder were executed by lethal injection. This latter method has been promoted as more humane, but the lethal injection of Tommie Smith in Indiana this year took one hour and seventeen minutes. The executioner could not find a vein in which to inject the poison chemicals. A doctor was summoned, and eventually the lethal injection was made through Smith's leg.

International Trends: The International Commission of Jurists released a report highly critical of the death penalty in the United States, based on its visit here. The report, entitled *Administration of the Death Penalty in the United States,* states: "By ratifying the Political Covenant and the Race Convention, the United States has accepted to submit its system of punishment for criminal offenses to the judgment of international opinion; and opinion in the Western democracies is unanimous that the death penalty offends civilised standards of decency." The Commission particularly singled out the racial disparities and due process violations evident in the use of the death penalty in the U.S.: "The Mission is of the opinion that . . . the administration of capital punishment in the United States continues to be discriminatory and unjust—and hence 'arbitrary'—, and thus not in consonance with Articles 6 and 14 of the Political Covenant and Article 2(c) of the Race Convention."

Other international rights groups, including Human Rights Watch and Amnesty International, issued reports before this year's Olympics in Atlanta criticizing the death penalty in the U.S.

Who Were Executed?

As usual, the death penalty in practice looks different from the death penalty in theory. Here are descriptions of a few who were executed in 1996:

Walter Correll—The first man executed this year was an inmate in Virginia with mental retardation. Correll had an IQ of 68. His two co-defendants blamed the murder on him and received lighter sentences.

Richard Townes, Jr.—The second man executed this year was also from Virginia. Mr. Townes represented himself at trial, questioned no witnesses, and presented no mitigating evidence regarding sentencing. The jury did not know that, had he been sentenced to life, he would never have been eligible for parole. The executioners searched 22 minutes for a suitable vein before injecting the poisonous chemicals into his foot.

Billy Bailey—Bailey was hung in the state of Delaware in January, the first hanging there in 50 years. Bailey's legs were tied with rope, and he wore a black hood which reached to his waist. When the trap door below Bailey was sprung, he dropped and twisted before being pronounced dead by a doctor.

John Taylor—was executed by firing squad in Utah in January. Five state law enforcement officers were paid $300 each to fire their rifles at Taylor's heart, which was marked by a white circle on his blue jumper. One of the five marksmen fired a blank. Taylor waived his appeals and asked to be executed by firing squad, just as the first person executed after the death penalty's reinstatement, Gary Gilmore, was also shot in Utah at his own request.

Stephen Hatch—was executed in Oklahoma for two murders in conjunction with a robbery. Hatch's co-defendant, the actual killer in this case, was sentenced to life in prison. Members of the victims' family watched the execution, thanks to a new law sponsored by one of the family who is now a state senator in Oklahoma. Allowing the victim's family members to view executions became a trend this year.

Ellis Wayne Felker—was electrocuted in Georgia this year. Felker's case attracted attention when the U.S. Supreme Court agreed to hear, on an expedited basis, his challenge to the new law curtailing federal review. Felker won his request to be able to file for review with the Supreme Court, despite apparent restrictions in the new law to such an approach. However, the Supreme Court did not accept his claim that new evidence of his innocence should stop his execution.

Commentary: Some Signs of Change

Although there were many executions in 1996, the long-predicted "flood" of executions has not occurred, and there was some movement away from the death penalty. The movie Dead Man Walking received wide acclaim and an Academy Award, generating much discussion about the wisdom of capital punishment. Sister Helen Prejean, the principal figure portrayed in the movie, traveled the country, engaging audiences with her stories and message of reconciliation. Rev. Jesse Jackson's first book, written with his son, Congressman Jesse Jackson, Jr., focused on the myriad of inequities presented by the death penalty in the United States. And shortly before his own death, Cardinal Joseph Bernadin, a strong opponent of capital punishment, demonstrated an act of compassion by visiting death row inmate Raymond Stewart in Illinois before Stewart was executed.

Virginia, which led the country in executions this year, saw its juries start to turn away from the death penalty once the alternative of life without parole became available to them. Only one person has been sent to death row in Virginia since the new sentence was instituted, whereas six people had been sentenced to death the year before, and ten the year before that. Indiana and Georgia, two other states which have recently instituted life-without-parole statutes, have also experienced a decline in death sentences. In Indiana, only 2 of 19 completed capital cases have resulted in a death sentence since its new law took effect in 1993. This positive movement away from the death penalty is in line with support in opinion polls for life-without-parole as an alternative to the death penalty.

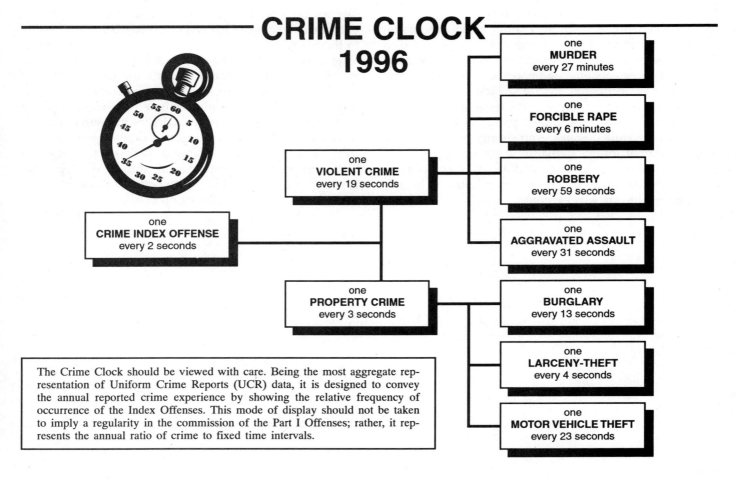

CRIME CLOCK 1996

one CRIME INDEX OFFENSE every 2 seconds	
one VIOLENT CRIME every 19 seconds	one MURDER every 27 minutes
	one FORCIBLE RAPE every 6 minutes
	one ROBBERY every 59 seconds
	one AGGRAVATED ASSAULT every 31 seconds
one PROPERTY CRIME every 3 seconds	one BURGLARY every 13 seconds
	one LARCENY-THEFT every 4 seconds
	one MOTOR VEHICLE THEFT every 23 seconds

The Crime Clock should be viewed with care. Being the most aggregate representation of Uniform Crime Reports (UCR) data, it is designed to convey the annual reported crime experience by showing the relative frequency of occurrence of the Index Offenses. This mode of display should not be taken to imply a regularity in the commission of the Part I Offenses; rather, it represents the annual ratio of crime to fixed time intervals.

Crime in the United States, 1996

The Crime Index total dropped 3 percent to nearly 13.5 million offenses in 1996, the lowest annual serious crime count since 1986 and the fifth consecutive annual decline. The decrease in serious crime was also evident among the Nation's cities, collectively. Within the city population groups, the greatest decrease, 6 percent, was reported in cities having 1 million or more inhabitants. In the suburban and rural counties, decreases of 4 and 2 percent, respectively, were reported.

By geographic region, the largest volume of Crime Index offenses was reported in the most populous Southern States, which accounted for 40 percent of the total. Following were the Western States with 24 percent, the Midwestern States with 21 percent, and the Northeastern States with 15 percent. Crime Index decreases in 1996 as compared to 1995 figures were recorded in the Western States, 8 percent; the Northeastern States, 7 percent; and the Midwestern States, 1 percent. In the South, the 1996 Index total increased 1 percent over the 1995 level.

Crime Index offenses occurred most frequently in July and August and least often in February.

Rate

Crime rates relate the incidence of crime to population. In 1996, there were an estimated 5,079 Crime Index offenses for each 100,000 in United States population, the lowest rate since 1984. The Crime Index rate was highest in the Nation's metropolitan areas and lowest in the rural counties. The national 1996 Crime Index rate fell 4 percent from the 1995 rate, 10 percent from the 1992 level, and 8 percent from the 1987 rate.

Regionally, the Crime Index rates ranged from 5,727 in the South to 3,899 in the Northeast. Two-year percent changes (1996 versus 1995) showed rate declines in all four regions.

Table 1. — Index of Crime, United States, 1987-1996

Population[1]	Crime Index total[2]	Modified Crime Index total[3]	Violent crime[4]	Property crime[4]	Murder and non-negligent man-slaughter	Forcible rape	Robbery	Aggravated assault	Burglary	Larceny–theft	Motor vehicle theft	Arson[3]
					Number of Offenses							
Population by year:												
1987-243,400,000	13,508,700		1,484,000	12,024,700	20,100	91,110	517,700	855,090	3,236,200	7,499,900	1,288,700	
1988-245,807,000	13,923,100		1,566,220	12,356,900	20,680	92,490	542,970	910,090	3,218,100	7,705,900	1,432,900	
1989-248,239,000	14,251,400		1,646,040	12,605,400	21,500	94,500	578,330	951,710	3,168,200	7,872,400	1,564,800	
1990-248,709,873	14,475,600		1,820,130	12,655,500	23,440	102,560	639,270	1,054,860	3,073,900	7,945,700	1,635,900	
1991-252,177,000	14,872,900		1,911,770	12,961,100	24,700	106,590	687,730	1,092,740	3,157,200	8,142,200	1,661,700	
1992-255,082,000	14,438,200		1,932,270	12,505,900	23,760	109,060	672,480	1,126,970	2,979,900	7,915,200	1,610,800	
1993-257,908,000	14,144,800		1,926,020	12,218,800	24,530	106,010	659,870	1,135,610	2,834,800	7,820,900	1,563,100	
1994-260,341,000	13,989,500		1,857,670	12,131,900	23,330	102,220	618,950	1,113,180	2,712,800	7,879,800	1,539,300	
1995-262,755,000[5]	13,862,700		1,798,790	12,063,900	21,610	97,470	580,510	1,099,210	2,593,800	7,997,700	1,472,400	
1996-265,284,000	13,473,600		1,682,280	11,791,300	19,650	95,770	537,050	1,029,810	2,501,500	7,894,600	1,395,200	
Percent change : number of offenses:												
1996/1995	-2.8		-6.5	-2.3	-9.1	-1.7	-7.5	-6.3	-3.6	-1.3	-5.2	
1996/1992	-6.7		-12.9	-5.7	-17.3	-12.2	-20.1	-8.6	-16.1	-.3	-13.4	
1996/1987	-.3		+13.4	-1.9	-2.2	+5.1	+3.7	+20.4	-22.7	+5.3	+8.3	
					Rate per 100,000 Inhabitants							
Year:												
1987	5,550.0		609.7	4,940.3	8.3	37.4	212.7	351.3	1,329.6	3,081.3	529.4	
1988	5,664.2		637.2	5,027.1	8.4	37.6	220.9	370.2	1,309.2	3,134.9	582.9	
1989	5,741.0		663.1	5,077.9	8.7	38.1	233.0	383.4	1,276.3	3,171.3	630.4	
1990	5,820.3		731.8	5,088.5	9.4	41.2	257.0	424.1	1,235.9	3,194.8	657.8	
1991	5,897.8		758.1	5,139.7	9.8	42.3	272.7	433.3	1,252.0	3,228.8	659.0	
1992	5,660.2		757.5	4,902.7	9.3	42.8	263.6	441.8	1,168.2	3,103.0	631.5	
1993	5,484.4		746.8	4,737.6	9.5	41.1	255.9	440.3	1,099.2	3,032.4	606.1	
1994	5,373.5		713.6	4,660.0	9.0	39.3	237.7	427.6	1,042.0	3,026.7	591.3	
1995[5]	5,275.9		684.6	4,591.3	8.2	37.1	220.9	418.3	987.1	3,043.8	560.4	
1996	5,078.9		634.1	4,444.8	7.4	36.1	202.4	388.2	943.0	2,975.9	525.9	
Percent change : rate per 100,000 inhabitants:												
1996/1995	-3.7		-7.4	-3.2	-9.8	-2.7	-8.4	-7.2	-4.5	-2.2	-6.2	
1996/1992	-10.3		-16.3	-9.3	-20.4	-15.7	-23.2	-12.1	-19.3	-4.1	-16.7	
1996/1987	-8.5		+4.0	-10.0	-10.8	-3.5	-4.8	+10.5	-29.1	-3.4	-.7	

[1]Populations are Bureau of the Census provisional estimates as of July 1, except 1990 which [is] the decennial census count.
[2]Because of rounding, the offenses may not add to totals.
[3]Although arson data are included in the trend and clearance tables, sufficient data are not available to estimate totals for this offense.
[4]Violent crimes are offenses of murder, forcible rape, robbery, and aggravated assault. Property crimes are offenses of burglary, larceny-theft, and motor vehicle theft. Data are not included for the property crime of arson.
[5]The 1995 figures have been adjusted.
Complete data were not available for the states of Illinois, Kansas, Kentucky, and Montana; therefore, it was necessary that their crime counts be estimated. An aggregate Florida state total for 1996 was supplied by the Florida Department of Law Enforcement.
All rates were calculated on the offenses before rounding.

Nature

The Crime Index is composed of violent and property crime categories, and in 1996, 12 percent of the Index offenses reported to law enforcement were violent crimes and 88 percent, property crimes. Larceny-theft was the offense with the highest volume, while murder accounted for the fewest offenses.

Property estimated in value at $15.5 billion was stolen in connection with all Crime Index offenses, with the greatest losses due to thefts of motor vehicles; televisions, radios, stereos, etc; and jewelry and precious metals. Nationwide, law enforcement agencies recorded a 38-percent recovery rate for dollar losses in connection with stolen property. The highest recovery percentages were for stolen motor vehicles, consumable goods, livestock, clothing and furs, and firearms.

Law Enforcement Response

In 1996, law enforcement agencies nationwide recorded a 22-percent clearance rate for the collective Crime Index offenses and made an estimated 2.8 million arrests for Index crimes. Crimes can be cleared by arrest or by exceptional means when some element beyond law enforcement control precludes the placing of formal charges against the offender. The arrest of one person may clear several crimes, or several persons may be arrested in connection with the clearance of one offense.

The Index clearance rate has remained relatively stable throughout the past 10-year period. In both 1992 and 1987, the clearance rates were 21 percent.

Total Crime Index arrests, as well as those of adults, dropped 3 percent in 1996 when compared to 1995 figures.

Juvenile arrests for Index crimes decreased 1 percent. By gender, arrests of males decreased 4 percent, and arrests of females showed virtually no change for the 2-year period.

Between 1996 and 1995, declines in the number of persons arrested were recorded for each of the individual offenses composing the Index. Decreases ranged from 10 percent for murder to 1 percent for larceny-theft.

As in the past years, arrests for larceny-theft, estimated at nearly 1.5 million in 1996, accounted for the highest volume of Crime Index arrests.

CRIME INDEX OFFENSES REPORTED

MURDER AND NONNEGLIGENT MANSLAUGHTER

DEFINITION

Murder and nonnegligent manslaughter, as defined in the Uniform Crime Reporting Program, is the willful (nonnegligent) killing of one human being by another.

TREND

Year	Number of offenses	Rate per 100,000 inhabitants
1995	21,606	8.2
1996	19,645	7.4
Percent change	–9.1	–9.8

Volume

In 1996, the estimated number of persons murdered in the United States was 19,645. The 1996 figure was down 9 percent from the 1995 count, 17 percent from the 1992 total, and 2 percent from the 1987 level.

As compared to 1995 figures, murder volumes reported in 1996 dropped 10 percent in the Nation's cities, 9 poercent in suburban counties, and 6 percent in rural counties. The greatest decrease—13 percent—was registered in cities with populations over 1 million and in cities with populations of 250,000 to 499,999.

When viewing the four regions of the Nation, the Southern States, the most populous region, accounted for 43 percent of the murders. The Western States reported 23 percent; the Midwestern States, 20 percent; and the Northeastern States, 14 percent. All regions showed declines in the number of murders reported from 1995 to 1996. The greatest drops were experienced in the Northeast and West, each with 13 percent. Decreases of 7 percent were recorded both in the South and Midwest.

Monthly figures show that in 1996 most murders occurred in August while the fewest were committed in March and April.

Rate

Down 10 percent from the 1995 rate, the national murder rate in 1996 was 7.4 per 100,000 inhabitants, the lowest since 1985. Five- and 10-year trends show the 1996 rate was 20 percent lower than in 1992 and 11 percent below the 1987 rate.

On a regional basis, the South averaged 9 murders per 100,000 people; the West 8 per 100,000; the Midwest, 6 per 100,000, and the Northeast, 5 per 100,000. Compared to 1995 rates, murder rates in 1996 declined in all of the four geographic regions, with the West experiencing the greatest change, a 14-percent decrease, and the Midwest, the smallest, a 7-percent drop.

The Nation's metropolitan areas reported a 1996 murder rate of 8 victims per 100,000 inhabitants. In both the rural counties and cities outside metropolitan areas, the rate was 5 per 100,000.

Nature

Supplemental data were provided by contributing agencies for 15,848 of the estimated 19,645 murders in 1996. Submitted monthly, the data consist of the age, sex, and race of both victims and offenders; the types of weapons used; the relationships of victims to the offenders; and the circumstances surrounding the murders.

Based on this information, 77 percent of the murder victims in 1996 were males; and 87 percent were persons 18 years of age or older. Forty-three percent were ages 20 through 34. The percentages of whites and blacks murdered were equal at 49 percent, and other races accounted for the remainder.

Supplemental data were also reported for 18,108 murder offenders in 1996. Of those for whom sex and age were re-

Murder by Month, 1992-1996
[Percent distribution]

Months	1992	1993	1994	1995	1996
January	8.1	8.1	8.2	8.3	8.7
February	7.5	6.7	7.6	6.8	7.7
March	8.2	7.9	8.8	7.6	7.6
April	8.0	7.6	8.1	8.4	7.6
May	8.5	7.8	8.2	7.9	8.4
June	7.9	8.6	8.3	8.2	8.7
July	9.1	9.3	9.0	8.9	8.8
August	9.1	9.2	9.2	9.9	9.0
September	8.7	8.3	8.3	8.6	8.3
October	8.0	8.4	8.5	8.8	8.5
November	8.1	8.2	7.9	8.0	8.0
December	8.8	9.8	8.0	8.6	8.8

Murder Victims by Race and Sex, 1996

Race of Victim	Sex of Victims			
	Total	Male	Female	Unknown
Total White Victims	7,647	5,596	2,048	3
Total Black Victims	7,638	6,201	1,434	3
Total Other Race Victims	425	310	115	—
Total Unknown Race	138	88	34	16
Total Victims[1]	15,848	12,195	3,631	22

[1] Total murder victims for whom supplemental data were received.

ported, 90 percent of the offenders were males, and 86 percent were persons 18 years of age or older. Sixty-nine percent were ages 17 through 34. Of offenders for whom race was known, 52 percent were black, 45 percent were white, and the remainder were persons of other races.

Murder is most often intraracial among victims and offenders. In 1996, data based on incidents involving one victim and one offender show that 93 percent of the black murder victims were slain by black offenders, and 85 percent of the white murder victims were killed by white offenders. Likewise, males were most often slain by males (89 percent in single victim/single offender situations). These same data show, however, that 9 of every 10 female victims were murdered by males.

FORCIBLE RAPE

DEFINITION

Forcible rape, as defined in the Program, is the carnal knowledge of a female forcibly and against her will. Assaults or attempts to commit rape by force or threat of force are also included; however, statutory rape (without force) and other sex offenses are excluded.

TREND

Year	Number of offenses	Rate per 100,000 inhabitants
1995	97,470	37.1
1996	95,769	36.1
Percent change	−1.7	−2.7

Volume

The 95,769 forcible rapes reported to law enforcement agencies across the Nation during 1996 represented the lowest total since 1989. The 1996 count was 2 percent lower than in 1995, and 12 percent below the 1992 level, but 5 percent higher than the 1987 volume.

Geographically, 39 percent of the forcible rape total in 1996 was accounted for by the most populous Southern States, 25 percent by the Midwestern States, 23 percent by the Western States, and 13 percent by the Northeastern States. Two-year

Forcible Rape by Month, 1992-1996
[Percent distribution]

Months	1992	1993	1994	1995	1996
January	7.0	7.7	7.5	7.7	7.9
February	7.6	6.9	7.3	7.1	7.9
March	8.6	8.5	8.3	8.5	8.1
April	8.5	8.2	8.4	8.0	8.1
May	8.9	8.9	8.9	8.9	9.0
June	8.7	9.2	9.2	8.5	8.8
July	9.4	9.7	9.7	9.4	9.5
August	9.6	9.3	9.6	9.9	9.1
September	8.7	8.3	8.7	8.8	8.8
October	8.4	8.1	8.5	8.7	8.5
November	7.6	7.5	7.3	7.8	7.4
December	7.0	7.7	6.5	6.9	6.9

trends show that forcible rapes declined 5 percent in the Midwest, and 3 percent in the West. Totals for the Northeast and the South remained virtually unchanged from the 1995 level.

Monthly totals show the lowest volume occurred in December, while the largest number of forcible rapes was reported during the month of July.

Rate

By Uniform Crime Reporting definition, the victims of forcible rape are always female, and in 1996, an estimated 71 of every 100,000 females in the country were reported rape victims. The 1996 female forcible rape rate was 1 percent lower than the 1995 rate and 15 percent lower than the 1992 rate.

The Nation's metropolitan areas recorded the highest forcible rape rate in 1996, 75 victims per 100,000 females. In cities outside metropolitan areas, the rate was 68 per 100,000 females, and in rural counties, it was 47 per 100,000 females. Although metropolitan areas record the highest rape rates, they have shown the only rate decline over the past 10 years (1987–1996), 10 percent. During this same period, the rate increased in cities outside metropolitan areas by 45 percent and in rural counties by 31 percent.

By region in 1996, the highest female rape rate was in the Southern States, which recorded 79 victims per 100,000 females. Following were the Midwestern States with a rate of 75; the Western States with a rate of 73; and the Northeastern States with a rate of 49. Since 1995, forcible rape rates declined 4 percent in the Midwest, 3 percent in the West and 1 percent in the South. The Northeast's rate remained the same.

Over the last 10 years, female forcible rape rate decreases were recorded in two regions. Rates in the Northeast and West showed 14- and 12-percent decreases, respectively, and those [in] the Southern and Midwestern States increased 4 percent each.

Nature

Rapes by force constitute the greatest percentage of total forcible rapes, 87 percent of the 1996 incidents. The remainder were attempts or assaults to commit forcible rape. The number of rapes by force decreased 3 percent in 1996 from the 1995 volume, and attempts to rape decreased 4 percent.

As with all other Crime Index offenses, complaints of forcible rape made to law enforcement agencies are sometimes found to be false or baseless. In such cases, law enforcement agencies "unfound" the offenses and exclude them from crime counts. The "unfounded" rate, or percentage of complaints determined through investigation to be false, is higher for forcible rape than for any other Index crime. Eight percent of forcible rape complaints in 1996 were "unfounded," while the average for all Index crimes was 2 percent.

Law Enforcement Response

In 1996, over half of the forcible rapes reported to law enforcement nationwide were cleared by arrest or exceptional means. Rural and suburban county law enforcement clearance rates, each at 53 percent, were slightly higher than the city law enforcement clearance rate at 52 percent.

By geographic region, forcible rape clearance rates in 1996 were 57 percent in the South, 53 percent in the Northeast, 49 percent in the Midwest, and 46 percent in the West.

Of the total clearances for forcible rape in the country as a whole, 12 percent involved only persons under 18 years of age. The percentage of juvenile involvement varied by community type, ranging from 11 percent in the Nation's cities to 13 percent in rural counties.

Participating law enforcement agencies throughout the Nation made an estimated 33,050 arrests for forcible rape in 1996. Of the forcible rate arrestees, 44 percent were under age 25. Fifty-six percent of those arrested were white.

The national arrest total for forcible rape fell 2 percent from 1995 to 1996. Arrests also declined 2 percent both in the Nation's cities and rural counties and 1 percent in the suburban counties.

ROBBERY

DEFINITION

Robbery is the taking or attempting to take anything of value from the care, custody, or control of a person or persons by force or threat of force or violence and/or by putting the victim in fear.

TREND

Year	Number of offenses	Rate per 100,000 inhabitants
1995	580,509	220.9
1996	537,050	202.4
Percent change	−7.5	−8.4

Volume

Nationally, the 1996 estimated robbery total, 537, 050, was the lowest since 1987. The robbery volume for 1996 was down 7 percent from the 1995 national total and registered an 8-percent decrease in the Nation's cities. The largest decline—10 percent—was reported by cities with 1 million or more inhabitants. During the same period, the robbery volume dropped 6 percent in suburban counties and fell 2 percent in rural counties.

Regionally, the Southern States, the most populous area of the Nation, accounted for 35 percent of all reported robberies. The Western States followed with 24 percent, the Northeastern States with 22 percent, and the Midwestern States with 19 percent. Two-year trends show the number of robberies in 1996 was down in all regions as compared to 1995 figures. The Northeast and Midwest marked an 11-percent decrease, the West an 8-percent drop, and the South a 3-percent decline.

In 1996, the number of robbery offenses was 20 percent lower than in 1992 but 4 percent higher than in 1987.

Monthly volume figures for 1996 show robberies occurred most frequently in January and December and least often in April.

Robbery by Month, 1992-1996
[Percent distribution]

Months	1992	1993	1994	1995	1996
January	9.0	8.8	8.7	8.6	9.0
February	8.0	7.1	7.7	7.3	7.9
March	8.1	8.3	8.6	8.0	8.1
April	7.8	7.4	8.0	7.5	7.7
May	7.9	7.5	8.0	7.8	8.0
June	7.9	8.1	8.0	8.0	8.0
July	8.4	8.7	8.5	8.5	8.3
August	8.6	8.8	8.8	8.9	8.5
September	8.3	8.4	8.3	8.5	8.3
October	8.7	9.0	8.8	9.3	8.7
November	8.3	8.5	8.2	8.7	8.5
December	9.0	9.4	8.4	8.9	9.0

Rate

The national robbery rate in 1996 was 202 per 100,000 people, 8 percent lower than in 1995. In metropolitan areas, the 1996 rate was 244; in cities outside metropolitan areas, it was 71; and in the rural areas, it was 16. With 674 robberies per 100,000 inhabitants, the highest rate was recorded in cities with populations 1 million and over.

Robbery rates per 100,000 inhabitants declined in all regions from 1995 to 1996. The rates of 232 in the Northeast and 161 in the Midwest were down 11 percent. The West's rate of 219 was 9 percent lower than it was in 1995, and the South's rate of 203 was down 4 percent.

Nature

During 1996, losses estimated at nearly $500 million were attributed to robberies. The value of property stolen averaged $929 per robbery, up from $873 in 1995. Average dollar losses in 1996 ranged from $487 taken during robberies of gas or service stations to $4,207 per bank robbery. The impact of this violent crime on its victims cannot be measured in terms of monetary loss alone. While the object of a robbery is to obtain money or property, the crime always involves force or threat of force, and many victims suffer serious personal injury.

More than half (51 percent) of the offenses in this category during 1996 were robberies on streets or highways. Robberies of commercial and financial establishments accounted for 24 percent, and those occurring at residences, 11 percent. The remainder were miscellaneous types. All robbery types declined in 1996 as compared to 1995 totals, with the exception

Robbery, Percent Distribution, 1996
[By region]

	United States Total	North-eastern States	Mid-western States	Southern States	Western States
Total[1]	100.0	100.0	100.0	100.0	100.0
Street/highway	51.2	65.6	60.3	44.7	47.0
Commercial house	13.5	8.3	11.1	14.2	16.3
Gas or service station	2.4	2.5	3.0	2.2	2.5
Convenience store	5.9	4.5	4.1	7.6	5.5
Residence	10.6	7.7	9.8	14.1	8.8
Bank	2.0	1.3	1.7	1.6	3.0
Miscellaneous	14.4	10.3	10.1	15.6	17.0

[1] Because of rounding, percentages may not add to totals.

of bank robbery which increased by 14 percent. Among the remaining robbery types, decreases ranged from 11 percent for those committed on streets and highways to less than 1 percent for commercial house robberies.

AGGRAVATED ASSAULT

DEFINITION

Aggravated assault is an unlawful attack by one person upon another for the purpose of inflicting severe or aggravated bodily injury. This type of assault is usually accompanied by the use of a weapon or by means likely to produce death or great bodily harm.

TREND

Year	Number of offenses	Rate per 100,000 inhabitants
1995	1,099,207	418.3
1996	1,029,814	388.2
Percent change	−6.3	−7.2

Volume

Aggravated assaults decreased in 1996, marking the third consecutive year of decline. Accounting for 61 percent of violent crimes in 1996, the total of 1,029,814 aggravated assaults represented a 6-percent drop for this offense.

Forty-one percent of the aggravated assault volume was accounted for by the Southern Region, the Nation's most populous area. Following were the Western Region with 24 percent, the Midwestern Region with 20 percent, and the Northeastern Region with 15 percent. All of the Nation's regions registered decreases in the number of reported aggravated assaults.

The 1996 monthly figures show that the greatest number of aggravated assaults was recorded during July while the lowest volume occurred during February and November.

The Nation's cities collectively experienced a decrease of 7 percent in the aggravated assault volume from 1995 to 1996. Among all city population groupings, decreases ranged from 9 percent in cities with populations from 50,000 to 99,999 to 4 percent in cities with 500,000 to 999,999 inhabitants. The number of aggravated assaults decreased 9 percent in suburban counties and 5 percent in the rural counties during the same 2-year period.

Five- and 10-year trends for the country as a whole show aggravated assaults 9 percent lower than in 1992 and 20 percent above the 1987 figure.

Rate

In 1996, there were 388 reported victims of aggravated assault for every 100,000 people nationwide, the lowest rate since 1989. The rate was 7 percent lower than in 1995 and 12 percent below the 1992 rate. The 1996 rate was, however, 11 percent higher than the 1987 rate.

Aggravated Assault by Month, 1992-1996
[Percent distribution]

Months	1992	1993	1994	1995	1996
January	7.3	7.5	7.2	7.6	7.8
February	7.3	6.5	7.0	7.0	7.5
March	8.0	8.1	8.3	8.1	8.0
April	8.7	8.3	8.5	8.3	8.2
May	9.2	8.9	8.8	8.8	8.9
June	8.9	9.1	8.9	8.8	9.0
July	9.4	9.6	9.5	9.4	9.3
August	9.1	9.2	9.4	9.4	9.2
September	8.6	8.3	8.9	8.9	8.6
October	8.5	8.5	8.7	8.7	8.5
November	7.6	7.4	7.7	7.5	7.5
December	7.4	8.6	7.3	7.4	7.6

Higher than the national average, the rate in metropolitan areas was 424 per 100,000 inhabitants in 1996. Cities outside metropolitan areas experienced a rate of 350 and rural counties, a rate of 177.

Regionally, the aggravated assault rate was 293 per 100,000 people in the Northeast, 331 in the Midwest, 428 in the West, and 454 in the South. Compared to 1995 rates, 1996 aggravated assault rates were down in all regions. The West marked an 11-percent decline, the Northeast and Midwest each recorded declines of 8 percent, and the South registered a 4-percent drop.

Nature

In 1996, 34 percent of the aggravated assaults were committed with blunt objects or other dangerous weapons. Personal weapons such as hands, fists, and feet were used in 26 percent of the assaults; firearms in 22 percent; and knives or cutting instruments in 18 percent.

When broken down by weapon, aggravated assaults in all four weapon categories decreased from the previous year's totals. Assault decreases were as follows: firearms, 10 percent; personal weapons (hands, fists, feet, etc.), 9 percent; knives or other cutting instruments, 7 percent; and other dangerous weapons, 3 percent.

Aggravated Assault, Types of Weapons Used, 1996
[Percent distribution by region]

Region	Total all weapons[1]	Firearms	Knives or cutting instruments	Other weapons (clubs, blunt objects, etc.)	Personal weapons
Total	100.0	22.0	18.1	34.4	25.5
Northeastern States	100.0	12.8	19.5	38.7	28.9
Midwestern States	100.0	25.0	19.1	36.6	19.3
Southern States	100.0	25.2	19.7	34.1	20.9
Western States	100.0	20.7	14.2	31.0	34.2

[1] Because of rounding, percentages may not add to total.

BURGLARY

DEFINITION

The Uniform Crime Reporting Program defines burglary as the unlawful entry of a structure to commit a felony or theft. The use of force to gain entry is not required to classify an offense as burglary.

TREND

Year	Number of offenses	Rate per 100,000 inhabitants
1995	2,593,784	987.1
1996	2,501,524	943.0
Percent change	−3.6	−4.5

Volume

During 1996, the estimated 2.5 million burglaries in the United States was the lowest total in more than two decades. Distribution figures for the regions showed that the highest burglary volume in 1996, 42 percent, occurred in the most populous Southern States. The Western States followed with 23 percent, the Midwestern States with 20 percent, and the Northeastern States with 14 percent.

In 1996, the greatest number of burglaries occurred during July while the lowest number took place in February.

The burglary volume dropped 4 percent nationwide during 1996 as compared to the 1995 total. By population group, the Nation's cities overall experienced a 4-percent decline; the largest decrease was in cities with populations of 1 million and over, which showed a 7-percent decline. Suburban and rural counties also recorded decreases, 6 percent and 3 percent, respectively.

Three of the four regions of the United States reported decreases in burglary volumes in 1996 as compared to the previous year's figures. The Northeastern States registered a 9-percent decline; the Western States, an 8-percent decrease; and the Midwestern States, a 2-percent decline. The Southern States recorded a 1-percent increase in burglary volumes.

Burglary by Month, 1992-1996
[Percent distribution]

Months	1992	1993	1994	1995	1996
January	8.6	8.3	7.9	8.4	8.3
February	7.7	6.9	7.1	7.2	7.6
March	8.2	8.2	8.2	8.2	7.8
April	7.8	7.7	8.0	7.7	7.8
May	8.2	8.0	8.5	8.4	8.3
June	8.1	8.4	8.3	8.3	8.2
July	9.0	9.0	9.2	9.0	9.1
August	9.0	9.1	9.4	9.2	9.0
September	8.4	8.5	8.6	8.5	8.6
October	8.3	8.4	8.6	8.8	8.8
November	8.2	8.1	8.4	8.3	8.0
December	8.3	9.3	7.9	8.1	8.5

Long-term national trends show burglary down 16 percent from the 1992 level and down 23 percent compared to the 1987 volume.

Rate

The burglary rate in 1996, lower than in any other year in more than two decades, was 943 per 100,000 inhabitants nationwide. The rate was 4 percent lower than in 1995, down 19 percent from the 1992 level, and 29 percent below the 1987 rate. In 1996, the burglary rate for every 100,000 in population was 993 in the metropolitan areas, 935 in the cities outside metropolitan areas, and 620 in the rural counties.

Looking at the Nation's regions, the burglary rate was 2,129 in the Southern States, 1,003 in the Western States, 817 in the Midwestern States, and 691 in the Northeastern States. A comparison of 1995 and 1996 rates showed declines of 10 percent in the West, 9 percent in the Northeast, 3 percent in the Midwest, and 1 percent in the South.

Nature

As in previous years, 2 of every 3 burglaries in 1996 were residential in nature. Sixty-six percent of all burglaries involved forcible entry, 26 percent were unlawful entries (without force), and the remainder were forcible entry attempts. Offenses for which time of occurrence was reported showed that 51 percent of burglaries happened during daytime hours and 49 percent at night. Fifty-nine percent of residential burglaries occurred during the daytime, and 65 percent of nonresidential burglaries occurred during nighttime hours.

Losses estimated at $3.3 billion in 1996 were suffered by burglary victims, and the average dollar loss per burglary was $1,332. The average loss for residential offenses was $1,350 and for nonresidential offenses, $1,296. Compared to 1995 losses, the 1996 average loss for both residential and nonresidential property increased.

Both residential and nonresidential burglary volumes declined 4 percent in 1996 from the previous year's figures.

LARCENY-THEFT

DEFINITION

Larceny-theft is the unlawful taking, carrying, leading, or riding away of property from the possession or constructive possession of another. It includes crimes such as shoplifting, pocket-picking, purse-snatching, thefts from motor vehicles, thefts of motor vehicle parts and accessories, bicycle thefts, etc., in which no use of force, violence, or fraud occurs.

TREND

Year	Number of offenses	Rate per 100,000 inhabitants
1995	7,997,710	3,043.8
1996	7,894,620	2,975.9
Percent change	−1.3	−2.2

Larceny–theft by Month, 1992-1996

[Percent distribution]

Months	1992	1993	1994	1995	1996
January	8.2	7.7	7.4	7.9	7.9
February	7.8	6.8	7.1	7.1	7.5
March	8.3	8.0	8.1	8.1	8.0
April	8.1	8.0	8.1	7.8	8.1
May	8.2	8.2	8.5	8.5	8.6
June	8.5	8.7	8.6	8.6	8.6
July	9.1	9.2	9.2	9.1	9.2
August	9.1	9.3	9.5	9.4	9.2
September	8.4	8.3	8.5	8.5	8.4
October	8.6	8.6	8.9	8.8	8.7
November	7.9	8.0	8.3	8.1	7.8
December	8.0	9.1	7.9	8.1	8.0

Volume

Estimated at nearly 7.9 million offenses during 1996, larceny-theft comprised 59 percent of the Crime Index total and 67 percent of the property crimes. Continuing the pattern of recent years, larceny-thefts were recorded most often during the months of July and August and least frequently in February.

The Nation's most populous region, the Southern States, recorded 40 percent of the larceny-theft total. Both the Western States and Midwestern States recorded 23 percent, and the Northeastern States, 14 percent.

In 1996, the volume of larceny-thefts nationwide was 1 percent lower than the 1995 total. By community type, decreases of 2 percent were recorded both in cities collectively and suburban counties. A 1-percent decline was experienced in the rural counties.

In two of the four geographic regions, incidents of larceny-theft decreased from 1995 levels. The decreases were 6 percent in the West and 5 percent in the Northeast. The South recorded an increase of 2 percent, and the Midwest showed an increase of less than 1 percent.

An examination of long-term national trends indicated larceny was up 5 percent when compared to the 1987 total. However, there was virtually no change when compared to the 1992 level.

Rate

During 1996, the larceny-theft rate was 2,976 per 100,000 inhabitants in the United States. Two-, 5- and 10-year trends show the rate was 2 percent below the 1995 rate, 4 percent lower than the rate in 1992, and 3 percent below the 1987 rate. The 1996 rate was 3,188 per 100,000 inhabitants of metropolitan areas; 3,695 per 100,000 population in cities outside metropolitan areas; and 1,083 per 100,000 people in the rural counties.

By Region, the 1996 larceny-theft rate per 100,000 inhabitants in the South increased 1 percent. The West recorded an 8-percent decline, and the Northeast marked a 5-percent drop. The Midwest's rate showed virtually no change from the 1995 level. The regional rates ranged from 2,181 per 100,000 people in the Northeast to 3,368 per 100,000 population in the South.

Nature

During 1996, the average value of property stolen due to larceny-theft was $532, down from $535 in 1995. When the average value was applied to the estimated number of larceny-thefts, the loss to victims nationally was over $4 billion for the year. This estimated dollar loss is considered conservative since many offenses in the larceny category never come to law enforcement attention, particularly if the value of the stolen goods is small. Losses under $50 and those over $200 jointly accounted for 77 percent of the thefts reported to law enforcement. The remainder involved losses ranging from $50 to $200.

Losses of goods and property reported stolen as a result of pocket-picking averaged $320; purse-snatching, $296; and shoplifting, $120. The average value loss due to thefts of motor vehicle accessories was $387 and for thefts of bicycles, $263. Thefts from buildings resulted in an average loss of $894; from motor vehicles, $518; and from coin-operated machines, $296.

Thefts of motor vehicle parts, accessories, and contents made up the largest portion of reported larcenies—36 percent. Also contributing to the high volume of thefts were shoplifting, accounting for 15 percent; thefts from buildings, 13 percent; and thefts of bicycles, 6 percent. The remainder was distributed among pocket-picking, purse-snatching, thefts from coin-operated machines, and all other types of larceny-thefts. Table below presents the distribution of larceny-theft by type and geographic region.

Larceny Analysis by Region, 1996

[Percent distribution]

	United States Total	Northeastern States	Midwestern States	Southern States	Western States
Total[1]	100.0	100.0	100.0	100.0	100.0
Pocket-picking	.4	1.1	.3	.3	.4
Purse-snatching	.6	1.0	.6	.5	.5
Shoplifting	15.4	15.5	14.4	14.5	17.1
From motor vehicles (except accessories)	25.3	23.6	23.5	23.1	30.4
Motor vehicle accessories	10.7	9.1	11.9	10.8	10.6
Bicycles	5.6	7.7	6.1	4.3	5.9
From buildings	12.7	16.9	15.9	9.9	12.5
From coin-operated machines	.6	.6	.5	.7	.6
All others	28.7	24.4	26.9	36.0	22.1

[1] Because of rounding, percentages may not add to total.

MOTOR VEHICLE THEFT

DEFINITION

Defined as the theft or attempted theft of a motor vehicle, this offense category includes the stealing of automobiles, trucks, buses, motorcycles, motorscooters, snowmobiles, etc.

TREND

Year	Number of offenses	Rate per 100,000 inhabitants
1995	1,472,491	560.4
1996	1,395,192	525.9
Percent change	–5.2	–6.2

Motor Vehicle Theft by Month, 1992-1996

[Percent distribution]

Months	1992	1993	1994	1995	1996
January	8.8	8.5	8.2	8.6	8.7
February	7.9	7.3	7.4	7.5	8.0
March	8.2	8.2	8.5	8.2	8.2
April	7.8	7.8	8.0	7.8	8.0
May	8.1	7.9	8.2	8.2	8.2
June	8.2	8.4	8.3	8.1	8.1
July	8.8	8.9	8.9	8.6	8.7
August	8.9	8.9	9.1	9.0	8.6
September	8.2	8.4	8.4	8.4	8.2
October	8.6	8.6	8.8	8.9	8.6
November	8.3	8.3	8.4	8.5	8.2
December	8.2	8.8	7.8	8.3	8.5

Volume

During 1996, there were nearly 1.4 million thefts of motor vehicles nationwide, marking the lowest total for that offense since 1987. The regional distribution of thefts in 1996 showed 35 percent of the volume was in the Southern States, 28 percent in the Western States, 20 percent in the Midwestern States, and 17 percent in the Northeastern States.

An examination of the monthly distribution of motor vehicle thefts reveals the highest percentage of vehicles was stolen during the months of January and July, and the lowest percentage was stolen in February and April.

In the Nation and in cities as a whole, motor vehicle thefts declined 5 percent from 1995 to 1996. Among city population groupings, the decreases ranged from 7 percent in cities 1 million and over in population and those with populations of 100,000 to 499,999 to less than 1 percent in cities with populations under 25,000. During the same 2-year period, a 6-percent decrease in the volume of motor vehicle thefts occurred in suburban counties, while rural counties registered virtually no change.

Geographically, decreases in motor vehicle thefts were recorded in the West, with 12 percent; in the Northeast, with 8 percent; and in the Midwest, with 1 percent. The South recorded virtually no change.

. . . [T]he volume of motor vehicle thefts in 1996 declined 13 percent from the 1992 volume.

Rate

The 1996 national motor vehicle theft rate—526 per 100,000 inhabitants—was 6 percent lower than in 1995 and 17 percent below the 1992 rate. The 1996 rate was less than 1 percent below the 1987 rate.

For every 100,000 inhabitants living in metropolitan areas, there were 616 motor vehicle thefts reported in 1996. The rate in cities outside metropolitan areas was 238 and that in rural counties, 126. As in previous years, the highest rates were in the Nation's most heavily populated municipalities, indicating that this offense is primarily a large-city problem. For every 100,000 inhabitants in cities with populations over 250,000, the 1996 motor vehicle theft rate was 1,223. The Nation's smallest cities, those with fewer than 10,000 inhabitants, recorded a rate of 247 per 100,000.

Among all regions of the country, motor vehicle theft rates ranged from 666 per 100,000 inhabitants in the Western States to 443 in the Midwestern States. The Southern States' rate was 524, and the Northeastern States' rate was 472. All regions registered rate declines from 1995 to 1996. The West reported the greatest rate decrease, 13 percent. The Northeast reported a decrease of 9 percent, the Midwest, a decrease of 2 percent; and the South, a decrease of 1 percent.

An estimated average of 1 of every 147 registered motor vehicles was stolen nationwide during 1996. Regionally, this rate was greatest in the West where 1 of every 114 motor vehicles registered was stolen. The other three regions reported lesser rates—1 per 147 in the Northeast, 1 per 149 in the South, and 1 per 191 in the Midwest.

Motor Vehicle Theft, 1996

[Percent distribution by region]

Region	Total[1]	Autos	Trucks and buses	Other vehicles
Total	100.0	78.3	16.5	5.2
Northeastern States	100.0	90.4	5.9	3.7
Midwestern States	100.0	81.5	13.5	4.9
Southern States	100.0	75.5	18.3	6.2
Western States	100.0	72.5	22.4	5.1

[1] Because of rounding, percentages may not add to total.

Nature

The estimated value of motor vehicles stolen nationwide in 1996 was nearly $7.5 billion. At the time of theft, the average value per vehicle was $5,372. The recovery percentage for the value of vehicles stolen was higher than for any other property type. Relating the value of vehicles stolen to the value of those recovered resulted in a 68-percent recovery rate for 1996.

Seventy-eight percent of all motor vehicles reported stolen during the year were automobiles, 16 percent were trucks or buses, and the remainder were other types.

Glossary

Abet: To encourage another to commit a crime.

Accessory: One who harbors, assists, or protects another person, although he or she knows that person has committed or will commit a crime.

Accomplice: One who knowingly and voluntarily aids another in committing a criminal offense.

Acquit: To free a person legally from an accusation of criminal guilt.

Adjudicatory hearing: The fact-finding process wherein the court determines whether or not there is sufficient evidence to sustain the allegations in a petition.

Admissible: Capable of being admitted; in a trial, such evidence as the judge allows to be introduced into the proceeding.

Affirmance: A pronouncement by a higher court that the case in question was rightly decided by the lower court from which the case was appealed.

Affirmation: Positive declaration or assertion that the witness will tell the truth; not made under oath.

Alias: Any name by which one is known other than his or her true name.

Alibi: A type of defense in a criminal prosecution that proves the accused could not have committed the crime with which he or she is charged, since evidence offered shows the accused was in another place at the time the crime was committed.

Allegation: An assertion of what a party to an action expects to prove.

American Bar Association (ABA): A professional association, comprising attorneys who have been admitted to the bar in any of the 50 states, and a registered lobby.

American Civil Liberties Union (ACLU): Founded in 1920 with the purpose of defending the individual's rights as guaranteed by the U.S. Constitution.

Amnesty: A class or group pardon.

Annulment: The act, by competent authority, of canceling, making void, or depriving of all force.

Appeal: A case carried to a higher court to ask that the decision of the lower court, in which the case originated, be altered or overruled completely.

Appellate court: A court that has jurisdiction to hear cases on appeal; not a trial court.

Arbitrator: The person chosen by parties in a controversy to settle their differences; private judges.

Arraignment: The appearance before the court of a person charged with a crime. He or she is advised of the charges, bail is set, and a plea of "guilty" or "not guilty" is entered.

Arrest: The legal detainment of a person to answer for criminal charges or civil demands.

Autopsy: A postmortem examination of a human body to determine the cause of death.

Bail: Property (usually money) deposited with a court in exchange for the release of a person in custody to ensure later appearance.

Bail bond: An obligation signed by the accused and his or her sureties that ensures his or her presence in court.

Bailiff: An officer of the court who is responsible for keeping order in the court and protecting the security of jury deliberations and court property.

Bench warrant: An order by the court for the apprehension and arrest of a defendant or other person who has failed to appear when so ordered.

Bill of Rights: The first 10 amendments to the U.S. Constitution that state certain fundamental rights and privileges that are guaranteed to the people against infringement by the government.

Biocriminology: A relatively new branch of criminology that attempts to explain criminal behavior by referring to biological factors which predispose some individuals to commit criminal acts. See also Criminal biology.

Blue laws: Laws in some jurisdictions prohibiting sales of merchandise, athletic contests, and the sale of alcoholic beverages on Sundays.

Booking: A law-enforcement or correctional process officially recording an entry-into-detention after arrest and identifying the person, place, time, reason for the arrest, and the arresting authority.

Breathalizer: A commercial device to test the breath of a suspected drinker and determine that person's blood-alcohol content.

Brief: A summary of the law relating to a case, prepared by the attorneys for both parties and given to the judge.

Bug: To plant a sound sensor or to tap a communication line for the purpose of surreptitious listening or audio monitoring.

Burden of proof: Duty of establishing the existence of fact in a trial.

Calendar: A list of cases to be heard in a trial court, on a specific day, and containing the title of the case, the lawyers involved, and the index number.

Capital crime: Any crime that may be punishable by death or imprisonment for life.

Career criminal: A person having a past record of multiple arrests or convictions for crimes of varying degrees of seriousness. Such criminals are often described as chronic, habitual, repeat, serious, high-rate, or professional offenders.

Case: At the level of police or prosecutorial investigation, a set of circumstances under investigation involving one or more persons.

Case law: Judicial precedent generated as a by-product of the decisions that courts have made to resolve unique disputes. Case law concerns concrete facts, as distinguished from statutes and constitutions, which are written in the abstract.

Change of venue: The removal of a trial from one jurisdiction to another in order to avoid local prejudice.

Charge: In criminal law, the accusation made against a person. It also refers to the judge's instruction to the jury on legal points.

Circumstantial evidence: Indirect evidence; evidence from which a fact can be reasonably inferred, although not directly proven.

Clemency: The doctrine under which executive or legislative action reduces the severity of or waives legal punishment of one or more individuals, or an individual exempted from prosecution for certain actions.

Code: A compilation, compendium, or revision of laws, arranged into chapters, having a table of contents and index, and promulgated by legislative authority. See also penal code.

Coercion: The use of force to compel performance of an action; The application of sanctions or the use of force by government to compel observance of law or public policy.

Common law: Judge-made law to assist courts through decision making with traditions, customs, and usage of previous court decisions.

Commutation: A reduction of a sentence originally prescribed by a court.

Complainant: The victim of a crime who brings the facts to the attention of the authorities.

Complaint: Any accusation that a person committed a crime that has originated or been received by a law enforcement agency or court.

Confession: A statement by a person who admits violation of the law.

Confiscation: Government seizure of private property without compensation to the owner.

Conspiracy: An agreement between two or more persons to plan for the purpose of committing a crime or any unlawful act or a lawful act by unlawful or criminal means.

Contempt of court: Intentionally obstructing a court in the administration of justice, acting in a way calculated to lessen its authority or dignity, or failing to obey its lawful order.

Continuance: Postponement or adjournment of a trial granted by the judge, either to a later date or indefinitely.

Contraband: Goods, the possession of which is illegal.

Conviction: A finding by the jury (or by the trial judge in cases tried without a jury) that the accused is guilty of a crime.

Corporal punishment: Physical punishment.

Corpus delicti (Lat.): The objective proof that a crime has been committed as distinguished from an accidental death, injury, or loss.

Corrections: Area of criminal justice dealing with convicted offenders in jails, prisons; on probation or parole.

Corroborating evidence: Supplementary evidence that tends to strengthen or confirm other evidence given previously.

Crime: An act injurious to the public, which is prohibited and punishable by law.

Crime Index: A set of numbers indicating the volume, fluctuation, and distribution of crimes reported to local law enforcement agencies for the United States as a whole.

Crime of passion: An unpremeditated murder or assault committed under circumstances of great anger, jealousy, or other emotional stress.

Criminal biology: The scientific study of the relation of hereditary physical traits to criminal character, that is, to innate tendencies to commit crime in general or crimes of any particular type. *See also* Biocriminology.

Criminal insanity: Lack of mental capacity to do or refrain from doing a criminal act; inability to distinguish right from wrong.

Criminal intent: The intent to commit and act, the results of which are a crime or violation of the law.

Criminalistics: Crime laboratory procedures.

Criminology: The scientific study of crime, criminals, corrections, and the operation of the system of criminal justice.

Cross examination: The questioning of a witness by the party who did not produce the witness.

Culpable: At fault or responsible, but not necessarily criminal.

Defamation: Intentional causing, or attempting to cause, damage to the reputation of another by communicating false or distorted information about his or her actions, motives, or character.

Defendant: The person who is being prosecuted.

Deliberation: The action of a jury to determine the guilt or innocence, or the sentence, of a defendant.

Demurrer: Plea for dismissal of a suit on the grounds that, even if true, the statements of the opposition are insufficient to sustain the claim.

Deposition: Sworn testimony obtained outside, rather than in, court.

Deterrence: A theory that swift and sure punishment will discourage others from similar illegal acts.

Dilatory: Law term that describes activity for the purpose of causing a delay or to gain time or postpone a decision.

Direct evidence: Testimony or other proof that expressly or straightforwardly proves the existence of fact.

Direct examination: The first questioning of witnesses by the party who calls them.

Directed verdict: An order or verdict pronounced by a judge during the trial of a criminal case in which the evidence presented by the prosecution clearly fails to show the guilt of the accused.

District attorney: A locally elected state official who represents the state in bringing indictments and prosecuting criminal cases.

Docket: The formal record of court proceedings.

Double jeopardy: To be prosecuted twice for the same offense.

Due process model: A philosophy of criminal justice based on the assumption that an individual is presumed innocent until proven guilty.

Due process of law: A clause in the Fifth and Fourteenth Amendments ensuring that laws are reasonable and that they are applied in a fair and equal manner.

Embracery: An attempt to influence a jury, or a member thereof, in their verdict by any improper means.

Entrapment: Inducing an individual to commit a crime he or she did not contemplate, for the sole purpose of instituting a criminal prosecution against the offender.

Evidence: All the means used to prove or disprove the fact at issue. *See also Corpus delicti.*

Ex post facto (Lat.): After the fact. An *ex post facto* law is a criminal law that makes an act unlawful although it was committed prior to the passage of that law. *See also* Grandfather clause.

Exception: A formal objection to the action of the court during a trial. The indication is that the excepting party will seek to reverse the court's actions at some future proceeding.

Exclusionary rule: Legal prohibitions against government prosecution using evidence illegally obtained.

Expert evidence: Testimony by one qualified to speak authoritatively on technical matters because of her or his special training of skill.

Extradition: The surrender by one state to another of an individual accused of a crime.

False arrest: Any unlawful physical restraint of another's freedom of movement; unlawful arrest.

Felony: A criminal offense punishable by death or imprisonment in a penitentiary.

Forensic: Relating to the court. Forensic medicine would refer to legal medicine that applies anatomy, pathology, toxicology, chemistry, and other fields of science in expert testimony in court cases or hearings.

Grand jury: A group of 12 to 23 citizens of a county who examine evidence against the person suspected of a crime and hand down an indictment if there is sufficient evidence. *See also* Petit jury.

Grandfather clause: A clause attempting to preserve the rights of firms in operation before enactment of a law by exempting these firms from certain provisions of that law. *See also Ex post facto.*

Habeas corpus (Lat.): A legal device to challenge the detention of a person taken into custody. An individual in custody may demand an evidentiary hearing before a judge to examine the legality of the detention.

Hearsay: Evidence that a witness has learned through others.

Homicide: The killing of a human being; may be murder, negligent or nonnegligent manslaughter, or excusable or justifiable homicide.

Hung jury: A jury which, after long deliberation, is so irreconcilably divided in opinion that it is unable to reach a verdict.

Impanel: The process of selecting the jury that is to try a case.

Imprisonment: A sentence imposed upon the conviction of a crime; the deprivation of liberty in a penal institution; incarceration.

In camera (Lat.): A case heard when the doors of the court are closed and only persons concerned in the case are admitted.

Indemnification: Compensation for loss or damage sustained because of improper or illegal action by a public authority.

Indictment: The document prepared by a prosecutor and approved by the grand jury that charges a certain person with a specific crime or crimes for which that person is later to be tried in court.

Injunction: An order by a court prohibiting a defendant from committing an act, or commanding an act be done.

Inquest: A legal inquiry to establish some question of fact; specifically, and inquiry by a coroner and jury into a person's death where accident, foul play, or violence is suspected as the cause.

Instanter: A subpoena issued for the appearance of a hostile witness or person who has failed to appear in answer to a previous subpoena and authorizing a law enforcement officer to bring that person to the court.

Interpol (International Criminal Police Commission): A clearing house for international exchanges of information consisting of a consortium of 126 countries.

Jeopardy: The danger of conviction and punishment that a defendant faces in a criminal trial.

Judge: An officer who presides over and administers the law in a court of justice.

Judicial notice: The rule that a court will accept certain things as common knowledge without proof.

Judicial process: The procedures taken by a court in deciding cases or resolving legal controversies.

Jurisdiction: The territory, subject matter, or persons over which lawful authority may be exercised by a court or other justice agency, as determined by statute or constitution.

Jury: A certain number of persons who are sworn to examine the evidence and determine the truth on the basis of that evidence.

Jury, hung: A trial jury which, after exhaustive deliberations, cannot agree on a unanimous verdict, necessitating an mistrial and a subsequent retrial.

Justice of the peace: A subordinate magistrate, usually without formal legal training, empowered to try petty civil and criminal cases and, in some states, to conduct preliminary hearings for persons accused of a crime, and to fix bail for appearance in court.

Juvenile delinquent: A boy or girl who has not reached the age of criminal liability (varies from state to state) and who commits an act which would be a misdemeanor or felony if he or she were an adult. Delinquents are tried in Juvenile Court and confined to separate facilities.

Law Enforcement Agency: A federal, state, or local criminal justice agency or identifiable subunit whose principal functions are the prevention, detection, and investigation of crime and the apprehension of alleged offenders.

Libel and slander: Printed and spoken defamation of character, respectively, or a person or an institution. In a slander action, it is usually necessary to prove specific damages caused by spoken words to recover, but in a case of libel, the damage is assumed to have occurred by publication.

Lie detector: An instrument that measures certain physiological reactions of the human body from which a trained operator may determine whether the subject is telling the truth or lying; polygraph; psychological stress evaluator.

Litigation: A judicial controversy; a contest in a court of justice for the purpose of enforcing a right; any controversy that must be decided upon evidence.

Mala fides **(Lat.):** Bad faith, as opposed to *bona fides,* or good faith.

Mala in se **(Lat.):** Evil in itself. Acts that are made crimes because they are, by their nature evil and morally wrong.

Mala prohibita **(Lat.):** Evil because they are prohibited. Acts that are not wrong in themselves but which, to protect the general welfare, are made crimes by statute.

Malfeasance: The act of a public officer in committing a crime relating to his official duties or powers. Accepting or demanding a bribe.

Malice: An evil intent to vex, annoy, or injure another; intentional evil.

Mandatory sentences: A statutory requirement that a certain penalty shall be set and carried out in all cases upon conviction for a specified offense or series of offenses.

Martial law: Refers to control of civilian populations by a military commander.

Mediation: Nonbinding third-party intervention in the collective bargaining process.

Mens rea **(Lat.):** Criminal intent.

Miranda rights: Set of rights that a person accused or suspected of having committed a specific offense has during interrogation and of which he or she must be informed prior to questioning, as stated by the Supreme Court in deciding *Miranda v. Arizona* in 1966 and related cases.

Misdemeanor: Any crime not a felony. Usually, a crime punishable by a fine or imprisonment in the county or other local jail.

Misprison: Failing to reveal a crime.

Mistrial: A trial discontinued before reaching a verdict because of some procedural defect or impediment.

Modus operandi: A characteristic pattern of behavior repeated in a series of offenses that coincides with the pattern evidenced by a particular person or group of persons.

Motion: An oral or written request made to a court at any time before, during, or after court proceedings, asking the court to make a specified finding, decision, or order.

Motive: The reason for committing a crime.

Municipal court: A minor court authorized by municipal charter or state law to enforce local ordinances and exercise the criminal and civil jurisdiction of the peace.

Narc: A widely used slang term for any local or federal law enforcement officer whose duties are focused on preventing or controlling traffic in and the use of illegal drugs.

Negligent: Culpably careless; acting without the due care required by the circumstances.

Neolombrosians: Criminologists who emphasize psychopathological states as causes of crime.

No bill: A phrase used by a grand jury when it fails to indict.

Nolle prosequi **(Lat.):** A prosecutor's decision not to initiate or continue prosecution.

Nolo contendere **(Lat., lit.):** A pleading, usually used by a defendant in a criminal case, that literally means "I will not contest."

Notary public: A public officer authorized to authenticate and certify documents such as deeds, contracts, and affidavits with his or her signature and seal.

Null: Of no legal or binding force.

Obiter dictum **(Lat.):** A belief or opinion included by a judge in his or her decision in a case.

Objection: The act of taking exception to some statement or procedure in a trial. Used to call the court's attention to some improper evidence or procedure.

Opinion evidence: A witness's belief or opinion about a fact in dispute, as distinguished from personal knowledge of the fact.

Ordinance: A law enacted by the city or municipal government.

Organized crime: An organized, continuing criminal conspiracy that engages in crime as a business (e.g., loan sharking, illegal gambling, prostitution, extortion, etc.).

Original jurisdiction: The authority of a court to hear and determine a lawsuit when it is initiated.

Overt act: An open or physical act done to further a plan, conspiracy, or intent, as opposed to a thought or mere intention.

Paralegals: Employees, also known as legal assistants, of law firms, who assist attorneys in the delivery of legal services.

Pardon: There are two kinds of pardons of offenses: the absolute pardon, which fully restores to the individual all rights and privileges of a citizen, setting aside a conviction and penalty, and the conditional pardon, which requires a condition to be met before the pardon is officially granted.

Parole: A conditional, supervised release from prison prior to expiration of sentence.

Penal code: Criminal codes, the purpose of which is to define what acts shall be punished as crimes.

Penology: The study of punishment and corrections.

Peremptory challenge: In the selection of jurors, challenges made by either side to certain jurors without assigning any reason, and which the court must allow.

Perjury: The legal offense of deliberately testifying falsely under oath about a material fact.

Perpetrator: The chief actor in the commission of a crime, that is, the person who directly commits the criminal act.

Petit jury: The ordinary jury composed of 12 persons who hear criminal cases and determines guilt or innocence of the accused. *See also* Grand jury.

Plaintiff: A person who initiates a court action.

Plea-bargaining: A negotiation between the defense attorney and the prosecutor in which the defendant receives a reduced penalty in return for a plea of "guilty."

Police power: The authority to legislate for the protection of the health, morals, safety and welfare of the people.

Postmortem: After death. Commonly applied to an examination of a dead body. *See also* Autopsy.

Precedent: Decision by a court that may serve as an example or authority for similar cases in the future.

Preliminary hearing: The proceeding in front of a lower court to determine if there is sufficient evidence for submitting a felony case to the grand jury.

Premeditation: A design to commit a crime or commit some other act before it is done.

Presumption of fact: An inference as to the truth or falsity of any proposition or fact, made in the absence of actual certainty of its truth or falsity or until such certainty can be attained.

Presumption of innocence: The defendant is presumed to be innocent and the burden is on the state to prove his or her guilt beyond a reasonable doubt.

Presumption of law: A rule of law that courts and judges must draw a particular inference from a particular fact or evidence, unless the inference can be disproved.

Probable cause: A set of facts and circumstances that would induce a reasonably intelligent and prudent person to believe that a particular person had committed a specific crime; reasonable grounds to make or believe an accusation.

Probation: A penalty placing a convicted person under the supervision of a probation officer for a stated time, instead or being confined.

Prosecutor: One who initiates a criminal prosecution against an accused. One who acts as a trial attorney for the governments as the representative of the people.

Public defender: An attorney appointed by a court to represent individuals in criminal proceedings who do not have the resources to hire their own defense council.

Rap sheet: Popularized acronym for record of arrest and prosecution.

Reasonable doubt: That state of mind of jurors when they do not feel a moral certainty about the truth of the charge and when the evidence does not exclude every other reasonable hypothesis except that the defendant is guilty as charged.

Rebutting evidence: When the defense has produced new evidence that the prosecution has not dealt with, the court, at its discretion, may allow the prosecution to give evidence in reply to rebut or contradict it.

Recidivism: The repetition of criminal behavior.

Repeal: The abrogation of a law by the enacting body, either by express declaration or implication by the passage of a later act whose provisions contradict those of the earlier law.

Reprieve: The temporary postponement of the execution of a sentence.

Restitution: A court requirement that an alleged or convicted offender pay money or provide services to the victim of the crime or provide services to the community.

Restraining order: An order, issued by a court of competent jurisdiction, forbidding a named person, or a class of persons, from doing specified acts.

Retribution: A concept that implies that payment of a debt to society and thus the expiation of one's offense. It was codified in the biblical injunction, "an eye for an eye, a tooth for a tooth."

Sanction: A legal penalty assessed for the violation of law. The term also includes social methods of obtaining compliance, such as peer pressure and public opinion.

Search warrant: A written order, issued by judicial authority in the name of the state, directing a law enforcement officer to search for personal property and, if found, to bring it before the court.

Selective enforcement: The deploying of police personnel in ways to cope most effectively with existing or anticipated problems.

Self-incrimination: In constitutional terms, the process of becoming involved in or charged with a crime by one's own testimony.

Sentence: The penalty imposed by a court on a person convicted of a crime; the court judgment specifying the penalty; and any disposition of a defendant resulting from a conviction, including the court decision to suspend execution of a sentence.

Small claims court: A special court that provides expeditious, informal, and inexpensive adjudication of small contractual claims. In most jurisdictions, attorneys are not permitted for cases, and claims are limited to a specific amount.

Stare decisis (Lat.): To abide by decided cases. The doctrine that once a court has laid down a principle of laws as applicable to certain facts, it will apply it to all future cases when the facts are substantially the same.

State's attorney: An officer, usually locally elected within a county, who represents the state in securing indictments and in prosecuting criminal cases.

State's evidence: Testimony by a participant in the commission of a crime that incriminates others involved, given under the promise of immunity.

Status offense: An act that is declared by statute to be an offense, but only when committed or engaged in by a juvenile, and that can be adjudicated only by a juvenile court.

Statute: A law enacted by, or with the authority of, a legislature.

Statute of limitations: A term applied to numerous statutes that set a limit on the length of time that may elapse between an event giving rise to a cause of action and the commencement of a suit to enforce that cause.

Stay: A halting of a judicial proceeding by a court order.

Sting operation: The typical sting involves using various undercover methods to control crime.

Subpoena: A court order requiring a witness to attend and testify as a witness in a court proceeding.

Subpoena duces tecum: A court order requiring a witness to bring all books, documents, and papers that might affect the outcome of the proceedings.

Summons: A written order issued by a judicial officer requiring a person accused of a criminal offense to appear in a designated court at a specified time to answer the charge(s).

Superior court: A court of record or general trial court, superior to a justice of the peace or magistrate's court. In some states, an intermediate court between the general trial court and the highest appellate court.

Supreme court, state: Usually the highest court in the state judicial system.

Supreme Court, U.S.: Heads the judicial branch of the American government and is the nation's highest law court.

Suspect: An adult or juvenile considered by a criminal agency to be one who may have committed a specific criminal offense but who has not yet been arrested or charged.

Testimony: Evidence given by a competent witness, under oath, as distinguished from evidence from writings and other sources.

Tort: A breach of a duty to an individual that results in damage to him or her, for which one may be sued in civil court for damages. Crime, in contrast, may be called a breach of duty to the public. Some actions may constitute both torts and crimes.

Uniform Crime Reports (U.C.R.): Annual statistical tabulation of "crimes known to the police" and "crimes cleared by arrest," published by the Federal Bureau of Investigation.

United States claims court: Established in 1982, it serves as the court of original and exclusive jurisdiction over claims brought against the federal government, except for tort claims, which are heard by district courts.

United States district courts: Trial courts with original jurisdiction over diversity-of-citizenship cases and cases arising under U.S. criminal, bankruptcy, admiralty, patent, copyright, and postal laws.

Venue: The locality in which a suit may be tried.

Verdict: The decision of a court.

Vice squad: A special detail of police agents, charged with raiding and closing houses of prostitution and gambling resorts.

Victim and Witness Protection Act of 1984: The federal VWP Act and state laws protect crime victims and witnesses against physical and verbal intimidation where such intimidation is designed to discourage reporting of crimes and participation in criminal trials.

Victimology: The study of the psychological and dynamic interrelationships between victims and offenders, with a view toward crime prevention.

Vigilante: An individual or member of a group who undertakes to enforce the law and/or maintain morals without legal authority.

Voir dire (Fr.): The examination or questioning of prospective jurors in order to determine his or her qualifications to serve as a juror.

Warrant: A court order directing a police officer to arrest a named person or search a specific premise.

White-collar crime: Nonviolent crime for financial gain committed by means of deception by persons who use their special occupational skills and opportunities.

Witness: Anyone called to testify by either side in a trial. More broadly, a witness is anyone who has observed an event.

Work release (furlough programs): Change in prisoners' status to minimum custody with permission to work outside prison.

World court: Formally known as the International Court of Justice, it deals with disputes involving international law.

SOURCES

The Dictionary of Criminal Justice, Fourth edition, © 1994 by George E. Rush. Published by Dushkin/McGraw-Hill, Guilford, CT 06437.

Credits/Acknowledgments

Cover design by Charles Vitelli

1. Crime and Justice in America
Facing overview—© 1998 by PhotoDisc, Inc.

2. Victimology
Facing overview—United Nations photo by P. S. Sudhakaran.

3. The Police
Facing overview—© 1998 by PhotoDisc, Inc.

4. Judicial System
Facing overview—© 1998 by PhotoDisc, Inc.

5. Juvenile Justice
Facing overview—© 1998 by Cleo Freelance Photography.

6. Punishment and Corrections
Facing overview—© 1998 by PhotoDisc, Inc.

ANNUAL EDITIONS ARTICLE REVIEW FORM

■ NAME: _____ DATE: _____

■ TITLE AND NUMBER OF ARTICLE: _____

■ BRIEFLY STATE THE MAIN IDEA OF THIS ARTICLE: _____

_____

■ LIST THREE IMPORTANT FACTS THAT THE AUTHOR USES TO SUPPORT THE MAIN IDEA:

_____

_____

_____

_____

■ WHAT INFORMATION OR IDEAS DISCUSSED IN THIS ARTICLE ARE ALSO DISCUSSED IN YOUR TEXTBOOK OR OTHER READINGS THAT YOU HAVE DONE? LIST THE TEXTBOOK CHAPTERS AND PAGE NUMBERS:

_____

_____

_____

_____

_____

■ LIST ANY EXAMPLES OF BIAS OR FAULTY REASONING THAT YOU FOUND IN THE ARTICLE:

_____

_____

_____

_____

■ LIST ANY NEW TERMS/CONCEPTS THAT WERE DISCUSSED IN THE ARTICLE, AND WRITE A SHORT DEFINITION:

_____

_____

_____

_____

*Your instructor may require you to use this ANNUAL EDITIONS Article Review Form in any number of ways: for articles that are assigned, for extra credit, as a tool to assist in developing assigned papers, or simply for your own reference. Even if it is not required, we encourage you to photocopy and use this page; you will find that reflecting on the articles will greatly enhance the information from your text.

We Want Your Advice

ANNUAL EDITIONS revisions depend on two major opinion sources: one is our Advisory Board, listed in the front of this volume, which works with us in scanning the thousands of articles published in the public press each year; the other is you—the person actually using the book. Please help us and the users of the next edition by completing the prepaid article rating form on this page and returning it to us. Thank you for your help!

ANNUAL EDITIONS: CRIMINAL JUSTICE 98/99
Article Rating Form

Here is an opportunity for you to have direct input into the next revision of this volume. We would like you to rate each of the 35 articles listed below, using the following scale:

1. **Excellent: should definitely be retained**
2. **Above average: should probably be retained**
3. **Below average: should probably be deleted**
4. **Poor: should definitely be deleted**

Your ratings will play a vital part in the next revision. So please mail this prepaid form to us just as soon as you complete it.
Thanks for your help!

Rating	Article	Rating	Article
	1. An Overview of the Criminal Justice System		19. 'We're in the Fight of Our Lives'
	2. The Real Problems in American Justice		20. A Little Learning
	3. What to Do about Crime		21. Restoring the Balance: Juvenile and Community Justice
	4. The Mystery of the Falling Crime Rate		22. Teen Crime
	5. African American Males in the Criminal Justice System		23. Controlling Crime before It Happens: Risk-Focused Prevention
	6. Restorative Justice: A Story Needing to Be Told		24. On the Streets of America
	7. Victimization and the Victim Industry		25. With Juvenile Courts in Chaos, Critics Propose Their Demise
	8. True Crime		26. Teen Court
	9. The Dynamics of Domestic Abuse		27. Can We Break the Pattern of the Criminal Lifestyle?
	10. Victims of Childhood Sexual Abuse—Later Criminal Consequences		28. Reinventing Parole and Probation
	11. Police and the Quest for Professionalism		29. Eddie Ellis at Large
	12. Reducing Stress: An Organization-Centered Approach		30. Ethical Considerations in Probation Practice
	13. Better Cops, Fewer Robbers		31. Prisons Grapple with Rapid Influx of Women—and Mothers
	14. Incorporating Diversity: Police Response to Multicultural Changes in Their Communities		32. To Keep Peace, Prisons Allow Race to Rule
	15. A LEN Interview with Prof. Edwin J. Delattre of Boston University, Author of "Character & Cops"		33. The Color of Justice
	16. Adversarial Justice		34. What Works? What Matters? Recidivism among Probationers in North Carolina
	17. Day of Reckoning		35. The Death Penalty in 1996: Year End Report
	18. Jury Nullification: A Perversion of Justice?		

(Continued on next page)

ABOUT YOU

Name _____ Date _____

Are you a teacher? ❑ Or a student? ❑

Your school name _____

Department _____

Address _____

City _____ State _____ Zip _____

School telephone # _____

YOUR COMMENTS ARE IMPORTANT TO US!

Please fill in the following information:

For which course did you use this book? _____

Did you use a text with this *ANNUAL EDITION*? ❑ yes ❑ no

What was the title of the text? _____

What are your general reactions to the *Annual Editions* concept?

Have you read any particular articles recently that you think should be included in the next edition?

Are there any articles you feel should be replaced in the next edition? Why?

Are there any World Wide Web sites you feel should be included in the next edition? Please annotate.

May we contact you for editorial input?

May we quote your comments?